Critical Theory and
the Teaching of Literature

W9-AOB-470

NCTE Editorial Board: Colette Daiute, Hazel Davis, Bobbi Fisher, Keith Gilyard, Gail Hawisher, Ronald Jobe, Richard Luckert, Karen Smith, Chair, ex officio, Marlo Welshons, ex officio

Two-Year College, Four-Year College, and University Section Committee: James L. Hill, Chair, Albany State College; Frank Madden, Assistant Chair, Westchester Community College; Pat Belanoff, SUNY–Stony Brook; Theresa Enos, CCCC Representative, University of Arizona; Gail E. Hawisher, University of Illinois at Urbana-Champaign; Dawn Rodrigues, Kennesaw State College; Tom Waldrep, Medical University of South Carolina; Demetrice A. Worley, Bradley University; Collett Dilworth, CEE Representative, East Carolina University; Louise Smith, ex officio, Editor, *College English,* University of Massachusetts at Boston; Miriam Chaplin, Executive Committee Liaison, Rutgers University; Miles Myers, NCTE Staff Liaison

Critical Theory and the Teaching of Literature

Politics, Curriculum, Pedagogy

Edited by

James F. Slevin
Georgetown University

Art Young
Clemson University

National Council of Teachers of English
1111 W. Kenyon Road, Urbana, Illinois 61801-1096

Manuscript Editors: Robert A. Heister, Frances M. Camarena
              Humanities & Sciences Associates

Production Editor: Michael Greer

Interior Design: Tom Kovacs for TGK Design

Cover Design: Martin Hertzel

NCTE Stock Number: 09632–3050

© 1996 by the National Council of Teachers of English. All rights reserved. Printed in the United States of America.

It is the policy of NCTE in its journals and other publications to provide a forum for the open discussion of ideas concerning the content and the teaching of English and the language arts. Publicity accorded to any particular point of view does not imply endorsement by the Executive Committee, the Board of Directors, or the membership at large, except in announcements of policy, where such endorsement is clearly specified.

Library of Congress Cataloging-in-Publication Data

Critical theory and the teaching of literature : politics, curriculum,
    pedagogy / edited by James F. Slevin, Art Young.
        p.   cm.
    Includes bibliographical references and index.
    ISBN 0-8141-0963-2 (alk. paper)
    1. Criticism. 2. Critical theory. 3. Literature—Study and
teaching (Higher) I. Slevin, James F., 1945. II. Young, Art,
1943–   .
PN98.S6C67   1995
801´.95—dc20   95-31257
                                                                          CIP

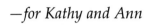

—*for Kathy and Ann*

Contents

Introduction

James F. Slevin
Georgetown University

Art Young
Clemson University

This book grew out of the work of two Summer Institutes for Teachers of Literature sponsored by the National Council of Teachers of English. In June 1991, and again in June 1992, hundreds of college teachers of literature gathered for what has become an important tradition in the NCTE. This book attempts to capture the dialogue that began there. The five main speakers at these conferences—Barbara Christian, Peter Elbow, Gerald Graff, Mary Louise Pratt, and Robert Scholes—initiated a conversation that continues in the pages of this volume. Other essays—by Keith Hjortshoj, Beverly Sauer, John Warnock, and Janice Wolff—incubated during the conference, generated as part of the many opportunities for conversation and collaboration made possible there. These and the other essays represent a variety of viewpoints, and they take a range of generic forms, ranging from formal arguments to personal reflections and dialogues. In selecting them, we have been guided by our commitment to providing a vital exchange of views on the issues raised at the Summer Institutes.

These issues are probably the central questions of our discipline at this time. If texts no longer organize the curriculum, then what does? If the "professor" is no longer the privileged agent of education, then who is? The essays in this book raise and respond to these pressing questions, which contemplate the end of coverage as a model, the end of the canon as an agreed-upon certainty, the end of the professor as the agent of learning, and the end of the classroom as a place where education is delivered. These "ends" have been much contemplated, indeed. But what arises in their place? What have we begun?

The new directions in literary theory and criticism that mark the last two decades can be seen as responses to these very concerns, reexamining the assumptions that underlie literary study. But this exciting, disciplinewide reappraisal of what we read, and why and how we read it, has not yet adequately addressed questions of curriculum and pedagogy. We have yet to consider fully how recent developments in theory and critical practice have influenced, or can influence, the way we teach, organize, and reflect upon undergraduate courses in language and literature. This book aims in part to fill this need. The essays collected here explore how curricular arrangements—the English major, interdisciplinary programs, and general education sequences—can be responsive both to new critical perspectives and to bodies of literature heretofore excluded from the academy. They are concerned as well with how individual courses can more effectively introduce students to new critical theories and help them make connections among the various critical perspectives that now mark literary studies.

In a book as many-voiced as this one, it is unlikely that any generalization will apply universally. But we will risk at least one. It seems to us that this book differs from others in the introduction of the student as a vital presence in the profession's reflections on critical theory. Unlike most theoretical work so far, even work that concerns itself with "teaching theory," this one asks us to see our students not as the receivers of our theoretical knowledge but as participants in the making of it. Many of the essays, then, set up a model of teaching literature that envisions education as a collaborative process between students and teachers; so, a concern with student voices is a central focus of what we take it to mean to be a teacher of literature. Teaching literature and getting students talking/writing are inseparable in this view of things; students play a central role as the makers of the meaning of literary education.

Politics

The first two essays set the tone and introduce many of the themes that the reader will find in the essays that follow. Mary Louise Pratt's "Daring to Dream" sets literary study and theory within the larger debates about national culture and language and the power relationships and struggles these debates inhabit. Proposing the ideal of the "polyglot citizen," she envisions the study of language and literature as a process of democratizing education. She proposes an educational renewal in which multiculturalism becomes a way of understanding and effecting change by reorienting our attention to the literatures and cultures of the Americas and therefore including all our students in the creation of a truly American culture. Building on Pratt's work, John Warnock's "What We

Talk about When We Talk about Politics" addresses the place of politics, and the talk about it, in our universities and classrooms. Warnock is concerned with the very real place of students in all this talk and with teaching as a process of inviting and enabling students' participation. Addressing the disjunction between theory and practice, he offers a compelling way of theorizing classroom practices and thereby restoring the work of teaching to a central place in our professional conversation.

The three essays that follow continue this concern with the active participation of students, with particular attention to student writing and how to read it, learn from it, think about it—in short, with how we might take it seriously as literature. Like Warnock's essay, Keith Hjortshoj's "Theory, Confusion, Inclusion" brings politics and theory (and the politics of theory) into the classroom and into the everyday lives of teachers and students. Like Pratt, Hjortshoj sets these considerations within the context of a diverse American culture. Situated firmly in his own experience as a teacher and arising out of his active participation at the two Summer Institutes, the essay draws on (and so now, in this volume, helps the reader to anticipate) the contributions of Barbara Christian, Gerald Graff, and Peter Elbow. By focusing on a particular student writer and the larger political and social contexts that mark the significance of that writer's work, Hjortshoj ties theory to the dynamics of teacher-student relationships. David Bleich, in "The Unconscious Troubles of Men," continues this concern with students, offering a model for reading student writing as cultural text as well as personal revelation. Through a series of readings of student papers, Bleich discloses the social and political struggles present in the classroom and teaches us how to read these struggles through his exemplary reading of student writing. In the pedagogy he makes available to us, we can learn how the ever-present politics of the classroom can become the subject of serious inquiry by students as well as teachers. Min-Zhan Lu's "Teaching Literature: Indoctrination vs. Dialectics" develops classroom strategies (particularly writing assignments) that deepen students' participation in such inquiry. She shows how student writing can be used to help students bridge the gap between their theories and their practices, enabling them to become more aware of the political implications of their own language and their own perspectives. At the same time, and by this very means, she helps teachers to reflect on the politics of the theoretical positions we take in our classroom and their implications for pedagogy.

If these first essays help us to work out social critiques in the classroom—particularly by showing how taking student writing seriously can help us learn from our students and reconceptualize the process of teaching and learning—the last two essays in this section move toward the curricular and institutional implications of this pedagogy. In his essay, "Standing in This Neighborhood: Of English Studies," Daniel Moshenberg broadens our notions of virtually everything we imagine ourselves to be doing: the site of learning becomes not just the classroom but the "neighborhood" (particularly *his* neighborhood, the Arlandria/ Chirilagua area of Alexandria, Virginia), where reading and writing are tied directly to efforts for political and social change. Learners here, primarily African American and Central American people, are also citizens and workers, struggling for justice and power—"standing." For Moshenberg, as for Pratt, the study of language and literature must address issues of national and international consciousness, of unequal economic and cultural power, and of communities of students far more diverse than currently acknowledged. By offering more inclusive ways of understanding our disciplinary aims, he extends our notion of scholarship and suggests ways of rethinking both our theory and our practice. In "Redistribution and the Transformation of American Studies," Eric Cheyfitz focuses considerations such as these on the politics of the curriculum, joining with Mary Louise Pratt in advocating a thoroughly revised notion of American studies. Both not only expand our notion of the canon and the "Americas" but also rethink literary study as a practice entailing larger social concerns and responsibilities. Like Moshenberg and others in this volume, Cheyfitz envisions the work of our discipline and the curricula we establish as incorporating, and reflecting upon, outreach beyond the campus. His essay thus constitutes a transition to the curricular issues that are the focus of the next section.

Curriculum

Gerald Graff's essay, like those in part I, derives from a very basic concern to include students more actively in the professional conversations now taking place apart from them. "Organizing the Conflicts in the Curriculum" moves beyond Graff's earlier, very influential work which delineated our disciplinary debates and which advocated that they be taught; here, he offers several concrete ways in which these debates can be brought into a course of study. In his essay, to which many of the subsequent essays explicitly or implicitly respond, the issues of politics in the classroom, the cultural and social contexts of literature, redefinitions of the canon, and considerations of gender, class, race and ethnicity are clarified and given shape in practical measures that institutions might adopt to involve students more fully in this wide-ranging professional discussion.

Jacqueline Jones Royster's "Literature, Literacy, and Language" reminds us that the curriculum serves people, not "Western Civ" or "the profession." She asks some fundamental questions: Who are we serving and what hopes for them inspire our educational plans? Keeping that focus allows her to develop alternative ways of thinking about how we organize and teach the knowledge students must have, and use, to lead their lives as readers, writers, and citizens. The pedagogy she advocates centers on open inquiry and the process of inviting everyone to participate in and to shape that inquiry. The curriculum she envisions is inclusive and dialogic, opening up a space for neglected literature to be read and for marginalized students to be heard. Anne Ruggles Gere and Morris Young continue this concern with expanding the canon and establishing curricular practices that develop a critical literacy which enables students to read not just texts but contexts. Attending to "Cultural Institutions," particularly the material conditions of textual production and reception, they connect theory with practice by bringing a cultural studies approach to selected works by Zora Neale Hurston, Leslie Marmon Silko, and Maxine Hong Kingston. Their essay not only illuminates these important texts but models a mode of inquiry that can be extended to other texts as well. By attending to the process of writing and publication as well as to the institutionalized readings (academic and other) that create a canon and shape our perceptions of writers and their work, Gere and Young clarify how culture is constructed and, perhaps more important, help us to invite our students to join in that essential project.

Robert Scholes and Gary Waller continue the discussion of reconceiving language and literary study as central to a college education by suggesting changes in the goals and practices of general education. In "A Flock of Cultures—A Trivial Proposal," Scholes argues that "Great Books" and "Western Civ" cannot anchor the college curriculum because they do not have an intellectual core and because they lack the coherence for pedagogically sound instruction. In arguing against the "Great Books" theory of general education, Scholes advances his own proposal based on two goals: helping students (1) to understand a usable cultural past and (2) to establish an active relationship with the cultural present. Scholes suggests a modern "trivium" of grammar, dialectic, and rhetoric—one centered on the English language and matters of textuality. In this curriculum, texts would be selected for study on the basis of their relationship to a canon of concepts and practices rather than because of their representation in a canon of "Great Books." Gary Waller also discusses what it means to theorize the general education curriculum, and he suggests another trio of contexts—the contemporary, the historical, and the ways to knowledge and power—designed to put literary study "out in the world" and to connect it to the intellectual and cultural forces that affect all our lives. What students do with what they read is perhaps more important than what they read. Waller is a college administrator as well as a teacher, and his essay, "Polylogue: Ways of Teaching and Structuring the Conflicts," describes the difficult process of building faculty consensus for interdisciplinary curricular change in the modern university organized by disciplines. Thus Waller addresses not only questions of why we should theorize the curriculum but also practical and political questions of how we might go about doing it. For Waller as well as Scholes, critical theory should not be an isolated course in the undergraduate English curriculum but rather should inform the entire college curriculum.

The final two essays in this section, by Wendy Bishop and James Phelan, focus specifically on how curricular matters affect individual teachers and their students. Bishop writes about how the faculty in her English department, influenced by the scholarly work of Gerald Graff and Robert Scholes, attempted to restructure their curriculum. Bishop's "Attitudes and Expectations" analyzes the impact of such a process on graduate students who are being socialized into the profession. Through a case study of "Dennis," a Ph.D. student in literature and an instructor of first-year composition courses, Bishop demonstrates how issues of theory, as integrated into a department's planning and curriculum, affect the lived experience of one student as both learner and professional-in-training. When theoretical and pedagogical conflicts exist within a departmental faculty but are not acknowledged, much less "taught," to graduate students, then how do such students process these conflicting messages? For Dennis, the conflicts between literature and composition, between theory and practice, between teaching and research, between competing theories of interpretation, all seem to be discrete issues to be navigated through in separate courses rather than professional issues to be understood through active participation in professional conversations. Through her case study, Bishop lets us see the implications of such unacknowledged theories in the professional life of one graduate teaching assistant.

We close this section on curriculum with James Phelan's "Teaching Theory/Theorizing Teaching," a dialogue among literature teachers trying to envision the place of theory in their classrooms. Through his characters, Phelan asks what a course in critical theory should be about. What texts should be taught? Is coverage an issue? Should theory be taught as content to be mastered or as the process of theorizing? What should students know and be able to do when they finish such a course?

Why? Can we teach the dialogic nature of discourse without changing the teacher's traditional role as disseminator of authoritative knowledge? Phelan's dramatic scenario enacts many of the conflicts discussed in this book—offering different approaches to theorizing the curriculum and, as well, different approaches to teaching a course in theory. In some ways, Phelan's coffee-room conversation imagines Wendy Bishop's GTAs on the far side of the Ph.D., finally talking about theory in ways that might lead to pedagogical and curricular change. Phelan constructs a dramatic scene which itself helps us see the implications of theory in individual classrooms, in departments, and in the profession—for theory is about talk, texts talking to one another, texts talking to us, readers talking to texts and talking to each other. Such "teacher talk" seems to lead from matters of theory to matters of curricular context to matters of pedagogy. How can we engage our students in this conversation?

Pedagogy

In our final section, Barbara Christian, Paul Lauter, and Peter Elbow reflect on the impact of theory on readers and writers in the classroom. All three are concerned that critical theory be used as a tool by teachers to enrich students' experience of reading literature; they do not want theory to become yet another barrier between the student reader and the literary text, a barrier that can only be overcome by reading more theory and less literature. Thus they set an important theme not only for this section but for the entire book: for the teacher of literature, examining how we teach is as important a pedagogical consideration as determining what we teach. Critical theory can help us undertake this examination, for understanding ourselves as teachers involves an understanding of how we read texts, and how we read our students.

Barbara Christian's "Does Theory Play Well in the Classroom?" cautions us that literary scholars' fascination with "high theory" might contribute to the alienation minority students feel toward theoretical discourse and the neglect that African American writers experience. She provides us with the personal context for her earlier, influential essay, "The Race for Theory," in which she argues that feminist, Marxist, and psychoanalytic critics interpret the works of contemporary African American writers without an adequate knowledge of African American history and culture. What concerns Christian is the silence of theorists in this regard, as if such knowledge is not needed to fully appreciate the novels of Toni Morrison and Alice Walker. For Christian, there are many theories—but African American theory must be one of the theoretical

tools for understanding African American literature. And as Christian
points out, African American theory exists and is most readily accessible
in the oral and written narratives of African Americans. She then discusses how she teaches Toni Morrison's *Beloved* from an African American perspective, what kinds of cultural knowledge she brings to her
reading, and how she opens up this novel to the students in her
multicultural classroom. In doing so, she opens up *Beloved* for all of us.

Paul Lauter, like Barbara Christian, demonstrates how new ways of
reading literary texts can be discovered in the texts themselves. For
Lauter, the issue is no longer the value of multiculturalism, "for it is here
to stay," but "the problem of translating multiculturalism into effective
classroom practice." In order to solve this problem, we need to free
ourselves from the "pedagogical canon" of "theoretical correctness"
established by the literary theory of T. S. Eliot and the New Critics. We
need to work with our students to discover new ways of teaching and
learning literature, and one way to do so is by reading together literary
texts that themselves challenge formalist assumptions about literature
and about teaching. Lauter examines poems by Amy Lowell and Sterling
Brown to demonstrate how they can be understood as theoretical as well
as literary texts and to suggest how such theoretical readings lead to
revision of the pedagogical canon. Indeed, different classroom practices
suggest different ways of hearing and making meaning of literary texts.

Further challenges to the pedagogical canon come from Peter Elbow.
"The War between Reading and Writing—and How to End It" questions
the unexamined pedagogy of most literature classrooms in which writing "serves" literature. In some sense, this often translates into the
student serving literature rather than the other way around. Elbow
follows Lauter in viewing this unfortunate situation as the legacy of New
Criticism, and he follows Christian in invoking Toni Morrison's concern
with the damage done to writers by postmodern critical theories: "for it
means that there is no way to talk about what we mean, because to mean
anything is not in vogue." One important way to make students active
readers of literature is to privilege the writing students do in literature
classes. When students view themselves as writers, when students feel
empowered to talk back to literature and to join the cultural conversation
engendered by literature, then they read as writers. Reading literature as
a writer of literature creates student readers who are "braver, more
lively, more thoughtful." Elbow goes on to give many practical ways in
which student writing can be effectively integrated into literature classrooms, ways which ultimately serve the interests of literary culture (as
well as the student) by creating critical and imaginative readers and
writers.

The process of reading—and the cultural knowledge that reading both provides and requires—is the basis from which Kathleen McCormick explores possibilities for a culturally situated reading pedagogy. McCormick brings together two areas of reading research, reading theory and literary theory, that do not often "read" each other. Indeed, most of the recent research in reading theory reviewed by McCormick is unfamiliar to college literature teachers. She offers a theory of readers as social subjects, suggesting that literature teachers need to bring reading theory and critical theory together to understand better what goes on in our students' minds as readers. Because reading is a socially constructed activity, what students write is a visible and accessible avenue into how they read. Thus McCormick, working with pedagogical conceptions from David Bleich and Peter Elbow among others, explores how teachers can help students locate themselves as reading subjects by becoming more self-conscious and culturally informed as readers.

The final three essays in the collection focus on teachers and students exploring together alternatives to the theoretically correct pedagogical canon. In doing so, they bring us full circle in our consideration of the interrelated issues of this volume: critical theory, politics, curriculum, and pedagogy. They bring us face to face with teachers in individual classrooms who seek to translate what they are learning from critical theory into classroom practices. Central to that process is each teacher's reading and talking about published literature and literary theory, and equally important, each teacher's serious reading of students' writing and talk.

Janice M. Wolff's "Teaching in the Contact Zone" employs the metaphor of the "contact zone" developed by Mary Louise Pratt to construct teacher knowledge of classroom experiences, such as discussing issues of racism with students who are reading Toni Morrison's *Beloved*. Wolff's reading of *Beloved* and its contact zone of "oral cultures" and "print cultures" assists her in developing her theory of the novel and her theory of pedagogy. Thus she follows Christian and Lauter in discovering theory in the reading of imaginative literature. The most illuminating moment in Wolff's classroom and in her essay occurs when she reads her students' writing and listens to their voices, for she discovers that what the students are learning from her teaching is quite different from what she intends. Her classroom experience thus reinforces the point made throughout this collection that a teacher can't define her role apart from her students' learning.

In "How Literature Learns to Write: The Possibilities and Pleasures of Role-Play," James E. Seitz asks us to confront the alienation we often feel as readers of students' texts. It may be that in assigning "pedagogically correct" writing to students, we unwittingly alienate them from their own writing as well as the literature we want them to read and enjoy. Furthermore, as writers and readers, we may alienate students from teachers. By asking students to participate in a performance model of role-playing, by asking students to assume various textual identities, by asking students to imagine historical and cultural possibilities and audiences, by asking students to write creatively in literature classes, Seitz constructs a classroom environment envisioned by Elbow when he recommended that students read literature as writers of literature and as contributors to the cultural tradition. Seitz wants to restore the pleasure of writing to students, the pleasure of reading student writing to teachers, and the pleasure of the literary experience to all concerned.

At the 1991 and 1992 NCTE Summer Institutes, Beverly Sauer conducted workshops each afternoon in which participants gathered to talk about the critical theories they had been reading prior to the Summer Institute and that they were hearing about in the presentations of Barbara Christian, Peter Elbow, Gerald Graff, Mary Louise Pratt, and Robert Scholes. The focus of these workshops was on translating the theoretical into the everyday life of college literature teachers: new courses, new curricular components, departmental politics, institutional cultures, redesigned syllabi, and new classroom practices. Sauer's concluding essay, "Making Connections," discusses many of the questions raised by the participants, ones that continue to be raised by literature teachers across the nation—questions about canon formation and redefinition, about multiculturalism, about the politics of theorizing the curriculum. Who is authorized to speak in the classroom? How does theory practiced in academic criticism reflect the kind of thinking we would like our students to do? The participants not only asked questions, but they came prepared to share experiences in the forms of bibliographies, new course syllabi, redesigned curricula, and innovative classroom strategies. As their discussions and syllabi revealed, these faculty are teaching and learning in the "contact zone" of their classrooms; they are learning from critical theorists, from the literature they read, from each other, and, most important, from their students.

Perhaps the learning that we and our students *can* undertake in this wide variety of contexts constitutes the central theme and the primary purpose of this collection of essays. Explicitly or implicitly, each of the essays here is concerned with the intellectual work students and teachers do together and with what that work can contribute to the *profession's* "conversation." These articles thus explore crucial professional relationships: between students and teachers, reading and writing, texts and contexts, one course and other courses, the academic world and the world beyond the academy. Through these explorations, our professional conversation is moved in new directions, considering the way pedagogies, curricula, and other institutional practices theorize literature and the literary knowledge that teachers and students produce. More than any particular theoretical perspective that might be introduced into a course, the way that course is taught, the place that course holds in the curriculum, and the politics of textual, cultural, and personal relations embedded in our pedagogies and curricula influence both what is learned and what literary study is taken, by students and teachers alike, to mean. This book is meant to contribute to this important professional consideration, probing and clarifying the meaning of what we do and thereby reconceptualizing the discipline of English studies to account for *all* that we do, as scholars *and educators* responsible to the future.

I Politics

1 Daring to Dream: Re-Visioning Culture and Citizenship

Mary Louise Pratt
Stanford UniversIty

A few years ago, when the affluent Bay Area suburb of Los Altos passed an "English Only" ordinance, the Chicano artist and poet José Antonio Burciaga asked his neighbors to reflect on the irony of their choice:

> I feel that Los Altos should have gone all the way and changed its Spanish name to **The Highs, Highlands,** or more appropriately, **The Tall Ones.** All across the country defenders of ye olde English would do well to authenticate, in English, all of the "foreign" names of our cities and towns.
>
> For example, here in California, we could begin by translating Los Baños to **The Bathrooms** and Sobrantes to **Leftovers.** San Francisco, of course, would be renamed **Saint Francis of Assisi,** Atascadero could become **Mud Puddle,** Manteca, **Lard,** Panocha, **Brown Sugar,** and Aromas could become **Smells,** California.
>
> Los Angeles? Anaheim already took away the city's baseball angels, so how about **Lost Angels** or **Lost Anglos?** (1)

Not inappropriately, Burciaga entitled his piece "The Tall Ones Are Ganging Up on Me." There are plenty of people today who, at least from time to time, feel like "Lost Anglos" is the contemporary reality of the United States. And since the political Right launched its highly orchestrated and well-financed campaign in 1990 against educational reform, plenty of scholars and teachers have shared the feeling that "the tall ones" are ganging up on us.

In our good moments, those of us so beset know that the vehemence of the reaction against educational reform means something of potentially great significance is underway. It is very important not to lose sight

This essay was the keynote address of the 1991 NCTE Summer Institute for Teachers of Literature and was also presented at a forum on "American Literary Pluralisms" at the Modern Language Association Convention, San Francisco, in December 1991, sponsored by the Commission on Literatures and Languages of the Americas. My sincere thanks to Rina Benmayor, David Palumbo-Liu, José Saldívar, Renato Rosaldo, James Clifford, and Herman Gallegos for their comments.

of this fact. A few years ago, I had the remarkable experience of seeing the planning documents for a first-year culture course I co-teach published (in strategically edited form) in the *Wall Street Journal*, along with a vehement, ill-informed editorial attacking "The Stanford Mind." After the initial shock and insult wore off, I found myself astonished that such a thing as an undergraduate course syllabus could be of any interest to the national business daily—even assuming a slow day on the market! Unfortunately, like most academics, I lacked the media competence to take advantage of the occasion.

That was seven years ago. Now, it is clear that what some see as a battle for the national will is also a process by which U.S. society is reimagining and redefining itself. At this point, it is essential that intellectuals pursuing the democratic renewal of society, institutions, and culture make a concerted effort to insert some terms and ideas into the public debate, terms that suggest where it is we are trying to go and why. Those of us arguing for democratic change face an opportunity and an imperative to articulate our visions clearly and forcefully. What sort of society are we looking for in these United States, in these Americas, on this planet? What sort of culture and what sort of institutions do we wish to inhabit? What do we see as the relationships to be developed between language and nation, among culture, education, and citizenship? If we abandon assimilationism and the idea of homogeneous cultural wholes, what will be the bases for our social bonds? In California, these questions have been posed with a new urgency ever since the Los Angeles uprising in the spring of 1992.

For many people, the search is for ways to undo deeply held assumptions that tie difference to subordination and social heterogeneity to social inequality. Difference, in other words, does not necessarily imply inequality—where it does, it does so as the result of a historical process. For some, it is a question of redefining social bonds so that homogeneity is not the only basis for solidarity or accountability. For many people it has become imperative to be able to live out particular identities and group histories *as part of one's citizenship*, rather than as an obstacle to citizenship—imperative to feel not just that one is entitled or allowed to be here, but that one *belongs* here, that one is entitled to proprietorship of the nation's institutions as fully as people of the traditionally dominant or normative group.

In the 1980s, following on the national and global upheavals of the 1970s and late 1960s, certain sets of monolithic linkages came unstuck in metropolitan culture, both in imagination and reality—notably, linkages that lined up the idea of a nation with the idea of *a* territorial state, *a* language, *a* culture, sometimes *a* religion, and *a* (masculine-defined) citizen-subject who defends the territory, embodies the language and culture, and serves the state. In particular, the three-layered monolith of nation, language, and culture, which defined the modern nation-state and the modern citizen-subject at the level of the imagined, came apart in what seems likely to be a permanent and global way. This is one lens for diagnosing the current upheavals both in actual social relations and in the ways nations represent themselves to themselves. Often, these disarticulations register themselves most dramatically in the realm of language.

The Polyglot Citizen

All parents have moments when they confront the fact that their children are growing up in a different world from the one they did. I recall picking my daughter up a few years ago at preschool and hearing that she had a new friend she wanted to ask over to play. "Great," I said, "get her phone number and I'll call her parents." "I can't," said Olivia. "Why not?" "She doesn't speak English." "Well, should we ask her in Spanish?" I said. "Momma," said Olivia impatiently, "We don't understand each other's *language*." (The intonation meant: "We understand everything else, just not the language.") The two four-year-olds, I realized, lacked an expectation of a common language as essential to constructing a relationship and indeed proved in the times they spent together that, for four-year-olds, it was not.

The incident stuck in my mind because it happened not long after I had attended a meeting of a professional organization at which two linguistic matters had come up for our consideration. One was whether and how to respond to the "English Only" initiatives that were being passed all across the country with varying effects, from undermining bilingual education programs to prohibiting workers from the using of their native languages in the workplace. At the same meeting, we received a briefing from some policymakers outlining the urgent need in American business and government for more adult speakers of second languages. The proposal was to begin a massive national initiative to teach foreign languages to adults who held advanced positions in the areas of business, diplomacy, and national security.

So we had a situation where simultaneously initiatives were being taken (a) to eliminate bilingualism among schoolchildren (for whom multiple-language learning is possible and perfectible) and (b) to try to create bilingualism among mature adults (for whom foreign language learning is extremely difficult and virtually never perfectible)! My fantasy at the time was to get the two groups together in the same room (almost certainly revealing, of course, that they were in fact the same people!). But that wouldn't do much good, really, because the crowd in such a room would not have included a lot of people who needed to be there for a valid discussion of what was possible and desirable in the way of a national language policy. As anyone who has been working on educational democracy knows, *everything* depends on who is in the room where the decisions are being made, on whether those seeking change and those expected to benefit from it are part of the process. (One of the significant openings created by the upheaval in Los Angeles was the appearance on mainstream TV of inner-city people analyzing their situation and the society as a whole. Their clarity, articulateness, and wisdom often contrasted with the ignorant wafflings of an officialdom who lacked all familiarity with the dynamics at work.)

What a difference it would make, then, if a national language policy were formulated by a group that corresponded to the linguistic realities of the U.S.—to the fact, for instance, that in California, half the children entering kindergarten now speak first languages other than English. As a scholar, a parent, and a teacher, I dare to dream about a public education system that sees this extraordinary multilingualism not as an educational handicap or a social impediment, but as an extraordinary endowment to be cultivated and preserved. Imagine a school system that made it a priority for children to become literate in all the languages they knew and for every monolingual English speaker to learn a second language early and well. In a generation, *without giving up a shared knowledge of English among its citizens,* the national self-understanding would, I suspect, be profoundly altered.

What could emerge might be a new national subject—a figure Renato Rosaldo has called the *polyglot citizen.* Let me use this term for a moment to reflect on this society's present and its past. On the one hand, as a purely linguistic entity, the polyglot citizen would be the result of changing realities in the U.S., notably the arrival of large, new immigrant populations—8.5 million in the 1980s alone, and that's the official figure. On the other hand, as Burciaga tried to remind his neighbors in Los Altos, such a concept would simply incorporate into the national understanding realities that have constituted American life and history for a very long time. For, of course, multilingualism, intercultural contact, radical social heterogeneity and discontinuity have been part of human history in the Americas for a very long time, certainly since before contact with Europe, and, of course, more dramatically since the shock of 1492 and its aftermath. Despite ideologies of homogeneity and assimilation, the polyglot American has been everywhere but never named as a model for citizenship. (When you read Willa Cather's *O Pioneers!*, did you or your teacher notice that every single character is bilingual, and there is not a single native speaker of English in the book? Did you know that in the 1850s, 60 percent of the newspapers published in the U.S. were *not* in English?) In the Southwest, people have to be reminded constantly that Spanish is not an immigrant language in the U.S., that Mexicans were here for three centuries before Anglos showed up, and that the dominant presence of English did not eliminate Spanish by the third generation, as the immigrant formula specifies.

In her courses on sociolinguistics at San Jose State University, linguist Patricia Nichols does a simple and revealing exercise to orient her students to the history of multilingualism in the United States (see "Language in the Attic"). Nichols has students reconstruct their linguistic biography to see how many generations back they go in their own family before encountering native languages other than English. This is a great exercise for something I call "unraveling the white synthesis" in the classroom. For most students, including Euramericans, it is only two or three generations back to bilingualism. In fact, among Nichols's students, the *group* with the longest history as native speakers of English is the African Americans. (Of course!—when you think about it.)

The other things those linguistic biographies revealed, to Nichols's surprise, was the violence of compulsory monolingualism. Many families had preserved horror stories about linguistic repression and forced language loss. In the United States, the polyglot citizen of all races has traditionally been subjected to considerable psychosocial violence. This was one of the costs of producing what I referred to above as "the white synthesis." As Nichols's classroom experiment suggests, that synthesis begins to unravel as soon as you tug it by a thread. Unraveling it is crucial to the unraveling of white supremacy itself.

Linguistic repression and enforced monolingualism are also old realities in the Americas. Walter Mignolo wrote recently about a literacy campaign conducted by the Spanish in the 1550s, led by Franciscan friars (see "Literacy and Colonization"). One of their tactics was to imprison children of the Aztec elite and prevent them from conversing with anyone in their own language, "especially not their mothers" (67). The authority of literate culture, the friars surmised, could only be established if the authority of oral culture was interrupted. (The Aztecs, it appears, were not entirely naive about what was afoot. Commentators revealed that some of them, suspecting the exercise, turned over not their own children but those of subordinates.) That history is still being lived out today. In the first-year culture course a group of us teach at Stanford (the one the *Wall Street Journal* wrote up), readings include a sacred, mythic text of the Maya called the *Popol Vuh*. This year, following the lecture on this text, a student came up to the professor with some comments, at the end of which he said, "My grandparents are Maya, you know. It's the only language they know, but they insisted my parents speak only Spanish to get ahead, so I've never learned it, though I've heard it all my life." Ironically, as he probably knew, north of the border, Spanish is the language parents tell their children to suppress, for the same reasons that his grandparents suppressed Maya. Of course, it was the presence of the *Popol Vuh* on the curriculum, and a Chicano professor behind the podium, that brought this student's Maya experience into intersection with the powerful structures of knowledge that reside in the university.

The idea of the polyglot citizen is intended, of course, to refer to cultural, and not just linguistic, consciousness. It does not mean simply a polity whose citizens speak more than one language, but a polity that is, and sees itself as, multiply constituted, as *consisting of* heterogeneity at the level of the individual and the collective. Citizens are constituted by the multiple and shifting parameters we all know by heart: region, gender, class, race, religion. People are bound by histories, but histories that they have lived out *in very different ways*. As anthropologist Renato Rosaldo has argued, fears that such multiplicity produces chaos are unfounded. Heterogeneous societies can hold together just fine, though what holds them together is not homogeneity. Rather, they are held together by the dense degrees of overlap between and among their various identifications and formations. The other great fear is of fragmentation or, as it is often called, "Balkanization." But this too cannot happen because *no one belongs to only one group*. The polyglot citizen, metaphorically speaking, identifies herself or himself as a point of intersection of multiple threads that weave in and out to make the dense fabric of society. As the L.A. rap group Aztlan Nation put it, "I didn't cross the border, the border crossed me." Perhaps here there is a richer and more inclusive model of citizenship than those which imagine social bonding as constituted by sameness and conformism.

Multiculturalism: Five Propositions

There is at least one term that all participants in the culture debates have a stake in: multiculturalism. For reasons that will become apparent in a moment, I will make no attempt to define this concept. In fact, I'll do the opposite. I propose to identify five of what I take to be the key dimensions of the term, thinking in particular about widespread concern over co-opted, bureaucratized, and watered-down versions of multiculturalism. So acute are these concerns that powerful voices committed to cultural democracy and educational reform now often back away from or even denounce multiculturalism, leaving colleagues who have taken great risks in its name dangling in a limbo of (il)legitimacy. The "Five Propositions" below are aimed at resolving some of the confusion generated by the multifarious evocations of the term.

Proposition 1: Multiculturalism has at least four narratives of origin.
(a) Civil Rights. Multiculturalism has its historical roots in the U.S. civil rights struggles and continues the battles for gender and racial equality that have been an ongoing part of U.S. social history since independence. With respect to people of color, women, gays, and other disenfranchised groups, one can characterize multiculturalism as a move from demanding the right to *be* here to demanding the right to *belong* here, from demanding representation to demanding co-possession of the nation's institutions.

(b) Immigration. Close to one out of every twenty-five Americans, by official statistics, arrived here within the last fifteen years from very disparate parts of the world. The actual numbers are probably greater. This extraordinary immigration has produced a cultural and linguistic landscape that is much more diverse than has ever existed previously. From this perspective, multiculturalism is not simply a movement but a reality. It is already here. Debates over education and diversity represent the pangs of adjustment and the struggles over how to adjust our institutions to these new realities.

(c) Globalization. The communications revolution, worldwide immigrant diasporas, and globalization of capital and markets mean that everyone's reality has diversified culturally and linguistically and that nearly everyone is experiencing increased demands for interaction with other cultures and societies. This is where multiculturalism intersects with international relations, where domestic projects in cultural diversity meet up with the demand for greater global cultural competence, often in the name of economic competitiveness in the global market.

(d) Academic "Business as Usual." Questioning, challenging, and revitalizing established traditions and structures of knowledge is business as usual in the university. In fact, such processes of renewal are central to the university's mission in society. Today's curriculum debates, for example, are strikingly similar to the heated struggles that occurred in the 1920s over whether American literature should be taught in

American universities. Many of the arguments used then against American literature are the same ones used now against "substituting" European classics with "inferior" works by women, people of color, or non-Europeans. In any scholarly discipline, paradigm shifts are inevitable and desirable, for though they occasion discord, they are the way new knowledge is incorporated, the way history works on the institution. Without them, universities would be attempting to live outside history—and would become instant anachronisms. There is, of course, a commercialized version of this: in the books and journals market, multiculturalism is a growth industry, and most big corporations today have professional diversity managers.

Having suggested four narratives of origin, I would like to privilege a particular orientation toward the future. The central core of the reformist projects referred to under the label "multiculturalism," I would argue, is the struggle in the domain of culture against forms of subordination that distort this society, that inhibit its thought and fail so many of its inhabitants: racism and white supremacy, sexism and heterosexism, ethnocentrism, intolerance and xenophobia, all based as often on ignorance as on prejudice.

Proposition 2: Multiculturalism is not a goal or a stopping-off place; like affirmative action, it is a <u>strategy</u>, not an end in itself. In the case of both strategies, it is crucial to keep in mind what they can and cannot do. They should not be attacked or blamed, as they often are, for what they cannot and never undertook to do. Affirmative action cannot eliminate racism and sexism, and those who designed it never thought it could. It was intended merely as an initial mechanism for intervening in situations understood to be distorted by racism and sexism. Yet affirmative action itself is often blamed for creating stigmas that should really be attributed to the persistence of racism and sexism themselves. Its "failure" to eliminate these prejudices has been effectively used by supporters of racial and gender inequality to divide and weaken groups committed to opposing inequality.

So it has been with multiculturalism, which is criticized, for instance, because it is compatible with a kind of uncritical pluralism, with a smorgasbord approach to culture, and with forms of consumerism. Again, such limitations have been used to divide groups committed to promoting a democratic and heterogeneous culture.

It is crucial to recognize these movements as strategies rather than goals and to keep one's eye on the prizes of equality, liberation, and social and cultural renewal. In the case of both affirmative action and multiculturalism, it is the burden of their critics to propose something better.

Proposition 3: Multiculturalism doesn't have a referent. Precisely because it denotes a strategy, it is a highly contextualized term. What it
"means" in a given instance will depend entirely on the context—who
the participants are, what is at stake, and what is possible. Such factors
determine what constitutes a "multicultural" intervention in a given situation. If one recognizes the context-boundedness of multiculturalism and
its status as a strategy rather than an end goal, then one worries less about
compromised or co-opted gestures that seem designed to appease rather
than transform. The productive response to such gestures is not necessarily to condemn or reject them as undesirable per se, but rather to demonstrate their limitations and to push in every instance for additional
change. The fact of co-optation does not discredit the goals or trivialize
the stakes nor should it be allowed to.

A related but somewhat different point concerns what one might call
the *horizontalness* of political language in the electronic-media age. Political terms tend not to retain specific empirical, ideological, or moral
referents, but rather to spread horizontally across the political and ideological spectrum, altering their meaning accordingly. Thus terms like
democracy, diversity, freedom, fairness, equality—and *multiculturalism*—are
used across the entire ideological spectrum in public discourse. In part,
this horizontal spread is due to the Right's habit of appropriating transformative or critical language as quickly as it enters public discourse. In
part, it is due to the fact that different sectors of the society are always
responding simultaneously, but differently, to changes in social conditions. So, in response to, say, an increased Hispanic clientele, a supermarket owner might hire more bilingual clerks, move the salsa out of
the "international foods" section, stock new items like tomatillos and
plantains, or add cumbias to the muzak. Of course, one can easily argue
that such actions are not at all emancipatory but simply designed to in-
tegrate the new clientele further into consumer society, and that would
certainly be true. But what follows from such a conclusion? That the store
owner should be expected to resist the impulse to respond to changes
in the clientele or be condemned for doing so? Would it not be absurd
to deny the obvious fact that the changes do make the store a more hos-
pitable place for the people who shop there? A more appropriate response, I submit, might be to open a dialogue with the supermarket
owner and to ask for funds to support multicultural initiatives in the
education sphere on the grounds that there exists a shared understanding of the changes taking place.

***Proposition 4: Multiculturalism is not a substitute for, nor a guarantee
of, economic justice.*** Its goals, nonetheless, will always be compromised
by the absence of economic justice. Multiculturalism is most immediately

about *consciousness* and *institutions*. These are what is at stake in the struggle, and these are the sites of intervention and renewal. Multiculturalists ask, what kinds of institutions are we going to inhabit in the future? How do we propose to represent ourselves to ourselves and to the world? How fully enfranchised will the populace be with respect to education, language, culture, and expression?

While multiculturalism will not directly bring about economic justice, it brings awareness of the workings and histories of inequalities and fosters more representative institutions through which to correct them. Multiculturalists call for scholarship that clarifies the links between economic injustice and cultural disenfranchisement, that brings the histories behind both to national consciousness, and that explores alternatives.

Proposition 5: Multiculturalism does not "Balkanize"—segregation does. Multiculturalism seeks to multiply the number of socially defined groups that have access to the society's dialogues about itself and to place those groups in dialogue with each other. Inevitably, the dialogue is initially anchored in the groups' differences from each other—but this does not constitute Balkanization; in fact, it constitutes the opposite, for the groups are *in the same room* and are talking and listening to each other. The real Balkanization is what we had before—the legal and de facto segregations around which this country's institutions were built. Nothing could be more Balkanized than American higher education in the 1920s or the 1950s. The momentum of multiculturalism is meant to counter fragmentation produced by social disenfranchisement and segregation.

The Colonized Imagination

I suggested that the breakup of cultural monoliths in the U.S. involves two processes. First, there is the response to new realities such as the communications revolution, the so-called immigrant implosion of the Third World onto the First, the globalization of markets, and the successful demands by women and people of color that their differences be decoupled from legacies of subordination and recognized as the basis for their belonging. Second, people in the U.S. (and in many other countries) are coming to grips with old realities that have been elided from official history.

It is on this latter process that I want to focus for the moment. I'm going to give it a name that may surprise some readers: *decolonization*. When the debates over Western culture broke out in the U.S. a few years ago, I found myself reminded over and over of my years growing up in

English Canada in the 1950s, when pictures of the Queen of England governed every home, courtroom, hockey arena and curling rink and received our morning pledges of allegiance in the classroom; where culture, history, art, reality itself lived somewhere else—not where we were, but on the other side of the ocean, where Britain ruled. These, I later realized, were the workings of the colonized imagination. Now, the United States is a world imperial power, and it is admittedly difficult to think of it as having a colonized imagination. But I am convinced that, in the domain of culture and national understanding, it does.

When it comes to culture, Europe has continued to possess the American, especially the Euramerican, imagination, to be its point of reference, regardless of the realities that surround us here. So it was in the 1920s that American universities debated intensely whether American literature should be taught there. So it was in the 1980s, at many American colleges, that the book lists adopted as representing the cultural heritage of American students included no Americans! These are symptoms, I would argue, of a much more general state of mind. Even when they know almost nothing about European high culture, *as cultural subjects,* I suggest, Americans remain to a significant degree colonial subjects for whom reality and value live somewhere else. They are so constituted by the national institutions of knowledge and culture, official and otherwise. Euramericans tend to experience this phenomenon, as ever in neocolonial contexts, as alienation, passivity, and a sense of disenfranchisement. Asked to define or describe their culture, for example, white American students often react with pain and anger, for they tend to know themselves as people without culture. They tend to envy and resent "ethnic" students who know themselves deeply as cultural beings, because in the absence of political and economic power, culture and community have been the sustenance of life for them. In U.S. ethnic communities, culture often plays the role it plays in anticolonial struggles—as a site and source of resistance to domination. This is very different from the sense of self-alienation and disenfranchisement which characterizes the cultural self-consciousness of many Euramericans and which readily leads people to use white privilege to ridicule culture and those who "have" it. Much of this, I suggest, is the legacy of European colonialism from which this country has still to emancipate itself. In a recent article exploring the term "postcolonial," cultural critic Anne McClintock similarly argues that the U.S. belongs to the group of what she calls "breakaway settler colonies" which "have not undergone decolonization" ("Angel of Progress" 92). Is it the colonized imagination that makes the soil here so fertile for the growth of a passive culture of consumption, spectatorship, and simulation? In the public polemics about canons and book lists, it is the colonized imagination that speaks when numerous writers, even distinguished intellectuals like C. Vann Woodward, denounce books they have never read, writers whose names they have never seen, simply because they are not European. It is, at least in part, the colonized imagination that sends intellectuals from the Americas to Europe for theories of society—even theories about America, like those of Eco, Baudrillard, Todorov—or for terms like "Balkanization" in which to mirror ourselves.

European cultural critics have created a tradition of talking about the sense of unreality they encounter in the United States, about the mania here for creating simulations, replicas, and artificial worlds like Disneyland or Heritage USA. (Eco wrote up his pilgrimage, documenting all the replicas of the "Last Supper" between San Francisco and Los Angeles [see *Travels*].) What is this mania for simulation which the Europeans do not seem to understand (they tend to conclude Americans cannot distinguish between fiction and reality because they have no history)? Perhaps it's what you get when you combine a technological superpower with a colonized imagination that experiences "real" cultural agency as being "somewhere else." Though this view runs counter to perceptions of the U.S. as the ultimate global cultural imperialist, the two facts are not at all incompatible.

What current educational reform movements are engaged in can be understood, in part, as a process of *decolonization* of culture and the national imagination. This involves recognizing the unique historical and cultural experience of the United States and the Americas and the claiming of that experience in all its specificity and complexity. It involves not erasing the European legacy (though that is the thing multiculturalists are most often accused of), but *situating* that legacy within the history of life and society on this side of the Atlantic, being accountable to that history from within.

What is to be gained from such a decolonization? The prospect of society here knowing its reality more fully, judging itself more wisely. It points to the possibility of a society *more fully grounded in its own reality and history*. This is the part I bring up most often when people ask me what is in all of this for the white middle class. An extraordinary cultural renewal, I say, an enrichment and an emancipation—emancipation, for instance, from the sense of being at the mercy of consumption and spectatorship; the possibility of a cultural subject that is more than a consumer. An emancipated imagination is a rich and powerful thing. Colonizers know this well, which is why colonialism tries to deprive the colonized of independent access to cultural institutions, particularly to the means of representing themselves to themselves.

The (U.S. in the) Americas

Earlier on I spoke about the fact that bilingualism, intercultural relations, radical social heterogeneity and discontinuity are old realities in the Americas, though not always part of official histories and national mythologies. This final point is about "the Americas" in the hemispheric sense. Of all the possibilities for cultural renewal offered by the current movements toward cultural enfranchisement, the one that strikes me as most promising is the possibility that the United States will reimagine and resituate itself *in the Americas*—that it will rewrite its history and rework its self-understanding so as to recover the specificity and uniqueness of the experience of this hemisphere. (Uniqueness and specificity are not simple, celebratory terms here: the experience to be recovered has horrendous dimensions which multiculturalists are always being attacked for bringing up.) The unique, specific experience of this hemisphere includes the history of the huge range of indigenous societies, both before and since contact with Europe; the European invasion and conquest and the establishment of white settler colonialism; the elaboration of African-based cultures out of massive forced emigration and slavery. European intellectual history, often accepted as the source of American social understanding, has an extraordinarily limited capacity to characterize the realities of the Americas, for its anchor points are in the history of European society. European theory is not going to tell us about colonialism, neocolonialism, dependency, and decolonization from the receiving end. (For that we must look to Latin American and Caribbean thought.) European social theory only peripherally knows or even cares about such questions as the structure of settler societies, the interactions between Christianity and indigenous religions, the plantation as a social order, the structure of intercultural relations on the frontier, institutional racism or the ways in which imperialism interacted with religion and patriarchy, the role land plays in the frontier imagination and in the consciousness of long-term subsistence societies. Yet these are matters of central concern to social understanding in the Americas.

As the examples suggest, the reidentification with the Americas which I am describing is part of what I referred to earlier as the *decolonization of consciousness*. As most Americanists (in the hemispheric sense) are aware, it is not a question of setting such a process in motion: it *is* in motion and has been for some time, accelerated by the social movements of the 1960s and foregrounded by the recent 1992 quincentennial. Within the United States, significant and often brilliant scholarship has sought to decenter the Euro-centered narrative of Western expansion as the backbone of national history and to view things from an intellectual center of gravity here. As U.S. multiculturalists know, the body of Canadian thought on these issues is much larger and more sophisticated than what has emerged in the U.S., partly because Canada has been dealing openly with these issues for a longer time and partly because Canada has staked its very constitutional viability on the possibility of a diverse and discontinuous conception of the nation-state. But I propose to end by looking southward and offering, in list fashion, a few examples of terms and concepts from Latin American and Caribbean intellectual dialogues on the social and cultural peculiarities of the Americas. See if you don't think there are inter-American conversations to be held on the subject of culture and American self-understanding.

(1) *Criollo* is the term in Spanish for a Euramerican. While this category has never functioned in U.S. social thought, it has been a basic term in Latin American vocabulary since colonial times, when it was used to distinguish people of European descent who were born in the Americas from those who were born in Europe and who, under Spanish colonialism, were given the positions of greatest power and privilege. The category has always functioned to distinguish the Euramericans from Europeans, especially in regard to their relationship to Europe. Equally important, it has functioned to distinguish Euramericans who, following independence, formed the elites of most countries, from indigenous, mestizo, and African-descended populations.

It can be enlightening to think of the United States as a multiethnic country ruled by a criollo elite, with significant indigenous, mestizo (especially in the West and Southwest), and African-descended populations. The term *criollo* is especially helpful in characterizing the *dependent* relations the Euramerican elites have maintained with Europe. In the multiethnic, heterogeneous social orders of the Americas, the European referent, however alienated it may be from the lived American reality, becomes the chief guarantor of criollo identity and the chief means of legitimating their privilege over others *to themselves*. The term thus names the alienated basis for white supremacy in the societies of the Americas.

(2) *Creole*, the English translation of *criollo*, is a broader term that denotes anything born in the Americas out of its intersecting cultural heritages. *Creole* refers specifically to the uniqueness of American-generated phenomena, whether language, music, race, culture, or dress, to their *difference* from European or African or Asian or Amerindian "originals." Creole, in a way, denotes the upstart, the unauthentic, mixed-around thing, that generates its own authenticity, often by being rooted in a particular, very local place: Jamaica, Trinidad, Antigua, and so on. In linguistics, *creole* is the name given to languages that began as pidgins— hybrid, simplified languages invented to enable communication

between historically discontinuous groups (like European slave traders in West Africa, or U.S. soldiers in Vietnam). When such languages develop into the full-fledged native language of a group, they are called *creoles*. The term thus embodies the improvised, transcultural character that many see as a central fact of culture and society in the Americas since contact with Europe and Africa.

American vernacular culture is often fruitfully analyzed as creole or creolized in this way. The term has the potential to go beyond the narrowness and alienation of hyphenated ethnic terminologies toward self-conceptions rooted in American reality.

(3) *Transculturation* is a term originally coined in the 1940s by the Cuban sociologist Fernando Ortiz, as he studied the workings of Afro-Cuban society and its development in the tobacco and sugar economies of the Caribbean. Anthropology had used the concept of acculturation to describe the ways subordinated groups absorbed materials from dominant cultures, but Ortiz found this term inadequate to depict the dynamics of Afro-Cuban culture which he observed. The traditional assumption was that, in situations of contact between dominant and subordinate or metropolitan and peripheral cultures, the subordinate or peripheral culture necessarily acculturates to the dominant or metropolitan culture, gradually abandoning its own practices and traditions. The assumption was that (a) culture tends to be a finite space in which new things must necessarily displace old things and (b) subordinate and marginal peoples absorb metropolitan or dominant cultures by something akin to osmosis, exercising no choice or agency in the matter. Ortiz's argument, later developed by the Uruguayan literary scholar Angel Rama, was that, in fact, subordinate groups are anything but inert when it comes to determinant relations with dominant and metropolitan cultures. Even in situations of extraordinarily unequal power, they argue, subordinate groups are highly *selective* and *inventive* in absorbing materials from the metropolis, and they develop many ways of maintaining cultural integrity. When processes of selection and invention are factored into the picture, what once appeared as a simplistic dynamic of acculturation is better characterized as a dynamic of *trans*culturation. (The absorption of Christian elements into preconquest religions, traditionally called *syncretism*, is perhaps the best known example of such selection and invention. The selective tendency of Latin American intellectuals to absorb resistant and critical currents of European thought, such as Marxism and radical Christianity, is another.)

Transculturation is a vital concept for characterizing the dynamics of culture in the Americas from a vantage point anchored in the Americas rather than in Europe. It forces into motion static pluralist paradigms that multiculturalists often find so confining.

(4) *Heterogeneity* is a term introduced by the Peruvian scholar Antonio Cornejo Polar to describe society and culture in the Andean countries, where Euramerican (criollo) minorities cohabit national territory with large indigenous populations whose language and traditions are Andean and large mestizo populations whose life ways draw on both. In contrast to the terms "difference" and "diversity" used in European and North American discussions, Cornejo Polar uses the concept of "heterogeneity" and *culturas heterogeneas* ("heterogeneous cultures") to name the conditions of drastic discontinuity and incommensurability that characterize societies where colonial invasion has brought together peoples with entirely separate histories, such as the Spanish and the Andeans. When one side does not eliminate the other, such societies articulate themselves in states of intractable conflict and profound incomprehension. The idea of a social synthesis or community is not an option, nor is the idea of a single national form of expression or representation that will speak to/for all. There is no shared discourse or concept of membership, no shared symbols, not even any stable meanings, for the signifiers constructed by one side will be transculturated and redefined by the other. More than a case of the proverbial slipperiness of signifiers, it is a case of profound semantic disjuncture. Such situations appear extreme from the perspective of a normative model of social homogeneity, but, as Cornejo Polar argues, they are normal conditions of existence and social structure in the Americas, and we can't intervene in them wisely until we have adequate theories of them.

In a way, Cornejo Polar's use of the term heterogeneity can be thought of as radicalizing (though not in the political sense) the more descriptive European-based vocabulary of difference, différance, heteroglossia, and polyphony so that it can express the physical and epistemological violence that follows on the shock of contact and invasion. There are many areas of the United States where the model of the *culturas heterogeneas* would help us recover the specific ways the history of colonial contact continues to determine reality.

I introduce these four concepts, *criollo, creole, transculturation,* and *heterogeneity,* along with the term *decolonization,* to encourage consideration of what it might mean for U.S. Americans to work out theories of society and culture which take American historical experience as the norm. Such theorizing would be grounded in an open encounter with American realities and anchored in the shared experience of this hemisphere, an experience that both divides us irrevocably from Europe and binds us historically to Europe (as well as to the rest of the world).

A few years ago, my son's fourth-grade class was given a copy of a letter Chief Seattle wrote to the president of the United States toward the end of the last century, protesting the violation of land agreements by white settlers. The settlers argued back that they needed the land to survive. The fourth graders were asked, of all things, to think about it and write up what they thought would be a fair solution. My son, a skeptic when it came to schoolwork, closed his door and, astonishingly, began to write. Pages flew, covering the floor. He emerged with a two-sentence paragraph that said something like, "There is no fair way to solve this problem. The Europeans must return to Europe and the Native Americans must agree to stay in America." I told him I thought he had probably reconstructed Chief Seattle's own conclusion. But what was to be Manuel's solution, as a Chicano-Jewish-Anglo-Canadian-California kid? How was he to situate himself with respect to that manichean history? There was no language for it in his classroom, no language better than that which Chief Seattle was able to lay his hands on over a century ago as he sought to negotiate with the conqueror in the conqueror's language. We can do better than this, I thought—and for Manuel's sake, we have to.

While the wholesale re-envisioning of society remains incomplete, few of us have any trouble envisioning the work that awaits us as scholars and educators. The picture is daunting and exciting. It is not necessary to dream to encounter scholars and teachers excited by new possibilities for understanding, driven by curiosity, eager to read the lost texts and the new ones, eager to branch out of their specializations and to devise forms of collaborative work that are accountable to heterogeneity and multiplicity. One need not dream to find teachers exploring new pedagogies for multiethnic classrooms, pedagogies where the teacher's role cannot be to unify the world or create homogeneously shared understandings. Everywhere, teachers are working to develop forms of classroom leadership that will shape, but not control, the development of understanding and foster in students a sense of excitement over the responsibility of creating a new vision of one's society. One still does have to dream, however, to encounter two elements still largely lacking at present. The first of these is translators, who are needed in the dozens to make the knowledge and insights from each part of the world available to others. Respect for the work of translation has not yet caught up in the U.S. with the vital need for it. One can only hope it will. The second element that still has to be dreamed could be called a science of cultural mediation, by which I mean a disciplined inquiry into the means by which intercultural understanding and communication are constructed and sustained. I believe it will not be long before such an inquiry consolidates itself. There is work to be done, lots of it. We know something about what it is and how to do it. The thing now is to get on with it.

Works Cited

Burciaga, José Antonio. "The Tall Ones Are Ganging Up on Me." *Estos Tiempos.* Stanford U, 1988. 1. Rpt. in Burciaga, José Antonio. *Weedee Peepo: A Collection of Essays.* Edinburg, TX: Pan American UP, 1989. 118–23.

Eco, Umberto. *Travels in Hyper Reality: Essays.* Trans. William Weaver. San Diego: Harcourt, 1986.

McClintock, Anne. "The Angel of Progress: Pitfalls of the term 'Postcolonialism.'" *Social Text* no. 31/32 (1992): 84–98.

Mignolo, Walter. "Literacy and Colonization: The New World Experience." *1492–1992: Re/Discovering Colonial Writing.* Ed. Rene Jara and Nicholas Spadaccini. Minneapolis: Prisma Institute, 1989. 51–96.

Nichols, Patricia. "Language in the Attic: Claiming Our Linguistic Heritage." *Diversity as Resource: Redefining Cultural Literacy.* Ed. Denise E. Murray. Alexandria, VA: TESOL Publications, 1990.

"The Stanford Mind." *Wall Street Journal* 22 December 1988, morning ed.

2 What We Talk about When We Talk about Politics

John Warnock
University of Arizona

In public discourse in the United States, we are schooled, assiduously, in how to keep "politics" out of the conversation, even in situations where politics is obviously the order of the day. If "politics" is mentioned at all in the pronouncements of our legislators, it is likely to be demonized. Recalcitrant compatriots are accused of engaging in "partisan" politics, as if there were some other kind. Our legislators may from time to time agree with each other, but events of the last ten years have made it clear, if it wasn't clear before, that many Americans outside the corridors of power can take little comfort from that fact.

There is one place, we are invited to believe, that ought always to be especially free of demon politics, a place where we are led to expect instruction, not rhetoric; "the transfer of knowledge," not "indoctrination"; general truths, not special pleading. That place is the classroom.

Certainly, we were invited to think of the classroom in this way by the former chair of the National Endowment for the Humanities, Lynne Cheney. Again and again, in her speeches and publications, she inveighed against "politics" in the classroom.

The proposition has an a priori appeal. For one thing, allowing politics into the classroom offends our peculiarly American (we may like to think) sense of fair play: it isn't fair that students, who are subject to their professors, should have to profess their professor's particular political beliefs to "get along." It isn't fair, either, that professors should be able to subvert the political commitments of taxpayers when the taxpayers are paying the bills. "The taxpayer" is, of course, a mythical creature. Everyone pays taxes, but not everyone has the same politics, and it may occur to us that we need to ask *which* taxpayers are having their values subverted. Again, the point is rarely raised when it is being claimed that "the taxpayer" has been aggrieved.

If "politics in the classroom" means teachers and professors demanding from their students avowals of particular political commitments as a condition of getting good grades, not many would defend it. In this scenario, a particular set of political commitments is promoted by force, or by a merely hortatory project. The politics are given, part of an "agenda," and the teacher's goal is simply to manipulate others into accepting those beliefs. The distaste that attaches to this kind of politics, in or out of the classroom, is the same distaste that attaches to "rhetoric," as the term is commonly employed in contemporary public discourse. "Politics," like "rhetoric," is here something you can be accused of.

But what if "politics in the classroom" means teachers and professors considering with their students the causes and consequences of inequalities of power in cultures past and present and the means by which those inequalities may be maintained and challenged? If that is what we mean by "politics," the motive for the argument against politics in the classroom has changed radically. We oppose or support the first kind of politics in the classroom because we believe that it unfairly promotes the interests of the powerful. But we will support or oppose the second kind of politics in the classroom for just the opposite reason—because we think it may help us see how to promote the interests of the powerless.

The ex-chair's consistent failure to recognize this equivocation in the word "politics" leaves us to wonder if she wasn't hoping that her audiences might miss the equivocation so that the distaste some of us might feel for the first kind of politics in the classroom might attach itself to the second, and very different, kind. If people insist, as the ex-chair did, that education should be free of "politics," and if they fail, as the ex-chair did, to say what they mean by the term, it seems entirely possible that they are trying not to free education from politics but to disable any criticism of their educational proposals themselves as an exercise of power.

Escape from "Agenda": The Move to Knowledge

The ex-chair was certainly correct in assuming that, in the United States, many of us believe that a teacher's particular political loyalties and beliefs should not be *imposed* in a classroom upon those who are subject to the superior power of the teacher. We are likely to believe this about the imposition of the teacher's "politics" even if we understand that students are imposed upon, and in many theories of education, *should* be imposed upon, in myriad ways. "Politics," we think, is a special case. People should be allowed to choose their "politics" freely. Education should educate, we say, not "indoctrinate," though upon reflection we may decide that we need to make certain exceptions to that principle.

As a teacher of literature and writing of twenty-five years' experience—often with students who, left to their own devices, would not have chosen to be in the particular class I was teaching—the idea that a professor might "impose" a set of political loyalties and beliefs on students strikes me as comical. I would guess that many of the parents who are concerned about such teacherly impositions are all too aware of how unsuccessful they themselves have been in imposing their own values on their own children. You have to wonder why they think professors— particularly *English* professors—would be more successful than they have been.

On the other hand, it is important not to overstate the independence of students or the powerlessness of professors and teachers. Students' powers of resistance to the blandishments of "others" are constrained in many ways, not least by the fact that, if they are adolescents, they are struggling to construct identities they can live with as adults. Furthermore, while teachers and professors may be characterized as ineffectual in any "real" world, their powers are considerable vis-à-vis the students. These powers are hardly absolute, and they may not be very strong at all relative to the powers of, say, advertising. But they are not insignificant. We who are professors and teachers might like to think our powers come from what we know, and this may, to some extent, be so. But surely the knowledge we may have "banked" must finally be seen as a good deal less significant as a source of power than our institutional standing. We can be silly and ignorant, yet still be accorded a great deal of power as long as we continue to be embraced by one of the established educational institutions. Teachers or professors who think their power comes from what they know can always test this proposition by quitting their jobs and hanging out a shingle.

In any case, very few of the professors and teachers I know want to impose their "politics" on their students—not all, but most would be horrified to think that that was what they were doing. This scruple may be taken as laudable (by liberals), or as lamentable (by critical commentators who see this attitude as a feature of complicity with the reigning order). In any case, professors who set about consciously to impose their politics on their students are far rarer than the coverage accorded to complaints from the right might lead us to believe.

The classic strategy employed by educators who wish not to impose their politics is the move to "knowledge." "Knowledge," posited as the foundation of the educational enterprise, erases "politics" of the sort that presupposes an "agenda."

A classic instance of the use of this strategy is found in the proposals of E. D. Hirsch concerning "cultural literacy," proposals eagerly embraced by the ex-chair, and also by the Exxon Foundation, which funded Hirsch's Foundation for Cultural Literacy. Professor Hirsch proposed that teachers should teach the "contents" of "cultural literacy." These "contents" could be established "scientifically"—that is, apolitically—by running surveys to find out "what literate Americans know" (see *Cultural Literacy*).

Hirsch did acknowledge that while the project of ascertaining the contents of cultural literacy might be scientific, the undertaking to teach those contents was "political," in that it amounted to an undertaking to preserve "the nation." "The nation" had not just a different future, but no future, he implied, if these "contents" were not taught. To this conservative political agenda, Hirsch added a liberal one by asserting that children deprived of an education in cultural literacy would also be deprived of any prospect of making it in the modern industrial world.

Colonizers have always found a way to convince themselves that they were doing their subjects good.

As Hirsch sets up the matter, the *only* obstacle to "effective communication" with the reigning order is this lack of common knowledge. Eliminating educational inequality is thus made into a merely technical problem—one that teachers and students can be blamed for not solving—once the "contents of cultural literacy" are known. Utterly absent from Hirsch's considerations are such matters as the "savage inequalities" in school funding documented by Jonathan Kozol, and the possibility they raise that educational inequality is neither an accident nor the product of a poor curriculum, so much as it is the product of a system that produces and maintains that inequality (see *Savage Inequalities*).

Professor Hirsch was often accused, wrongly, of arguing that we should teach the "canon." Actually, he was promoting, as he often protested, something much more like a vocabulary list. This seemed to those of us who were concerned about the politics of Hirsch's proposals to be anything but consoling. We might at least hope that literary works would contribute to their readers' liberatory political educations despite how they were taught (as Shakespeare's writing did in Huxley's *Brave New World*); vocabulary lists have no such built-in resistance to the suppression of politics. Once we accept Hirsch's vocabulary list in the terms in which it is offered—as the scientifically established knowledge that is necessary to anyone who would communicate effectively with "literate culture"—all we have left to do is update these "contents" in minor respects from time to time and to look for "effective" teaching methods. We don't have to trouble our little heads about politics at all.

To propose to establish a curriculum for cultural literacy in a way that is "scientific" will be seen as reassuring if the alternative to "scientific" is taken to be "arbitrary" or "by fiat." But it is not so reassuring if we see the promise of a "scientific" approach as a way of suppressing the inescapable political dimensions of such a project and a refusal to accept the task of working out, and with, those politics.

When we object to the mystifying way in which Hirsch proposes to establish a curriculum for "cultural literacy" and the mystified status he gives such "knowledge," we need not also to be understood as objecting to *any* such curriculum at the national or the local level. If an effort to establish a curriculum for cultural literacy were made part of an inquiry into relations between knowers and what they know, teachers and students, teachers and their sponsoring institutions, the sponsoring institutions and other cultural institutions, and if it were understood that these relations necessarily involve domination, appropriation, resistance, and what Mary Louise Pratt calls "transculturation" (see *Imperial Eyes*), then this proposed national curriculum for cultural literacy might amount to something other than just another colonial project.

Curricularizing Politics: The Move to Theory

Another strategy for curricularizing politics—but one that is not nearly so safe as the move to knowledge—is the move to theory. "Theory" can have many meanings, and one of them is very much like the meaning of "knowledge," as when we speak of a theory that has been "validated," which we may then go on simply to "apply." Sometimes "theory" has a much more contingent quality than does "knowledge." A "theory" is *a* way of seeing, not *the* way, and this implies other ways of seeing, which may be not only possible but preferable, depending on the situation in which we find ourselves.

Fundamentalist thinkers will sometimes consider that they have scored a point by characterizing some set of proposals—those in the theory of evolution, for example—as "only" theory. They are, of course, presupposing an accessible realm of propositions that are not "theorized" but "known," by faith, perhaps, or, if one is a certain kind of hardheaded realist, by empirical observation. The "theorist" does not operate in this realm.

When we propose to deal with theory, then, we place ourselves in a realm that may be less safe from politics than are the realms of "knowledge." A theory may be discussed in a way that puts at issue more than what is and isn't part of the "contents" of "cultural literacy" and how we may "transfer" them. From this point of view, we can understand why the ex-chair and others like her in education have consistently done what they could to demonize "theory."

Gerald Graff, on the other hand, has proposed that we accept the contingency of "theory" in "English" and make a virtue of it. Graff recognized that a number of different theories—some quite incompatible with each other—are at work in contemporary academic English departments (see *Beyond the Culture Wars*). Over the years, though, he claimed, we in "English" have hidden our professional disputes from our students in a curriculum that is based upon the principle of "coverage," even though it offers courses that differ not only in content, but in what is presupposed about the nature of "English." We know about these differences, but we make no effort to come to terms with them in the curriculum. Our differences with each other, said Graff, in what seems to me a very happy analogy, have been like those family secrets parents keep from the children, or think they do. We could revitalize English studies, he claimed, if we acknowledged these differences forthrightly and brought them into the curriculum, perhaps by making our classes look more like our conferences. In short, he says, we should "teach the conflicts."

Graff's proposals are obviously not as containable as Hirsch's. They acknowledge conflict and thus open up the possibility of political awareness. If we ask "Whose conflicts?" Graff's answer is clear: the conflicts are those that may be located in the arguments of professionals in English studies. Well, the arguments of *some* professionals in English studies. Certainly not the arguments of teachers of English in the schools, where the disputes that exercise academics can seem more than a little strange. But not even of all academic professors of English, many of whom have little time for the conflicts that Graff and others in the academy (including me) think are so interesting and significant.

For our present purposes, the question of "Whose conflicts?" is of less import, however, than questions that might be raised about the words "teach" and "the" in the formula. The "the" implies that what we will be dealing with here is an objectifiable subject matter. Consider the difference if the formula were "teach conflicts." Further, the word "teach" suggests a relationship to this subject matter and to students that simply reproduces standard assumptions about the "natural" relations of professors, students, and subject matter that themselves should be questioned. Consider the difference if the formula were, say, "locate" or "enact" or "embody" conflicts.

Graff's proposals are not as safe from politics as Hirsch's, but in their apparent satisfaction with locating the conflicts that we are to address— in what certain academic professionals in certain situations concern themselves with in their conversations with each other—they may be safer than some of us might wish.

Today, the word "theory" is often found in company with the adjective "critical," as in the title of this book. The adjective "critical" bespeaks among other things an aspiration to make theory *active*, not merely the kind of thing that might be "learned." Critical theory thus has an essential relation to practice, but not one in which it is merely "applied." Its role is to help us reflect *upon* practice—"cultural" practice, typically, as manifested in everything from material culture, to advertising, to the media, to the products of "high" culture. It aspires to help us discern agendas in these cultural practices—typically the agendas of racism, sexism, and classism—and thus it offers itself as a way of doing politics in educational settings that is not itself a mere matter of promoting an agenda, which professional educators—and not just critics of education—tend to consider unprofessional. As such, critical theory may also offer a kind of consolation to those educators who, while they don't want to promote an agenda, also do not want to serve passively as agents for the reigning order.

Though critical theory is usually seen as something new, its educational goal has a long and respectable tradition: Aristotle urged the study of rhetoric for most people as a way of enabling them to resist the rhetoricians.

Students, as well as professional educators, can become very excited by this kind of study and exhibit a growing sense of their power to resist sexism, racism, and classism in the myriad forms in which they are incorporated into our cultural practice. But for those who wish to find a way to "do" politics in educational settings without descending to the mere promotion of particular political agendas, it seems apparent to me that critical theory will not provide the answer. To begin with, the practices of those authors who establish reputations as critical theorists almost always participate in two biases built into our sense of what it is to do good academic work: the bias against practice and the bias against the local. It is telling that while critical theorists analyze and interpret practice, they describe themselves as critical *theorists*, not as practitioners. They write and teach with the goal of "understanding" certain practices, not with the goal of changing practice, their own or that of others, except insofar as an understanding of the agendas of the cultural practices under scrutiny—which usually are neither personal nor local—itself changes practice. Further, although the practices they study are not always those of elite culture, they tend to be located at some distance from their own practice and their own situations.

I have seen brilliant critical theorists utterly baffled at questions about how they reflect their critical theory in their teaching. Usually, the problem seems to be not that the brilliant critical theorist feels that this is a hard question to answer, but rather that the question seems to be one of stunning irrelevance, as if one were to ask Tolstoy how he reflected the values of his novels in his relations with his wife.

In academic literary study, we tend to enforce the view that ethics is irrelevant to and less important than poetics, and, by analogy, that practice is of less importance than theory. We do this not by accident but because our standards of professionalism require it. In the schools, this disjunction is also enforced, but in the schools the emphasis tends to be on a sort of denatured ethics—"interpersonal skills"—rather than on poetics. In both situations, this disjunction can lead us into embarrassing situations which, like the brilliant critical theorist, we may or may not notice *as* embarrassing.

On a brief visit to Piaget's Rousseau Institute in 1977, I read an editorial in the student newspaper that asked how the professors reconciled what they were teaching about development (that children learn to be intelligent by acting intelligently, perhaps) with the fact that these lessons were being delivered in lectures to hundreds of note-taking students in huge halls.

The point here is not to lodge an accusation of hypocrisy, with an adjuration implied that what we need to do is to get our theory and our practice into line. When practice is brought into line with theory, the result can be inane, as when the student writes the essay according to the formula for the five-paragraph theme, or comical, as when Malvolio dresses the way he thinks a lover is supposed to dress. It can also be horrific, as when Pol Pot displaces and kills millions of people in Cambodia to enforce his vision of the way things ought to be.

When it comes to theory, including critical theory, it is crucial to keep in mind the caveat memorably expressed by Kenneth Burke:

> Even if any given terminology is a **reflection** of reality, by its very nature as a terminology it must be a **selection** of reality; and to this extent it must function as a **deflection** of reality. (45)

In academic theorizing, our strength is our weakness. We are smart; we can "understand" this stuff; we can use it to "bring out" what is not obvious to others. Unfortunately, we sometimes write as if we believe that our theories are to be understood entirely as reflections of the reality we are dealing with, and not also as selections and deflections of it. This failing is characteristic of us in the academy, not just of those benighted souls who may not have developed to the point of being able to understand their theories *as* theories. In the academy, the failing arises not out of simplemindedness, but out of a susceptibility to the "poetics" of theory (in Burke's sense; see Burke 25–43). We in the academy are permitted and in some respects obligated to live and work in a domain where we are, in fact, insulated from much of what "ordinary" people have to deal with, especially if we are the sort of people who involve ourselves in the conflicts Graff and other important critical theorists are interested in. Our susceptibility to the poetics of theory—which in another light might be called a weakness for totality—is something we academics are *supposed* to have. It is a quality that can make us useful to parties who may stand to benefit from our actions, irrelevant outside our specialized contexts, and dangerous when we get to be in a position to enforce our theories broadly.

Politics (Weak Sense) and Politics (Strong Sense)

It seems to me that we can protect ourselves to some extent against the lure of poetics in our critical theory by understanding that the politics that critical theory will be able to comprehend is politics in the weak sense, by which I mean those politics that we are able to "know," not necessarily as "knowledge" or "final truth," but as a matter of conscious awareness.

Politics (weak sense) is something that it might at least be *possible* to keep out of a classroom, or at least out of the topics of explicit conversation in the classroom. We might at different times decide that it is also *desirable* to keep it out of the classroom, perhaps because it might place our students at special risk, or because we happen to be teaching a course in calculus. At other times, we might decide that it is important to introduce politics (weak sense) into a classroom where it is not "expected," even a classroom in calculus, just as Paolo Freire decided it was important to introduce this kind of politics as part of his effort to "alphabetize" Brazilian peasants.

Politics (strong sense), however, is the politics that works through us in our actions, whether we are aware of this work or not, and in ways of which we can be aware only partially and belatedly.

This is the politics that works in our selections and deflections, not just our reflections, not just in virtue of who we know ourselves to be but who we wish we were or who we are afraid we might be; not just in virtue of what we know, but in what we know that isn't so, what we wish were the case, what we wish not to know, what we consider not worth knowing. Politics (strong sense) is always already with us in our human relations, whether we think of these relations as with others or ourselves. Our relations with our students can't not be affected by our politics (strong sense). We cannot keep them out of the classroom since they are part of what brings us, our students, the classroom itself into being.

It might seem that the politics I have designated here as "weak" should be considered "strong" (because "known") and vice versa. Certainly, those of us who see the highest human achievement as knowledge would tend to reverse the terms. But I wish to make the point that the politics of which we are conscious must be but an instance of the politics which we enact at all levels, conscious and other than conscious.

When it comes to *knowing* our politics (strong sense), we encounter a conundrum that has been recognized with respect to *knowing* our own culture. We *must* know our culture, in one sense, or it wouldn't be ours, but in another sense, we cannot know it since it is the very system of significance by which we know. It is not a difficult matter to "criticize" the "factual" statement that "Columbus discovered America in 1492." If we were paying attention at all during the quincentenary, we learned to question the word "discovered" (since human beings were already here), and it may even have occurred to us to question the idea that "Columbus" did the discovering when it was probably a crew member who first saw the "new" land, and because we have learned to question the attribution of such feats to one person, since projects like that exploratory journey are inconceivable without the work of many hands and the coalescence of many historical and social factors. We may even have gone so far as to question the notion that the event happened in 1492, since we have learned that even the calendar is not politically innocent. It wouldn't be 1492 if the Mongols had conquered Europe, as they very nearly did.

But having developed these political criticisms of what we might once have taken to be an innocent claim, where are we? What do we replace that claim with? I invite readers to try out different sentences. I think the undertaking will demonstrate that while we can think *about* our culture, we must also think *through* it, and that in this thinking we will never be entirely outside of it.

Considerations like these reflect only part of the challenge of coming to terms with politics (strong sense). The challenge less often acknowledged (perhaps because it might remind us of certain scandals in our professional conduct) is the challenge adumbrated in the discrepancy between our theory and our practice, or, if you like, between what we preach and what we practice. Unfortunately, as argued above, the scandals are not to be addressed merely by forcing our practice into line with our theory. Forcing practice into line with theory is the aspiration of one who would totalize a politics (weak sense), not the aspiration of one who would wrestle with the angel of politics (strong sense).

If we wish to make our classrooms a place for such wrestling, we can begin by turning around the standard relation between theory and practice, to hold that practice (or, if you like, "action"), not theory, is the larger notion, that while theory and knowledge can help us criticize and develop practice, they must always be criticized finally in terms of practice.

It is important to remember here that what we are calling "practice" is something that is, by definition, not entirely "known" to us. We are recognizing that when we "act," we do so without knowing entirely why, or wherefore, or what the outcomes will be. This is the stuff of comedy, and of tragedy, and of much that does not attain to either of these distinctions.

We may then want to see questions of pedagogy as questions of practice (or action) and not, as they may be even by critical theorists, questions of "technique," and thus as questions of limited interest, irrelevant to the critical project. In categorizing pedagogical questions as questions of technique, one shares the politics of Professor Hirsch, who insisted that once the "contents" of cultural literacy were ascertained, many techniques for teaching them might be developed. Professor Hirsch may have wished to make (and indeed was making) a gesture of liberal tolerance here, but more importantly, he was making the old move of locating questions of pedagogy outside the realms of real significance—characterizing them as merely technical questions—*how* to teach—as against questions of substance—*what* should be taught. This is a classic move by which politics-busters have forever attempted to secure their programs against the demon.

To those who hope to wrestle with politics (strong sense) in their actions in the classroom, knowledge of different techniques of teaching can be helpful. But it is important to realize that no pedagogical technique, as such, is a sure way of achieving this end—not "process teaching," not "collaboration," not "group work." All these techniques can be given over to other than liberatory purposes, as indeed can any technique.

As mysterious as this new relation to practice may be in some respects, I do not see it as a relation for which we must seek heretofore unimagined models. It seems to me very like the relation between the writer and the draft. The writer engaged with the draft knows there is no place outside the evolving draft where he or she may stand and dictate outcomes. The writer engaged with the draft knows that the tedious, the everyday, can embody as much mystery as the momentous. The writer engaged with the draft knows that what the writer experiences as unexpected, unplanned, grotesque may come to be seen as the result of a door opening, a burden being laid down, a call answered. The writer engaged with the draft understands that the struggle is sometimes to act, knowing that while you know something, what you know is never enough and may not even be so. And so it will have to be enough to believe that there is something here, or not here yet but within reach, worth striving for, something to do not just with oneself but with other people. And not just with "who I am" or "who they are," but with what I, and other people, might be, not somewhere over the rainbow, but in some place I might make here, now, and there, then, in this language, this world.

Works Cited

Burke, Kenneth. *Language as Symbolic Action: Essays on Life, Literature, and Method.* Berkeley: U of California P, 1966.

Graff, Gerald. *Beyond the Culture Wars: How Teaching the Conflicts Can Revitalize American Education.* New York: Norton, 1992.

Hirsch, E. D., Jr. *Cultural Literacy: What Every American Needs to Know.* Boston: Houghton, 1987.

Kozol, Jonathan. *Savage Inequalities: Children in America's Schools.* New York: Crown, 1991.

Pratt, Mary Louise. *Imperial Eyes: Travel Writing and Transculturation.* New York: Routledge, 1992.

3 Theory, Confusion, Inclusion

Keith Hjortshoj
Cornell University

In that place, where they tore the nightshade and blackberry patches from their roots to make room for the Medallion City Golf Course, there was once a neighborhood.

—The opening sentence in Toni
Morrison's *Sula*

When I returned from the NCTE conference at Myrtle Beach in 1991, sunburned and overstimulated, I immediately drafted an account of the ways in which the main speakers' arguments had helped to clarify my own position, as an anthropologist who teaches writing in interdisciplinary programs at Cornell, at the confluence of literary and social theory, literary and cultural studies. Some of the themes of the 1991 conference led me to explain, at the beginning of this draft, that I had been troubled for several years by social constructionist pedagogies, especially in the field of rhetoric and composition, that subject students to the authority of hypothetical "communities" of academic discourse. Gerald Graff's suggestion that we should "teach the conflicts" within and among these communities seemed preferable to the myths of consensus that subordinate undergraduates to several conflicting delusions of grandeur each semester. I went on to argue, however, that any pedagogy that locates the construction of knowledge in privileged discourse communities remains deaf to the intersubjective resonance through which learning actually occurs. In reference to Barbara Christian's observation that values are embodied in the sounds of language, I was developing this concept of intersubjective resonance, as the basis for a truly *social* constructionist pedagogy, when I learned that related discussions would continue at Myrtle Beach in 1992, with contributions from other scholars and teachers I admire. I set this draft aside, then, to find out how it would look in the light that Mary Louise Pratt and Peter Elbow might shed on it.

After the 1992 conference, my arguments rang false to me in an unexpected, interesting, and ironic way, as first drafts often do. The summaries and critiques I had constructed still seemed accurate. The theoretical position I had carved out for myself was still credible, I felt, and still faithful to the way I teach. When I put that essay to rest, I had come to believe that it represented the way the conference had led me to reposition myself. It was a good story about theoretical realignment, of the sort that passes for dialogue in our professional journals, and even now I'm reluctant to part with it.

While I was reading this old draft, however, I also noticed that in deference to the conference speakers and organizers, I had done precisely what our students (or, at any rate, the cleverest ones) continually do for us. By positioning myself in relation to the arguments of the main speakers and to the stated goals of the conference, I had helped to maintain a theory of learning and change that I don't accept—one I was even arguing against in the essay itself. This theory of learning constructs an almost irresistible, circular genealogy of illusions that begins, we'll say, when conference speakers construe their teaching experience and scholarship into positions that correspond with conference topics, much in the way that teachers construct lectures, assignments, and reading materials for specific courses. These speeches and the discussions they stimulate help participants to construct theoretical and pedagogical positions of their own, which they carry back to their institutions and use to redesign their courses. The new directions from which these teachers approach the classroom then shape the learning experiences of their students. According to this model, theory governs practice, which structures the learning experience according to the teacher's intentions.

As long as everyone involved agrees to account for experience along these lines, learning and change appear to occur along these lines as well. So our students struggle to represent what they learned as a rendition of what we intended for them to learn and to demonstrate that they changed in the ways we hoped they would change: that what they got out of the course was a version of what we put into it. In fact, students are often more interested in one another than in their teachers, and they often learn the most from one another too. Their most profound learning experiences can result from something another student says or writes, from a passage in the readings that we consider unimportant, from the answers they discover to questions we didn't ask, from questions they ask that we can't answer, or from the silent ways in which they resist us. When we ask students to tell us what they got out of the course, however, their assessments rarely include the types of learning that occur outside the conventional lines of transmission, in which theories of teaching, the practice of teaching, and learning appear to make sense together.

I found it interesting, then, that my initial account of the 1991 conference conformed so closely to the overt structure and purpose of the event: that I chose to construe the effects of highly theoretical speeches in theoretical terms and that I defined my position in relation to those of the main speakers. No one told me to do this. Participants were encouraged to write and speak freely, from any perspective. Yet the structure of an academic conference, like the structure of a course, implicitly distinguishes responses that seem relevant and coherent from equally authentic responses that seem irrelevant or incoherent. My first draft represented a version of the truth that would make the easiest kind of sense in this frame of reference. It also demonstrated that, like a good student, I was paying attention and was smart enough to summarize and criticize the speakers' arguments. Other versions of the truth are more erratic and difficult to explain, but they also represent more authentic accounts, I believe, of the peculiar, unruly ways in which we and our students come to new understandings.

Much of what we notice *is* irrelevant, I suppose, to the communities in which the experiences of individuals acquire social or cultural meaning. Before a couple of the morning sessions at the conference, I spent some time on the footbridge to the beach watching a green heron, the sneakiest creature on earth, stalking minnows from the bank of Ocean Creek at low tide. There, just beneath the resort's snack bar and condominium towers, this little heron went about its ancestral business, undaunted by the morning traffic of joggers and beachcombers, and oblivious to the accretions of a history so bizarre, I thought, that this true native of the area seemed alien, displaced, and irrelevant: not worth mentioning, in itself, except as an odd example of irrelevance.

At the end of the conference in 1991, however, another unruly experience intensified my fascination with the ways in which the themes of this conference played against its location, where everything larger than an acre is called (and was once part of) a "plantation." Before we left Myrtle Beach, my wife and I drove through the tidal marshes and river deltas around Georgetown to the remains of the Hampton Plantation, which Archibald Rutledge, the descendant of the original owners, still occupied and farmed in the 1960s with the help of a hundred African American laborers, many of them direct descendants of Hampton's slaves. Around 1970, Rutledge donated the place to the state, which installed a few picnic tables and called it a state park.

When Marty and I arrived, no one was there but a sleepy park ranger, dozing on the steps of the columned porch. The whole estate had an abandoned, haunted look, the cavernous mansion and outbuildings unrestored among the live oaks, pines, and cypress swamps, where hundreds of slaves once cultivated rice and indigo. Rutledge himself lay under a slab along the path to the Santee River, which forms the southern border of Georgetown County. Left to explore on our own, we tried to enter the kitchen building and encountered an enormous red-bellied snake coiled by the door. When we called the park ranger to see it, and moved too close, the snake lunged and sent all three of us running in terror across the yard. Hampton seemed pretty determined to remain empty.

Rutledge wrote several books about the area surrounding the Santee, and when I got back to Ithaca, I read a couple of them, along with Toni Morrison's *Sula* and *The Bluest Eye*, other novels by writers Barbara Christian recommended during the conference, some histories of Georgetown County, and several volumes of slave narratives, including many accounts from South Carolina. I began to read this material not to construct or question any theory, and not with the intention to write, but to relieve a freshly nagging sense that I was terribly ignorant of African American literature and history. Once I got started, I just wandered, over the next two months or so, from one reference to others almost at random, to satisfy unfettered curiosity—the undisciplined, irresponsible cousin of scholarship. And this is the kind of reading I most enjoy, when I let myself dig around here and there like an amateur archaeologist, without plans or intentions, among texts that were never meant to be read together. Reading in this haphazard fashion, you can't get lost because you don't imagine you are going anywhere in particular; and when you aren't looking for anything, whatever you find seems to have been looking for you. Here, I'll sort a few of these artifacts into a loosely chronological order.

The official antebellum history of Georgetown County describes the politics, fortunes, marriages, and parties of a few extended families of Scots and Huguenots who owned just about everything and everyone around them. When these planters had figured out how to use the tides to flood and drain rice fields, through elaborate systems of channels and sluices, their demand for labor stimulated the importation of slaves to Charleston, which remained the largest North American port for the African slave trade throughout the eighteenth century. Africans, these rice planters found, were most likely to survive the ordeal of clearing and farming malarial, snake-infested swamps, and the development of the lucrative indigo production, in the middle of the eighteenth century, increased the demand for African labor. By 1840, the river delta plantations in Georgetown County produced half of the rice grown in the United States. In 1850, 98 percent of this massive crop of some 47 million pounds was produced on only 91 plantations, each with a labor force of between 100 to 1,000 slaves. In that year, the population of Georgetown

District consisted of 18,253 slaves of African descent, 201 free persons of color, and only 2,193 free whites. Excluding slave quarters, there were only 575 "dwellings," occupied by the same number of free families, in the entire county (Rogers 253).

The contemporary testimonies of fugitive slaves from this area recall some of the misery, brutality, and terror these people experienced. The flat, factual accounts of their lives, published to fuel the abolitionist movement, contrast in tone, most of all, with the language in Toni Morrison's novels—that gorgeous dignity and "muscularity" (as Barbara Christian called it) of embodied language, written in the pulse of moving blood. Because she makes those embodied voices so vibrant and accessible to us in fiction, Morrison also makes it easy to ignore the very message she wants to convey: that the actual voices of slaves were silenced and ignored, distorted, objectified, and ultimately lost. Moses Roper's eyewitness account (in 1836) of the sadistic execution of a fellow slave near Greenville, South Carolina (for the crimes of preaching and escaping from a plantation in Georgia), sounds, especially in its use of the passive voice, like a police report or a set of technical instructions:

> The manner in which George was burnt was as follows: a pen of about fifteen feet square was built of pine wood, in the centre of which was a tree, the upper part of which had been sawn off. To this tree George was chained; the chain having been passed round his neck, arms, and legs, to make him secure. The pen was then filled with shavings and pine wood up to his neck. A considerable quantity of tar and turpentine was then poured over his head. The preparations having been completed, the four corners of the pen were fired, and the miserable man perished in the flames. (Blassingame 25)

This description gathers its horrible power in the absence of horror, imagination, anger, fear, or even inference. Roper establishes credibility with white audiences by adopting the detached persona of the expert witness who simply recounts the "facts," deleting all traces of human consciousness embodied in the moment he describes. Morrison, by contrast, represents her characters in the whole of that consciousness made clear. In language that makes the most remote depths of experience accessible, we hear even what Sula is imagining but not saying as she makes love to Ajax, in "the drift of her flesh toward the high silence of orgasm":

> *If I take a chamois and rub real hard on the bone, right on the ledge of your cheek bone, some of the black will disappear. It will flake away into the chamois and underneath there will be gold leaf. I can see it shining through the black. I know it is there . . . .*
> How high she was over his wand-lean body, how slippery was his sliding sliding smile.

> *And if I take a nail file or even Eva's old paring knife—that will do—*
> *and scrape away at the gold, it will fall away and there will be alabaster.*
> *The alabaster is what gives your face its planes, its curves. That is why*
> *your mouth smiling does not reach your eyes. Alabaster is giving it a gravity*
> *that resists a total smile.* (130)

So facts become lifeless, fictions full of life, and the truths between them inaccessible. Even if we could hear the fully embodied voices of slaves now, across all that time and change, I doubt that we could understand them. When the Federal Writers' Project of the WPA tried to record the memories of former slaves verbatim, in the vernacular, their voices conveyed both the strangeness and the remoteness of lives that had already, in the 1930s, become almost unimaginable.[1]

Forty-four rice plantations lined the Waccamaw River, which flows south, just inland from the coastal King's Highway, into Winyaw Bay at Georgetown. The largest of these estates was Brookgreen, now a sculpture garden and roadside attraction just a few miles south of Myrtle Beach. This was one of six plantations owned by Joshua Ward, who, in 1850, produced almost four million pounds of rice with the labor of 1,092 slaves. Next to Brookgreen was The Oaks, owned by the governor of South Carolina, Joseph Alston, and his wife Theodosia Burr Alston, the daughter of Aaron Burr.[2] On his "Southern Tour" in 1791, President George Washington spent an evening at Brookgreen, on his way to Georgetown, Hampton Plantation, and Charleston. Overlooking the vast expanses of green rice in the valleys of the Waccamaw and Pee Dee Rivers, from the porch of the Clifton Plantation (also owned by the Alston family), Washington remarked that he felt he was in a "fairyland." Later, in Charleston, he expressed to the governor his astonishment that the rice planters in the area had brought agriculture to such "perfection" (Devereux 21–22).

"Mom Hagar" was born at The Oaks during the Civil War. When the Federal Writers' Project interviewers found her at Murrell's Inlet, in 1937, she was 77 years old and could recall only fragments of what her mother told her about the lives of the slaves owned by the Alstons. Like others recorded for the WPA, these scraps of memory emerge from such a deep well of loss that images flash briefly against a darkness, as though everything in that time occurred at night by flickering candlelight:

> Ma say some dem plan to run way. "Less run! Less run!" Master
> ketch dem and fetch dem in. Lay 'em cross barrel. Beat dem till they
> wash in blood! Fetch 'em back. Place 'em cross the barrel—hogsket
> barrel—Christ! They ramp wash in blood. Beat Ma sister. He sister
> sickly. Never could clear task—like he want. My Ma have to work
> he self to death to help Henritta so sickly. Clear task to keep from
> beat. Some obersheer mean. Oaks labor.

Stay in the field! [she sang]
Stay in the field!
Stay in the field till the war been end! (Rawick 2: 110–11)

By the time Archibald Rutledge wrote *The World Around Hampton,* published in 1960, the vestiges of the plantation system in his own backyard had simply reverted to "nature," from his perspective. Although he still referred to the black women who lived on his estate as "my good girls" and recalled their shy pleasure when his father allowed them the rare "privilege and honor" of taking refuge on the porch of The Great House during a violent storm, Rutledge refers in the same passage to "their natural freedom and happiness." Like the owls, the egrets, and the alligators, the hundred loyal, happy black people who lived on his estate just belonged there, had always been there. Their songs blended perfectly with the sigh of the wind in cypress boughs and swamp grass in the lazy, soft, unruffled flow of time. As the "Master of Hampton," Rutledge liked to think of himself as the steward, not the owner, of this natural order. "There are many," he wrote, "to question my undisputed ownership of the land, what is on it and under it: the Negroes who work the land, the wild animals that make it their home, the silent ancestors buried in the ancient churchyard—all have claim to the place" (13).

While I was thumbing through the *USAir Magazine* on the way to the NCTE conference in 1992, I found an article called "Rhett Butler's Hometown," by Jolee Edmondson, that brought Rutledge's nostalgia a step closer to the ethos of Myrtle Beach. In the opening spread, a heart-shaped film clip of Clark Gable and Vivien Leigh in a passionate embrace is superimposed on a panoramic photograph of the avenue of oaks leading to the Boone Hall Plantation. If Rhett Butler had existed, the article suggests, he would have felt right at home on one of these plantations near Charleston, which still "recall the splendor of the *Gone with the Wind* era." The carefully edited histories and descriptions of these estates do not describe the plantation system, for the words "slave" and "slavery" are never mentioned in the article. Nor are there references to agriculture. Instead, the elegant remains of this system are supposed to remind us of the movie, which has become their history. In effect, Boone Hall Plantation has become "the quintessential Old South," as a caption describes it, because it resembles Tara.

Built upon all of these images and voices, the drained, landscaped developments along Myrtle Beach look like sets for a different kind of movie with imported actors: vacationers, retirees, and legions of white teenagers who come to work at the restaurants, resorts, and golf courses, or at the Bikini Bottom Car Wash up on the North King's Highway. Here the descendants of slaves make brief, minor appearances in the roles of maids and busboys. And across this improbable landscape, nothing could pass more lightly, improbably, and unmemorably than a national conference of English teachers who convene to talk about literary theory and multiculturalism.

Talk about theory always stimulates this shift of attention to my surroundings. Our students tend to attribute similar reactions to boredom. When discussions become abstract, they become fascinated with their pens and notebooks, with their clothing and hair, with the details of the room, and with one another. But I don't find theory boring, and I just said that theoretical discussions *stimulate* interest in my surroundings, along with curiosity, memory, and fantasy. One reason, which accounts for our students' reactions too, is purely cognitive and linguistic. Every abstract noun, such as "multiculturalism," attempts to represent thousands of other nouns, more specific and concrete. That single word assumes meaning in reference to an entire world of cultural variation. Sustained discussions at the rarefied pinnacle of language—where the world is subsumed by a few -*isms* and -*tions*—create a kind of sensory deprivation that *should* stimulate awareness of who and where we are, and why, and what we are doing, and with whom. I think that's what theoretical language is good for: it's a way of informing and illuminating practice or of stimulating awareness and change. When you turn on that kind of light, you also need to open your eyes and pay attention.

I was dissatisfied with my first draft, in part, because it described the way theory sheds light on theory, as though an academic conference were a bunch of floodlights installed in outer space. When we become absorbed in those discussions, words such as *student* and *class* become abstractions too—hypothetical categories, "imagined communities"— even in our discussions of multiculturalism, differentiation, conflict, contact, and inclusion. Teachers from research universities, liberal arts colleges, and two-year community colleges throughout the country begin to sound as though they are all talking about the same creatures in the same contexts, much in the way that politicians talk about their *constituents,* or about *Americans* at large. We begin to imagine that if we assemble the right theoretical apparatus and approach the classroom from just the right angle, theory will govern practice. We will know in advance what will happen when we get there, who our students are, what they need, and how they should change. Then, we begin to talk about using this theoretical equipment for the purpose of "hammering," "chiseling," or "chipping" away at some kind of hard, homogeneous substance, as though our primary goal were to convert our students into the effects of our causes. In this dreamy, collective dislocation from our lives and jobs, we begin to imagine that when we enter the classroom on the first day of the next term, we will really know what we are doing.

When I start to believe that, I've found, my teaching and my students always suffer. They suffer because there's a special kind of confusion and vulnerability that occurs when people who hold power over our lives behave as though they know what they are doing when they don't. Political leaders continually affect us in this way. Doctors and lawyers often do. And so do teachers, especially when they attribute motives, values, and levels of ability to their students without really taking their students into account—without asking questions, listening, and paying attention. We can perpetrate this confusion just as easily from the Left as from the Right, with or without cynicism. The term "safety net" doesn't really catch anyone. Hypothetical "points of light" provide neither hope nor warmth. So theories of inclusion, in themselves, don't include anyone, and I could use them to exclude students just as easily as I could use any other theoretical approach to teaching. I could also "teach the conflicts," as Gerald Graff recommends, in ways that convince students that these debates have nothing to do with them, or I could design a multicultural curriculum that leads students to believe that multiculturalism is just a liberal political gesture to appease "minorities."

So I agree only in part with Mary Louise Pratt's suggestion, during the 1992 conference, that theory alienates people because it accounts for experience from an oblique angle, that it has to be alienating in order to explain things in ways other than those in which things explain themselves. I recognize this potential value of theory to dislocate understanding and disturb common sense. I think most of our students need, first of all, to become more confused.

But so do we. It's just as important for us to let experience destabilize theory and return us to that condition of creative bewilderment from which new understandings emerge. When I start to believe that I have everything figured out, I'm sure to be at least partly wrong. In practice, I can maintain the integrity of my theories only by becoming increasingly oblivious to the people and circumstances to which they are supposed to apply. I think we need to remind ourselves constantly, therefore, that our words and ideas resonate on the unknown, in chords different from the ones we struck, if they resonate at all. That's why we need first of all to include students, with recognition that we know almost nothing about them, and then listen. Otherwise, we'll hear nothing but the echoes of our own voices inside our heads, or their halfhearted, unpracticed efforts to play along in harmony.

This was the mistake I almost made a few years ago with an African American student, a senior sociology major, in an advanced expository writing class. In response to the first formal, analytical assignments in this course, Paul wrote in an extremely stilted, convoluted, billowing style. His diction was inflated with what my students call "thesaurus words," and his efforts to construct elaborate sentences led to frequent errors in punctuation (primarily by avoidance) and sentence division. Paul began his comparison between two articles written for different audiences with this passage:

> These papers are a contrast in purpose of design. They contrast in their purpose insofar as the article written for popular reading is essentially designed with the main idea being of providing entertainment and at the same time reaching and appealing to a broad base of people. . . . Its base is in a material incentive. It ignores the idea of unselfishness in that it does not merely simplify the findings for popular digestion but involves itself heavily into marketing for its own personal magnification. The consequence being that we read further and further in an attempt to satisfy our curiosity but with the catch that our curiosity is not allowed to be satiated.

In a paper about his previous experiences as a writer, however, Paul's voice became relaxed, lively, fluent, and sometimes genuinely funny. In one passage, for example, he described his efforts to meet the expectations of an English teacher who had asked her urban students, in a pre-college program for "minorities," to "characterize a snow pea pod" in writing. "I resigned myself to the fact that this teacher was just off in her own world," he wrote, "and filled three-quarters of a page with information I found in an encyclopedia. Needless to say, this did not suffice. It seemed we battled and fussed for the rest of that semester." Paul appeared to have lots of control over the language he used in this paper, and the types of errors that appeared in his previous essays vanished.

Our students also theorize, as Barbara Christian reminded us, and Paul appeared to be using two different theories for writing that led him to adopt two, very different voices. My professional experience, in turn, led me to adopt theories of my own about the causes of this variation. The poise and precision of Paul's speech in the classroom suggested that autobiographical and descriptive topics allowed him to maintain a lively, comfortable connection between writing and speech. When he used that voice in writing, his ear for language worked; he could accurately hear the natural pauses and breaks in the flow of language, along with the qualities of the words he used.

I concluded that Paul viewed the academic essay, by contrast, as a highly structured, visual, literary object—a "thing" he had to fabricate from language he wouldn't ordinarily use and thus couldn't effectively hear himself using. According to this theory, which I attributed to Paul, whatever language he would ordinarily use to discuss a topic seemed automatically inadequate—too informal, colloquial, and effortless—for a type of writing he perceived to require fancy words (such as "afore-mentioned") in complex sentences and long, meandering paragraphs. I assumed that he acquired this notion of academic writing from reading social scientific articles and textbooks. The stilted, convoluted quality of his prose resulted from what David Bartholomae described, in "Invent-ing the University," as the "imitation or parody" of academic discourse conventions that still seemed alien to him and altogether disconnected from speech. Because Paul was exposed to this style almost entirely through reading academic texts, in voices that were not yet his own, he couldn't accurately regulate the sound and flow of academic prose.

This is a very popular theory among teachers who flatter themselves with the assumption that our students want most of all to write, think, and become like us. In Paul's case, it just happened to be false. In the following weeks, my efforts to help him produce a smoother, more con-vincing imitation of academic writing failed miserably. When I tried to restructure a particular sentence, the entire passage collapsed around it like a punctured balloon. I could help Paul to reconstruct a new passage in my voice and style, but this work had no effect on the next ornate, impenetrable essay he composed. What I had presumed to be a nascent, misbegotten rendition of sociological prose seemed to have a stubborn integrity of its own.

When I called Paul in to talk with me about this problem, he waited politely and patiently for me to tell him what was wrong with his writ-ing and what he should do to improve it. I was about to explain the theo-ries I described above (and I suspect he would have pretended, at least, to believe them), but something about them rang false. Instead, I just admitted my confusion, read passages he had written in those two styles out loud, and asked him if he could explain the differences. "Why do you make academic writing so *complicated*," I asked, "when you can obviously write smoothly and clearly in this other voice?"

Paul thought about this question for a while, and then his face lit up with amusement. "I just realized," he said. "That's the way the men in my family *talk!*"

Although Paul was raised in New York, he explained, his family was from Barbados, where most of his male relatives were lawyers and public officials. On formal occasions, or when they argued about politics, his father, uncles, and grandfathers spoke in the inflated, deliberately im-pressive voices of nineteenth-century English barristers—very different from the voices they used in casual conversation. Two other students from Barbados have since told me that they called a version of this style of speech "Being Great": a kind of playful formality they used in verbal sparring matches with their friends.

As a consequence, almost everything I had concluded about Paul's writing was wrong. What I read as an inept attempt to imitate an alien, detached style of writing turned out to represent a displaced but deeply familiar, playful style of speech. Paul had difficulty controlling this voice in writing not because he had acquired it from reading, but because he had never seen it written and didn't speak that way with his friends and family. The language he used did not represent a deliberate effort to appropriate (or, in Bartholomae's terms, to "be appropriated by") the discourse conventions of our communities in the hope that he might one day be allowed to join them. Instead, he adapted, almost unconsciously, familiar speech patterns to writing when he encountered situations in which he felt he should sound formal, professional, and impressive. The model he was trying to use was not culturally alien to him; it was culturally alien to me.

When Paul recognized the origins of this voice, he could also hear its contextual peculiarity, which he suddenly found very amusing. From then on, he wrote all of his papers in what he called his "American voice" instead, with greater success in all of his courses. This change occurred only when I abandoned my theories and admitted bewilderment. Paul immediately filled this space I left for him with his own lively intelligence and presence. When I stopped trying to work on his writing, we began to work together for the first time that semester.

This is the kind of moment in teaching that I've since learned to cherish: when a new understanding emerges from misunderstanding, and the student and teacher change at once. To experience it, though, you first have to let yourself become openly confused—a condition that our conventional roles lead us to avoid or to conceal. You have to believe that confusion, for teachers and for students, is a wonderful opportunity.

Inclusion, multiculturalism, transculturation, and *interaction* aren't just principles for constructing a reading list or a syllabus, or ways in which we talk about teaching, or ideas we bring to the classroom, or invitations we extend to our students. They are also experiences that students either have or do not have in the classroom. So I found myself thinking about theory from the opposite direction. If students of all types could feel at once differentiated and included—free to address and to challenge me, or the readings, or one another—what kind of approach to teaching would create this environment? What kind of theory of teaching would account for it?

From this inverted perspective, one of the most significant moments for me in the 1992 conference occurred when I arrived late for a workshop that Cynthia Selfe led on the development of assignments. Because the participants had already formed a closed circle of chairs, I settled down on the floor by the doorway, where I could listen without disturbing the session. Cynthia immediately told me there was an empty chair back in the corner, so I made my way to it and sat down outside the circle, behind Peter Elbow.

That position felt comfortable enough to me, as a passive observer, but it obviously bothered Peter. There wasn't room for me in the circle, but he kept looking back at me and moving his chair to the side and back in increments, until the people around him became uncomfortable and began to move their chairs too, in little chain reactions of disturbance. Gradually, silently, the circle expanded and opened until there was a perfect space I was invited to fill—couldn't refuse to fill, really, because the circle had already broken open to include me. And suddenly, having felt content to sit outside the group, watching and listening, I wanted instead to be a part of it and to participate. My attitude toward the context and my relation to it changed because Cynthia and Peter, especially, altered the context in a way that made room for me. Having entered as a tardy spectator, I became an active participant.

As a little illustration of good teaching, this experience was most instructive to me, especially when I think of students who position themselves at (or off) the margins of the class, doing their best to become invisible, as though they were watching everything through a one-way mirror. What needs to happen for the class to include these students? Somehow, the idea of sharpening my theoretical tools for the purpose of chiseling away at them, or at the power structure at large, doesn't seem very helpful. If I pay close attention to what Peter and Cynthia *did*—and ignore much of what was *said* during the conference about students as the objects of our ideological "projects"—I get the opposite message. That message tells me that if I want to include these students, I need to interrupt my own "project" and assume, first of all, that it can't go on without them—that it's theirs as much as mine. If I want them to join the class, I have to move aside. If I want them to change, I have to be willing to change as well. If I want them to learn, I need to learn too. If I want them to speak, I need first to listen.

Notes

1. George Rawick assembled the transcriptions of these WPA interviews by state into nineteen volumes, entitled *The American Slave: A Composite Autobiography.* For discussions of the value and validity of the WPA interviews, see essays by Paul Escott and John Edgar Wideman in *The Slave's Narrative,* edited by Henry Louis Gates and Charles T. Davis.

2. This uncomfortable marriage is the subject of Anya Seton's historical novel, *My Theodosia*.

Works Cited

Bartholomae, David. "Inventing the University." *When a Writer Can't Write: Studies in Writer's Block and Other Composing-Process Problems.* Ed. Mike Rose. New York: Guilford, 1985. 135–65.

Blassingame, John W., ed. *Slave Testimony: Two Centuries of Letters, Speeches, Interviews, and Autobiographies.* Baton Rouge: Louisiana State UP, 1977.

Devereux, Anthony Q. *The Rice Princes: A Rice Epoch Revisited.* Columbia, SC: State Printing, 1973.

Edmonson, Jolee. "Rhett Butler's Hometown." *USAir Magazine* (June 1992): 78–87.

Gates, Henry Louis, Jr., and Charles T. Davis, eds. *The Slave's Narrative: Texts and Contexts.* New York: Oxford UP, 1985.

Morrison, Toni. *Sula.* New York: Knopf, 1973.

Rawick, George P., ed. *The American Slave: A Composite Autobiography.* Vol. 2. Westport, CT: Greenwood, 1972. 19 vols.

Rogers, George C., Jr. *The History of Georgetown County, South Carolina.* Columbia: U of South Carolina P, 1970.

Rutledge, Archibald. *The World Around Hampton.* Indianapolis: Bobbs, 1960.

Seton, Anya. *My Theodosia.* New York: Grosset & Dunlap, 1941.

4 The Unconscious Troubles of Men

David Bleich
University of Rochester

One of the interesting features of the theory-glut in trendy academic zones has been renewed attention to psychoanalysis. Derrida reread Freud, other Francophile critics textualized his work, and American feminists have tried to transform his Victorian boldness and daring about individual psychology into contemporary social and political courage. Through all of these rereadings, two original features of psychoanalysis remain especially useful in today's postsecondary classrooms: its dependence on language as a substantive feature of human relationships, and the detection, through language use, of important feelings and forces of which we were at first unaware: unconscious feelings, attitudes, fantasies, assumptions, and so on.

In spite of the interest in the French use of Freud, only the feminist revision of psychoanalysis retains both its basis and reference points in lived experience. In the feminist critique of society, we recover a sense of the linguistic locus of unconscious activity. In English courses—that is, those courses in which students examine carefully and produce different forms of language—we may not only make use of the feminist critique as a subject in and of itself, but we may also make use of a long-neglected feature of psychoanalysis: the presumption that psychoanalysis will examine language use collectively in order to teach and learn collectively about social relations.

My advanced undergraduate course, "Seminar in Writing: Telling the Truth," had as its substantive concern writing and language use as "telling the truth," in the sense of making what is unconscious conscious in public, as this process appears in a variety of contexts in daily and professional life. As a hardly concealed subtext, the matter of a feminist critique of society was represented in one of the course's texts, Adrienne Rich's *On Lies, Secrets, and Silence,* while a different viewpoint was offered in Lynne Cheney's pamphlet, written for the government and outlining her sense of the humanities academy today, entitled, *Telling the Truth*. The feminist critique was purposely juxtaposed with more familiar and traditional academic senses of telling the truth given by Cheney. Between these two perspectives, a variety of issues were considered, including, for example, hedging, euphemism, and jargon as ways of obscuring the "true" meanings, as well as different contexts, which determine what "truth" is in different ways. This, at least, was the "planned" curriculum.

Because of an accident of enrollment, this course "unconsciously" had as one of its principal subject matters what is happening, recently, collectively, to men as society reexamines traditional masculine roles. Particularly, "unconscious" came to seem an accurate description of the trouble men feel as our assumed privileged status is measured for revision. By studying the work of some of the men in my course, one gets a hint about what may be happening collectively on a larger scale. Some men accept the need for political change, while others answer its challenges with personal defenses, describing their own "sensitivity," their history of feeling responsive to the claims and interests of women and other politically active groups. In most men, there is a new level of personal and social uncertainty, previously masked by such behaviors as macho bravado and military truculence. Men's traditional unconscious uncertainty about roles, authority, knowledge, and justice, for example, previously obscured by fluent and simple assumptions about self and society, is now becoming conscious.

The "accident of enrollment" referred to above was the student population of the seminar: six white men, two women, and me, the white male teacher. In their presentational manner, five of the seven men were extremely talkative and loud; two of the men were soft-spoken and not given to interrupting. The two women were extremely reserved, visibly reluctant to chime in, sometimes raising their hands to speak, but tending to stay silent while male shouting, including my own, proceeded. I sometimes interrupted male shouting matches and urged the two women to share their thoughts, which they did, more often than not, but briefly. Here is an instance, given by one of the two female students, Ms. P:

> Mr. G would ask Bleich about the presidential election or vice versa and suddenly there was a debate on which candidate would win and then a bet over beer was being worked out to see who could guess the winner. Someone would ask what kind of beer and the loser should buy. . . . I suddenly found myself in left field. I didn't know whether I should say something because I felt that I had been gradually pushed out of the conversation, out of the circle, out of the field, and onto the bleachers as a spectator. I was no longer a

player. I was flustered because the males could introduce and carry
on any conversation they wanted to and I could not. I wanted to be
a participant because it was more fun.

Not a new story. On the other hand, the frustration this course had for
Ms. P led to a final essay detailing the above events and several others
that caused her frustration. Furthermore, in spite of the generally inhibited feelings held by both women, each wrote hard-hitting essays that
were shared with the whole class and were discussed and debated in
public. Most of my efforts in the class were to make room for the women
to speak, but probably too many times, as suggested above, I was part
of the problem. However, Ms. P observes the following:

> I knew Bleich was aware of Ms. F's and my feelings. He was careful
> of what he said and more attentive to what we said. I know that
> Bleich was even "nicer" to us. He had raised his voice so often to
> the guys, especially to Mr. G. When Mr. R mumbled, Bleich would
> say, "Speak up!" but when Ms. F whispered like a "mouse," he either
> looked like he was straining his ears or he would say something in
> a gentle voice. I didn't mind the special treatment even though I
> knew it was unfair for the guys. I may have stepped into a man's
> shoes when I saw the unequal treatment by Bleich yet I did not say
> anything; in fact I liked it. It was great to be on the other end for a
> while. I had the desire to agree with Mr. S vocally [about the unequal
> treatment] but I also thought it was unfair at the same time how once
> women or non-whites get preferential treatment, it becomes so
> obvious and white men are quickly up in arms.

Into this atmosphere class members were invited to "tell the truth"
and to explore the ways our language helps us to conceal "true" things
from ourselves and others. There is no doubt that the men perceived the
women as secondary in some sense, even though the people treated one
another with respect. Much of my time was, in fact, spent making sure
that the women had the chance to speak and that their work was studied. At the same time, the men did feel that they could "learn" in public,
that the atmosphere was finally safe for them to share thoughts and feelings that do not normally emerge for discussion in school: the women
and the teacher were, by and large, to be trusted. In the following discussion, I will explore the work of three male students, trying to show
what counts as the disclosure-for-discussion of what is rarely discussed
about masculine psychology: how the "normal" masculine identity generally presupposes violence, misogyny, and homophobia, all connected
with one another but ultimately unmentionable as values which are
psychosocially necessary to "normal" male identity in today's society.

Mr. B was one of the soft-spoken members of this class but was close
friends with the others, especially with the loudest and most politically

conservative in the class. He was from a well-to-do family, and he went to a fancy preparatory boarding school in the East before coming to this university. Mr. B nevertheless led an offbeat life as a student: he was particularly proud of his campus radio show in which he presented himself as an African American rap disk jockey. He was also an amateur rap artist. In a sense, Mr. B was already "bilingual" or bicultural in that he could easily shift back and forth between a white and an African American entertainment mentality. In his essay on hedging and euphemism, Mr. B came to a new level of understanding about his own history of language use and contributed significantly to our common project of understanding the political roles and uses of hedging and euphemism as linguistic tropes.

Mr. B first cites an episode of "Star Trek" which presents a race of genderless people. In this fictional society, he continues:

> Anyone who claims to have the feelings of either the male or female gender is quickly arrested and "cured" (brainwashed) of their "problem." As the show progresses we see one of the alien people begin to express female feelings. She expresses an attraction for one of the male heterosexual members of the Enterprise. (Reiker, for all you Trekkies.) At one point, she reveals her oppressed feelings to the man. She describes how she lives in fear of her own people. She describes how she has no control over her natural desires and how it is unfair that her kind is persecuted. During this scene, she is identified as the heroine of the show. The audience sees the message that people should not be punished for the sole reason of having different wants and needs.

Mr. B reads the reversal of sexual orientation identities in this episode as a "euphemism for the plight of the homosexual in the world today." Why is this reversal to be understood as a euphemism instead of just a metaphor? He explains.

> In accordance with the government's FCC laws of censorship, we can see a man and a woman kiss on television, yet, we cannot see a man and a man kiss. Therefore the episode is able to show us a heterosexual relationship much more easily than it could show us a homosexual one. The show hedges around the issue by being able to give a positive heterosexual example of homosexuality. Instead of disregarding the issue, the show uses hedging in order to discuss it within the censorship boundaries. . . .
>
> By using euphemism, the viewer is not only able to hear an opinion from the homosexual point of view, but is also able to see an example of the ugly persecution that goes with it. The euphemism is able to draw upon a common theme in humanity.

How about that phrase, "a positive heterosexual example of homosexuality"? In "Star Trek," heterosexuality is a euphemism for homosexuality. What might this mean? Well, "passed away" is a euphemism for "died." "Settled your account" is a euphemism for "paid your bill." "Internal revenue" for "government's taxes" and so on. In each case, a "euphemism" actually also means the very same thing as the item it replaces. If, with Mr. B, you read heterosexuality as a euphemism instead of a metaphor—that is, instead of as a reversal of some sort—we may perceive, at some level, unconscious though it may be, that heterosexuality, like homosexuality, can be understood as one orientation among others and as neither more nor less right for all people than is homosexuality. Reading heterosexuality as a euphemism made it possible for Mr. B to announce his sense of the equivalence of the two categories, as opposed to the conventionally perceived unequal status of the two social identities. This, in any event, is how I read Mr. B's reading of the television episode. With this reading in mind, consider, now, another instance of hedging and euphemism which Mr. B offers in the same essay: his retrospective reading of his own interpersonal language in high school. Here is his report:

> I was a student at a boarding school. During my Junior year I met a female named Marge. She and I began to see each other regularly. I had sexual intercourse for the first time with Marge. In fact, we had it regularly. During the time we spent together (one and one-half years), Marge and I bonded closely.

Mr. B relates in the next few paragraphs how he would try not to admit in public, when asked by his friends, that he was seeing Marge regularly "because I was not mature enough to be able to deal with a relationship that included love and sexual relations." He felt he had to pretend not to be involved. He writes:

> Over time, this pretending grew. Shrugging off responsibility and claims to my serious relationship made other immature males think I was some kind of "stud." Euphemisms for love became rampant. My false show of apathy turned me into a cocky bastard. I began hearing questions like, "Are you fucking her?" "You bet I'm fucking her," I would respond. Even though this answer seems harsh to me now, it was definitely a euphemism (for my male friends) in high school. "I'm fucking her" was a much more acceptable and prevalent term than "I love her." ... My entire nonchalant attitude in front of my friends was a sexist euphemism for love, something I could never publicly express for fear of being ridiculed.

Once again Mr. B surprises me with his sense of what a euphemism is. It had not occurred to me to read men's bragging about sex as a euphemism. Yet many have observed that men have trouble facing their actual feelings of tenderness. If Mr. B's account is to be believed, heterosexual men's harsh speech about sex and women is actually a softening of what to men are much more difficult verbal acts: describing feelings of tenderness, dependency, and vulnerability to passion.

Mr. B's juxtaposition of instances is extremely suggestive, to wit: He observes that both heterosexuality in the "Star Trek" episode and heterosexual bragging are euphemisms for homosexuality on the one hand and tender feelings toward women on the other. In a recent, short book, *Homophobia: A Weapon of Sexism,* Suzanne Pharr outlines how homophobia derives from sexism, a conclusion similar to what I see in Mr. B's juxtaposition of euphemisms. What is particularly noteworthy in Mr. B's case is that his insight came from an inquiry into the ways hedging and euphemism are used in society today. He was considering a familiar language-use style, and he found instances in both popular culture and in his own life that, first, changed slightly the sense of what a euphemism is, but, more importantly, enlarged its meaning in a way that gives insight into how sexuality is now changing its identity in society: feelings of understanding and tolerance for homosexual behavior and respect for tenderness in heterosexual relationships have been concealed in similar ways for similar reasons. Young men, even privileged white males like Mr. B, can, by interrogation of their own language-use styles along with their own cultural texts, find enough space in the classroom to participate in the wider movements of cultural change. Because Mr. B is himself somewhat unusual, in addition to his being a bona fide member of the most privileged group in America, he is in a good position to influence his less-understanding friends. Perhaps another, if uncertain, index of change in the gender-identity consciousness in young men could be the unusual announcement by Mr. B of "the first time" he had intercourse, an announcement I have never seen before in student essays and have rarely heard even in the intimate confines of my own all-male conversations among adolescents in the 1950s.

Mr. B's moment of growth reflects one item that is only part of what is unconscious among men, yet almost always what is at the forefront of women's thoughts: the likelihood that heterosexual men will become violent toward women and with each other when communication doesn't yield quick solutions—and sometimes, even, for no good reason at all. Worse, the tendency to be violent is admitted as a solution itself, or at least as an acceptable choice, in any dispute. Heterosexual violence has an erotic component in both heterosexual and homosexual situations. The language cited above by Mr. B—"Are you fucking her?"—suggests this feeling, as do other slang words used in the same situation, like "banging," "poking," "nailing," and so on. However, consider this passage from Robert Cormier's *The Chocolate War*, which characterizes Emile Janza, a bully in the all-male parochial high school that is the main scene of the novel:

> For instance, when he went to the john at school he seldom flushed the toilet—and got a kick out of picturing the next kid who'd go in and find the mess in the bowl. Crazy. And if you told anybody, it would be hard to explain. Like how he sometimes felt actually horny when he roughhoused a kid or tackled a guy viciously in football and gave him an extra jab when he had him on the ground. How could you tell anybody about that? (42)

Two items are pertinent in this passage: "he felt actually horny" and the tacit sense that this feeling can't be told or explained. The passage describes what we recognize as sadism, which is not merely pleasure in another's pain but sexual pleasure gained through the act of inflicting the pain. In this instance, the pleasures are homoerotic, and the inflicting of the pain is, in a sense, a sexual act.

There is reason to understand the heterosexual tendency to violence in just this way: as a repression of homoerotic feelings—in the novel, the repression being the sense that it "can't" be explained or is otherwise "crazy." Relative to women, male heterosexual violence is a repression—and perhaps even a conscious suppression—of one's own feelings of tenderness and / or vulnerability, as in the case of Mr. B above. This tender feeling, in turn, is clearly related to homoerotic feeling: the impulse to be tender is common to both sexes, as when parents and siblings have the same kind of tender feelings toward family members of either sex. The case of Emile Janza suggests that male physical strength is used violently toward others in order for the individual to conceal from himself the socially unacceptable fact that he may have tender feelings for both sexes. In the novel, Janza has affectionate feelings for other young men in the "ruling" school junta. That one should become sexually excited in the act of inflicting pain on someone else is the perverse outward manifestation of the feeling that it is perverse to be tender and even more perverse to feel tenderly toward other men. In this context of men's psychology, consider the discussions of the language of football given by Mr. F, another member of our "Telling the Truth" seminar.

Mr. F wrote his discussion of language use in high school football in a loose partnership with Mr. S, another student in the seminar. They explored "two sides of the coin," namely, Mr. F's discussion of the language actually used by the coaches to motivate the teams, which was combined with Mr. S's discussion of how he and his father conversed around their many games of tennis with one another. Their common introduction cites the following exhortation as being ordinarily given by coaches of male athletic teams: "Be a man; don't play like a damn pussy." This command combines the two sides of Mr. F and Mr. S's study: the exhortation toward physical bodily violence described by Mr. F and the conscious, almost passionate, attempt by Mr. S's father to use tennis to separate himself and his son from the three women in their family. In other words, this study suggests the combination of interpersonal physical violence, misogyny, and homophobia that names what I am referring to in this essay as the "unconscious troubles of men."

Mr. F is a biology major and respects the standards of detachment that are used in writing descriptions of work in the biology laboratory. As a result, he tends to report things with only a minimum of comment and to let the "factual" narrative speak for itself. First, he describes his coach—"a good ol' boy from Oklahoma, with a pack of chewing tobacco in his pocket and a really big mouth"—as a man whose own athletic career was ended by an injury in high school. He then cites several of the principles of motivation regularly given by this coach and which, after six years, "remain embedded in my mind": "If they don't score, we don't lose!!!"; "Go out there and knock his jock off"; "I want you to rip them some new assholes!!"; "If he holds you again, rip his fucking head off"; "If they score one more touchdown, I'm gonna run your guts till you chuck [vomit]." At the end of his account, Mr. F observes: "I realize this may seem a bit violent or hateful, but when I was on the field during a game, I wanted for the other team to lose and hurt more than I wanted to win. This was not my normal attitude, but . . . football changed my mind set."

Perhaps a surprising disclosure in this group of comments is that the shame of losing is a greater motivator than the pride of winning. It is as if winning were normal and losing were some form of degeneration or corruption of this normalcy. As is well known, in this society, all major sports programs, from the major colleges to the professionals, require a certain degree or frequency of winning to remain viable: people do not pay to watch a losing team. In society, this situation helps to explain, in part, the desperate character of the coach's exhortations. Economic coercion and male gender identity become part of a single fabric of values that govern our society.

Mr. F describes how the individual player, himself in this case, learns that it is not only permissible, but required, to hurt others, simply to maintain the sense of normalcy. Mr. F comments on the need to avoid losing:

> During the game the main threat [to cause us to lose] was their quarterback. . . . My chance to end the threat (take the quarterback

> out of the game) was given with the coach's play call . . . [in which]
> the two defensive ends [would] crunch the quarterback; I was one
> of these defensive ends. As the ball was snapped and we rushed in,
> the quarterback noticed the other defensive end first and this
> exposed his back to me, I couldn't resist, I speared him in the lower
> back with my helmet and I could hear a grunt leave his lungs along
> with the rest of his air. As the trainers came on the field to help the
> quarterback off, with his now broken rib, my coach and fellow
> teammates were ecstatic. I just seriously injured another person and
> my peers were saying, "Nice fuckin' hit!!" I must admit, I too was
> happy with my performance, I realize how violent it was, but I so
> loved a "Nice fuckin' hit." I was a very violent player.

I shortened this long and breathless account: uncharacteristically for Mr.
F, there were repeated comma splices, as if he could not contain his excitement, even in writing this account, long enough to punctuate according to his usual standard to date.

This was his final essay of the semester. For Mr. F, the mere retelling
of these events recreated the actual excitement generated by the combination of pleasing the coach, avoiding humiliation, and gaining the admiration of the team—something was gained in high school; something
is gained now by Mr. F, even in this retelling. There is a momentary re-
experiencing of the sadistic pleasure of having produced the grunt, the
loss of air, the broken rib, in another person. Spearing (hitting with one's
helmet) is illegal and understood to be a weapon on the football field,
yet the coach's counsel was to do anything to avoid losing. The players
tacitly understand that any penalty is far less damaging than, in this case,
merely letting the "threat" of losing remain legitimately in the game. Mr.
F's account suggests that football is actually governed by standards and
practices that are outside the accepted rules. These standards and practices are like those of war and are the opposite of what we take to be
sports.

Mr. F was also the victim of this style of behavior on the field. Here is
his account:

> The game was against the defending state champions . . . an all black
> team . . . . We were playing an away game in a stadium that was by
> far filled predominantly with African-Americans. Anyway, he [the
> opposing defensive lineman] started the little chat while waiting for
> the snap of the ball, "I'm gonna run your ass over cracker!!" a cracker
> being a derogatory term for white people. So I responded in my
> usual instigating manner with an extremely racist offensive remark,
> "Isn't your mother my maid?" Needless to say, this pissed him off
> and with his forty pound weight advantage, he proceeded to "knock
> my ass off the ball" along with snapping my head back with his
> forearm. I decided not to instigate verbally again.

> Reflecting upon the racist comment I made, I realize that my
> language use had again changed because of football. I was in no way
> racist and his mother did not look anything like my maid because
> we didn't have a maid at the time, but something inside my head
> told me to piss this guy off and I guess my statement did just that.

Of course, Mr. F is not an innocent victim. This account documents how
all the players, not just those on one side or the other, were participating in the regular practice of stepping outside the boundaries of the game
in order to avoid losing—actually hurting or destroying the opposition,
not simply defeating it.

Mr. F's remark was sexist as well as racist: it alluded to the humiliat-
ing place held in society by black people in general, as well as the
extrasubordinate place of black women. Mr. F knew this would "piss
off" his opposite number because of their common understanding that
the terms of battle are *men only:* having an opponent's mother as one's
maid implies having dominion over that opponent's women relations.
Obviously, the actual fate of black women is of consequence to neither
player. The issues are who has power over whom and who has power
over whose women. Mr. S's comments on this part of Mr. F's essay are
also noteworthy:

> Mr. F claimed his language went through a change when he spoke
> to the opponents during the game. It was his tactic of motivation to
> insult the other team. This was his justification for "slipping" when
> he retaliated to his opponent. But I believe his reply "Isn't your
> mother my maid?" implied more than just a change of scenes. It
> indicated the constant reminder of the unconscious racism that
> plagues our society. Although he said these words in the heat of
> battle, it was his way of gaining the upper hand on his "black"
> opponent. This easily could have been done without answering with
> a racial comment. He could have said, "You overweight piece of shit.
> I'm goin' to knock you so hard you're not goin' to know what hit
> you. You slow mother-fucker."

Noteworthy, of course, is that Mr. S's presumed better alternative strategies for insulting the opposition include deriding his body, his physical ability, and calling him a "mother-fucker," a term that implies that
the mother either desires or has no choice about participating in the in-
cestuous situation. In proposing this term as a point of solidarity between
black and white men (itself a questionable assumption), Mr. S disclosed
the unconscious sexism we are discussing, even as he accurately observes
Mr. F's unconscious racism. To further document his point, moreover,
Mr. S might have commented on what can only be a sudden lapse of
logic on Mr. F's part: would the opposing lineman's mother have had to
actually "look like" a particular person for Mr. F's wisecrack to have its
effect?

Mr. S, like Mr. F, wrote a description of family life that discloses his struggle to remove himself from the perversions that mark the scenes of male athletic effort. However, neither writer stopped to wonder about the frustration he may be having; both gave their accounts with a sense that they are now enlightened and beyond the struggles of their youth. Where Mr. F "resolved" his struggle by moving out of football, on through water polo with its female coach, to settle finally on weightlifting, where the cheering is only of the encouraging kind, Mr. S "resolved" his presentation of his family and gender-identity struggle by finally paying attention to relations with African Americans, demonstrating that he had no history of racism and that he had been, in fact, speaking the same "hip-hop" language of his black friends on the basketball court. Ultimately, while both Mr. F and Mr. S presented materials which showed their trouble with masculine gender identity, neither finally faced this trouble in his work in this course—but if you asked them, each would say he'd been unusually candid, to the point where he overcame whatever trouble he may have had in the past.

Here, now, is how Mr. S describes his relationship with his father:

> My relationship with my father revolved around sports. We never talked about the world. We never conversed about my education except with grades. And, we never, never talked about the family. That was the forbidden topic. If I brought something up with relation to the family, I was crossing over the boundary. I learned to keep quiet when I had a problem. My confusion had to be solved with my own intelligence.

Mr. S is the youngest child in his family. He recounts that his father was aggrieved because, having had two older children who were both female, he had to suppress all of his previous interest in and thinking about sports within the family. When Mr. S was old enough, he attracted his father's strong attention, but mainly with regard to his being a partner in sports as well as in conversation about sports: "I guess he believed sports were men's games. Women could try it but they could never be good, I mean really good." Because of this principle, Mr. S's father did not involve himself with his daughters, either in sports activities or in other ways. Mr. S reports that his sisters were always longing for their father's attention, but instead he directed his attention toward Mr. S, though only in the one narrow sense: the path, through sports and competition, to separate family—that is, female family members—from the world of men and male sports.

As Mr. S describes it, even when this separation was achieved, it was, in a heartbreaking way, itself unsatisfying, marked as it was by the frustration the rest of the family felt toward the father. Much as Mr. F observed that "it seemed as if my IQ dropped about fifty points when I was in the company of my teammates"—his speech "filled with curses, slang, and yes, a more violent tone"—Mr. S observed that "I always said 'ain't' when I wasn't around my mother. I acquired the habit from my father who, although very well educated . . . [at] Cornell University and Harvard Law School, seemed to use the word frequently when talking about sports." His mother, correctly perceiving the origin of Mr. S's changed speech habits, "took it upon herself to blame my father for my bad habits." However annoying his mother's reminders may have been, they were additionally painful because the discourse between Mr. S and his father was itself troubled:

> The conversations between my father and me usually lasted for about two hours but they always ended on a bad note. Whatever topic we were on, it always led into my tennis game, and this was my forbidden subject. I hated talking about this particular sport because it represented more than a game. It involved my entire family. . . . It resembled gambling in the sense that my father neglected his other responsibilities in life for his selfish pleasures [of playing with his son and paying large sums for his tennis lessons and training].

Mr. S cites many revealing instances of actual conversation between his father and himself, and even though this was the late 1980s, his father's tone and approach to Mr. S sound like that of Willy Loman's in the 1940s: "You never see a Jimmy Connors looking up before his hits. You're not going to get anywhere playing the way you are." Even though Mr. S's father pays cash for his son's expected athletic achievement, the ideal is no different from Willy's hopes for Biff's athletic stardom. For Mr. S, his father's financial sponsorship—to advance his own wishes for his son—contributes the element of coercion that sullies even this all-male sports relationship. In addition to the sense of obligation instilled in Mr. S due to his father's idealism and sponsorship, another factor also damaged the integrity of Mr. S's athletic identity:

> "Dad, do we have to talk about tennis? I'm sick of hearing about it . . . ." My voice would begin to rise every time the subject of tennis was the focus of conversation. I become very impatient talking about the game that dominated my life since I was seven. I wasn't sure why, but I refused to take criticism from my father. . . I felt I couldn't enjoy the game if he was part of it. It took something away from my advancement in the sport. . . . My progress was so hindered by his involvement that I contemplated quitting the sport. But also, I hated the idea that I was better than him. . . . It was difficult to think of my father in a less than dominant role. It was too fantastic of an idea. How could I be better than him, the man who governed my life? . . . My skills were being hidden to appease my father.

Mr. S describes how both "the game. . . dominated my life" and how he could not imagine his father "in a less than dominant role." In a sense, there was a total governing of Mr. S's life by his father through sports and through tennis in particular. While his father's actions did not overwhelm Mr. S altogether, the space of his own autonomy was nonetheless small and emotionally reduced, a reduction marked, in part, by reduced language—a stutter ("sometimes it took me three or four times to get out the first word when I was conversing with my family about sports"), the use of "ain't," and his own reduced usage, "bees" for "because."

As Mr. S reports it, his mother responded to this reduction, but in ways not fully explained by Mr. S in the essay:

> My mother . . . wasn't bothered by my stuttering as compared to the misuse of my language. She seemed to accept the fact that the stutter was a lack of maturity. But I didn't understand why she didn't put forth an effort to analyze it. . . . I became embarrassed by the thought of stuttering. I found it easier to avoid any discussion that involved sports. . . . The only time I felt free was at school and on the courts with my friends. That was the only place where I talked all the jargon [including hip-hop, or Black English, in this case] without hesitation.

In other words, Mr. S believes that his mother did not connect his stutter to his relationship with his father, to whom she connected his other language reductions. But he seemed to feel that all of his peremptory (unconsciously initiated) actions with the language were bound up in some way with the element of, say, sports servitude to the masculine ideals and psychology of his father.

I noted earlier that in responding to Mr. F's essay, Mr. S considered the inertia of Mr. F's racism but did not reflect on the sexism that accompanied it. His essay suggests that, in spite of his awareness of the painful struggle with his father's narcissism, he senses that there is something wrong at home and can't quite identify it. Mr. S demonstrates this just-below-the-surface problem while telling of two moments in his family where the sports imperative conflicted with another social event. Mr. S was about to see the first Rambo movie, *First Blood*, with a few of his friends, but his father reminded him of a previously scheduled tennis date they'd made:

> I was confused by the thought that I couldn't do my own thing. I wasn't happy with this obligation to my father. At that moment, I felt more like a puppet than his own son. He was pulling the strings and I had no defense. His presence was too great for me to revolt. There was no way I could change the things that corrupted the house.

His sister observed his agitation, and when she asked what was disturbing him,

> I yelled at her to relieve some of the frustration. My mom always hated when I treated my sisters in this way. She said it was just another influence from my father. To take the anger out on the woman.

Although Mr. S probably knows not to get angry at innocent parties in cases like this, only six months before his essay was written, he told of events that involved this same sister, who was graduating from a very fine undergraduate school. His whole family went to the graduation, and

> My parents were most proud of her accomplishment. But their display of joy was short-lived when I decided to play basketball at the gym. My whole family followed me to the courts and on my sister's graduation weekend, we watched me play basketball. It was true that we were all bored, but this was obviously not the answer. It was an exact replica of how things were. I was the center of attention trying to impress everybody who watched, as my sister looked on wondering how this was possible. She graduated from one of the toughest schools in the country and she wasn't even acknowledged for her accomplishments. . . . Her emotions were controlled by the familiarity of the situation. The scene was so depressing. . . .

Although it is clear from his own narrative that Mr. S is deeply implicated in creating this depressing scene, one cannot discern just how disturbed he is by what happened. It looks as if he had his own response to the boredom, did not himself demand that everyone follow, but unconsciously understood that his father would follow, his mother would follow his father, and then so would his sister. The women would not take an initiative, as Mr. S did, on their own without first consulting the others. I offer this reading of the narrative because of Mr. S's repeated mention of the familiarity of the situation, his sense of its representative character, and his belief that his sister was able to cope with it at all because of its familiarity.

This is a demonstration of the unconscious character of "the things that corrupted the house." Mr. S is unconsciously inhibited from opposing his father. I say unconsciously here because he did not need to oppose his father in this story. Because of this inhibition, described earlier in the essay—in fact the Rambo story just preceded the graduation story—it looks as if he is acting on his own to relieve the boredom. But being unconsciously fixed in the "exact replica of how things were," Mr. S actually takes the initiative to recreate it. Even his own understanding of his sister's needs is not enough to change anything. He implied in his essay that one need not even worry about how badly his sister may feel because she

> no longer needed a father figure. She had adapted to her situation. She had no more expectations.

What a remarkable claim: to observe on the one hand that his sister "looked on wondering how this was possible," and on the other to declare that she "adapted to her situation."

In other words, it is not enough to say that Mr. S's father is the villain or the cause of whatever may be corrupting Mr. S's household. It seems that Mr. S is receiving the actual heritage of his father and using it on his own and that to some degree, at least, other family members do not or cannot take the initiative to change a situation that causes them frustration and pain. My claim is only that Mr. S is unconscious of his own relatively strong role in perpetuating the corruption that he otherwise finds so disturbing. His playing of basketball at that moment is itself the result of the long momentum of his adolescence; it is the result of his habitual use of the athletic field, with its "reduced" language demands, its freedom to use other languages to build solidarity with black men his own age so as to escape home and family. Mr. S wants himself and us vaguely to understand this interracial bond as a progressive step against racism. But he is not aware that this step is, in turn, the grounds for remaining unconscious not only of Mr. F's sexism, but of his own responsibility to become a different kind of a person on behalf of his sister's needs for attention and recognition, needs which, as cited above, Mr. S is well able to identify and sympathize with.

It might be the case that all three of these young men—Mr. B, Mr. F, and Mr. S—are thinking along lines that can help them grow toward less troubled values and futures. But we cannot tell at present. The dramatic material that these writers disclose is the new combination of insight and inertia, self-examination and smugness that causes many men to feel troubled without being able to decide why. Perhaps most important from the perspective of those who are striving to combine awareness of social critique and the teaching of English, we find that attention to the use of oral and written language is virtually certain to guide us to the unconscious struggles taking place within ourselves and between one another, struggles now "coming out" to us as individuals and as citizens.

Finally, I want to recall now how this discussion was made possible by an accident, and not by theoretical and curricular planning beyond our sense that this was an English course with its attention to writing and language use. The issues raised in this course and in this essay got their pedagogical force from the fact that we in our class had to cope with a continuing run of contingencies: class members' responses to and opinions about the readings and about one another. The classroom atmosphere welcomed the reduction of inhibition. But what we did with the readings and with each other's writings could not be decided by either theoretical or curricular principle. Each class member had to speak and write out of social and political consideration, foresight, and respect for an ever-changing interpersonal situation. One might call this a "contingent curriculum" in consideration of the fast pace of social and political change that almost all English courses are now trying to face. Our contingent curriculum retained our interest in truth telling, but this subject was focused by the class demography, interest, and effort: we got to sports, homophobia, violence, and how to tell the truth about them.

Of the title elements in this volume, pedagogy emerges as the critical term. To take teaching seriously is to do, perhaps, the opposite of "theorizing" it: once in class, see who is there, think of what people want, examine what people actually do, and find the curriculum, backwards, in retrospect, after the moment has been seized and class members have faced one another over time. In part, this essay is the retrospective description of my curriculum. Mr. S concluded his essay with a redefinition, perhaps, of our course's curriculum, observing that "It seems all sports are played on the same field." We were unconscious of this thought when we went into the course. Now we are conscious of it: the curriculum is what we know after the course is over. That's something to write about. It may even be telling the truth.

Works Cited

Cheney, Lynne. *Telling the Truth: A Report on the State of the Humanities in Higher Education*. Washington, D.C.: NEH, 1992.

Cormier, Robert. *The Chocolate War: A Novel*. New York: Pantheon, 1974.

Pharr, Suzanne. *Homophobia: A Weapon of Sexism*. Inverness, CA: Chardon, 1988.

Rich, Adrienne. *On Lies, Secrets, and Silence: Selected Prose, 1966–1978*. New York: Norton, 1979.

5 Teaching Literature: Indoctrination vs. Dialectics

Min-Zhan Lu
Drake University

Let me start with a scenario that might ring a bell for those of you whose teaching has been influenced by the theories of feminist, Marxist, and poststructuralist critics. You are teaching an introductory-level, writing-intensive literature class. The central goal of the class is not only to ask students to read and write about a body of texts but also to (1) help students perceive the politics of interpretation and to (2) help them deliberate over the kinds of political decisions each of them makes when reading and writing. To that end, you have asked the class to read, discuss, and write about several critical essays which deal with the nature of language and interpretation. About midterm time, to remind your students that one of the goals of your course is to work against some of the formalist and intentionalist assumptions underlying their habitual ways of approaching a text, you jokingly threaten your class that you will fail students who end their midterm papers with disclaimers such as "This, I believe, is the true meaning of the text" or "As we all know, different people interpret texts differently. The above is just my personal interpretation of the text." And you and your class laugh.

I have noticed that when my class and I laugh at moments like this, we usually laugh loudly but nervously. We laugh, I believe, to tell one another that we know not to take my threat literally. That is, by this point in the term, we are "in" enough to get the joke: the authority of Truth with a capital "T" or the sovereign "personal" has lost its hold on us at the level of theory. The uneasiness of our laughter, however, comes from our realization that our having gained the ability to critique the assumptions behind these disclaimers does not necessarily mean that we would know how to fight against our habitual reliance on them when we read and write about a specific text. That is, vowing not to use such disclaimers does not automatically lead us to carry out the activities we have come to value: (1) to consider a whole range of alternatives to one's habitual ways of approaching a text; (2) subsequently, to take a position among these diverse and often contradictory approaches; and (3) to reflect on the politics of the position one is taking.

This essay explores ways of using assignment writing to help students bridge the gap between theory and practice, between their developing understanding of the politics of interpretation and their ability to apply such an understanding in their actual writing. I'll do so by posing three types of assignments, which, I argue, are based on different assumptions about why some of our students continue to have difficulty reflecting on the politics of their own views in their actual practice. Thus, each type of assignment would serve different functions at different points in a writing-intensive literature class. I will explore the pedagogical implications of designing assignment sequences which incorporate all three types by discussing each one's ability to involve students in the dialectics of theory and practice and to help them enact a critical dialogue when reading and writing. That is, to enable students to participate actively in a negotiation with "others" across the ideological spectrum by not only respecting the "differences" between "self" and "other," but by not being afraid to confront all forms of inequality, including forms of indoctrination, intellectual as well as political.

When teachers like me encounter the type of disclaimers I mentioned earlier, one common explanation of why students use them is that they are complacent about their own views—which they have often inherited from some sort of authority figure, such as a critic, teacher, or parent—and that they are too lazy to look for alternative ones. With this explanation in mind, some of us look for assignments which will help students perceive the limitations in their existing ways of approaching a text and develop new understandings of what is involved in the act of interpretation. Thus, we often ask students to read and write texts which explore the nature of interpretation, assignments such as the following:

Assignment A

For this assignment, read Steven Mailloux's essay "Interpretation" (*Critical Terms for Literary Study* 121–34).
    Write a paper in which you first discuss your understanding of Mailloux's claim that "interpretation is always a politically-interested act of persuasion" (127). Then, use the working definition Mailloux offers on page 121—"interpretation" is "acceptable and approximating translation"—to analyze the politics of claiming that one is merely setting forth "the true meaning" of a text or claiming that one is merely setting forth "one's personal interpretation" of a text.

This assignment asks students to carry out two activities: to formulate some understanding of the politics of interpretation through reading and discussing Mailloux's essay and to use their developing understanding of the politics of interpretation to critique certain assumptions about the nature of reading and writing which are common among themselves. The chief goal of this type of assignment is to help students become better versed in their understanding of the nature of interpretation. Used appropriately, this understanding could help students to critique their habitual views, such as their submission to the power of the Author, the Critic, or the sovereign "personal" when trying to interpret a text. It might help them to see the need to reflect on the ways in which all forms of interpretation are politically interested, including their own. Thus, it foregrounds the dialectics of theory and practice by asking students to view their critical practices from the perspective of a particular theory.

But since the question of how we might interpret is raised as the topic for the paper, and not as a method that the students must act out in their actual reading and writing, I don't think doing Assignment A, alone, would necessarily help students translate such a theoretical understanding into their actual critical practice. Let me use another assignment, which I think is also common in literature classes, to illustrate what I mean:

Assignment B

World domination, as everyone knows, is divided between demons and angels. But the good of the world does not require the latter to gain precedence over the former (as I thought when I was young); all it needs is a certain equilibrium of power. If there is too much uncontested meaning on earth (the reign of the angels), man collapses under the burden; if the world loses all its meaning (the reign of the demons), life is every bit as impossible.

— Milan Kundera (*The Book of Laughter and Forgetting* 61)

For this assignment, write a paper in which you discuss what this statement about "angels," "demons," and "power" might be said to mean within the context of Part Three (53–76) of *The Book of Laughter and Forgetting*.

In the past few weeks, when discussing Mailloux's "Interpretation," workshopping some of the papers written by members of this class in response to the essay, and reading Hurston's *Their Eyes Were Watching God* and Jacob Riis's *How the Other Half Lives*, we have considered the importance of keeping in mind the politics of interpretation, including one's own, when trying to read and write about a text. Make sure that you continue to do so when doing this assignment.

This assignment is one which I have used a few times after an assignment similar to Assignment A. The purpose of having students do Assignment B is to see if they can apply to their reading the understanding they've developed when doing A. Aside from asking the students to translate their theoretical understanding into actual critical practice, an assignment like B also foregrounds the dialectics of theory and practice by helping students to use their practice to put the theory to the test. Thus, their experience in using the theory might provide them with a critical edge from which to resist their potential indoctrination from the theory promoted by the critic (Mailloux) and by the teacher (me) who assigns the critical text.

I have two reasons for frequently asking my students to write about texts like Kundera's right after they have written an essay about the politics of interpretation. First, I look for texts which force the students to deal with what Bakhtin calls the "living heteroglossia" (*The Dialogic Imagination* 272). Throughout Part Three of *The Book of Laughter and Forgetting*, and especially in the paragraph cited in the assignment, Kundera uses the metaphor of "angels" to criticize fanatics who maintain that there exist some "uncontestable meanings" in the things they endorse; he uses the metaphor of "demons" to criticize those who find absolutely no meaning in anything; and he explores the burden of living in a world dominated by either an "angelic" or a "demonic" attitude toward institutionalized meanings. This use of the words "angels" and "demons" appears alien to most of my students because of their previous exposure to Western Judeo-Christian discourse. Thus, their reading of the book has to take place in response to the gap between Kundera's use of these words and the ways they are accustomed to using them.

Second, I look for texts which problematize various popular stances that a majority of my students identify with. For example, in Part Three of his novel, Kundera uses the imagery of angels and demons to critique not only the political dictatorship of Russian and Czech communists after the 1968 Russian occupation of Czechoslovakia, but also to critique the cultural practices of people from cultures like that of my students. One of the subplots in the chapter involves two American students—whom Kundera names after the angels Michael and Gabriel—taking a summer course on the French Riviera. As part of the course, these two American students, Michelle and Gabrielle, are assigned an oral presentation on Eugene Ionesco's play *Rhinoceros*. They proceed to prepare their presentation in the same way a lot of my students prepare their papers at the beginning of the term: they rack their brains for what the teacher has said about the play. After one of them remembers that the teacher had said the play has "comic effect," they use "comic effect" as the master code to decipher everything in the play (Kundera 55–56, 64). Every time one of the two comes up with a question about the play which could potentially push them beyond that master narrative, the other smugly puts an end to that line of inquiry by reminding the other that their teacher, Madame Raphael, believes the play has "comic effect." Using the metaphor of "angels," Kundera explores the similarity between these students' submission to the authority of Madame Raphael and the ways in which some Czechoslovakians responded to the political dictatorship of the Russian and Czechoslovakia governments during the late 1960s (Kundera 74). Thus, the book explicitly challenges a popular master narrative disseminated by the America media, which usually alternates between euphoric celebration of Western democracy and demonization of communist dictatorships. Some of these reports had left deep impressions on my students, such as the media's coverage of the student protest in Tiananmen Square and the collapse of the Berlin Wall. In highlighting the parallel between a student/teacher relationship set on the French Riviera and the Russians' colonization of Czechoslovakia, Kundera directly challenges the kind of dualistic thinking that underlies such political master narratives. Thus, students are forced to take a position between two conflicting authoritative voices on issues of power and domination: the voice of the Author, in this case Kundera, and that of the popular media.

In short, I choose texts with these two aspects because they pose challenges for students as they attempt to test their notions of the politics of interpretation, which is what Assignment B asks them to do. However, it has often been the case that, when doing Assignment B, most students tend to skirt around rather than take up the two challenges posed by such texts. Most students tend to focus their attention on the narrator's critique of the dictatorship of the Russian and Czechoslovakian governments. Very few connect that aspect of the book with the narrator's criticism of the teacher/student relationship of Madame Raphael and her American students. The few students who discuss the plot line involving the teacher and students tend to interpret the narrator's portrayal of the girls' "angelic" qualities as referring to their goodness and purity and, then, to contrast them with what they see as the demonic qualities of the communists, even though the narrator explicitly uses "angelic" imagery to portray both the students and the blind followers of the communist government. In many ways, the following passages from a paper written by a student, whom I shall call Ken, exemplify the approach taken by students who demonstrated a fairly sophisticated understanding of the political nature of the act of interpretation when doing Assignment A. That is, this paper characterizes the kind of gap between one's theoretical understanding and the actual practice of a critical perspective which is likely to surface when students like Ken are asked to do Assignment B:

. . . Kundera states that good and evil must achieve a certain equilibrium of power or life loses its meaning and "man" is unable to function. He tells us that total submission to one cause or idea is harmful and people must have the right to challenge institutionalized meanings. Kundera illustrated this by contrasting Michelle and Gabrielle's roles in the circle they form with their teacher Madame Raphael and the role of "Kundera" (a character in Part Three) outside the circle of Russian government and its Czechoslovakian followers. In this context, the circle represents the harmful security that a group can have.

. . . Michelle and Gabrielle focus their energy on pleasing Madame Raphael and doing well for the class. They spend all of their time trying to understand her ideas and doing what she wants. The girls do not explore their own ideas and feelings. . . . They were so concerned with doing "good" that they were absorbed by Madame Raphael and became archangels. . . . In the passage on page sixty-one, Kundera says that if there is too much uncontested meaning on earth, man collapses under the burden. This is saying that if no one contested meaning then we would all be like slaves, doing exactly what we were told whether we thought it was right or not.

"Kundera" focused on not being part of the circle—the communist people dancing in rings to keep themselves together and to keep unwanted people (like "Kundera") out. "Kundera" felt he belonged with the people who were against the evil government and its followers, which is demonic in nature. He says on page fifty-eight that he will never betray to the communists his friends who helped him when the government would not let him work. This is saying that he is contesting the reign of the demons.

These two stories shows Kundera's thought that extremes, either "good" or "evil," will ruin a life. All people must find a mid-point at which to live.

Let me make clear that what bothers me about this type of reading is not just that my students performed an "approximating translation" of the text, which I find unacceptable because of the difference in our political interests. Rather, what I find disturbing is the students' seeming lack of awareness that they have made a deliberate decision to "misread" the text, not to mention the absence of any reflectiveness on the politics of having made such a decision, especially given the fact that they have just responded to Assignment A. For example, there is no evidence in Ken's paper that he is aware of a potential gap between the codes of the writer (Kundera) and the reader (Ken) when approaching the story of "Kundera" and the government. While Kundera consistently uses "angelic" imagery to depict both the behavior of the two American students and their teacher and that of the Russian dictators and their Czechoslovakian followers, Ken only acknowledges this use of imagery in the former. Furthermore, he attaches adjectives such as "demonic" and "evil" to the behaviors of the latter group without either acknowledging or reflecting on the politics of such a switch in codes. Ken's paper suggests that, even if we succeed in increasing our students' understanding of the political nature of interpretation, they might still have difficulty enacting such an understanding in their writing.

We might want, therefore, to consider also using another type of assignment, one which provides an occasion for students to act out a method of interpretation that situates the making of meaning in the midst of heteroglossia—the potential distance and conflict between the language of the author and that of the student writer, as well as between the political interests of the student writer and those of the teacher or the other members of the class:

Assignment C

For this assignment, reread Part Three of *The Book of Laughter and Forgetting*. Then write a revision of the paper you wrote for your previous assignment.

Before beginning this paper, take notes in answer to the following questions (Please attach your notes to your paper):

(1) Prior to reading Kundera's book, in what type of texts and social contexts have you most often encountered words such as "angels," "demons," and "communism"? What type of meanings were usually attached to these words on these occasions?

(2) In the paper you wrote for Assignment B, to what extent have you used these words in the same way that they are used in the texts and contexts you discussed above? To what extent do they differ?

(3) Reread the passage on page 61 and Chapter 3. Take notes on elements in the text which indicate that the narrator is using these key words in very different ways than you did when you write the paper and/or in the kind of texts and contexts you are familiar with.

(4) To what extent would the narrator's usage be considered acceptable by people who tend to use these words in the sense you are familiar with? Why? Unacceptable? Why?

(5) Given your thoughts on the above questions, what part of your initial interpretation in your last paper would you like to take back, qualify, change, or develop? How? Why?

(6) To what extent might the decisions you made when revising your last paper be said to have advanced the interest(s) of a specific social group? Which group? What interest(s)? How?

Assignments like the one I call Assignment C challenge the notion of a reader or writer who is capable of taking only one fixed position toward the text, say the position taken by Ken when doing Assignment B. It asks the student to use revision as an occasion to reimagine alternative positions and, consequently, to reposition himself or herself in relation to a range of possible positions. For example, the first question asks the student to take notes, before writing the revision, on the kinds of connotations he or she habitually associates with words such as "angels," "demons," and "communism" and to locate such connotations in relation to a specific body of texts and social contexts. Such notes aim at helping students contextualize the kind of codes or master narratives which are familiar to them, as well as those which are likely to be invoked by some of the key words in Kundera's book. The second question then asks the student to reflect on the degree to which he or she has identified with this particular set of codes when writing the previous paper. Questions three and four ask the student to examine the potential distance between the codes and master narratives the student writer is familiar with and those employed by the narrator and Kundera. Then, questions five and six ask the student to approach that distance from the perspective of the politics which underlie the conflict between these two sets of codes and the conflict between the student writer's initial interpretation of the text and the interpretations of the teacher and other students that surface during class discussions of the text and the student papers written in response to Assignment B. That is, the questions help the student to take a position toward these two ways of using words from the perspective of social interests and concerns.

In trying to address questions one and two, Ken became aware that he had used the words "demon" and "evil" in the same ways as most people around him when they talk about communism in relation to American democracy. Yet, in discussing the relationship of the two "girls" with their teacher, he had changed the way most people he knew would use the words "angel" and "good." Questions three and four led Ken to speculate on why he was willing to go along with Kundera's use of these words in the context of only one of the stories. Ken wrote that it was easy for him to see eye to eye with Kundera's point that blind eagerness to do "good" is not necessarily best for the "good of the world" in the case of the "girls" because:

> I disliked Michelle and Gabrielle, who are bonded to Raphael and feel they are above their peers. They reminded me of my sister. I identified with Sarah, who was brave enough to kick the girls during their oral presentation and made the whole class laugh. When I was fourteen, I was completely oppressed by overprotective parents. To show them they could not control me like they thought they could, I kicked, and shaved my hair into a mohawk and dyed it white. They knew then! I too, had contested meaning.

Ken goes on to say that he probably unconsciously switched codes when discussing the story of the "communists" because he "truly believes that communism is bad," and that it is only the "good deeds" of people like "Kundera" and the "good examples" set by countries like the United States that have brought democracy to countries like Russia and Czechoslovakia. As a result of taking notes in response to these five questions, Ken acknowledges, in his revision, the ways in which Kundera uses the imagery of the angel to depict the classroom scene on the French Riviera and the political scene in communist Czechoslovakia, thus establishing a parallel between a student/teacher relationship in a Western culture and the government/citizen relationship in the Eastern bloc. Then, Ken uses his earlier reading of the political scene to reflect on and qualify the political stance he had taken toward "communism" (evil) and "democracy" (good) in his earlier paper:

> Kundera is saying that the Russian communists and their followers are not very different from Michelle and Gabrielle in their concern with doing "good." Kundera likes "kickers" ("Kundera" and Sarah) who dare to contest dictatorship. I think that the degree of harm these two groups of "angels" can do to the world is different. To that extent, I believe that the communist "angels" are much more evil than the school "angels." I don't think Kundera will agree with my black and white view of democracy and communism. Maybe Kundera is saying that in a democratic country like ours, there are also Madame Raphaels in the government and a lot of us are more like Michelle and Gabrielle than Sarah. This shows Kundera's political interest, which I ignored when I first read the book because I want to believe in American democracy. . . .

There is still quite a distance between Ken's translation of the text and mine. I find a lot of his comments on the book hard to accept. Yet, I want to argue that his revision is successful in the context of the course and the three assignments. His writing is beginning to show efforts to apply his understanding of the politics of interpretation to both Kundera's and his own approach to the political scene represented in the book.

To encourage my students to further explore the relationship between theory and practice, I usually follow Assignment C with a class discussion aimed at getting them to reflect on and theorize about the method by which they have performed their two readings and to work out the connections between the method they have just enacted and the critical perspectives discussed in essays such as Mailloux's "Interpretation." For example, we might use the two papers and notes Ken wrote for Assignments B and C to articulate methods for addressing the ways political interests mediate our interpretive acts in the process of reading and writing. Students are more likely to be able to continue practicing such a method in their future writing because they have synthesized it on the basis of their own performance. As the term progresses, when I hand out writing assignments similar to Assignment B, I will also invite students to design, in groups, assignments modeled after Assignment C— that is, I encourage them to take the initiative to use the method built into B and C to monitor their interpretive acts. I think that following assignments like A with ones like B and C is useful precisely because, together, they form a mini-sequence of assignments structured on a dialectic between practice and theory. The sequence provides the students with occasions not only to understand the politics of interpretation but also to practice that understanding and to theorize about their own practice. The dialectic between practice and theory built into the sequence counters the danger of the mere indoctrination of a theory of language, which is latent when an assignment such as A or B is used by itself.

At the same time, attention to the dialectics of theory and practice can also push the teacher to locate some gaps between her own theoretical perspectives and pedagogical practice. For example, reading students' interpretations of Kundera's book and listening to them talking about their experience in doing Assignment C—especially their difficulties in making socially responsible decisions when negotiating with the codes of a more powerful "other"—have prompted me to revise my assignments as well as my reading of Kundera's book. To encourage students to talk back to the critic, I added a section in Assignment C which asks them to use their experience in applying a theoretical stance to comment (on a separate sheet, after they have finished their revision) on both the limitations and strengths of that stance. Papers like Ken's have also taught me to reflect more carefully on the politics of my own interpretation of Kundera's book and the effects of those politics on my assignment writing as well as the kind of interpretations the assignment elicits. For instance, Ken's identification with the "kickers" made me rethink the appeal of Kundera's portrayal of the two American students, which I initially found "powerful." Does the "power" of Kundera's depiction tell me more about my susceptibility to portraits of students as helpless dupes than about the power of teachers like Madame Raphael to indoctrinate students? If so, does it also point to a potential gap in my theoretical interest in resistance theory—the belief that the dominated want to and can confront power—and my actual perception of "students"? Considering these questions has helped me to be more attentive to the subversive interests of my students and more watchful of the discrepancy between how I abstractly and actually perceive things. Student papers written in response to these assignments have also called my attention to the way in which my own reading of Kundera's book has delimited the readings of students. For example, through assignment writing and class discussion, my interest in the educational and political dynamics of power seems to have focused students' attention on certain sections of the book but away from others, such as Part Two, in which the behavior of several characters challenges some of the master narratives concerning the relationship of mother/child and husband/wife to which I subscribe. This realization has pushed me to follow Assignment C with another assignment, Assignment D, which asks students to locate aspects of the book which were "overlooked" in class discussion and their previous writings and to revise their papers with these aspects in mind. The purpose of this type of assignment is to explicitly invite the students to move beyond my own socially interested reading and thus to negotiate with my power as the teacher. Explicitly inviting students to negotiate with authority figures—including me as teacher and the critic of my choice—has, ironically, also enabled me to become more comfortable in voicing my observations on forms of sexism in Kundera's writing—such as his portrayal of a male character's admiration for a woman ally's ability to tolerate contradictions in terms of his desire to "rape" her (75), which students like Ken, with his view of "girls," seem to find acceptable.

The importance of accompanying assignments such as A and B with C and D is especially relevant in the context of recent debates over "political correctness." Conservative critics like D'Souza gain currency by presenting themselves as the defenders of academic freedom—that is, they tend to couch their attack in terms of an academy dominated by a group of radical teachers who impose their version of politically correct texts and interpretations on colleagues and students and, in the process, suppress the freedom of speech of those who dare to disagree. For teachers like me, who are interested in calling students' attention to the politics of interpretation, the core of our conflict with these conservatives is never merely over determining and disseminating a body of politically correct texts or interpretations, although it is undoubtedly in our interest to expose our students to such texts and interpretations. The center of the conflict is, rather, to call our students' attention to the politics of reading and writing, to help them locate their decisions over what texts to read and how to read these texts in the context of the power struggle among conflicting cultures. Therefore, it is important that we find ways of making clear that in our classrooms, "PC" stands for power and conflict, politics and commitment, as well as political correctness. The central message for a classroom such as ours is that no position, textual or otherwise, can be taken in isolation from the power relationships among diverse cultures with conflicting political interests. While there are good reasons for why the teacher needs to make her view of what is the politically correct position clear to the students, it is also important that we, as teachers, make it clear that, for each of our students, the ultimate decision of what is politically correct is and can only be theirs. It is their responsibility and not ours to make that decision, although it is our responsibility to ensure that they reflect on the politics of their reading and writing in the very process of generating it.

It should not be surprising that—in a culture which privileges product over process—our struggle to help students reflect on the process by which they have come to their viewpoints or the particular political commitments they have made in enacting such viewpoints when reading and writing is reduced by conservatives to the mere indoctrination of a particular viewpoint. Neither should it be surprising that, in a culture such as ours, our students come to us with more experience in imbibing and regurgitating viewpoints programmed and disseminated by the institution and those with institutional power and that they seldom come to us with any exposure to methods which they can use if they want to explore new, alternative, alien views or to form positions out of a range of contradictory views which transform all of them. Therefore, one of the challenges facing those of us who are committed to oppositional pedagogy is to provide occasions for students to explore and theorize such methods. That is, we need to look for assignments which make it impossible for students to generate a reading without also having to consider alternative viewpoints, without having to reflect on the politics of choosing one, but not other, viewpoints. We need to experiment with ways of designing assignments which call attention to the process in which political commitments are made in the context of polyvalency— the power struggle among conflicting cultures.

Works Cited

Bakhtin, M. M. *The Dialogic Imagination: Four Essays.* Ed. Michael Holquist. Trans. Caryl Emerson and Michael Holquist. Austin: U of Texas P, 1981.
Kundera, Milan. *The Book of Laughter and Forgetting.* Trans. Michael Henry Heim. New York: Penguin, 1980.
Mailloux, Steven. "Interpretation." *Critical Terms for Literary Study.* Ed. Frank Lentricchia and Thomas McLaughlin. U of Chicago P, 1990. 121–34.

6 Standing in This Neighborhood: Of English Studies

Daniel Moshenberg
George Washington University

It is often said that there are more than six centuries of English literature. It is not often said that there are less than two centuries of English literacy. Of course, "English" in those two statements has different meanings. The first refers primarily to the language, the second to the people. But then it is the ordinarily unexamined relation between these meanings that can reveal a central problem in English studies. The idea of literature, throughout, has been so closely connected with the condition of literacy that it can hardly be said that this deeper relationship needs to be forced. Powerful social and cultural conventions control or displace what is otherwise an obvious connection. What then is "English literacy," for professional students and teachers of English? Is it their own condition and that of people much like them, currently and retrospectively applied? Or is it the diverse and changing conditions of their whole nominal people? To approach two centuries of English literacy means restricting ourselves to a bare majority. General literacy has a bare century, and within that many are still disadvantaged. In relation to what is seen as "our" literature, where then do students and teachers of English stand?

> —Raymond Williams
> (*Writing in Society* 212)

Where do students and teachers of English stand? In his essay, "Beyond Cambridge English," Williams describes and reflects upon the "awkward stand" he made, an uneasy contract between literacy and literature (*Writing in Society* 212). Instead of considering either the stands that we, students and teachers of English, make or the legal and political standing of English studies, I want to look, simply, at "where" we stand. As teachers and students of English elaborate a new critical lexicon of borders

The author wishes to thank Susan Lanser, Sammie Moshenberg, and You-me Park for close readings and friendship, and the 1992–93 George Washington University Writing Program Staff Seminar for support. This essay is part of a larger project tentatively entitled, "Being in a Neighborhood, and Playing with Earth."

and boundaries, emerging from earlier critiques of the operations of territory and of community, I want to see how all that stuff plays in the places in which I live. What happens to concepts such as the inoperative community, sites of articulation, and borderland epistemology when they are linked to the ways in which my neighbors and I get from here to there? What does the *neighborhood* offer us, the teachers and students of English?

In "Notes toward a Politics of Location," Adrienne Rich says,

> When I was ten or eleven, early in World War II, a girlfriend and I used to write each other letters which we addressed like this:
>
>> Adrienne Rich
>> 14 Edgevale Road
>> Baltimore, Maryland
>> The United States of America
>> The Continent of North America
>> The Western Hemisphere
>> The Earth
>> The Solar System
>> The Universe
>
> You could see your own house as a tiny fleck on an ever-widening landscape, or as the center of it all from which the circles expanded into the infinite unknown.
> It is that question of feeling at the center that gnaws at me now.
> At the center of what? (*Blood, Bread, and Poetry* 211–12]

Where is Edgevale Road? How can we learn to see 14 Edgevale Road as an integral part of something of which it is not the center? This is Rich's question as she constructs a world geography of women's bodies in motion and struggle. I propose a linked interpretation in which we read the social space between the second and third lines. Although Rich enjoins us to "begin . . . not with a continent or a country or a house" (212), I want to proceed with the neighborhood that identifies Edgevale Road to those who know Baltimore.

The location 14 Edgevale Road is in the heart of Roland Park, a wealthy, tree-lined neighborhood, a neighborhood that used to be called "exclusive"—and you know what that means. Because I know Baltimore, having lived there once for over two decades and having immediate family still living there, I can tell you that Rich's childhood, her life as a girl, was profoundly affected by the unwritten component of neighborhood. I am not suggesting that that ten- or eleven-year-old girl consciously suppressed her neighborhood; she merely followed the proper format as dictated by the U.S. Postal Service. People don't put their neighborhoods in their addresses; neighborhoods as corporate, state-authorized entities do not exist. They only exist in the minds, languages, cultures, and habits of everyone who lives in the area. What happens if we locate ourselves in writing, in addressing one another, as we often do when we speak, by the neighborhoods in which we live? What happens if we write the names of our neighborhoods on the envelopes, across the maps, between the lines on the pages?

People don't just live and work on streets; those streets rise and fall in the context of their named neighborhoods. Certainly, Adrienne Rich knows this, as a cursory reading of her earlier "Teaching Language in Open Admissions" makes clear. In this essay, Rich describes her life in the SEEK program in the City College of New York. She describes the "three ways in which the white middle class could live in New York: the paranoiac, the solipsistic, and a third" (*On Lies, Secrets, and Silence* 54). The third is love. As a lover of the city, she exclaims,

> The streets were rich with human possibility and vicious with human denial (it is breathtaking to walk through a street in East Harlem, passing among the lithe, alert, childish bodies and attuned, observant, childish faces, playing in the spray of a hydrant, and to know that addiction awaits every brain and body in that block as a potential killer). In all its historic, overcrowded, and sweated poverty, the Lower East Side at the turn of the century had never known this: the odds for the poor, today, are weighted by heroin, a fact which the middle classes ignored until it breathed on their own children's lives as well. (54–55)

What are the naming practices here? The unnamed Roland Park is metonymically recalled as Edgevale Road. East Harlem, named, is metonymically traversed, in the present tense, as "a street" and "that block." And the Lower East Side operates as a transhistorical metaphor for East Harlem, a way of reading, through the similarities of poverty and housing, the differentiated present of heroin. When does the neighborhood sublime, the "breathtaking," become murderous? Where exactly is Bensonhurst in English studies? How does the name of Yusef Hawkins affect our understanding of the sublime? People live and die on unnamed streets in East Harlem, on the Lower East Side, as well as on named streets in unnamed Roland Park. The neighborhood is where we live; it is, and its name is, a site of cultural-political practice.

This method of reading as interventionary revision, this complication of a simple address into a differentially related social event and meaning, is what Ernesto Laclau and Chantal Mouffe call *articulation*. For Laclau and Mouffe, articulation is "any practice establishing a relation among elements such that their identity is modified as a result of the articulatory practice" (105). But what is articulatory practice?

> The practice of articulation . . . consists in the construction of nodal
> points which partially fix meaning; and the partial character of this
> fixation proceeds from the openness of the social, a result, in its turn
> of the constant overflowing of every discourse by the infinitude of
> the field of discursivity. Every social practice is therefore—in one
> of its dimensions—articulatory. As it is not the internal moment of
> a self-defined totality, it cannot simply be the expression of
> something already acquired, it cannot be **wholly** subsumed under
> the principle of repetition; rather, it always consists in the
> constructions of new differences. The social is articulation insofar
> as "society" is impossible. (113–14)

Lawrence Grossberg suggests that

> articulation is the construction of one set of relations out of another;
> it often involves delinking or disarticulating connections in order
> to link or rearticulate others. Articulation is a continuous struggle
> to reposition practices within a shifting field of forces, to redefine
> the possibilities of life by redefining the field of relations—the
> context—within which a practice is located. (54)

Articulation is the process of "analyzing an event . . . [by] (re)-
constructing or, in Foucault's terms, fabricating the network of relationships into which and within which it is articulated" (Grossberg 54). It is
a way of reading texts, events, the world, history, "the struggle for language and the struggle against perfect communication, against the one
code that translates all meaning perfectly" (Haraway 176).

Let me offer a brief example. In his delineation of relationships among
articulation, culture, and cultural studies, Grossberg writes, "A particular site is defined by 'the exteriority of its [neighborhoods]'" (Grossberg
53).[1] How am I to read, or understand, [neighborhoods]? How can I not
read the brackets and their "over-inscribed" contents as an invitation to
"fabricate" a contextual network? My articulation of Grossberg's statement begins with the question, "What can I make of [neighborhoods]?"

How does Grossberg rewrite *vicinity* as [neighborhoods]? I am not concerned with the matter of accuracy in translation, with the silencing claim
of worthlessness. I am interested in the relations between these two terms
as they begin to construct a practical context, the precarious "blank
space" from which I read and thus speak these texts.

Michel Foucault published his version of this sentence as follows:

> C'est définir un emplacement singulier par l'extériorité de ses
> voisinages; c'est—plutôt que de vouloir réduire les autres au silence,
> en prétendant que leur propos est vain—essayer de définir cet espace
> blanc d' où je parle, et qui prend forme lentement dans un discours
> que je sens si précaire, si incertain encore. (*L'Archéologie* 27)

What changes from [neighborhoods] to *vicinity* to *voisinages*, what differences do these changes make, and how would you characterize the

ensemble? For example, how does the shift in number from plural *voisinages* to singular *vicinity* affect the attempt to define the particularity of the "blank space"? What are the political geographies of *neighborhoods* and of *vicinity*? Which disciplinary discourses are invoked or employed in each of the three terms? Which personal experiences are called upon as you read the three terms? Finally, what name(s) would you give to the networks emerging from your reading of the zone of contact formed by [*neighborhoods*]—*vicinity*—*voisinages*—and with which "struggles," to recall Grossberg's formulation, would you link the network(s)?

These questions offer preliminary access into articulatory practices. To answer them here would take too long; I simply note that a preliminary distinction between neighborhood and vicinity, according to at least three dictionaries, is the difference between a place where people live near one another and the quality or state of being near one another. Grossberg then points toward the problematics and the politics of metaphysics, the inscriptions of being and presence.

From this, articulating English studies would mean constructing new differences, new antagonisms, in a constantly, self-consciously nonredundant here and now. For Raymond Williams, here and now is located on the line that separates and unites literature and literacy; for Rich, I am suggesting, the here-and-now impossibility of "society" can be seen in the ungraspable dimensions of the cosmos *and* in the space between the remembered places.

This is about reading history. In Archer and Costello's *Literacy and Power: The Latin American Battleground*, Paolo Freire tells a story from his days working with the Workers Party in Brazil. He describes how easy it is to assume one's own historical illiteracy. Freire says,

> The other day I talked with Lula [Luis da Silva] after a television conversation where a very good intellectual said to him, "Lula, it is a surprise to me because I know you do not have time to read but still you speak very seriously about the historical moment of Brazil especially the situation today."
> Then Lula said, "I really don't read."
> I said to him after that I disagreed with him. I said: "Lula, you are for me one of the best readers of Brazil today, but not readers of the word, readers of the world. That is, you are reading the history you are making every day. You are understanding it, grasping it to the extent that you are making it also. Please, don't say anymore that you are not reading. You can say that you are not yet reading books. But you are reading history." (Archer and Costello 199)

How does one read history? For Freire, since *Pedagogy of the Oppressed*, reading history has meant engaging in the production of critical consciousness through an ongoing activity that involves the cultural practice of renaming the world as a necessary part of individual and national liberation struggles. In "Teaching Language in Open Admissions," Rich described this process succinctly: "Language is . . . a weapon, and what goes with language: reflection, criticism, renaming, creation" (*On Lies, Secrets, and Silence* 68).

What kind of weapon are we talking about here? When does language as renaming the world, as reading history, go ballistic? Freire's response relies on the written and lifework of Amilcar Cabral, the African revolutionary philosopher and participant in the liberation of Guinea Bissau. In a speech entitled "The Weapon of Theory: Presuppositions and Objectives of National Liberation in Relation to Social Structure," offered January 6, 1966, to the First Solidarity Conference of the Peoples of Africa, Asia, and Latin America, Cabral noted that

> the national liberation of a people is the regaining of the historical personality of that people, it is their return to history through the destruction of the imperialist domination to which they were subjected. . . . The basis of national liberation . . . is the inalienable right of every people to have their own history; and the aim of national liberation is to regain this right usurped by imperialism, that is to free the process of development of the national forces. (Cabral 130)

For Freire, Rich, and Cabral, the role of culture is understood within the context of the ambition of national liberation. To talk of language, or theory, or culture, as a weapon is to locate oneself within the contested terrain of domination and resistance, of hegemony and antagonism. According to Ngugi wa Thiong'o, the Gikuyu Kenyan novelist, playwright, and popular educator, the writing of the African revolutions of the 1960s (and presumably the liberation struggles in the Western Hemisphere that looked to them for theoretical and tactical guidance) are a footnote to Frantz Fanon's *Wretched of the Earth,* especially the two central chapters, "The Pitfalls of National Consciousness" and "On National Culture" (*Writing Against Neocolonialism* 6–8; *Decolonising the Mind* 63–64).

I want to come home with this skeletal genealogy, Freire—Rich—Cabral—Ngugi—Fanon. Fanon ends "On National Culture" with my neighborhood praxis:

> If a person is known by her acts, then we will say that the most urgent thing today for the intellectual is to build up the nation. If this building up is true, that is to say if it interprets the manifest will of the people and reveals the eager African peoples, then the building of a nation is of necessity accompanied by the discovery and encouragement of universalizing values. Far from keeping aloof from other nations, therefore, it is national liberation which leads

the nation to play its part on the stage of history. It is at the heart of national consciousness that international consciousness lives and grows. And this two-fold emerging is ultimately only the source of all culture. (Fanon 247–48)

At the heart of national consciousness, international consciousness lives and grows. I take that sentence literally and receive it as a call to one version of a fairly traditional form of the articulation of the study of literature, the neighborhood. I suggest that this genealogical cadre invites us to work with the people who live at and construct the heart of national consciousness and, as traditionally trained intellectuals, to connect the local with the international, both by bringing the contacts and by soliciting the international aspects of the local.

It is this last notion that I suggest is actually very traditional. As a discipline, English literature / literacy studies have always been divided between accumulators and speculators. On the side of accumulation, we have had those who want to add on more units, be they more national units or more disciplinary units. I see this as the basically liberal discourse of cultural literacy. On the speculative side, we have had the philological tradition that wants to excavate, or solicit, "hidden" or "repressed" elements within a word or term. While I see this as part of a radical tradition of critical literacy, epitomized by the Freire—Rich—Cabral—Ngugi—Fanon cadre, it also includes scholars such as Leo Spitzer.

I call the latter tradition radical because, as it pulls material out, it heightens the tension of submersion and struggle as a method. According to Laclau and Mouffe, this kind of cultural criticism is both the instrument and the short-term goal for those working toward a radical and plural democracy: "This moment of tension, of openness, which gives the social its essentially incomplete and precarious character, is what every project for radical democracy should set out to institutionalize" (190). Williams, at the end of "Beyond Cambridge English," offers English studies as a practical means of understanding and enacting articulation as connection: "In English studies, and in its convergences with other humanities and human sciences, there is so much active knowledge, so many active skills, which are very valuable in themselves and which really can connect with a world of practice and choice and struggle" (*Writing in Society* 226).

Where does all this connecting go on? For Williams, the neighborhood, as linked to and yet distinct from the community, was the primary contested place of significant, working-class, progressive connections.

In Williams's experience as a student and teacher of English, the neighborhood was the physical and social space specifically rejected by traditional, institutional English studies. On at least three occasions, he told the story of his discovery of that rejection: once in a 1958 essay, "Culture Is Ordinary" (see *Resources of Hope*); once in an interview conducted in the summer of 1977 (*Politics and Letters* 67); and once in a lecture, "The Importance of Community," given to the Plaid Cymru Summer School at Llandudno, on 13 July 1977 (see *Resources of Hope*). In *Politics and Letters*, Williams offers the shortest version of this story, which he identifies as an "incident . . . which anticipated what was eventually my key disagreement with him [the English critic, F. R. Leavis]" (67). Twenty years after the incident, Williams recalls:

> (Wolf) Mankowitz and I went to hear L. C. Knights give a talk on the meaning of "neighbour" in Shakespeare. Leavis was leaning against the wall at the back of the room. When Knights said that nobody now can understand Shakespeare's meaning of neighbour, for in a corrupt mechanical civilization there are no neighbours, I got up and said I thought this was only differentially true; there were obviously successive kinds of community, and I knew perfectly well, from Wales, what neighbour meant. Mankowitz . . . then attacked me bitterly for sentimental nonsense. Leavis was nodding approvingly while he was doing so. (*Politics and Letters* 67)

In "Culture Is Ordinary," Williams recalls this event as one in which "I even made a fool of myself, or was made to think so" (*Resources of Hope* 9). Here, he relates some of his experience of neighborhood:

> When my father was dying, this year, one man came in and dug his garden; another loaded and delivered a lorry of sleepers for firewood; another came and chopped the sleepers into blocks; another—I don't know who, it was never said—left a sack of potatoes at the back door; a woman came in and took away a basket of washing. (9)

Finally, in "The Importance of Community," Williams offers more detail as well as definition. In response to the proclamation of the incomprehensibility of neighborhood, Williams arose:

> Well, then I got up, straight from Pandy, so to say, and said I knew perfectly well what "neighbour," in that full sense, means. That got hissed—it was a remark so against the common sense that here was something in literature which was not now socially available: the notion of that kind of recognition of certain kinds of mutual responsibility. Now this was not to idealize my own place. I do not mean that people . . . all liked each other. I do not mean that people didn't play dirty tricks on each other sometimes. I do not mean that people didn't have disputes. I mean that there was nevertheless a level of social obligation which was conferred by the fact of seeming to live in the same place and in that sense to have a common identity. And from this sense there were acts of kindness beyond calculation, forms of mutual recognition even when they were wild misinterpretations of the world outside. My father had to go to the

local pub to stop them taking up a collection for me when I won a
scholarship to Cambridge. He had to explain to them that having
won a scholarship I had enough money to go. People assumed that
going to a strange place like that . . . I mean the one thing they could
identify about Cambridge was that you'd need a lot of money up
there. And so a collection was taken up, to try to look after me.
(*Resources of Hope* 114)

Williams felt that "a distinct working-class way of life . . . , with its
emphases of neighbourhood, mutual obligation, and common better-
ment, as expressed in the great working-class political and industrial
institutions, is in fact the best basis for any future English society" (8).
His tale of public humiliation at the hands of the leading lights in Cambridge English studies in the late 1940s indicates that *neighborhood* might
also be seen as the best basis for any future English studies, precisely
because it complicates the representation of the social as a uniform totality. Some people, living in neighborhoods, understand the concept of
neighborhood, despite the advances or incursions of industrial, or
postindustrial, capital.

Adrienne Rich's childhood suppression of her Roland Park neighborhood operates within the rules of one version of English studies, that in
which the state and civil society become fused. You live at home, and
your home is in the city. What might it mean to resist this fusion, to suggest that I live in a neighborhood, and, specifically for teachers and students of English, that that neighborhood might inform my work?

I work with the Tenants Support Committee in the Arlandria/
Chirilagua neighborhood of Alexandria, Virginia. It is a small place,
populated primarily by low-income African American and Central
American people, most of whom used to work on construction sites and
in restaurants; in hotels, offices, and in housekeeping; or as babysitters.
The housing and other property is owned primarily by absentee landlords who seek to "improve" the neighborhood through mass evictions,
personal harassment, poor maintenance, and rent increases.

Here is the international consciousness at the heart of the national
consciousness. Of course there is the mix of languages, predominantly
Salvadoran campesino Spanish; Middle Atlantic, working-class Black
English; and Middle Atlantic, middle-class White English. There is also
the international consciousness of struggle at the heart of a national consciousness that calls itself democracy.

But listen to Detroit African American community activist James
Boggs's description of that democracy:

The truth is that the democracy of which Americans have been so
proud is based on the worst kind of class system in the world, a class
system that is based on the systematic exploitation of another race.

Racism is the philosophy which pursues or condones the systematic
oppression of another race because that race is inferior or subhuman.
If the American people had not been racist, they could never have
boasted about American democracy all these years. (Boggs 125)

Working at the neighborhood level, we are trying to create an appropriate international-local model for democratic culture in the service of
national liberation. In large terms, this means constantly wondering
whether national liberation means emancipation of or from the nation.
Immediately, it means reading and renaming the ways in which we co-
inhabit small places. This occurs in three stages. In the first, we see and
study each other and learn to read history in a new mode. We acknowledge that we are in the same place and different, in this case African
American and Central American, and that we can construct a neighborhood out of that. We begin our study with the everyday domestic practices of neighbors, with the knowledge we already have of our
neighborhood and with the insistence that working people, and especially women, are something other than victims. In the second, we learn
to step out of the small place, to make our views public, to publish them.
This involves creating opportunities for public speaking, such as rallies,
celebrations, classes.

The third stage involves full community action. On Tuesday, March
12, 1991, the Tenants Support Committee hosted a luncheon for the
homeless of Arlandria. With little prior notice, about eighty people
showed up, mostly men, mostly Salvadoran, along with print and broad-
cast journalists. After an hour of eating and circle testifying, about forty
of us marched about a mile and a half down to the Alexandria Office of
Human Services to ask for or demand assistance. The primary push was
for a shelter in our neighborhood. We had been told before that we
couldn't have a shelter because there really weren't any homeless people
in the area. Well, there we were.

Here the two paradigms of English studies articulation—accumulation and speculation—come in. The Office of Human Services brought
out eight or so Spanish-speaking bureaucrats to talk at the crowd. While
we preferred Spanish-speaking to non-Spanish-speaking bureaucrats,
this did not resolve the issues of housing and food. The city officials
continued to speak the language of scarcity of resources and of poor
geography. You know the language of poor geography: "What you say
is interesting, but that's not really our department. You have to go somewhere else, somewhere higher, somewhere where decisions are made."
This is the cartography of myth and simulation that Barthes, Wittig,
Baudrillard, and Virilio have already instructed us in.

This was intoned, in one form or another, twenty or thirty times. It takes a while to learn the language and the discourse. Finally, one of us said, "Listen. We're talking about a crisis. The recession has hit this neighborhood in a big way. People are desperate. Times have changed; I repeat this is a crisis, and we want to know how you are going to change with the changing times. We want to know how you as individuals and as a group are going to act."

This is interventionary revision. The top functionary leaned forward and explained that resources were scarce and that they weren't going to do anything. Another one explained that while it is difficult to imagine someone calling the police to be taken to a distant shelter, if someone was on the street and clearly in distress, the police would take them. This was offered as helpful information.

Finally, we were told, in Spanish, that even if we brought a hundred people down to the Office of Human Services, that would not prove their existence. They would have to go to shelters all over the city and be turned down or be found frozen near to death on the street and transported by police, if they were to be counted.

So what? My point here for English studies is simple. The terms of inclusion and exclusion are inadequate to the history that I read every day. People are not being kept out; they are struggling against being wiped out, evicted, eliminated, or, if they are lucky, jailed. In Arlandria, we are constantly confronting the attempts of state and parastatal institutions to deny the very existence of people living here. In the story above, it's the homeless. A local community college charges out-of-state fees to immigrants who have legal residence and work permits, even when they demonstrate that they have been living in the state for years. We bring a group of prospective Hispanic applicants to interview the people in charge; they form a culture circle to investigate and write a letter. The city claims apartments are "overcrowded." We form a neighborhood research project and find that apartments are not overcrowded; they are undersized. Despite our efforts, landlords have insisted on building only one-bedroom apartments. In the end, the landlords go bankrupt, and we assume cooperative ownership of 300 apartment units. The examples are everywhere and everyday, because the neighborhood is African American, Salvadoran, and poor.

The examples within the neighborhood also link with examples in other, similarly attacked neighborhoods. For example, in June 1993, the Alexandria Redevelopment and Housing Authority (ARHA) floated a proposal to sell off an entire, traditionally African American, low-income neighborhood known as the "Berg." ARHA claimed the process was democratic because "at the third stage of deliberations, after the concept is developed and the City Council is informed," the residents would have their turn. When the residents and their supporters took over the June 1993 ARHA Board of Commissioners meeting to express dismay and anger at their exclusion from the decision-making process, the chair "patiently tried" to explain "the process" and how it works. He was greeted with howls. Residents and supporters tried to explain "the process" from their perspective—personal and collective histories of mass dislocation, of deteriorating dwellings, of the meaning of hope in a culture of institutional and individual violence directed against them as African Americans, low-income people, women, women heads of households, children. They spoke of their deep desire to stay put in a neighborhood that is theirs, that no one wanted before the wealthy and white started moving into adjoining neighborhoods. They spoke and shouted about the dignity of permanence, of respect for their history, of staying still.

Although no one threatened any of the commissioners with physical violence, the commissioners freaked out. Concerning the meeting, the commission chair later told a local newspaper reporter, "I've never witnessed anything like that in my adult life. I thought I was in 'Jurassic Park'" (Jacobson A/A 1). When he went two days later to the City Council, he was surprised by residents' "extreme" response to being described as "beasts."

Rhetorically and strategically, this particular story, which continues as I write these words, echoes Paul Virilio's descriptions of popular defense in an age of military cultural hegemony. After all, when landlords, be they public agencies or private corporations, threaten to evict entire populations, they are reenacting a specifically military drama. In this context, according to Virilio,

> The principle aim of any truly popular resistance is thus to oppose the establishment of a social situation based solely on the illegality of armed force, which reduces a population to the status of a *movable slave*, a *commodity*. The domestic condition is scarcely better than that of an animal herd, and in fact, the proletarianization of the . . . working classes only reproduced the progressive reduction of the deterritorialized countryman *to the condition of movable or immovable.* (Virilio 54)

The struggle here is for the double sense of the *bur* that lies at the root of neighbor, that is dwelling and being. We need to develop both a rhetoric and methodology within the English studies communities that acknowledges the violence that is being perpetrated—as a constitutive and primary element of the national culture—and studies the various responses. The Rodney King video—and its ongoing aftermath—is a narrative of state-authorized violence against an African American male trying to get home. Likewise, as Patricia Williams has noted, the extended story of Howard Beach—from the assault on December 20, 1986, on through to the representation of events and the trial—is about neighborhoods, racism, and how our domestic, contemporary brands of cultural, or civil, society pass laws. For Williams, the investigators, legal and otherwise,

> assume that black people (and I have never heard the same public assumption about white people) need documented reasons for excursioning into neighborhoods where they do not live, for venturing beyond the bounds of the zones to which they are supposedly confined" (*Alchemy of Race* 68).

I propose an Afrocentric base for reading English from a neighborhood perspective. If we are talking about English studies and neighborhoods, we can begin with those places of the African-derived working classes, because they continue to serve as a self-conscious political and cultural model for neighborhood. In the United States, for example, "most black neighborhoods have existed only as long as whites have permitted them to; blacks have been this society's perpetual tenants, sharecroppers, lessees" (Williams 71). The African American struggle for decent and secure housing is a historical struggle for neighborhood, one that has been denied by the courts as much as by the realtors. When it comes to African Americans moving into a predominantly white neighborhood, the courts have established boundaries that distinguish between the rights of a few individual black families to move in and the "threat" of a whole bunch of black families moving in. As Derrick Bell notes, "Courts have tailored tenant racial balance to levels consistent with the refusal of whites to live in predominantly black residential districts" (Bell 152). When do individuals become too much of a mass, and what happens then? What happens to notions of authorship, readership, text, when they are located on borders that proliferate throughout predominantly African American neighborhoods?

Consider Lorraine Hansberry's *A Raisin in the Sun* as a kind of exemplary text. What are the exact neighborhoods involved? What are the racial, gender, and class bases for central terms such as freedom, identity, personhood? What do *you* make of the differences between Adrienne Rich and bell hooks on the subject of Lorraine Hansberry? For Rich, writing in 1979, Hansberry is "a problem to me. . . because even as I read *A Raisin in the Sun* I am aware of the inner and outer contradictions spawned when a writer who is both black and female tries with passionate intent to make a statement which can be heard by those who are neither" (*Blood, Bread, and Poetry* 14). Rich goes on to explain that as a white, lesbian, feminist writer, she can sympathize with the struggles Hansberry may have faced against external and internalized censors.

bell hooks, on the other hand, begins "Liberation Scenes: Speak This Yearning" with a different construction of the problem of Lorraine Hansberry:

> When it was first produced, *A Raisin in the Sun* was in many ways a counter-hegemonic cultural production. The play 'interrogated' the fear within black people that being out of our place—not conforming to social norms, especially those set by white supremacy—would lead to destruction, even death. On a basic level, the play was about housing—the way racial segregation in a capitalist society meant that black folks were discriminated against when seeking places to live. It made it clear that the Younger family was not interested in being a part of white culture, in assimilation; they wanted better housing. (hooks 1).

The problem is housing. The problem of housing, in African American United States, is neighborhood development or constitution or construction. The neighborhood can offer a base for an English studies program committed to a multicultural praxis that is always eager to explode race-neutral interpretation as it provides a cultural and institutional place for hooks, Hansberry, and Rich, as feminist women, to converse and act.

If we consider the neighborhood from the working-class, African American base, the struggle for decent and affordable housing that becomes the struggle for safe and legitimate neighborhood is underwritten by the political narrative of land. Even in urban areas, the African American struggle for space is described as a desire, or yearning, for land. Land as a constitutive community trope binds African Americans to the "grand narratives" of Native American, Hispanic American, Asian American, and certain European American communities. These are the subaltern and suppressed narratives that crisscross the nation and the idea of the nation, as well as the texts we read and write and the classrooms in which we teach and study English.

The cultural study of the struggle for space is a study of language, speech, and voice production within a critique of ownership and residence. It makes dialogics dialectic by insisting that every dialogue occurs in a place in which articulation entails not only the visible actors but also, often, invisible owners. In the Washington D.C., metropolitan area, for example, the majority of neighborhoods of color are owned by white, male, absentee landlords. Is the preponderance of efficiencies and one bedroom apartments in Arlandria a consequence of simple (and inaccurate) economic projections, or does this superabundance of too-small apartments also speak to the gender, race, and class of the land-lords who never took a walk down the street, who never asked the residents what they wanted, or what they might even pay more for? The plan was to remove African American and Salvadoran working-class people, mostly families. Reading neighborhood owner—tenant relationships puts everything into a historical relation that helps us avoid the trap of what Patricia Williams calls "the pain of word bondage," the notion that "the best way to give voice to those whose voice has been suppressed [is] to argue that they had no voice" (*Alchemy of Race* 156).

Reading textual and pedagogical practices through a neighborhood base further implies

> a recognition that the dimensions of space and time matter, and that there are real geographies of social action, real as well as metaphorical territories and spaces of power that become vital as organizing forces in the geopolitics of capitalism, at the same time as they are sites of innumerable differences and othernesses that have to be understood in their own right and within the overall logic of capitalist development. Historical materialism is finally beginning to take its geography seriously. (Harvey 355)

How we, as students and teachers of English, begin to take our geographies seriously is a matter of where we stand and how we, in each instance and across a given span of time, articulate the sites of our standings. I am not arguing for, nor against, sending students into "socially marked" neighborhoods to perform some sort of "field research." I am suggesting, more simply, that the neighborhood, and neighborhoods, can serve as interpellative resources for the design and understanding of individual courses and curricula, as well as of textual interpretation and interpretative methods.

For example, where I live, we are trying to create opportunities to promote the international consciousness at the heart of the national culture. Concretely, this means studying and teaching English in the context of the rights and literacy promoters of contemporary Central American popular education projects, of the SCLC Freedom Schools in the South, or of the ANC Solomon Mahlangu Freedom College in Tanzania. It means placing my Salvadoran and African American neighbors' cultural-historical traditions of critical literacy, postliteracy, and popular education at the center of my work and negotiating that center with those of others who come from different places. It means extending critiques of literary production and cultural materialism to neighborhood publications, including newsletters, flyers, and group letters, and bringing those analyses to class. It means trying to talk, every time you and I meet, about culture, education, and democracy in our own neighborhoods and in the neighborhoods represented in the works we study and

produce. In a classroom, it can mean something as simple as conceptualizing the participants as members, or rememberers, of neighborhood
cultures; that we come together as residents as well as readers, writers,
critics, scholars; and that the relationships between our literary practices
and our residential practices might bear intensive scrutiny.

When we take stands inside and outside the university, our scholarship informs and is informed by neighborhood praxis. Instead of seeing
ourselves as institutionally circumscribed intellectual workers, we can
learn to see ourselves as popular culture workers. One model for this
transformation is provided by Amilcar Cabral, in a speech entitled "National Liberation and Culture," offered at Syracuse University in February 1970. Having explained the ways in which national liberation is a
cultural process, Cabral then specified the culture work that needed to
be performed:

> development of a people's culture and of all aboriginal positive
> cultural values;
>
> development of a national culture on the basis of history and the
> conquests of the struggle itself;
>
> development of the technical and technological scientific culture;
>
> development of a universal culture, aiming at perfect integration in
> the contemporary world and its prospects for evolution;
>
> constant and generalized raising of feelings of humanism, solidarity,
> respect, and disinterested devotion to the human being. (Cabral 153)

For Cabral, there are no small places in the sense that Jamaica Kincaid
offers: "For the people in a small place, every event is a domestic event;
the people in a small place cannot see themselves in a larger picture, they
cannot see that they might be part of a chain of something, anything"
(Kincaid 52). Neighborhoods are neither isolated havens of myth and
magic nor naturally abandoned backwaters. The reason for English studies, understood as local internationalist articulation, is to stand, as students and teachers of English, among people struggling, politically and
culturally, to stay alive and secure in one place, to live and become as
"just human beings" (Kincaid 81).

Note

1. According to Grossberg's footnote 23, this citation comes from "M. Foucault, *The Archaeology of Knowledge*, p. 17" (Grossberg 408). On page 17 of the 1972
edition of *The Archaeology of Knowledge*, Foucault's "original" sentence reads, "It
is an attempt to define a particular site by the exteriority of its vicinity; rather
than trying to reduce others to silence, by claiming that what they say is worth-
less, I have tried to define this blank space from which I speak, and which is

slowly taking shape in a discourse that I still feel to be so precarious and so unsure" (Foucault *Archaeology* 17).

Works Cited

Archer, David, and Patrick Costello. *Literacy and Power: The Latin American Battleground.* London: Earthscan, 1990.

Bell, Derrick A. *And We Are Not Saved: The Elusive Quest for Racial Justice.* New York: Basic, 1989.

Boggs, James. *Racism and the Class Struggle: Further Pages from a Black Worker's Notebook.* New York: Monthly Review, 1970.

Cabral, Amilcar. *Unity and Struggle: Speeches and Writings.* Trans. Michael Wolfers. New York: Monthly Review, 1979.

Fanon, Frantz. *The Wretched of the Earth.* Trans. Constance Farrington. New York: Grove, 1968.

Foucault, Michel. *The Archaeology of Knowledge.* Trans. A.M. Sheridan Smith. New York: Random, 1972. [Translation of *L' Archéologie du Savior.*]

———. *L' Archéologie du Savoir.* Paris: Gallimard, 1969.

Freire, Paolo. *Pedagogy of the Oppressed.* Trans. Myra Bergman Ramos. New York: Continuum, 1970.

Grossberg, Lawrence. *We Gotta Get Out of This Place: Popular Conservatism and Postmodern Culture.* New York: Routledge, 1992.

Hansberry, Lorraine. *A Raisin in the Sun.* New York: Signet, 1987.

Haraway, Donna J. *Simians, Cyborgs, and Women: The Reinvention of Nature.* New York: Routledge, 1991.

Harvey, David. *The Condition of Postmodernity: An Enquiry into the Origins of Cultural Change.* New York: Blackwell, 1989.

hooks, bell. *Yearning: Race, Gender, and Cultural Politics.* Boston: South End, 1990.

Jacobson, Abbe. "Protesters Want Berg Renovated." *The Alexandria Journal* 30 June 1993: A1, A7.

Kincaid, Jamaica. *A Small Place.* New York: Plume, 1988.

Laclau, Ernesto, and Chantal Mouffe. *Hegemony and Socialist Strategy: Towards a Radical Democratic Politics.* London: Verso, 1985.

Ngugi wa Thiong'o. *Decolonising the Mind.* London: J. Currey, 1986.

———. *Writing Against Neocolonialism: The Politics of Language in African Literature.* Middlesex, UK: Vita, 1986.

Rich, Adrienne. *Blood, Bread, and Poetry: Selected Prose, 1979–1985.* New York: Norton, 1986.

———. *On Lies, Secrets, and Silence: Selected Prose, 1966–1978.* New York: Norton, 1979.

Virilio, Paul. *Popular Defense & Ecological Struggles.* Trans. Mark Polizzotti. New York: Semiotext(e), 1990.

Williams, Patricia J. *The Alchemy of Race and Rights.* Cambridge, MA: Harvard UP, 1991.

Williams, Raymond. *Politics and Letters: Interviews with New Left Review*. London: New Left Review, 1979.

———. *Resources of Hope: Culture, Democracy, Socialism*. London: Verso, 1989.

———. *Writing in Society*. London: Verso, 1983.

7 Redistribution and the Transformation of American Studies

Eric Cheyfitz
University of Pennsylvania

> What counts today, the question which is looming on the horizon, is the need for a redistribution of wealth. Humanity must reply to this question, or be shaken to pieces by it.
>
> —Frantz Fanon (*Wretched of the Earth* 98)

I

Fanon composed this statement in 1961 in *The Wretched of the Earth*. Today, thirty-four years later, the question stands with the same force and remains unanswered. It is the central question. The debates over multicultural curricula that in recent years have focused public attention on university campuses, and more recently on primary and secondary schools, are, I want to argue in section II of this essay, driven by Fanon's question.[1] But Fanon's question is not only the question of a highly visible Third-World revolutionary, of a black man from Martinique. It is also the central question of a highly visible American liberal, a white woman from Illinois, Jane Addams, who, in *Twenty Years at Hull House,* her account of the beginning of the settlement house movement in the U.S., theorized her project in the following way:

> The Settlement, then, is an experimental effort to aid in the solution of the social and industrial problems which are engendered by the modern conditions of life in a great city. It insists that these problems are not confined to any one portion of a city. It is an attempt to relieve, at the same time, the overaccumulation at one end of society and the destitution at the other; but it assumes that this overaccumulation and destitution is most sorely felt in the things that pertain to social and educational privileges. (*Twenty Years* 98)

The difference between the redistributive projects of Fanon and Addams is clear. For Fanon, a Marxist intellectual and activist, redistribution means economic redistribution through socialist revolution. For,

93

from a Marxist point of view, it is upon such basic redistribution that
the redistribution of what Addams calls "social and educational privileges" depends. On the other hand, for Addams, who theorizes progressive change within a democratic-capitalist vision, the redistribution of
"social and educational privileges" must be imagined as an issue that
can be, to a significant if not total degree, separated from the redistribution of economic privilege. Addams worked for the reform of the economic system of the United States, most effectively through her support
of and work for progressive labor legislation and her participation in the
burgeoning labor movement, particularly as it affected women and children—she was one of the first officers of the Women's Trade Union
League founded in 1903 (see Foner 228); she did not envision or act for
the system's transformation as did, for example, the socialist movements
of her day. In this respect, Christopher Lasch, who generally admires
her social agenda, can place her within the United States liberal tradition, where this agenda could lend itself to co-optation through incor-
poration into what Althusser calls "the ideological state apparatus" by
the very forces it opposed:

> . . . the new liberalism advocated by Edward A. Ross, Herbert Croly,
> Richard T. Ely, Newton D. Baker, and even by Jane Addams and
> John Dewey sought not so much to democratize the industrial
> system as to make it run more efficiently. These reformers wished
> to substitute "education" for older and cruder methods of social
> control, techniques that appeared to them not only offensive in
> themselves, since they rested on coercion, but inexcusably inefficient.
> (Lasch 10)

The projects of both Fanon and Addams are multicultural in vision
and action. Fanon worked across the cultural boundaries of Europe and
the Third World, from the Caribbean to Africa. Within the Chicago neighborhood of sweat shops where Hull House was established, Addams
worked with a range of cultural and ethnic differences inclusive of Europe and the Middle East, and, beyond this, she supported the agenda
of African American equality, though she compromised this support in
her support of the Progressive Party in 1912.[2] Both Fanon and Addams,
however, saw cultural difference finally subsumed under the political
and cultural unity of their visions. Addams put it this way:

> . . . the things which make men alike are finer and better than the
> things that keep them apart, and . . . these basic likenesses, if they
> are properly accentuated, easily transcend the less essential
> differences of race, language, creed, and tradition. (*Twenty Years at
> Hull House* 89)

At the end of his crucial book on racism, *Black Skin, White Masks*, Fanon
put it this way:

I find myself suddenly in the world and I recognize that I have one right alone: That of demanding human behavior from the other. (229)

Today, working through a paradigm of difference in a world of increasingly conflictive ethnicities (as capital becomes increasingly international, human groups are becoming increasingly nationalized and Balkanized), we may be powerfully skeptical of or at least puzzled or troubled by the notion of some "common humanity" invoked by Fanon and Addams, even as we try to imagine this humanity anew in terms of the poststructuralist interplay between identity and difference.

Both Fanon and Addams, I also want to emphasize, are American, in the crucial sense that we can no longer identify America with the United States but must see the United States as part of the Americas, North and South. This point will become specified in the third and fourth parts of my essay, where I want to propose, theoretically and practically, an American studies curriculum framed by the questions of redistribution posed by Fanon and Addams and figured by the radical opposition of their answers to these questions.

II

Allan Bloom's book, *The Closing of the American Mind*, which attacks what he construes as the historic drift of U.S. values into a radical relativity, figures most visibly in what have become known generally (in the years following its publication) as the "PC" debates. Those debates, whatever issues they have raised from free speech to affirmative action, have been driven by the forces that have taken on the name of "multiculturalism."[3] Because of its visibility and position in establishing the Right's perspective in these debates, I want to use some passages from Bloom's book as exemplary of the issue of redistribution that, for me, generates these debates. And I want to emphasize that the way I read these passages in what follows composes the kind of pedagogical strategy that drives the curriculum I suggest in parts III and IV.

As a way into the discussion of redistribution, I want to define as far as possible what I mean by the political designations "Right" and "Left." In my understanding, the Right consists of those discourses that in one way or another—from the politically *conservative*, even reactionary, to the politically *liberal* (terms I use here in the contemporary sense)—rationalize or naturalize, in a mode fundamentally derived from the founding ideology of the United States—that is, "liberal" ideology in the classic, not contemporary, sense of the term (though the two senses overlap)—what I will read later in this essay as a generative contradiction, a contradiction contained in the phrase *capitalist democracy*. Thus, fundamentally, a work of self-ascribed contemporary political liberalism, Arthur Schlesinger's *The Disuniting of America* (though at critical moments Schlesinger, with a decidedly anti-Bloomian tone and emphasis, enthusiastically pronounces his belief in multicultural values) does the same work as the conservative Bloom, which, it is clear, understands itself as a classically liberal discourse. (It should be noted here that Bloom, at least in his rhetorical strategy, which is typical of the rhetorical strategy of the Right in the PC debates, is not simply against any kind of multiculturalism. He is against the kind that suggests or argues for a relativity of values. Another way of putting this is that he supports a multiculturalism firmly under the control of what he understands as Western values; that is to say, no multiculturalism at all. In fact, multiculturalism does not propose, as Bloom reductively argues, a simple relativity of values. What it does do, in its strongest forms, is call into question the "natural" hegemony of any particular value system.)

In *The Disuniting of America,* Schlesinger, apparently out to reform multiculturalism, makes African American studies the paradigm for an unreformed multiculturalism and then makes Afrocentrism the paradigm for African American studies (compounding the distortion by making Leonard Jeffries the paradigm for Afrocentrism). Thus, when Schlesinger states, "The excesses of Afrocentrism are now threatening to discredit the whole field of African-American studies" (96), he makes *his* condemnation, of *his* partial construction of the part of a part, figuratively stand in for the condemnation of the whole. The polemical tactic employed here, consciously or not, hardly conforms to the model of objective history that Schlesinger argues for in his book. In fact, from beginning to end, like the Bloom book and its other progeny (Dinesh D'Souza's *Illiberal Education* and Roger Kimball's *Tenured Radicals*)—all of which base their arguments on radically decontextualized and often unsubstantiated anecdotes, even as they criticize what they characterize as the distorted scholarship of the Left—Schlesinger's argument lacks fundamental integrity. In effect, it rationalizes the racist status quo, which it seems to oppose, by scapegoating multiculturalism (through the highly partial logic I have just summarized) for the historic brutalities—economic, political, cultural, and social—of U.S. capitalism against minorities and women. So when Schlesinger, in an enthusiastically progressive moment, proclaims, "Let us by all means teach black history, African history, women's history, Hispanic history, Asian history. But let us teach them as history, not as filiopietistic commemoration" (99), the generosity of tone seems forced and rings hollow—for it springs from a classically liberal paternalism that reserves for itself the right to determine what "history" is. This liberal paternalism, which espouses "multiculturalism" in order to undermine multiculturalism, is characteristic of the position of the Right in the PC debates.

Both the Bloom and the Schlesinger books, and this is true of the Kimball and the D'Souza books as well, demonstrate what happens when arguments about culture are cut off from the political/economic contexts that generate them; and let me emphasize here that politics cut off from economics is not politics but "pure" culture masquerading as politics (Bloom is continually invoking the political as an essential category of thought, but it is a pristine "political" to say the least). What these purely cultural arguments produce are a hallucination about equality, which is read in these arguments as equally distributed throughout the polity. This hallucination then allows those who produce the arguments to blame the "victim" for the policies that have led to the victim's disempowerment because, if everyone is equal and yet some have failed to succeed, then those who have failed must necessarily bear the responsibility for their failure. This kind of argument, for example, with its own particular twists, forms the basis for the foundational first chapter of D'Souza's book. Following the logic of such an argument, the chapter is aptly entitled "The Victim's Revolution on Campus," and it is echoed by other chapter titles in the book: "More Equal than Others," "The Last Shall Be First," and "Tyranny of the Minority." What these titles suggest is a crucial psychological component of the argument I am describing, one which enables a responsibility-free blaming of the "victim." This component reads: the relatively disempowered are actually in power because they or their representatives have overturned the just mechanisms of equality for those of an unjust affirmative action, which is now in need of reformation, that is, a return to the status quo. Thus, the victims, who are, contradictorily enough, seen at the same time as victors in a stridently oppositional language that lacks any sense of dialectical interplay (they are at once totally passive "victims" and totally aggressive "victors"), are victim-victors because they have abused this equality, either through malice, ignorance, or combinations of both. So Schlesinger, like Bloom and D'Souza, can write of the segregation of minorities on college campuses as self-segregation, a free choice made outside of the context of a continuing history of abusive white power and minority resistance to that power. Within the contexts of these purely cultural arguments, communal political/economic issues get reduced to purely personal issues, issues between decontextualized, and hence formally equal, "individuals."

For example, in *Illiberal Education*, D'Souza reduces the complex of affirmative action issues that have taken shape in recent years on the Berkeley campus of the University of California to a verbal cartoon he constructs from the decontextualized fragments of conversations he claims to have held (he offers no field notes or field methodology to the reader to verify, that is, contextualize, these conversations) with two "[c]ontrast[ed]" (34) individuals: "Thuy Nguyen, a cheerful woman who turned out to be a student at UC–Davis" and who had come "to this country in 1980 as a Vietnamese boat person" (33), and Melanie Lewis, a "middle-class," "vivacious," African American woman who is a student at Berkeley and "a strong supporter of preferential treatment for blacks," though "she could not remember a single incident in which she was a victim of prejudice" (34).

At the center of this story, as we might expect, are clean, whole numbers:

> Nguyen revealed that her high school GPA was 3.8 (out of a possible 4.0) and her SAT score was 1,000 (out of a possible 1,600). She had a decent list of extracurriculars. Although her grades were excellent, her relatively mediocre SAT put Nguyen below the mean at Berkeley; she was not assured of automatic acceptance. Berkeley's average SAT score is around 1,200. (33)

Nguyen, who, D'Souza tells us, lived the hard life of a refugee and whose family came to the U.S. with "nothing" and "even now. . . hold menial jobs," who speaking virtually no English when she emigrated "ten years ago," now "seemed just as articulate as any of her peers" (33) did not get into Berkeley, whereas Lewis did with virtually the same numbers (her grade-point average was "slightly lower" at 3.6), produced, it is shown the reader, at least in part, by an advantaged socioeconomic and cultural position.

Nevertheless, Nguyen, whose "modesty and courage," D'Souza tells us, "it was easy to admire," does not complain about what we are to understand as this *clear* inequality, whereas Lewis, whom we are to understand as the *clear* beneficiary of it even as we are told to "sympathize" with her because affirmative action kept her from "get[ting] credit for her accomplishments" (35), continues to complain about a racism that is *clearly* nowhere evident in her life. Indeed, this unmotivated complaining becomes for D'Souza "an unwitting argument *against* affirmative action, because it raises the question of how preferential treatment can possibly help such a person," who "will still be oppressed" (35) no matter what she achieves, simply by virtue of being black. But, we should note, this fable of the black woman and the Asian woman was pointed against affirmative action from the beginning: "The examples of these two women . . . reveal how affirmative action has largely abandoned its original objective of giving a break to disadvantaged students to enable them to enjoy the same opportunities as their more fortunate peers" (35).

Thus, D'Souza, following the strategies of the Right on which I have been remarking, can discredit affirmative action (the political manifestation of multiculturalism) while appearing to be for it, in a putative, pristine, or original form, of course.

D'Souza's fable, grounded in a profound meanness of spirit that masks itself in a liberality of tone, does its work of discrediting affirmative action/multiculturalism, by individualizing, that is, erasing the historicity of, particular ethnic/racial groups, in this case Asian Americans and African Americans. It then asks us to take these racial cartoons as fairly representative of the groups they distort. The first effect of this allegory, for those who buy into it, is to enable the denial of the *ongoing* history of racism against blacks in the United States, a history manifested in radically unequal forms of capital distribution. For, as the driving logic of the allegory goes, if Melanie Lewis is representative of these blacks and she "[can]not remember a single incident in which she was a victim of prejudice," then it follows on the allegorical plain that such prejudice does not exist. Therefore, the oppression that Melanie Lewis says all blacks experience must be a hallucination (the allegory, in its general manifestations, does not, of course, deny slavery; it denies its ongoing force, effectively derealizing this force, which it reads as coming to an end with what it also reads as the success of the Civil Rights Movement by 1970). Further, the logic continues, if this racism is a hallucination, then the perception that blacks in the United States have of their historic and ongoing inequality is itself a hallucination. Ergo, blacks, whatever their protestations to the contrary, are in fact equal, a "fact" enforced allegorically by the middle-class status of Melanie Lewis. "See," the allegory seems to be saying, "all blacks are, like all Americans, middle class." But it is not saying this literally, for that would be preposterous. Rather, it is saying that all blacks, like all Americans, *should* be middle class, and if they haven't achieved this status, then this lack of achievement must be located in some individual lack or failure to take advantage of this equality, a lack or failure apparently more widespread in some groups than in others, rather than in the historical development of institutions that, as we will read when we arrive at Federalist 10, naturalize economic inequality even as they proclaim their devotion to political equality, without realizing the inseparability of these two forms of equity.

The kind of fiction about equality which informs the Right's allegories that go under the title of "Political Correctness" makes affirmative action/multiculturalism appear as an unjust distributive intervention subverting the uniform equity of a system based purely on individual merit. In fact, the U.S. system has always been based on groups competing legislatively for the benefits of affirmative actions, ever since the white, male property holders who wrote the Constitution affirmed to their class's advantage, as I will detail in my reading of Federalist 10, the inequalities in property—inequalities that Addams, a hundred years later, saw reflected in the cultural sphere, and Fanon, a hundred and fifty years after the fact, saw in all spheres. And this affirmative action was founded, as we know, on the erasure, to begin with, of Africans, Indians, and Euramerican women, as well as those white working-class men who could not afford to hold property, from this legislative competition. These erasures, we should emphasize, are still in search of an equitable writing that fully comprehends that the articulation of individual merit is dependent on the ability of communities or groups to institute affirmative actions, mechanisms of capital accumulation, on the behalf of their members.

What naturalizes/normalizes for a significant audience the kind of allegory that D'Souza tells us about affirmative action/multiculturalism is that the kind of thinking this allegory represents is itself enforced throughout the educational institutions of the United States. It is what I would call an "individualizing" habit of thought that bases itself in what it takes to be the unproblematic category of a "universal experience" or "common sense," which operates from an unacknowledged or unexamined metaphysics. The primary postulate of this metaphysics— which naturalizes or universalizes the specific race, gender, and class interests of the dominant ideology— is that individuals precede groups and therefore always transcend the power and the constraints that constitute these groups. This is invariably, if not always, the habit of thought I encounter in students when we begin our discussions of race, gender, and, particularly, class, as they operate historically in the United States.

It is, for example, the habit of thought informing Schlesinger in a culminating moment in his argument about Afrocentrism:

> Low self-esteem is too deep a malady to be cured by hearing nice things about one's own ethnic past. History is not likely to succeed where psychiatry fails. Afrocentrism in particular is an escape from the hard and expensive challenges of our society—the need for safer schools, better teachers, better teaching materials, greater investment in education; the need for stable families that can nourish self-discipline and aspiration; the need for jobs and income that can nourish stable families; the need to stop drugs and crime; the need to overcome the racism still lurking in the interstices of American society. (101–2)

In the curious syntactical structure of this sentence, Afrocentrism, reduced from an intellectual movement to a problem in individual character development (a problem in "self-esteem"), is not a particular effect of or response to the conjunction of capitalism and racism in the United States, represented by Schlesinger's list of social dysfunctions, but is this conjunction's cause (and the racism, we note, is not posited as central but as "lurking in the interstices of American society," like a mugger in the shadows of urban night). Further, we should note that this list of dysfunctions appears for the first time about two-thirds of the way through *The Disuniting of America* and is passed over without any analysis of its relation to the cultural situation that is being blamed for it in this topsy-turvy logic (a logic we find, unsurprisingly, in D'Souza as well, where affirmative action is not seen as an effect of and a *legitimate* response to the unequal distribution of capital enforced by racism, but, in effect, as racism's cause). Thus, in this instance, and this instance is exemplary of the Right's strategy in the PC debates, cultural issues are separated from political/economic issues, with the result that the phrase *capitalist democracy* remains coherent. And it is the defense of capitalist democracy that Schlesinger is undertaking in this book, as his concluding pages makes clear:

> Our democratic principles contemplate an open society founded on tolerance of differences and on mutual respect. In practice, America has been more open to some than to others. But it is more open to all today than it was yesterday and is likely to be even more open tomorrow than today. The steady movement of American life has been from exclusion to inclusion. (134)

But the narratives of growing economic discrepancies between the rich and the poor—discrepancies that impact disproportionately on certain minorities (principally Hispanic, African, and Native Americans) and women—that one can read daily in the newspapers contradict this progressive vision of history. And we should note that these discrepancies have radically destabilized the white middle and working classes as well. "Downsizing," that wonderful euphemism for the displacement of productive human life by profit, has spread rapidly from the permanently depressed, those groups who have been economically marginalized historically, to those Euramerican blue- and white-collar workers who in the post–World War II era right through the magically distracting reign of Ronald Reagan thought they could dream the American dream forever. So, to take two crucial examples culled from recent stories in the *New York Times:* the Census Bureau reports that "[t]he percentage of all Americans working full time but earning less than the poverty level for a family of four, about $13,000 a year, has risen by 50 percent in the past 13 years" (DeParle A1); and a study done for the Carnegie Corporation of New York "notes that three million children, nearly one-fourth of all American infants and toddlers, live in poverty" (Chira A1). To maintain in the light of narratives like these that "[t]he steady movement of American life has been from exclusion to inclusion" is surely a sign of delusion, a sign that one has disarticulated the economic from any notion of political justice, and thus disarticulated the political from the cultural, in order to maintain the coherence of the phrase *capitalist democracy.*

However, perhaps the kind of disarticulation I am describing can be read most forcefully not on the Right in the PC debates, but in the discourse of one of the most visible opponents of the Right in these debates. I refer here to Stanley Fish, in his book, *There's No Such Thing as Free Speech, and It's a Good Thing, Too.* As Fish tells us in a preamble to a significant section of the book: "Chapters 3 through 7 were written for a series of debates between Dinesh D'Souza and me that began in September 1991 and ended in March 1992" (51). These debates are reminiscent in their own small way of the show put on a few years back by Timothy Leary, former drug guru of sixties hippie culture, and Gordon Liddy, former operative of the Nixon administration in the Watergate affair, in which the two staged themselves as representative figures of the Left and Right, opposing each other fiercely if histrionically for the public, while professing a personal respect and even affection for one another, suggesting in the process, however inadvertently or unconsciously, that political differences can always be reconciled in personal, that is, individual, relationships. In its totality, then, the Leary/Liddy spectacle was structured by what I have referred to as an "individualizing habit of thought," in this case disarticulating the political and the personal, the political and the cultural, by suggesting that what is essential is the individual, while the political is no more than an illusion, the theatre of shadows in Plato's cave. The viewer, one takes it, was not meant to notice that the personal here was as much a part of the show as the political.

In his preamble to chapters 3 through 7, Fish reminisces about his professional and personal relationship with D'Souza:

> However harsh the accents either of us fell into on stage, our personal interactions were unfailingly cordial. We dined together, traveled together, and played tennis whenever we could. . . . In May I danced happily at his [D'Souza's] wedding, and we have since appeared together on a panel discussing First Amendment questions, about which we are pretty much in agreement. (In fact, the areas of agreement between us are wider than one might have expected.). Neither of us, I think, changed the other's mind on the issues we debated, but it is fair to say that both of us sharpened our arguments in the course of the rapid-fire thrust and parry that characterized our exchanges. . . . It was short-lived, but it was a great show. (52)

The nostalgic tone of this, located as it is in a reverie of male camaraderie (the good fight fought between equals that transcends in its personal aspects any ideology), strikes me as unmistakable, although it also
strikes me that, in fact, D'Souza's ramshackle arguments in *Illiberal Education* are no match for the deconstruction of them that Fish carries out
with admirable cogency in his book. But "it" would not be a "great show"
if one's opponent was perceived as overmatched, so, I suppose, under
the terms of the spectacle, one must provide publicity for the other side.

If this gesture of camaraderie were simply an aside in Fish's otherwise strong opposition to the Right in the PC debates, however, I would
not be bothering with it. What I want to argue, then, is that the dynamics of the aside which I have been describing structure Fish's opposition
to, or deconstruction of, the Right, so that in the end, the goals of Fish
and the Right appear curiously in concert. And these goals are precisely
to maintain the status quo.

In the introductory chapter to his book, Fish summarizes the essays
contained in it and interprets their overall import. His critique of the
Right in the PC debates proceeds in part on a premise that informs my
own critique. That is, the Right conducts its attack on multiculturalism
by decontextualizing, which is to say, dehistoricizing or depoliticizing,
a particular terminology in order to make it appear that this terminology has a transcendent, universal, or neutral status. And Fish, as I have
done, identifies this terminology of "fairness," "merit," and "neutrality"
as "the vocabulary of liberalism, and it is the structure of liberal thought
that is my target in every one of these essays" (16). Underpinning Fish's
critique of liberalism is a notion that has become a commonplace in a
certain segment of the humanities: that "the truths any of us find compelling will all be partial, which is to say they will all be political" (8).

Fish's evocation of the political as a universal category, however, turns
out to be in the service of the erasure of the political as a political category; that is, as a force active in the differential specificities of the material world:

> The essays in the second half of the book pretty much take the
> unavailability of nonpolitical modes of being as a given and go on
> to the next question: What follows? What does this mean for the way
> we live? My answer is "not very much," and it is an answer that will
> be distressing both to the forces on the intellectual left and to their
> opponents. (19)

Indeed, Fish deconstructs the transcendent agenda of liberalism not to
oppose the liberal political agenda politically but "to remove the sting
of the accusation from the word *politics* and redefine it as a synonym for
what every one inevitably does" (19). Because the political is everywhere,

the logic goes, the political is, effectively, nowhere. This logic, let me emphasize, is purely formal, decontextualized, dehistoricized, depoliticized; it is precisely the logic of the liberalism of which Fish stages himself as an opponent. This logic allows Fish to argue for the status quo in both legal and literary studies and to read liberalism and the Left as "mirror images of each other," precisely because he has suspended any historical reckoning in his argument. That is, like his stage opponent, D'Souza, and the other members of the Right, Fish disarticulates the political and the economic, thus containing the "culture wars" within the space of a purely formal theatricality, where the question of the co-herency of the phrase *capitalist democracy* is never raised (one notes that, in the index of Fish's book, the forms of the two words do not appear). And because Fish never questions the coherency of this phrase, his an-swer about the ubiquity of the political, far from "distressing both . . . the forces on the intellectual left and . . . their opponents," accommodates itself quite comfortably to the agenda of the latter. Given the ubiquity of the political, Fish's attempt to project himself into a third or "neutral" position in the PC debates must fail.

It has been and remains the work of the Left, the historic Lefts, on the other hand, to articulate the disarticulations of the cultural, the politi-cal, and the economic, thereby articulating the incoherencies of the phrase *capitalist democracy* in order to suggest concrete ways of imple-menting social justice both in the United States and also worldwide.

From the perspective of the Left, the issue of redistribution is read quite clearly as generating the PC debates, though no one, as far as I know, has read it as a theoretical and historical constitutional issue, which is the claim I make for it. Michael Denning, for example, observes in passing: "Underneath the Right's uproar over multiculturalism and Western civilization, one finds a persistent and insistent argument against affirmative action, an argument about who should have access to the resources and cultural capital controlled by the university" (34). And Ruth Perry puts it even more succinctly: "For that's what the stakes are [in the PC debates]. . . how to redistribute power, knowledge, and resources in this country" (78).

From the perspective of the Right, on the other hand, as I will argue in the generative case of Bloom, the issues underlying the PC debates have always been Constitutional. What remains repressed in the Right's social vision, as I will also argue (and as I have argued in the case of Schlesinger and D'Souza), is the conflict over redistribution that founds the Constitution. George Will, for example, writing of Lynne Cheney, the head of the NEH under Reagan and Bush, says: "She even more than a Supreme Court justice, deals with constitutional things. The real Constitution . . . is the national mind as shaped by the intellectual legacy that gave rise to the Constitution and all the habits, mores, customs, and ideas that sustain it" (25–26). Like that of Will, the loudest voices on the Right in the PC debates have without reflection equated capitalism with de- mocracy, an equation, as I will suggest, that is a sign of the repression of the conflict over redistribution that founds the Constitution. Thus, any one who tries to raise questions about this equation is suspect, for the Right, whether in the equivocal sublimations of Schlesinger or the in- sidious allegories of D'Souza, reflexively equates any form of anticapi- talism with being totalitarian and anti-Western (as if socialism wasn't itself part of a Western tradition or as if the West hadn't developed to- talitarian forms of government itself). So D'Souza can claim in a typical moment of pure ideological thinking (thinking that exhibits neither a sense of history nor theory) that

> liberal arts students, including those attending Ivy League Schools, are very likely to be exposed to an attempted brainwashing that deprecates Western learning and exalts a neo-Marxist ideology promoted in the name of multiculturalism. Even students who choose hard sciences must often take required courses in the humanities, where they are almost certain to be inundated with an anti-Western, anti-capitalist view of the world. ("The Visigoths" 12)

It is the historical and psychic origins of D'Souza's oppositions that I now want to explore.

In the "Preface" to *The Closing of the American Mind,* Bloom articulates the constituency upon which his educational philosophy is founded. This constituency is composed of "the kind of young persons who populate the twenty or thirty best universities" and who consequently "have the greatest moral and intellectual effect on the nation." These are "students of comparatively high intelligence, materially and spiritually free to do pretty much what they want with the few years of college they are privi- leged to have" (22). Bloom's paratactic syntax represses any questions about the hypotactic relation between material and spiritual freedom, while it supports a vision of cause and effect that is radically reductive to the concerns of a single class, a class whose interests he also implic- itly and unproblematically homogenizes in the process.

The result of this vision is that the relation of education to social jus- tice becomes immediately and formatively a non-question: "There are other kinds of students whom circumstances of one sort or another pre- vent from having the freedom required to pursue a liberal education. They have their own needs and may very well have very different char- acters from those I describe here" (22). While Bloom doesn't specify the composition of the intellectual elite he has in mind, this elite has been historically composed of predominantly white, middle-class, Protestant males. Even as this elite has been compelled by feminist and minority interests to open its ranks, particularly since World War II, this opening has not been large enough to change this elite's historic control of cultural and economic resources. In any event, this control could not be changed by any simple numerical shifts, but would require a change in the present ideology, which, as I try to explain in what follows, has not been or cannot be flexible enough to articulate questions of redistribution in a way that would make them central to the interlinked economic, political, social, and cultural agendas of the United States.

Bloom's characterization of the "other kinds of students" in the passage just cited is implicitly racist, and thus exclusionary, in the profoundest meaning of the term *racism,* for he figures these "others" almost as another species: "other kinds of students" who "have their own needs and may very well have very different characters from those I describe here." Bloom's characterization also curtly writes off the majority of Americans by abrogating any questions about the "circumstances" that "prevent [them] from having the freedom required to pursue a liberal education," questions that would interrogate the relationship between material and spiritual freedom and the appearance of such qualities as "high intelligence." (We can read just how profound, by which I mean deeply unconscious, Bloom's racism is in the section of his book on "Race" [see Bloom 91–97], where he both blithely inflates the numbers of black students and faculty in his "major" universities; unashamedly blames blacks, as previously noted, for the de facto social segregation on university campuses; and attacks affirmative action programs with the stereotypes that have become typical of the racist reaction against them [stereotypes that infer that blacks, and particularly African Americans, just don't have the intellectual equipment to succeed in higher education].)

Having written off the majority, while still claiming to write in the name of a true or founding U.S. democracy, Bloom, caught up in the kind of unrigorous contradictions that always mark the repression of "the other," proceeds to write, with apparent unconsciousness, his elite, intellectual minority as the "dominant majority. . . [which] gave the country a dominant culture with its traditions, its literature, its tastes, its special claim to know and supervise the language, and its Protestant religions" (31). Bloom confuses dominance with democracy by taking a part for the whole: those relatively few who control the economic resources of the country and hence the workings of its major cultural institutions become the whole country.

This confusion comes from a fundamental U.S. confusion, that of capitalism and democracy. I call this confusion fundamental because it informs the founding document of the United States, the Constitution, and inaugurates the separation of political rights from the economic sphere that keeps the prospects of social justice for all ever deferred even as the rhetoric of "America" continually promises these prospects. This confusion is most forcefully and rigorously articulated in Federalist 10, the most famous and arguably the most fundamental of the *Federalist* papers, the one that broaches and deals with the problem of faction, what we might term the earliest articulation of complaints about "affirmative action" or interest-group politics. It is Bloom's remarkably unrigorous reading of this paper that grounds the fundamental confusions of his own argument. And so I want to take a look, first, at the paper and, then, at Bloom's reading of it as a way of introducing the question of redistribution as not only driving the PC debates but making them a useful figure for understanding the relation of U.S. education, at its moment of encountering multiculturalism, to U.S. history.

In Federalist 10, James Madison defines *faction* in the following way:

> By a faction I understand a number of citizens, whether amounting to a majority or minority of the whole, who are united and actuated by some common impulse of passion, or of interest, adverse to the rights of other citizens, or to the permanent and aggregate interests of the community. (405)[4]

Further, Madison defines "the most common and durable source of factions . . . [as] the various and unequal distribution of property. Those who hold, and those who are without property, have ever formed distinct interests in society" (406). In the remainder of the paper we find that the kind of faction the Founders fear most is not the minority faction, which can be defeated "by regular vote" (407), but majority faction.

The notion of a *majority faction* may strike contemporary readers of Federalist 10 as paradoxical. For how in a democracy, which is how "we, the people" have come to think of the United States, can the majority, whose will is supposed to govern, be considered a faction, a special interest? Isn't the will of the majority identical with what the Founders termed the "public" or "common good"? This was certainly the notion held by an antifederalist like "Brutus," who argued in the pages of the *New York Journal* during the Constitutional debates that the system of representation proposed would lead to the displacement of representative democracy by oligarchy, that is, by a particular kind of minority faction.[5] But as Federalist 10 tells us, the Founders interdicted this identity between the will of the majority and the public good. The public good, everywhere evoked by them as the ground of their decisions and nowhere defined by them, paradoxically transcends the interests of any group in the body politic and yet must somehow be represented by the representatives who come from these groups, whether elected directly or appointed by the elected. The public good would seem to be a kind of eternal consensus that, like Socrates's idea of the good, can nowhere be exactly articulated but is everywhere understood, at least, in the words of Madison, by "a chosen body of citizens, whose wisdom may best discern the true interest of their country, and whose patriotism and love of justice, will be least likely to sacrifice it to temporary or partial considerations" (409). The public good is beyond the ken of ordinary people and yet somehow must be discerned by them if they are to recognize and elect the people who can represent it. This is another way of articulating the paradox that structures the philosophy that drives the U.S. Constitution.

This paradox articulates a conflict that is historically inherent in the Constitution and in the governments it has generated: the conflict between democracy, trust in the will of the majority, and the republican form of government that the Founders agreed upon, which was intended both to represent this will and guard against it in its form of faction, in order to protect what society might define as the legitimate interests of minorities. From a contemporary perspective, the paradox or conflict represented by Federalist 10 can be read as generating the legislation that has come to protect the political rights of ethnic and racial minorities as well as women. This is the reading of the paper made strikingly legible by Lani Guinier, whose reading was then ironically repudiated by President Clinton because it was not consistent, in his misreading, with the democratic principles of the republic (see "Who's Afraid"). Certainly anyone who knows Constitutional history must agree with Guinier's reading, with the understanding that this contemporary reading is embedded in the Founders's reading of the term *minority*, which interprets the term within the context of class interests based in property ownership, and, further, suggests that the conflict between democracy and republicanism figures a conflict between democracy and capitalism, a conflict between political rights and the economic sphere, that is both articulated and repressed in what I will term now "U.S. ideology."

As Federalist 10 makes clear, the Founders did not want to control the problem of factions by tampering with its principal cause: the "unequal distribution of property." For they believed that this cause of faction was inherent "in the nature of man" (406), that "the rights of property originate" in the "diversity" of "the faculties of men" and that the "protection of these faculties is the *first* object of government" (405;

my emphasis). Indeed, influenced by the specter of recent rebellions by indebted farmers in western Massachusetts, Madison, at the end of Federalist 10, condemns a "rage for paper money, for an abolition of debts, for an equal division of property" as "improper or wicked project[s]," "diseases" in the body politic that "a Republican remedy" is meant to cure (411).

To risk a certain kind of compression in historical analysis for the sake of space, I would propose that Federalist 10 represents the *naturalization* of a class system based on inequalities of wealth that is still with us and growing more inequitable all the time, as the statistics of growing discrepancies between the top and the bottom tell us. In naturalizing this system, Federalist 10, or the U.S. ideology it represents, implicitly equates capitalism with democracy by powerfully blurring the conflict between republicanism and democracy that the paper articulates. Further, in equating capitalism with democracy, U.S ideology has historically severed political rights from the economic sphere; that is, this ideology represents the realm of economics as a natural or ultimately self-regulating realm, untroubled by, or unrelated to, the political realm, where issues of equality arise and are adjudicated. So, clearly, while certain matters of economics have been governmentally regulated since the founding of the U.S., no *sustained* national debate on redistribution of wealth has occurred because of the limits inscribed in the possibility of such a debate by U.S. ideology, though such debates have begun at certain historical moments: the intertwined development of the U.S. labor and socialist movements from the second half of the nineteenth century through the 1930s; Martin Luther King, Jr.'s recognition of the tie between the economic sphere and political justice just before his assassination; Jimmy Carter's call for an economic bill of rights prior to his defeat by Ronald Reagan; or the agenda of the Rainbow Coalition in the late 1980s, as just a few examples. The presence of such beginnings, along with local visions and enactments of what I would call "redistributive communalism," of which Native American societies are the oldest ongoing example, suggest that while U.S. ideology has throughout its history been powerful, it has also been and continues to be contradicted. I will turn to the cultivation of these contradictions as the basis of a multicultural American studies curriculum. But first, I want to turn to Bloom's reading of Federalist 10 to suggest how these contradictions are repressed.

As I have noted, Bloom rewrites an elite economic/cultural minority as the majority, and so represses the central conflict represented and *theoretically* resolved by Federalist 10. Having manufactured a majority from a minority, Bloom then manufactures an anti-American intellectual/academic minority that opposes the legitimate agenda of the majority he concocts:

> Much of the intellectual machinery of twentieth-century American political thought and social science was constructed for the purposes of making an assault on that majority. It treated the founding principles as impediments and tried to overcome the other strand of our political heritage, majoritarianism, in favor of a nation of minorities and groups each following its own beliefs and inclinations. In particular, the intellectual minority expected to enhance its status, presenting itself as the defender and spokesman of all the others. (31)

One way of reading Bloom's revision of United States history is to understand the "intellectual minority" he conjures up as the enemy of the people as an ironic, if unconscious, double of the Founding Fathers, that intellectual minority which becomes Bloom's "majority" through his transfiguration of power into numbers. This reading can tell us something about the unconscious processes by which the Right in the PC debates has projected a demonized, powerful, and subversive Left that, in the Right's vision, has co-opted the intellectual life of the United States through its control of the universities, through—to use ironically some of Bloom's language cited previously—"its special claim to know and supervise the language," a claim and a knowledge that in this fantasy it has wrested from the legitimate Founders.

In the unconscious political imagination of the Right, then, the Left appears as fallen Founding Fathers, satanic sons and daughters, who have transformed the majoritarian agenda of the legitimate Fathers into an illegitimate minority agenda, where the demands of race, gender, and class are rioting. We are dealing with a Manichean vision here, where this new social and political thought that Bloom alludes to is a simple "reversal of the founding intention with respect to minorities" (31). "For the Founders, minorities are in general bad things, mostly identical to factions, selfish groups who have no concern as such for the common good" (31). But, as we have read, things do not appear to have been so Manichean in the Founders' minds, where, in the first place, we might note, "minorities" do not have the same definition that they do in Bloom's anachronistic use of the term. For the Founders, as I have noted, "minorities" as a term was restricted to the idea of special economic interests specified in Federalist 10, and so implied questions of class, whereas for Bloom the term carries the contemporary definition that expands its meaning to issues of race and gender as well. Bloom's usage tries to put the Founders on his side in ways they could not have imagined.

Further, and crucially as we have read in Federalist 10, minorities were *not* for the Founders "in general bad things." They were, however troublesome, "natural" things based in an unequal distribution of property that was itself based in the "diversity" of "the faculties of men." And, we remember, it was "the first object of government" to protect this diversity over and against a putative majority faction that might seek to overturn this system in proposing and carrying out an equal distribution of property.

Now, the kind of reading of Federalist 10 that Charles Beard has given us in his *Economic Interpretation of the Constitution of the United States,* a reading in keeping with the political critique of "Brutus" cited previously, might say that the Founders were not interested in minority rights in general, but in the rights of a particular minority, of which they formed a part, the minority of relatively large property holders; and that, in addition, they implicitly identified this minority with what they termed the "common good." In this reading, the reference we have read to "a chosen body of citizens, whose wisdom may best discern the true interest of their country" is both self-reflexive and self-interested, and serves, in equating the "common good" with this minority, to translate what are minority interests into a transcendent will of the majority, which is opposed to an earthly or fallen majority that is represented by this minority as merely another faction, that is, as equivalent to no more than a minority.

I would argue that Bloom's reading of the Constitution, which, converting a minority into a majority, grounds his attack on multiculturalism, follows *unconsciously* the strategies of identification I have just outlined, and in so doing represses the contradictions in the founding document, with little regard for either its historical or theoretical situation, contradictions that if *read* raise the questions of redistribution that I claim are at the core of the multicultural debates.

III

In *The Closing of the American Mind,* Bloom acknowledges the political function of a curriculum: "Every educational system has a moral goal that it tries to attain and that informs its curriculum. It wants to produce a certain kind of human being"(26). It is neither the Right nor the Left who politicizes education. Education *is* political, as Socrates knew quite well. The question that confronts us, then, is not that of depoliticizing education, but of what political form we want our education to take—that is, the question that confronts us is: What kind of human beings do we want to produce? The curricula we devise are answers to this question.

Let us say "we, the people" of the United States, want to produce human beings who are acutely and critically aware of multiculturalism because, simply enough, we live in a multicultural world, as we have historically, and we need to be aware of it. Our curriculum must work then to define the term *multiculturalism* in all of its *equivocality*, a word I use in its most literal sense to define both the productive and destructive conflicts of multiple voices in historical and visionary terms.[6] Within the educational context of the United States, multiculturalism means the representation of "minority" interests in the curriculum ("minority" in terms of numbers and/or power, as in the case of women), interests as inscribed within the conflicts of race, gender, and class. And as I have suggested in this essay, if we trace the term *minority* back to our founding document, the Constitution, we find that it is embedded in the issue of redistribution of wealth that itself articulates and is articulated by complex figures of the relation between majorities and minorities.

Both historically and theoretically, the terms *majority* and *minority* are inseparable, as we have read in the entangled ironies of the "common good" inscribed in Federalist 10. What this implies is that "our" projected curriculum will not inscribe a canon or canons within it. For such inscription carries with it the *ontological* separation of *majority* and *minority*. This canceling of canonicity as a principle, though not as an area of historical and theoretical study, is the way of having our curriculum figure in its form, which at this moment is certainly Utopian, a redistribution of cultural wealth. For canons have traditionally figured a radically unequal distribution of this wealth. Let us be clear. We do not stop reading the "classics" with this move. Rather, we make visible their historic cultural entanglement with a whole range of texts that have traditionally been rendered invisible by the politics of canon formation, and in doing this, we obliterate the notion of the "classic." This, however, does not stop us from ascribing value to texts. What it does do is make us as conscious as possible of the politics of such ascription, its strategies.

The American studies curriculum I am theorizing is founded, then, in the issue of redistribution, which it claims is the generative force in the production of the United States as a *contradictory* field of endeavor, a field where *capitalism* and *democracy*, traditionally taken to be synonyms, work not simply in concert but also in conflict. This curriculum also claims that the historical locus of this conflict lies in the linked European imperatives of the enslavement of Africans and the dispossession of American Indians, both of which commence in the fifteenth century, and in the resistance to these imperatives and their aftermaths, which are still with us. While, clearly, all issues of American race, gender, and class are not confined to this locus, I would argue that at one point or another they touch it, and so this locus is the most comprehensive base for our curriculum.

In this curricular vision, the United States is not an exception to European expansion, a "New World," but its apotheosis and alibi, as I have argued at length elsewhere (see Cheyfitz, *Poetics of Imperialism*). Within the traditional curriculum of American studies, the curriculum governed by the notion of "American exceptionalism," the United States is identified as "America," a figurative space of pure and always progressing freedom that, under the pressure of U.S. ideology, is read without irony, that is, literally. Within the curriculum I am articulating, this identification is broken. The United States is no longer "America" but is only part of the historic Americas, with their European and ultimately global entanglements, a space of conflictive narratives, where no master narrative governs, except, of course, the master narrative of redistribution. This narrative, let us say with a sense of irony and paradox, is the master narrative that contradicts the notion of master narratives. For it projects its own centrality neither as organic nor transcendent but as functional or strategic, remaining open to continual revision through the contradictory or conflictive movement of the *voices* who narrate. For this master narrative, paradoxically enough, is equivocal, not univocal. Let us say, merely by way of illustration, that the voices of this narrative might be figured by the conflictive concert of the texts of Fanon and Addams or by a reading of Federalist 10 that cultivates its contradictions in the name of equivocality rather than represses them in the name of univocality.

We might name this curriculum "The American Literature of Social Action and Social Vision," in that it will seek to articulate in its syllabi both the forces that have maintained such unequal distribution in the Americas historically and the forces that have resisted, continue to resist, and might be imagined to resist and transform this inequality. To accomplish this articulation, this curriculum must be rigorously historical, theoretical, and interdisciplinary. *And it must be activist*—Utopian figure working toward political fact—both in terms of affirmative-action initiatives within the university and community-action initiatives that link the university to the community at large which needs its resources as resistance to those forces that maintain inequality, of which, currently, the university is one. The university, then, must begin by resisting itself. Multiculturalism as pure curriculum, that is, social vision without action, risks becoming an alibi for the status quo. Hazel Carby says it with force:

> We need to ask ourselves some serious questions about our culture and our politics. Is the emphasis on cultural diversity making invisible the politics of race in this increasingly segregated nation,

and is the language of cultural diversity a convenient substitute for
the political action needed to desegregate? . . .While the attention of
faculty and administrators has been directed toward increasing the
representation of different social groups in the curriculum or the
college handbook, few alliances have been forged with substantial
forces across this society that will significantly halt and reverse the
declining numbers of black, working-class, and poor people among
university student bodies or faculty. (13–14)

The warning and the challenge of her words to our curricula are clear.

IV

Let me conclude this essay with one example of the kind of curriculum
I have been theorizing. In the spring of 1992, a group of about twenty
students, with the support of a few faculty and administrators at Southern Methodist University (where I taught in the Department of English
from 1990–1993), began a tutoring project, with the acronym of ICE (In-
ter-Community Experience), principally for primary school children in
an east Dallas community, composed of Mexican American and African American families, with the large majority of the people in the former
group. These families, some single- and some two-parent, work at jobs
that keep them close to the poverty line. But Habitat for Humanity, which
supports the tutoring project, has been developing the area, and so a significant number of these families live in decent housing. The project also
has the support of the largest church in the area, the Munger Avenue
Methodist Church, which is engaged in community outreach.

What distinguishes this project from the typical volunteer efforts that
we find on university campuses (and SMU has a very committed volunteer program under the guidance of Beatrice Nealy, who also supports
this project) are two things. First, during the academic year, at least four
of the students, at least one of whom is fluent in Spanish (as are a few
other tutors in the program), live in a house in the community and so
can get to know the families on a day-to-day basis and interact with them
on a number of community issues. And second, the tutoring project is
integrated into the regular SMU liberal arts curriculum through a three-
credit course, a seminar taught by SMU faculty for the tutors in the
project. The seminar is taught once a week for three hours in the eve-
nings at the Munger Avenue Methodist Church. Lynn Johnson, an urban historian who has also now left SMU, taught the course in the spring
of 1992; I taught it in the fall of 1992, when I joined the program as its
second faculty advisor.

Ideally, the course should be team-taught (and given the amount of
work required from faculty and students, should be worth six credit

hours), so that while one faculty member is leading the seminar, the other can be working on a regular basis in the community with the tutors, who, dividing the time, staff the tutoring program on a five-day/two-hours-a-day basis (there are also frequent Sunday field trips for the children). This team-taught structure, which would require more faculty to teach in the program, would allow for an optimum coordination between the seminar and the tutoring, as well as providing greater continuity from semester to semester in the tutoring program and more time for the development of the program, including its extension into other areas, such as English as a second language (the community has expressed a pressing need for this latter curriculum, which, clearly, among other things, would allow many of the parents to participate more fully in the formal education of their children). At the time I left SMU, because of routine teaching demands and the lack of general faculty interest in the program, the committed faculty could only maintain a minimum presence in the tutoring program and the community, even as the seminar asked the student tutors to relate, both in their writing and in class discussion, the theoretical and historical problems that the seminar addressed to their experience in the community. And I want to emphasize here that news I get from an informed source at SMU does not bode well for the progressive thrust of the program:

> Next year [1994–95] the ICE Board will fall under the purview of the Dean [James R. Jones, Jr.—a man who in my experience speaks progressively and acts regressively]; he will select the other members of the Board, and the faculty will serve in an advisory capacity only. It's clear that the Dean intends to use ICE as a powerful fundraising tool. So a new chapter in the ICE Program begins. The bottom line is that a few people are doing great work and making a difference, but it is maddening to see how power has come to appropriate progressive energies.

From the beginning, it was my sense of the upper administration at SMU that it used the ICE program to give the university the veneer of progressiveness that it lacked at its core, a lack well-evidenced by the refusal of the administration to commit substantial funds to the development of needed multicultural programs in women's and ethnic studies, particularly in the areas of hiring African American and Hispanic American faculty.

The title of the course I taught in conjunction with the tutoring was "The American Literature of Social Action and Social Vision." Let me say that, ideally, the course would have included members of the east Dallas community whose children we were tutoring but that this ideal (for various reasons included in but not limited to the problems of translation suggested immediately above in my mention of the need for an

ESL program) can probably only be realized in the long-range intensification of this project, an intensification I doubt will come about for the
institutional reasons just elaborated. My constituency for the course,
then, were the tutors, twenty SMU students, largely middle-class men
and women from, predominantly, the South and Southwest, largely
Euramerican, though with the participation of one Chicano, one African American male, and one woman from South America.

The course focused on issues of redistribution as these issues are articulated in the interplay of cultural and economic forces. Necessarily,
for a group of university students and faculty engaged in teaching forms
of literacy to a group of people alienated from the cultural and socioeconomic situation of the university, issues of language and power both
globally and locally were central to any discussion of redistribution.

Before proceeding to sketch in the texts for this course, let me add that
what I am sketching is a composite. For prior to teaching the course in
the tutoring project, I taught the course in various venues, both in conjunction with the work of social action and independent from it.

The course begins with a discussion of some documents that have
dominated and continue to dominate what I have termed elsewhere in
this essay "U.S. ideology." My reading of Federalist 10 in conjunction
with the multicultural debates is one way of opening such a discussion.
Two texts that I have cited in the course of my reading, the fall 1992 issue of the *Radical History Review* and the anthology *Beyond PC*, provide
useful materials for the discussion. Other dominant documents that the
seminar examines in this critical context are, for example, John
Winthrop's "A Model of Christian Charity," Benjamin Franklin's *Autobiography*, The Declaration of Independence, and Jane Addams's *Twenty
Years at Hull House*.

The question framing this examination is: What are the limits of
capitalism's imagination as it responds, historically and theoretically, to
issues of social justice? These limits, I propose, are inscribed by the fundamental separation of politics and economics in U.S. ideology that I
have mentioned. This separation, I ask the students to consider, has resulted in the institutionalization of poverty both in the United States and
around the world, through the continuing legacy of colonialism supported by the United States. And this institutionalization appears to be
increasing and intensifying, even though, as Michael Harrington pointed
out forcefully in what was the classic text on poverty for the 1960s, *The
Other America*, which the seminar reads, poverty costs a lot more money
than ending poverty through full employment would. Considering this
development of poverty around the world, in turn, raises questions about
what Max Weber understood in *The Protestant Ethic and the Spirit of Capi-*

talism as the irrational basis of capitalism's claim to the "rational," both in the sense of quantitative rationalization and in the sense of ethical reason. Franklin, as a self-styled exemplar of the rational in both these senses, is particularly vulnerable to a close reading in this context, as Weber has shown us. After reading the Weber, part of the work of the seminar is to consider how Franklin makes his claim to reason (a claim that he offers with a certain irony) through the erasure of race, gender, and class conflict.

In raising questions about the limits of capitalism's imagination, I have found no book more strategically useful than Patricia J. Williams's *The Alchemy of Race and Rights*, which from the explicit perspective of an African American female lawyer, a perspective Williams generously opens to all her readers, powerfully probes the way issues of race, gender, and class motivate the "neutrality," or "reason," of U.S. law.

As the title of the course suggests, the seminar is not simply concerned with articulating the *limits* of capitalism's vision of social justice, but with offering alternative American visions, visions that transgress, or contradict, these limits, as both the Harrington and the Williams books do. I have found *The Graywolf Annual Five: Multi-Cultural Literacy* a useful beginning here, offering, as it does, a selection of Asian American, African American, Caribbean, Euramerican, and Hispanic American writers of both genders. From this point, the class can concentrate on periods, areas, and issues of particular urgency.

Because, but not only because, we are engaged in a tutoring project, the seminar reads Paolo Freire's *Pedagogy of the Oppressed*, which has been so generative in developing revolutionary teaching methodologies in the Americas. And this text leads us into a discussion of the ways that U.S. capitalism has historically helped institutionalize poverty in Latin America and the socialist revolutionary responses to this institutionalization. We read, for example, two texts on the civil war in Salvador that is currently at a formal if not definitive end: Manlio Argueta's novel about peasant resistance to U.S.-sponsored repression, *One Day of Life*, and, to provide an historical context for the novel, Robert Armstrong and Janet Shenk's *El Salvador: The Face of Revolution*. Eduardo Galeano's *Open Veins of Latin America: Five Centuries of the Pillage of a Continent* is an eloquent narrative that can be read as an historical introduction to this section of the course. And as a theoretical introduction to these materials, Fanon's *The Wretched of the Earth* can be read at this moment and related to issues of redistribution raised by both Addams and Harrington.

Through these readings students can begin to think about the structural relationship between poverty in and outside of the U.S., and they can begin to encounter the historical and theoretical force of socialism at a time when U.S. ideology is proclaiming the triumph of capitalism around the world. At this moment, the class reads *The Communist Manifesto*, written and published by Marx and Engels in 1848, and compares and contrasts it to some examples of American literature written during the same period.[7] Specifically, we read Thoreau's "Civil Disobedience" along with the first chapter of *Walden* ("Economy") and Emerson's "Self-Reliance," which seems to me to be very much about how the intellectual *work* of everyone is *alienated* in the notion of "genius." We read these works within two contexts: the contemporary one generated by Frederick Douglass's *Narrative of the Life of Frederick Douglass, An American Slave, Written by Himself,* and Harriet Jacobs's *Incidents in the Life of a Slave Girl, Written by Herself;* and a modern one provided by Emma Goldman's essay "Anarchism" (and for Goldman, anarchism was a form of socialism, as the essay makes clear), which in part asserts its authority through the work of Emerson and Thoreau. Reading Emerson and Thoreau in these contexts is one way to begin the work of dislocating the classic *topos* of U.S. ideology, "individualism."

Our study of socialisms brings us to its specifically U.S. forms and in particular to the forms it took during the 1930s. The text we currently read in this excursion is an anthology of fiction, poetry, and theory: *Writing Red: An Anthology of American Women Writers, 1930–1940,* edited by Charlotte Nekola and Paula Rabinowitz. This text is, pedagogically speaking, economical, for it allows a focused discussion of class issues within the contexts of gender and race as they concern black and white women in particular.

Finally, the course ends by focusing on what, from a Euramerican perspective, as I have argued in *The Poetics of Imperialism,* is the most radical form of redistributive communalism, that found in "traditional" (a term that involves a complex politics of vision and revision) Native American communities. For historical and theoretical context, the class reads a selection of essays by Native American scholars and activists found in the collection *The State of Native America: Genocide, Colonization, and Resistance,* edited by M. Annette Jaimes. In closing we read Leslie Marmon Silko's novel *Ceremony,* with its story of American Indian resistance to the kind of individualism enforced by Euramerican capitalism.

Every curriculum and every syllabus within a curriculum are necessarily partial. We must count on others to complete us and the completion is never done. What I have just offered, then, is both a literal instance of work that is done and a figure for work in progress. Before I left SMU for the University of Pennsylvania, I thought of the class as becoming part of a cultural studies program that I had designed with other interested SMU faculty from the Departments of English, History, Anthropology, and Theater. One of the projected functions of this program was to mobilize concerned faculty in support of recruitment of minority faculty and students, particularly in Dedman College (the liberal arts college of the university), where such recruitment in terms of faculty has been almost nonexistent, and in support of the existing programs in ethnic studies and women's studies, which traditionally have gone begging for money and, in the former case, faculty. My point here is simply to illustrate how American studies/cultural studies programs might function as organizing tools for crucial educational issues both within the university community and in relation to the community in which the university resides and on which it has an impact, both positive and negative.

In conclusion, I should add that from our conversations with the east Dallas community, those of us who have worked in the tutoring program find that the community welcomes it and would like to see it remain and grow. My own teaching and writing activities have been energized by the activity that I have sketched in this essay, and I am grateful to the people (students, faculty, administrators, children, and parents) who shared this activity with me. I continue to believe in the surprising energies that are released in people as they begin to engage themselves and the world critically, that is, as they begin to denaturalize their own perceptual processes, to historicize, which is to say, to theorize and politicize them through the urgent work of what I have suggested as American studies.

Notes

1. Since the time when I wrote this essay, John Guillory's book *Cultural Capital: The Problem of Literary Canon Formation* has appeared, which discusses canon formation as a question of the distribution of cultural capital, the means of production necessary to reading and writing, that is, literacy. Guillory's argument, which has certainly helped sharpen my own, points in important ways to the socioeconomic entanglements of the current "crisis" in the formation of the literary canon, that is, to culture as politics, even though at times this argument seems more focused on its own formal operations than it does on the political operations it says it has in view. This kind of narcissistic focus manifests itself in Guillory's lack of awareness of or refusal to engage the radical and progressive work that is being done in pedagogical theory and practice both nationally and internationally at all levels of the "school," which he posits as the primary site of his critique. This lack or refusal tends to position Guillory, as the narrator of his discourse, as a kind of isolated, educational guru, who sees what virtually no one else sees, producing, typically, this kind of statement: "So long as

this movement ['to open or expand the canon'] fails to recognize the social relation between writing and speech, or the institutional relation between literature and composition, it will not be capable of understanding the historical forces which compel the literary canon to manifest itself as *linguistic capital*" (81). But, of course, the relations that Guillory refers to are not news in the radical or progressive educational community, which has been aware of them for many years (one could begin by invoking the influential name Paolo Freire, which does not appear in the index of Guillory's book). Nor is there some homogenous "movement to open or expand the canon" (81) as Guillory's rhetoric continually suggests. There are instead a range of institutional sites at which the canon and, crucially, the idea of canonicity itself are being contested in various ways, some of which I articulate in this essay. By positioning his narrator in isolation from these specific political/theoretical forces, Guillory impoverishes the cultural capital of his own discourse by severely limiting the range of its exchanges.

2. For Addams's explanation of her compromise, see "The Progressive Party and the Negro."

3. Tim Brennan has remarked on the centrality of multiculturalism in focusing the PC debates:

> From the point of view of nonacademic power, the humanities debates . . . were particularly (if unconsciously) about race and the Union, about fear of immigrants from the world's Southern (and Eastern) regions coupled with the new openness among educators to teach the "non-West." These fears are not so much about an invaded aesthetic value as a ruptured polity with its nightmarish demands for an equality that would jeopardize the profits of discrimination. It is, therefore, multiculturalism that has been the chief target of the anti-PC partisans and the one that held the others together in people's minds, even if it was never announced as playing this role in the numerous exchanges of the ensuing struggle. (631)

4. I am using *The Debate on the Constitution: Federalist and Antifederalist Speeches, Articles, and Letters During the Struggle over Ratification,* Part One. The page numbers in the body of my text are from the 1993 edition.

5. See in particular "Brutus" the *New York Journal* 29 November 1787 (*The Debate on the Constitution,* Part One 423–30).

6. For an elaboration of the term *equivocal,* see Cheyfitz, *The Poetics of Imperialism.*

7. For an important discussion of the relationship between socialist revolution in mid-nineteenth-century Europe and "classic" American literature, see Reynolds, *European Revolutions and the American Literary Renaissance.*

Works Cited

Addams, Jane. "The Progressive Party and the Negro." *The Social Thought of Jane Addams.* Ed. Christopher Lasch. Indianapolis: Bobbs, 1965. 169–74.
———. *Twenty Years at Hull House.* 1910. New York: New American Library, 1981.

Argueta, Manlio. *One Day of Life.* New York: Vintage, 1983.

Armstrong, Robert, and Janet Shenk. *El Salvador: The Face of Revolution.* Boston: South End, 1982.

Beard, Charles A. *An Economic Interpretation of the Constitution of the United States.* New York: Macmillan, 1913.

Bloom, Allan. *The Closing of the American Mind.* New York: Simon, 1987.

Brennan, Tim. "The Education Debate: A Postmortem." *American Literary History* 4 (Winter 1992): 629–48.

"Brutus." *New York Journal* 29 November 1787. Rpt. in *The Debate on the Constitution: Federalist and Antifederalist Speeches, Articles, and Letters During the Struggle over Ratification.* Part One. New York: Library of America, 1993. 423–30.

Carby, Hazel V. "The Multicultural Wars." *Radical History Review* 54 (Fall 1992): 7–18.

Cheyfitz, Eric. *The Poetics of Imperialism: Translation and Colonization from The Tempest to Tarzan.* New York: Oxford UP, 1991.

Chira, Susan. "Study Confirms Worst Fears on U.S. Children." *New York Times* 12 April 1994: A1, A13.

The Debate on the Constitution: Federalist and Antifederalist Speeches, Articles, and Letters During the Struggle over Ratification. Part One. New York: Library of America, 1993.

Denning, Michael. "The Academic Left and the Rise of Cultural Studies." *Radical History Review* 54 (Fall 1992): 21–47.

DeParle, Jason. "Sharp Increase Along the Borders of Poverty." *New York Times* 31 March 1994: A1.

Douglass, Frederick. *Narrative of the Life of Frederick Douglass, An American Slave, Written by Himself.* Boston: Published at the Anti-Slavery Office, 1845.

D'Souza. Dinesh. *Illiberal Education: The Politics of Race and Sex on Campus.* 1991. New York: Vintage, 1992.

———. "The Visigoths in Tweed." *Beyond PC: Toward a Politics of Understanding.* Ed. Patricia Aufderheide. St. Paul: Graywolf, 1992. 11–22.

Emerson, Ralph Waldo. *Self-Reliance.* Ed. Gene Dekovic. St. Helena, CA: Illuminations, 1975.

Fanon, Frantz. *Black Skin, White Masks.* Trans. Charles Lam Markmann. 1952. New York: Grove, 1967.

———. *The Wretched of the Earth.* Trans. Constance Farrington. 1961. New York: Grove, 1968.

Fish, Stanley. *There's No Such Thing as Free Speech, and It's a Good Thing, Too.* New York: Oxford UP, 1994.

Foner, Philip S. *The Policies and Practices of the American Federation of Labor, 1900–1909.* Vol. 3 of *History of the Labor Movement of the United States.* New York: International, 1964.

Franklin, Benjamin. *The Autobiography of Benjamin Franklin.* Ed. R. Jackson Wilson. New York: Modern Library, 1981.

Freire, Paolo. *Pedagogy of the Oppressed.* Trans. Myra Bergman Ramos. New York, Continuum, 1970.

Galeano, Eduardo. *Open Veins of Latin America: Five Centuries of the Pillage of a Continent.* Trans. Cedric Belfrage. New York: Monthly Review, 1973.

Goldman, Emma. *Anarchism, and Other Essays.* New York: Mother Earth, 1917. Rpt. New York: Dover, 1969.

The Graywolf Annual Five: Multi-Cultural Literacy. Ed. Rick Simonson and Scott Walker. St. Paul: Graywolf, 1988.

Guillory, John. *Cultural Capital: The Problem of Literary Canon Formation.* Chicago: U of Chicago P, 1993.

Harrington, Michael. *The Other America: Poverty in the United States.* New York: Macmillan, 1962.

Jacobs, Harriet. *Incidents in the Life of a Slave Girl, Written by Herself.* Ed. L. Maria Child. Boston: Published for the Author, 1861.

Jaimes, M. Annette, ed. *The State of Native America: Genocide, Colonization, and Resistance.* Boston: South End, 1992.

Kimball, Roger. *Tenured Radicals: How Politics Has Corrupted Higher Education.* New York: Harper, 1990.

Lasch, Christopher. *The Agony of the American Left.* New York: Knopf, 1969.

Marx, Karl, and Friedrich Engels. *The Communist Manifesto.* 1848. Centennial Ed. Authorized Trans. Samuel Moore. New York: New York Labor News, 1948.

Nekola, Charlotte, and Paula Rabinowitz, eds. *Writing Red: An Anthology of American Women Writers, 1930–1940.* New York: Feminist, 1987.

Perry, Ruth. "A Short History of the Term *Politically Correct.*" *Beyond PC: Toward a Politics of Understanding.* Ed. Patricia Aufderheide. St. Paul: Graywolf, 1992. 71–79.

Reynolds, Larry J. *European Revolutions and the American Literary Renaissance.* New Haven, CT: Yale UP, 1988.

Schlesinger, Arthur M., Jr. *The Disuniting of America.* 1991. New York: Norton, 1993.

Silko, Leslie Marmon. *Ceremony.* New York: Viking, 1977.

Thoreau, Henry David. *Walden and Civil Disobedience: Authoritative Texts, Background, Reviews, and Essays in Criticism.* Ed. Owen Thomas. New York: Norton, 1966.

Weber, Max. *The Protestant Ethic and the Spirit of Capitalism.* Trans. Talcott Parsons. New York: Scribner, 1930.

"Who's Afraid of Lani Guinier?" *New York Times Magazine* 27 February 1994: 38–44, 54–55, 66.

Will, George F. "Literary Politics." *Beyond PC: Toward a Politics of Understanding.* Ed. Patricia Aufderheide. St. Paul: Graywolf, 1992. 23–26.

Williams, Patricia J. *The Alchemy of Race and Rights.* Cambridge, MA: Harvard UP, 1991.

The Winthrop Papers: 1498–1649. Boston: Massachusetts Historical Society, 1929–1947. 5 vols.

II Curriculum

8 Organizing the Conflicts in the Curriculum

Gerald Graff
University of Chicago

In one sense, the war over the literary canon is over. It is becoming increasingly clear that the usual alternatives in which the debate is posed—should we teach the traditional canon of Western culture, or a multicultural canon reflective of the increasing diversity of our society—are misleading. The next generation is going to be exposed *both* to the traditional canon and a new and more multicultural canon. Debates will continue to go on about how much of this should replace how much of that, and certain schools, departments, and colleges will resist change longer than others. But the cultural diversification of the curriculum is powered by the cultural explosion of publishing, the demographic realities of the larger culture, and the most important new trends in the disciplines. For these reasons, I do not think it is likely to be reversed.

On the other hand, debates over the merits, implications, and proper strategies of diversifying the curriculum are not likely to go away. In this sense, the curriculum debate is not over at all, but is likely to be with us for a long time. I have been arguing recently, and I will restate some of the argument here, that we are missing a major opportunity if we do not turn our energies to making positive educational *use* of these debates by incorporating them into our object of study. If we do not begin viewing the debates as an opportunity instead of a disaster, they will not only continue to generate ill antagonism and rage, but will make education more confusing to students.

For even though the cultural diversification of the curriculum has enormously enriched the content of education, there is no evidence that this diversification in and of itself has done anything to alleviate the fundamental learning problems of students. On the contrary, there is reason to think that in the past, whenever there have been increases in the

This essay originally appeared in the *Journal of the Midwest Modern Language Association* 25.1 (Spring 1992): 63–75. Used by permission of MMLA and the author.

cultural and intellectual diversity of education, they have only posed new problems for the many students who have trouble making sense of the clashes of viewpoints and values to which they are exposed. Including new texts and approaches in our classes is a necessary and salutary thing, but it is not the only thing, and in some ways it is no more than a starting point—for those students who have had problems reading the texts of the traditional canon are likely to have just as many problems reading those of the newly opened and revised canon.

There is a danger of losing sight of this fact amid the sound and fury of the culture war. It is easy to get so caught up in the fight for one list of books against another list of books that we forget that for many of our students the problem is *books, period,* regardless of which side gets to draw up the syllabus. It is easy to get so caught up in the conflict between traditional and revisionist canons that we forget that for these students the very words "traditional," "revisionist," and "canon" are mysterious and intimidating.

What is true for literature courses holds for composition courses as well. However the controversies over freshman composition may have been resolved at places where they have erupted, like the University of Texas, the fact remains that the freshmen who find it a struggle to write compositions about traditional topics will find it no less of a struggle to write compositions about issues of racism and sexism. This is not an argument for giving up the battle to bring those political issues into the composition course. It is, however, an argument for recognizing that to many students a theme assignment on racism or sexism will look pretty similar to a theme assignment on God or patriotic duty: to those students, a theme is a theme is a theme, just as an English course is an English course, regardless of whether the topic is provoked by the work of an Allan Bloom or a Catharine MacKinnon. At least this is the case for those students for whom the distance between any two intellectuals like Bloom and MacKinnon seems far less great than the distance between those intellectuals and nonintellectuals like themselves. For these students, the generic terrors of the English essay, which force you to try to sound like the intellectual you know you are not and perhaps do not want to be, are a far more fundamental problem than whether to take either Bloom or MacKinnon as a model.

The rule that applies here I call Graff's Law of the Low Visibility of Intellectual Differences: it holds that to non-eggheads, any two eggheads, however far apart ideologically, will look more similar to one another than to people like themselves. What is easily lost sight of, in other words, is that it is academic intellectual culture *as such* that intimidates or alienates many students today, as it intimidated and alienated earlier generations of students long before any canon revisionists or antirevisionists came on the scene. It is not books per se that have always given students problems, but the special ways in which books are analyzed and discussed in the intellectual vocabularies of the academy. When students have trouble with these vocabularies, that trouble is likely to have very little to do with the particular texts or other materials being taught, and attempts to solve the problem simply by changing the texts and materials have always ended up being superficial.

We expect students not simply to *read* texts in the academic setting, but to find things to *say* about texts, to engage in book-talk or intellectual-talk, to contribute to an intellectual discussion, to join an intellectual community and produce its special kinds of discourse. Some, of course, say there is our problem right there—our teaching is overly intellectualized, overly fixated on getting students to sound like us, to replicate the forms of academic discourse. But this anti-academic line of argument seems to me self-defeating and a betrayal of students' interests. Students need to master academic discourse not only in order to make their way through the university, and not only in order to get ahead in an information-oriented culture which increasingly rewards those who can use analytic and argumentative forms of speaking; they also need to master academic discourse to become more critical as thinkers and more reflective as citizens. The problem as I see it anyway is not that we are trying to turn students into intellectuals but that we are not succeeding very well. It is not that we are perversely trying to recruit students into our academic intellectual community, but that we are not doing it as effectively as possible.

I believe a large part of this failure stems from our own ambivalence about our academic intellectual community, our uncertainty about whether we really want students to become intellectuals like us or not. Being ambivalent about our own discourse, we partly withhold that discourse from students—and then we punish them for failing to possess what we have withheld from them.

To take an example of what I am talking about from the study of literature, we generally do not expect undergraduates in literature classes to read literary criticism, even though, when you think of it, literary criticism is precisely what we expect them to *produce*. Some teachers actually discourage undergraduates from reading criticism and they certainly discourage them from reading literary theory, on the grounds that criticism and theory can only distract students from literature itself. This is disastrous reasoning, since it is students' lack of a critical and theoretical vocabulary for dealing with literature itself that makes literature so frightening to many of them, keeping them tongue-tied in the face of it and sending them to *Cliffs Notes* to get the critical discourse that is not taught to them in class. By a bizarre paradox, the defenders of literature itself turn out to be keeping *Cliffs Notes* in business. But what we are withholding from students in these cases is not only criticism and theory, but the discourses of the intellectual community, those discourses that, as I say, we then punish students for not being able to speak.

I trace the problem, however, not to any deficiency on the part of individual teachers, but to our collective failure to construct for students the intellectual community that we expect them to join. Here is why concentration on the individual components of the curriculum—texts, authors, traditions, theories, and so forth—is counterproductive unless attention is also paid to how the components fit together, whether they form an intelligible conversation or set of conversations in the minds of the students who experience them. Students do not just study texts, ideas, and other materials in a vacuum; they study these things as part of a socialization into a set of community practices, practices which, to those not already familiar with them, often seem as mysterious and arbitrary as an initiation into a secret club. The club analogy is not a bad one, despite its overtones of snobbery, for entering the intellectual world is as much an initiation rite as joining a social club.

If the mysteries of the intellectual club remain out of reach for many students, I believe a good deal of the blame falls on educational institutions for representing the club very poorly. And here is the essence of my complaint about the established curriculum, both the old curriculum before the flood and the new improved curriculum being reshaped by multiculturalism. If this new curriculum does not do more than incorporate new texts and subjects, if it does not put the old and the new texts and subjects into a new and more coherent shape, then like the old curriculum it will end up doing more to obscure than to clarify the nature of the intellectual club for students.

For even in its reformed state, with the new women's studies courses and cultural diversity requirements in place, the curriculum still represents itself to students not as a collective or club-like social practice at all, but as a series of courses. Even when these courses are excellent and culturally diverse, and even when they achieve a club- or community-like atmosphere within themselves through a "collaborative learning" format, they remain structurally isolated from other courses and from the rest of the academic intellectual community. The sum total of students' exposure to a series of good courses rarely adds up to a helpful sense of what the community of a given discipline is all about, much less the community of the intellectual life as a whole.

I have elsewhere told some exemplary stories that illustrate this point. There is the student who took an art history course and whose instructor observed one day, "As we now know, the idea that truth can be objective is a myth that has been exploded by postmodern thought." It so happened this student was also enrolled in a political science course in which the instructor spoke confidently about the objectivity of his discipline, as if the news that objectivity had been exploded had not reached him. What did you do, the student was asked?

"What else could I do?" he replied. "I trashed objectivity in the one course and presupposed it in the other."

Another story concerns a student in a history course where the teacher insisted on the superiority of Western culture in developing the ideas of freedom, democracy, and free-market capitalism that the rest of the world was now clamoring to imitate; she was also taking a course with a literature teacher who described Western culture as a hegemonic system that had unjustly arrogated to itself the right to police the world. When asked which course she preferred, her response was, "Well, I'm getting an A in both."

For some today, the moral of these stories would be that students have become cynical relativists who care more about grades than about learning to form convictions. In fact, if anything is surprising it is that more students do not behave in this cynical fashion, for cynicism is precisely what the curriculum asks for. A student today can go from a course in which the universality of Western culture is taken for granted to a course in which it is taken for granted that such universalism is fallacious and deceptive. Such discrepancies can be exciting for students who come to the university already skilled at synthesizing ideas on their own; others, however, become confused and, like the two students I just described, try to protect themselves by giving each teacher whatever he or she seems to want, even if it contradicts what the last teacher wanted.

Nor is it even easy to infer what the teacher wants, for this can be hard to guess in an environment in which there is increasingly less unspoken common ground. Since students do not want to be exposed as naive, they will often hesitate to ask questions about the assumptions that are taken for granted in a course, finding it less trouble to conform.

Take something seemingly as trivial as the convention of using the present tense to describe literary and philosophical ideas while using the past tense for historical events. As Susan McLeod has pointed out, for a historian, Plato *said* things, for a philosopher or literary critic he *says* them. McLeod observes that practiced writers become so accustomed to these tense shifts that they seem innocent, but they may well reflect potentially controversial assumptions about the disciplines. Presumably Plato speaks in the present in philosophy and literary criticism because in these fields ideas are considered timeless; only when we move over to history does it matter that Plato is dead. English teachers write "tense shift" in the margin when student writers betray uncertainty on this matter, but how do we expect them to "get" it when they pass through the very different time zones of history and philosophy / literature without seeing any engagement of the issue? The issue could only be engaged if the teaching of history were somehow connected with that of philosophy and English.

One of the oddest things about the university is that it calls itself a "community of scholars," yet it organizes itself in a way that conceals the intellectual links of the community from those who do not already know what they are. The courses being given at any moment at a school or campus represent any number of rich potential conversations across courses and disciplines. But since students experience these conversations as a series of monologues, these conversations are only rarely actualized, and when they are it is only for the minority of students able to make the connections on their own.

Then, too, when students are exposed to disparate assumptions that never engage one another, they may not even recognize that these assumptions are in conflict. If a student does not know that "positivism" has in some circles become a hostile buzzword for "objectivism," he or she may not become aware that the art history and political science teachers in my above example are in disagreement. If a student goes from one teacher who speaks of "traditional moral themes" to another who speaks of "hegemonic discursive practices," it may not occur to that student that the two teachers are actually referring to the same thing. These students are being exposed to some of the most important cultural debates of their time, but the conditions of exposure are such that it may be impossible to recognize them as debates, much less to enter them. It is as if you were to try to make sense of a telephone conversation by overhearing only one side.

No conscientious educator would think of deliberately creating a system designed to keep students dependent on their teachers. Yet this is precisely the effect of a disconnected series of courses, which systematically deprives students of a clear view of the community comprised by those courses and thus throws them into dependency on the individual teacher and what he or she "wants." We talk a lot nowadays about "empowering" students, but I would argue that the very structure of a disconnected set of courses disempowers students and makes them dependent on teachers, even when individual courses have empowering effects.

This last point should indicate the bearing of my argument on the question of "oppositional discourse." Though current theorists of oppositional pedagogy invoke the ideal of democratic education, too often they conceive their project as a direct *transmission* of "transgressive" ideas and practices. The followers of Paulo Freire's "pedagogy of the oppressed," for example, assume an audience that is already converted to an oppositional social program—instructors who desire to become "transformative intellectuals" and presumably lack only the lesson plan to find out how it is done, and students who are interested in (or at least not resistant to) becoming radicalized. Presupposing an already converted clientele of teachers and students, this model only provokes resentments among ideologically mixed faculties and student bodies like the ones most of us know. The goals of oppositional pedagogy seem to me to have more chance of being realized by the strategy of making political debate more central in the curriculum rather than trying to turn courses or curricula into extensions of radical thought. Such a strategy makes for a more coherent curriculum as well as a more democratic culture.

I recognize that my critique of curricular fragmentation rehearses some old and familiar complaints. In some ways, I have only been echoing today's educational conservatives, who lament the atomization of the curriculum into a pluralistic cafeteria counter of disparate items. And up to a point, the conservatives are right. They have exposed the consequences of a century of liberal pluralism in educational thinking, which has operated on a principle of live and let live. Liberal pluralism says, in effect, I won't try to stop you from teaching and studying what you want if you don't try to stop me from teaching and studying what I want. Conservatives are right to point out the bad educational consequences of this live-and-let-live philosophy, which has resulted in a curriculum that offers a great diversity of subjects but virtually abdicates the responsibility to help students make sense of it. The trouble is that, having identified a real problem, the conservatives would cure it by superimposing a higher order on the curriculum, an order that they like to call "the tradition" or "the common culture," but that is essentially *their* idea of order and common culture, which is only one contender among many.

Modern educational history has been one of alternating pendulum swings between the liberal pluralist solution, everyone do their own thing, and the conservative solution, everyone do the conservatives' thing. We would seem to be in a conservative phase of the pendulum swing at the moment, with cultural literacy programs in the schools and core curricula in the colleges. But I believe it would be closer to the truth to say that both the liberal pluralist and the conservative solutions have run out of gas. Everyone doing their own thing has made a mess of the curriculum, but cleaning up the mess by returning to a traditional curriculum would make a far worse mess, if only because it would have to be imposed by force.

The liberal pluralist and the conservative visions are actually only two sides of the same coin, for neither vision is able to imagine any positive role for *conflict* within the curriculum itself. Conflict for the conservatives is a symptom of nihilism, decline, the disintegration of the common culture. But liberals are almost equally ill at ease in the face of conflict. Liberals like to glorify "diversity," but when diversity leads to conflict they too are at a loss. And today the conflict has become so deep, antagonistic, and overtly political that the old conflict-avoidance strategies no longer work as well as they used to—that is, parceling out the curricular spoils to the conflicting factions and then keeping them in separate departments, courses, and offices so that no unseemly disagreement can break out. The dirty linen is showing anyway despite the silent agreement not to wash it in public.

That is why it seems to me that the best way to deal with the present educational conflicts is to start turning them to our advantage, not simply by teaching the conflicts in isolated courses, however, but by using these conflicts as a new kind of organizing principle to give the curriculum the clarity, focus, and common ground that almost all sides agree that it lacks and to engage our students in our most fundamental disputes. Conflict as a form of common ground? It sounds at first like a strange and threatening idea—we think of conflict as something that divides us when what we want is to come together; it smacks of traditional agonistic male competition. We need to distinguish, however, between unproductive conflict, which fails to rise above the level of antagonism and put-downs and the kind that can bind people into a new kind of community. In this latter sense, the term "conflict" is not opposed to "community" but presupposes it. I believe the conflicts that are now compounding the confusions of students have the potential to help those students make better sense of their education and their world.

Trying to practice what I preach, I have lately begun reorganizing some of my literature courses around the current culture war. As we know, the last several years have seen a sudden increase in the number of articles, editorials, and angry polemics attacking the ideology of "political correctness" that allegedly has been running roughshod over dissent in the academic humanities. Every time a new attack or counterattack appeared during a semester, I would add it to my Xerox packet and assign it (one advantage of teaching this way is you never have to worry about running out of material).

It so happened that the first week of our quarter coincided with the reprinting of an essay of mine in *Harper's* in which I described a debate in the faculty lounge between a traditionalist and a feminist professor over Matthew Arnold's "Dover Beach."[1] In the piece I suggested that the students whom the traditionalist professor complains about who are left cold by "Dover Beach" might have found the poem more interesting and accessible had they been able to witness his debate with his feminist colleague, who questioned the gender assumptions about the poem. After all, "Dover Beach" hadn't been doing all that well with students before any feminists and deconstructionists arrived on the scene.

I suggested that the traditionalist's feminist colleague was doing both him and "Dover Beach" a favor by attacking the poem in a way that made both the poem itself and his traditional way of teaching it more mean- ingful than they were before. Traditionalists should be grateful to theo- rists for giving their position more legibility than it had before. I have discovered to my surprise that it is much easier to explain the *universal- ity* claimed by traditional canonical authors like Matthew Arnold once you introduce the feminist challenge to this idea, since students now have something to compare it with. By the same principle of contrast, I have found that reading non-Western novelists like the Nigerian Chinua Achebe makes it easier for my students to understand the "Western" qualities of a writer like Joseph Conrad. Whereas previously the concept of "Western" seemed puzzling—Western as opposed to what?—they now have a point of comparison.

I concluded in my *Harper's* essay that the best way to rescue poems like "Dover Beach" was not to try to protect them from the critical con- troversies about their value, but to use those controversies to give them new life. I also concluded that, far from diverting students' attention from reading literary works in themselves, such controversies were a good way to give students entry into those works by raising the question of what it means to read a literary work "in itself" and how one goes about it. The debate over "Dover Beach" that I had described in my article could be used to introduce the traditional skills of close reading while at the same time inviting the questions about those skills that the new theo- rists raise—to what extent does the close reading of any text inevitably involve the reader's culturally induced assumptions? To what extent is textual representation a scene of power and conflicts of power?

I was struck by the eagerness with which my students entered into the debate over "Dover Beach," some taking the feminist's side, some the traditionalist's, some arguing that neither position was adequate or that the issues themselves needed to be reframed. In one class, the most severe criticism of the feminist's interpretation came from a student who was taking a feminist theory course and who found her interpretation of "Dover Beach" simplistic and reductive. As in any good discussion, the original polarization of Left vs. Right was displaced as third, fourth, and fifth positions emerged and as those who began on one side ended up on the opposing one or somewhere else entirely. One student acknowledged that though he was not convinced by the feminist's critique of "Dover Beach," struggling in his paper to refute her interpretation made the poem seem more interesting to him than when he had read it in high school, where it had been presented simply as an example of poetic greatness.

It was clear that my class' interest in the debate over "Dover Beach" came partly from the public prominence of such controversies, which have made the issues of the humanities suddenly seem more *real* to students than they have seemed in the past. But I believe their interest also came from the fact that they had been exposed to these clashing theories and interpretations in a fragmentary way throughout their college careers and were finally getting a chance to see what was at the bottom of them. And contrary to widespread fears, the revelation that their teachers are at odds did not seem to destroy the students' respect for them. It was as if the sight of their teachers becoming passionate and angry made us seem a bit more human, less the image of remote imperturbability that so often makes teachers seem strange and forbidding to students.

So much for how in my own teaching I have been feeling my way into organizing literature courses around the culture war. But for reasons I suggested earlier, I think we need to move beyond the confines of the individual course and begin using such debates as a means of overcoming the isolation of courses, departments, and university divisions and opening up a dialogue between them.

In a way, I was already moving beyond the confines of my course insofar as I identified the different positions in the debate over "Dover Beach" as ones my students could recognize in their other teachers. Your colleagues do not have to be physically present in your classroom in order for you to teach their debates with one another or yourself. But if I am right in arguing that students need to experience an intellectual community in order to be able to join one, then there are limits to how much you can accomplish through even the best solo performance.

How, then, can we begin to link our courses, assuming this has to be done with a minimum of cumbersome administrative red tape and without limiting the freedom of choice of teachers and students? I believe one very promising model is at hand in our professional *conferences* and symposia, which have a great deal of untapped educational potential. Conferences make creative drama out of intellectual activity in a way that the more restricted setting of the course does not. One senses in the heightened atmosphere of conferences that the eagerness with which they are attended stems from their ability to provide the kind of intellectual community that is so sadly missing from the home campus and the everyday routine of teaching. The conference format, however, can be used to inject some of that community into that everyday routine.

Too often, we tend to think of these conferences as preliminary to what we do in "the classroom," when the kinds of conversations we have there would often be more illuminating to our students than any strategies we take home *from* them. In fact, we teachers feel we learn a great deal from these conferences, we are increasingly making them a part of graduate education, and there is nothing about them in principle that would prevent us from adapting them to the interests and needs of undergraduates.

Here, then, are some specific conference ideas that can be used to turn courses into conversations and conflicts into communities. Imagine, say, that as few as two or three instructors or as many as a whole department or college agree that in the fifth, the eighth, and the eleventh week of a semester, they will suspend their regular class meetings and hold a series of multicourse symposia, each of which will be based on one or two common texts agreed on in advance by the instructors. All the students in the courses involved will be expected to take part.

An ambitious department or college might even declare a theme for a whole semester: a semester that was actually *about* something such as the battle over the humanities or political correctness would figure to generate tremendous excitement and community without in any way forcing anyone to conform to anyone else's beliefs, and the theme could change from one semester to the next to keep diverse interests satisfied. (Faculty should be free to decline to adapt their courses to the theme, though dropping out would now acquire meaning, for once.)

Some possible topics for these symposia:

1. "Writing and Culture": This symposium would combine composition and literature courses around the issue of utilitarian vs. aesthetic concepts of writing, a conflict buried in the great division between literature and composition. A good text might be the opening chapter of Robert Scholes's book, *Textual Power*, which points out that the very identities of composition and literary study are defined by the invidious hierarchy of low practical communication

in composition and high aesthetic communication in literature (see Scholes 1–17). If the budget allows, Scholes or some other author (whether a critic or creative writer) could be invited to speak at the symposium.

2. "The Multiculturalism Debate: Pros and Cons," or, a variant: "Poetry, Nationality, and Gender": The publicity flier for the new world studies program at Queens College, New York, suggests an excellent topic for this one: "Do women writing poetry in Egypt, Latin America, and the United States have more in common as women or as poets?" Poets and critics could be invited from outside.

3. "Are Art and Scholarship Political?" or, "The Conflict over Political Correctness, in the Disciplines and in Student Life": *Heart of Darkness*, Achebe's critique of it, and his *Things Fall Apart* would be a natural for this one.

4. "Academic Cultures and Student Cultures": Lots of possibilities here; the very concept of "student culture" bridges the gulf between student discourse and academic discourse, encouraging students to think like anthropologists about their own lives and to take stock of their often ambivalent relations to the academy.

5. "Truth, Objectivity, and Subjectivity in the Sciences and Humanities": This one sounds dry, but a good conference would figure to make it less so.

6. "High and Popular Culture": This could be based, perhaps, around a classic novel and the film treatment or on readings of literature and readings of advertising.

Though they would take their starting point from contemporary debates, such conferences could be aimed at exploring the history of whatever debate is chosen: Is the current challenge to traditional culture unprecedented? How might the twentieth-century culture war compare, say, to the seventeenth-century battle between the ancients and moderns (as dramatized in Swift's *Battle of the Books*) or to later conflicts over the advent of romanticism or the modern avant-garde? How does the present debate over "the canon" compare to the debates which raged in periods when that term referred to religious rather than secular texts? Ideally, these issues would not draw attention away from literary and other texts but would provide points of entry into them that students now tend to lack.

It is obviously crucial that steps be taken to combat the deadly syndrome in which professors speak only with professors and students sit by passively as spectators. To prevent this from happening, students should be assigned definite roles with increasing degrees of involvement:

Conference 1: Students write papers *about* the conference.

Conference 2: Students give formal papers or critical responses *in* the conference.

Conference 3: Students organize the conference, choose the topic, plan the program, invite inside and outside speakers, and so forth. Students figure to become less timid, more intellectually aggressive in such a communal situation, having some models to imitate of how disagreements are acted out and negotiated while a single professor is no longer the sovereign authority in the room. As one instructor put it after teaching an introductory course with several of his colleagues, "Our students were able to disagree with us because they saw us disagreeing with each other."

An advantage of the conference idea is that almost any group of teachers can implement it at any time, without the need for exhausting faculty meetings, changes in requirements, and bureaucratic red tape. Instead of wrangling fruitlessly for hours trying to agree on the content of a new introductory course, a department or college might be wiser to convene a conference on "The State of the Discipline Today" and channel the wrangling into a discussion—keyed to a list of readings—that will introduce students to the issues the department would not have been able to agree on anyway.

I want to conclude by addressing some objections that have been made to these proposals. It has been objected that teaching the conflicts in this fashion would only add yet another obligation onto the shoulders of already overworked and burned-out teachers. But teaching the conflicts is not a matter of adding a new obligation, but of doing something we are already doing now in a way that would help us as well as our students get more out of it. It is not a matter of an adding another extra task, but of performing existing tasks in relation to our colleagues rather than in a vacuum. Nor is it a matter of *adding* theoretical debate to teaching literature but of embedding the teaching of literature in our theoretical differences. It is really the existing system of disconnected courses that is the prescription for burnout, since it results in immense duplication of activity while leaving teachers with no means of helping one another.

A second objection is that teaching the conflicts involves a kind of relativism or skepticism: the university throws up its hands and says, "Ah, well, it's all relative. . . ." But this objection confuses relativism with disagreement. The real prescription for relativism is to expose students, as we do at present, to a series of disparate perspectives which never engage one another. Disagreement is the opposite of relativism: we would not engage in it unless we assumed there was some consensual truth to be gained at the end of the process. When truth is contested, it is by entering into debate that we search for it.

A third objection is that today's undergraduates do not possess the basic cultural literacy that would be needed to understand today's major cultural debates. What good would it do to expose students to a debate over poetry in Egypt and Latin America if he or she thinks Egypt is a planet and Latin America a neighborhood in New York? It is true that we do need to know some information in order to enter into it. But the best way to learn the facts about Matthew Arnold and "Dover Beach" is not to memorize such items as dead information but to be exposed to an interesting discussion that gives you the incentive to want to learn those things.

A fourth objection is that power differences and hierarchy would make debate impossible. Would an untenured assistant professor risk challenging the department chair? Would part-timers risk challenging senior faculty? The answer is yes, I think, at least some of the time in some departments. You can fail to get tenure by *not* challenging your superior, by not speaking up. Power differences would not be eliminated by the sort of thing I am recommending but would become part of the agenda of discussion—instead of, as usually now, building up repressed resentments.

Finally, I have been told that we do not want to turn the curriculum into a shouting match and further polarize an already overly polarized discussion. But the fact is, the curriculum is *already* a shouting match, and it can only become a more antagonistic one if we do not find productive ways to engage our differences. The hostility in the atmosphere at present is all the more reason for bringing the conflicts to the level of open discussion rather than let them further deepen and fester.

I would respond similarly to those who scold me for using pugilistic or other adversarial images and tell me that conflict is inherently male. Feminists who object to adversarial discourse can only do so adversarially—I think we need to talk about this double bind. On the other hand, the question of how controversy and debate *are* gendered in our culture is serious and important. It would make an excellent question for a multicourse symposium, with suitable texts perhaps by Carol Gilligan, Deborah Tannen, and others.

The point that all these objections miss is that we are *already* "teaching the conflicts" right now. We are teaching the conflicts every time a student goes from one teacher's course to another or from one department to another. I am only suggesting that we stop teaching the conflicts randomly and haphazardly and start doing it in a controlled way that gives students a chance to join our conversations. We are already teaching the conflicts now, but to do it well we need to do it together.

Note

1. See Graff, "Debate the Canon in Class"; this essay is excerpted and adapted from a longer essay, "Other Voices, Other Rooms"; a further revised version appears in *Beyond the Culture War* 37–41.

Works Cited

Achebe, Chinua. *Things Fall Apart.* London: Heinemann, 1958.

Graff, Gerald. *Beyond the Culture Wars: How Teaching the Conflicts Can Revitalize American Education.* New York: Norton, 1992.

———. "Debate the Canon in Class." *Harper's* 282.1691 (April 1991): 31–35.

———. "Other Voices, Other Rooms: Organizing and Teaching the Humanities Conflict." *New Literary History* 21.4 (Autumn 1990): 817–39.

Scholes, Robert. *Textual Power: Literary Theory and the Teaching of English.* New Haven: Yale UP, 1985.

9 Literature, Literacy, and Language

Jacqueline Jones Royster
Ohio State University

In 1892, Anna Julia Cooper, a teacher, scholar, community activist, and the first African American woman to be named president of a college, stated:

> Our money, our schools, our governments, our free institutions, our systems of religion and forms of creeds are all first and last to be judged by this standard: what sort of men and women do they grow? How are men and women being shaped and molded by this system of training, under this or that form of government, by this or that standard of moral action? You propose a new theory of education; *what sort of men does it turn out?* [emphasis mine] . . . I care not for the theoretical symmetry and impregnable logic of your moral code, I care not for the hoary respectability and traditional mysticisms of your theological institutions, I care not for the beauty and solemnity of your rituals and religious ceremonies, I care not even for the reasonableness and unimpeachable fairness of your social ethics,— if it does not give us a sounder, healthier, more reliable product from this great factory of *men* [her emphasis]—I will have none of it. I shall not try to test your logic, but weigh your results—and that test is the *measure of the stature of the fullness of a man* [her emphasis]. (Cooper 282–83)

Just as Anna Julia Cooper believed in 1892, I believe a century later that the fundamental reason for valuing a course of study and for teaching as we do is that we like the kind of human beings that it makes. By the same token, then, the fundamental reason for a change in teaching, in course content, in text selection, or in a curriculum is that by one process or another, the current framework is ineffective, or inefficient, or inadequate, or perhaps even incapable of making the kind of human beings that we deem it important, necessary, reasonable to make.

If such a perspective can be used, even momentarily, as a reasonable point of departure in looking at the intersection of theory and practice, then the initial question is not what or how do we teach, but what kind of person do we want to make? Initially, the question is not what balance of traditional English, American, or other literature there will be, nor even how much time will be devoted to building knowledge rather than skills or to developing a sense of identity and self-direction rather than enhancing levels of performance and achievement. Initially, the question is, given the realities of the world in which we live, what kind of people do we ideally want, need, must have to emerge from a particular course or course sequence after they have experienced it? What do we want to guarantee? What do we allow ourselves to hope for?

Like Anna J. Cooper, I believe that this is really the hard part. I believe that this is the measure that we are really held to. I can make a case for valuing works like Paule Marshall's *Brown Girl, Brownstones*. I can suggest strategies and resources for teaching, but the more critical case to make, in my opinion, is how such texts might help us engender ways of thinking, ways of being, ways of behaving that support, ideally, how we would prefer human beings to be. Such a perspective allows for a whole range of possibilities for how to choose and shape content and how to facilitate growth and development.

So, what kind of person, essentially, would I like to see emerge annually from our literature courses across the nation? The answer begins, of course, with the way that I see the world. What's out there?

When I look across the global landscape, I see that we are facing what my people (i.e., people of African descent) call tryin' times. We face difficult conditions and complicated choices. We are having to live with the mess that we've made of things. There are the legacies of slavery, imperialism, and colonialism. These chickens are coming home to roost, and we're getting quite loud about it. There are the legacies of the unbridled, undeliberated uses of our natural resources. We have now, on this small blue planet in the middle of nowhere, the potential to use up ourselves and everything else and then to have no place to go. There are legacies of war, aggression, inequity, and injustice. Around the globe, including in our own United States of America, we are experiencing, in untold numbers, homelessness, hunger, disease, illiteracy, poverty, as well as the devastation of ever-present drugs and violence.

I see despair and hopelessness and an increasing need for four C's —no, not the Conference on College Composition and Communication— but compassion, communication, cooperation, and courage. The fundamental human challenge has written itself boldly on our walls: We must be able to live, learn, work, grow, and prosper in the midst of others who may be quite different from ourselves. Our little world is in a mess, a mess that was created, in large part, by our own hands. If we are to survive we will most certainly need to draw on all our human talents and potential. We will need to think our way out, talk our way out, and support ourselves physically, spiritually, intellectually as we do so.

At this very minute, we need to demonstrate some special skills:

1. We need the ability to resist closure, i.e., to resist the urge to come to conclusions too soon. Instead, we should concentrate more on being careful observers who intend to hone our abilities to look inside and outside ourselves to other ways of seeing and experiencing the same situation. In other words, we need to be able to listen to our own voices and to the voices of others; to think; to examine carefully values, opinions, and behavior—our own as well as those of others.

2. We need the ability to express our thoughts, feelings, ideas, and concerns, clearly, effectively, and we also need the ability to respond to the thoughts, feelings, ideas, and concerns of others respectfully, conscionably, effectively.

3. We need the ability to be analytical about everything, to see what situations and circumstances are and are not, as well as what they could be. Imbedded in this skill is a recognition of the need to look consciously for both similarities *and* differences. In doing so, we can learn to take into account history, context, power, privilege, entitlement, authority; to take into account the specifics, not just the generalities of human lives, conditions, experiences, contributions.

To my mind, the combination of such skills helps to stretch our imaginations to unknown limits. With well-used imagination, we have a better chance of adjusting more flexibly to the hard work of living and breathing in the presence of others. Within this schema, then, I see English studies (which I define here as the study of literature, literacy, and language) filling a critical role. It is an area that seems perfectly suited to all educational levels (see, for example, *The English Coalition Conference*), but particularly to the college level, to support the development of the types of flexibility that would allow human beings to participate in a world in which compassion, communication, cooperation, and courage might operate systemically, vibrantly, and productively.

In recent decades, many teachers, researchers, and scholars have noted, particularly in the face of the contemporary scene, a need for reflection in English studies. In actuality, however, we are really just beginning to reconsider how and why we think of ourselves as a discipline in the ways that we do, and we are really just beginning to explore the broad landscape of possibilities for how we might operate in terms of curriculum, pedagogy, and assessment. Across the nation, we are struggling with the apparent reality that the old constructs just aren't keeping pace with either academic or social needs. In particular, our understanding of what constitutes a text and what constitutes knowledge is changing. What is also changing is our understanding of the impact of power, authority, and responsibility on people, knowledge, and action.

If we recognize these winds of change, and if we consider the curriculum as the entity that must modify itself in response (the tree that must learn to bend in the wind to preserve both itself and us), then this image allows us to see a particular moment of change not just as revolutionary, but perhaps more often than not as evolutionary. We are able to see that a change in shape or a shift in direction originates from prior conditions. These conditions, as they transform themselves, then, encourage change or, in some instances, demand it. Always, tensions exist, but we can use these tensions to invite, make room for, and nourish new ways of thinking.

I believe that viewing this process as evolutionary rather than revolutionary is a proactive, rather than a reactive, stance. It conjures images of growing, developing, unfolding, rather than images of chaos and destruction. Assuming a place for both continuity and change allows for the possibility of flexible and productive models in response to pressing needs. An evolutionary stance encourages us to bring both critical and creative thought to bear on problems and conditions since the goal is to evolve, not to revolt. It allows us to put aside some of our anxieties because, in the wide-ranging view of past, present, and future, the question of what to teach can be recognized not as a new one but a continuing one. We see clearly that it is a question that we have had in the past. It is a question that we have now. It is a question that we will have again and again and again as both the contexts and the impulses for learning, acculturation, and human survival change, as in our situation today.

With this wide-ranging view, we can envision this moment in our discipline as the retelling of an old story for a new generation. With this focus, curriculum becomes a mechanism for storytelling, a tool by which we shape and direct a *story* of truth and beauty, achievement and accountability, a story that points out pathways to knowledge and understanding. Using this perspective, we can recognize that the ways we conventionally use the word *change* often imply a need to tell a different story, a new story, another story. If, however, the goal is to think anew, with more enlightening theoretical constructs, then a primary task, as demonstrated, for example, by many contemporary scholars who speak from a race, class, gender, or cross-disciplinary perspective, is not to tell a new story but to tell the same story differently. The effort is to reconsider voice, audience, context, purpose; to take into account the convergences and divergences of crosscurrents; to raise questions like: Whose story, whose curriculum is it or is it not? What is the pretext, subtext, metatext? For whom was the course or the curriculum crafted or not crafted? How does the tradition out of which this curriculum, this literature, this story comes connect or not connect with other stories, other traditions, other curricular or scholarly impulses?

Clearly, the type of change that we are talking about is not a lateral one. The suggestion is not that we just put in *Brown Girl, Brownstones* and take out something else. The change is not simply exchanging one story for another. Lateral changes somehow seem not to account adequately for the complexities of either storytelling, as I have come to appreciate it, or the complexities of the contemporary context from which the current needs for change emerge. The essence of this suggestion is not displacement. It is more than just changing the artifacts, the books, the texts. *New texts* are not enough *to renew, to revitalize, or to reconfigure a curriculum.* As I see it, the demand is more for a change in vision, in pedagogy, in the sequencing of experiences, in assessment, and, ultimately, in content.

A Cautionary Tale

My take on the difference in the task between just changing from story to story and changing the whole way that we envision storytelling—the curriculum-making process—is rooted quite clearly in my personal experience of going through a course in graduate school which professed to be American literature after the Civil War. This course told its story through novels, starting with John William Deforest's *Miss Ravenel's Conversion: From Secession to Loyalty* and including more familiar works like Stephen Crane's *The Red Badge of Courage,* Theodore Dreiser's *Sister Carrie,* Mark Twain and Charles Dudley Warner's *The Gilded Age,* Willa Cather's *My Antonia,* Frank Norris's *McTeague,* and six or seven others that I don't especially remember now. The course did not include assignments, or discussions about, or references to any texts other than ones from this particular American literary tradition. There was also no initial acknowledgment of the place from which the professor claimed his intellectual authority or of his having created a world among other worlds. He did not acknowledge other Americas or the oppressions which permitted his America. He did not recognize other traditions or other stories which could have been used as point or counterpoint. What would have happened, for example, had he created a little intertextuality by using *Our Nig,* or *Clotel,* or *Contending Forces?* How might students' understanding of "American" literature have been broadened or deepened?

The professor gave, however, no indication of multiple experiences of the same or similar events. He showed no sensitivity as to how his anointed world, his privileged world, might intersect with or impact upon other lives. He did not even acknowledge the particularities of the lived experiences which made the chosen texts "true," or representative, or imaginative. He did not acknowledge "good" by articulating consciously that his choice of analytical criteria deliberately excluded an acknowledgment of context. What this professor did was to privilege twelve texts from one set of American experiences without even a peripheral glance at other analytical possibilities or at the Americans who were not represented or privileged through his choices, or even at those individuals, in all their specificity, who were there in his classroom.

Even so, the classroom of his world was *the* world for me until the very last day of the course. On that day the teacher turned to me and to a friend from my undergraduate institution (we were the only two African Americans in a room with no other racial minorities present), and he said to us something like, "Maybe you can tell us if there was anything happening with black people during this time." At that moment, I realized (although I certainly didn't have the vocabulary for it at the time) that, in that classroom, I had had to create for myself an imaginary place from which I could observe an image that I knew, from my own experience, was a distorted one. I had somehow found a way to listen and pretend that the story being told there was "representative" of *American* reality. I had had to create a space which allowed me to leave most of myself outside the door and to exist in an environment which gave no credit to me or to the fact that something, anything might have been left out of this classroom conversation.

What this teacher's question on that last day did for me was to knock me right out of that comfortable seat and remind me that the class was not designed with my history, my culture, my people in mind (although my people, the Americans that they are, are his people), and that our history, our culture, and even our literature are indeed part of his history, his culture, and his literature too. Our worlds collided. In one sense, we were both victims of the oppressions of race and gender and ignorance. In another, he didn't notice the extent of the injustice, the inequity, and the ignorance, but I did. Therein lies one tension between what we have come to call *margin/center* relationships and the multiple visions that marginalized people must always carry with them in this world—

while others remain significantly unconscious and insensitive and un-accountable.

The result, of course, was that neither he nor the class was able to benefit from the multiple experiences of converging lives, and I was unable to benefit from a well-informed, culturally conscious classroom leader who was authorized enough, empowered enough, and respon-sible enough to help me think again about American literature as if I too were an American, as if I too were a central part of the dialogue, as if my experiences belonged to the experience of a classroom focused on *American* literature, as if my experiences as an American counted and that there was indeed a place for my American life. I am not suggesting that we must always, deliberately politicize every classroom experience. I do believe, however, that classrooms are very much political places in the ways that we negotiate space, participation, power, and authority, as well as in the ways that we establish value. I am suggesting that the least we, as the makers and shapers of classrooms, can do with courses and curricula is to acknowledge openly, for ourselves and our students, that politics have always been and are still inextricably bound to the conceptual framing of classrooms and curricula because values, visions, and assumptions are inextricably imbedded in the intellectual author-ity which supports their framing.

Not only did I not benefit in this *American* literature course from be-ing exposed to theoretical or pedagogical constructs that encouraged me to bring my American self to this subject matter, I also did not benefit from being exposed to theoretical or pedagogical constructs that admit-ted their own strengths and their own limitations. In fact, such questions just never came up in class until they were hinted at by the professor (who, I suppose, was making some effort to be liberal) on the very last day when he asked my friend and me to speak for our race. In the case of the professor, I believe that he considered himself a good person with good intentions. What I understand now from my experiences as a stu-dent, as a teacher, and also as a scholar is that good intentions are no-where near enough to relieve us of the responsibility of being well-informed and thoughtful.

A Look at the Future

I believe that there is a message in this little anecdote for all of us, given the demographics of this country, given the historical realities of con-verging systems of oppression in this country, given the critical need to maximize talents and abilities in this country. I believe that meaningful curricula, which have within them well-deliberated course content, pedagogy, and assessment, swing at will by the ways in which we acknowledge the genesis of our intellectual authority and by the ways in which we allow for the sharing of the multiple experiences that constitute our national reality and, by extension, realities around the globe. Multiple accounts, like multiple readings of a single text and critical questioning, enable us to see converging and diverging worlds. They help us to fashion conceptual frames that are broad enough and deep enough to hold what I like to call expandable insights as we explore, analyze, and make meaning of the chaos of knowledge and also the chaos of human beings.

Such processes help us, I believe, to see a text, or situation, or problem space in bolder relief and also to value difference for the personal and intellectual benefit not only of those who operate in the margins, but of those at the center as well. A basic challenge in our classrooms may indeed be in finding ways to encourage people who are always automatically placed or who place themselves so arrogantly at the center to unlock the barriers to their own marginality, their own "otherness." We really need to talk to these people. Good learning in the context within which we find ourselves is not just paying attention when women talk about gender issues, or when people of color talk about issues of race and ethnicity, or when people with limited resources talk about the impact of economics. All of these issues belong to all of us. We're not being generous to others by being sensitive to other people's concerns. They are not just other people's concerns. They seem never to stay that docilely in place. One of the most critical questions, as articulated so well by Toni Morrison in her collection of essays, *Playing in the Dark,* for people who are white, Anglo-Saxon, male, middle to upper class, Protestant, heterosexual, physically able, or privileged in other ways, is the extent to which their privileges exist either because of, in the context of, or at the expense of others who are not one or more of those things.

We must search for ways to rise to an occasion that demands the recognition of how each human being in relation to other human beings is sometimes, if not always, "other" for any number of reasons. We need to get people out of central territory so that they can see what's really there and not there, so that they can see that even people who take tremendous comfort in occupying central territory show evidence themselves of distinctions that are worth noting—if we are ever going to recognize that there is no such thing as a generic human being, a generic American, or a generic student. Even when we look pretty much the same, we're not.

We could actually be bold and imagine a culture which can grow and prosper from the collective authority of our individually "felt senses" of "other," rather than just from the specifically delineated and often arrogant sense of "center" that we traditionally find in educational settings. Our challenge, then, is to create an evolutionary space that supports an interfacing of people, knowledge, and context; to fashion a curriculum that responds positively and productively to current needs, which recognizes that conditions and circumstances change, that encourages critical and creative thinking, and that can make it possible for us to take risks, live through the process, and come to understand with a more powerful lens. Our challenge is to create a curriculum and pedagogy that can help us not to feel overwhelmed by future needs because they also enable us to expect change, to expect strength to emerge from change, and to expect to have to keep focusing and refocusing our vision.

In the search to understand ourselves more fully, which I believe to be a fundamental advantage in the study of literature; to understand our connections to the known and the knowable more fully, which I believe to be an advantage of having cultural variety in literature; to transmit what we understand to our young more meaningfully and more productively, which I believe to be more likely with a dialectical vision— we must give considerable thought to a careful accounting of multiple realities. We must focus with more precision on what the world needs from students and on what students need from us so that they become well-equipped to fill those needs. We must think more flexibly about what it is that we want a course or a curriculum to do and why we want it to do that. Based on which and whose assessment of needs? In response to what demands? In keeping with what visions, values, attitudes? On what intellectual authority? Toward what ends, outcomes, expectations? Visions, values, attitudes, outcomes, expectations all inform how and why we shape and direct our teaching and constitute the genesis of intellectual power, authority, and also responsibility.

So, the questions are where are we and where do we go from here? What should the curriculum, the story, the texts account for? What else needs to be accounted for in our conceptualizations of curriculum if the texts, the embodiment of our ways of seeing, being, and doing, are to work productively, meaningfully. It seems to me that we face challenge, we face opportunity, and we face choice. One choice may be to do something like changing *the canon*, the texts, the stories; adding some texts; maybe even taking some away; including a few, perhaps, that are being retold in various ways. We could choose to do that—along with other things, like *changing the theoretical constructs which produce canons and changing the strategies that we use to teach, to help students to learn, and to assess levels of performance and understanding*. We could actually try to be innovative, adventurous, and open to possibilities and try to think differently about the whole curricular enterprise. We could look for new ways of being, not just new ways of doing. We might even consider that the opportunity to think anew is one that we should not miss.

Obviously, I am not really foolish enough to think that I have *the* magic answers to anything. What I'm most confident about is that I've got some darn good questions. My hope is that, among whatever other strengths any of our decisions may yield, we choose curricular mechanisms and designs which invite, affirm, and celebrate both consonance and dissonance, margins and centers. I hope that they model and shape visions that embrace inquiry, growth, development, and change as normal phenomena, phenomena to which our students can and should adjust.

I hope that our choices sustain multiple images that are balanced by race, ethnicity, class, gender, etc. I hope that these constructs minimize our tendencies toward dualistic thinking, hierarchies, binary relationships. I hope, even, that they blur dichotomies like margin and center. I hope that these mechanisms and designs increase our peripheral vision so that our classroom, departmental, and institutional visions of what we are doing are more flexible and more inclusive. I hope that they broaden the assumed territory of learning and achievement so that we are looking not just on the lines, as we have so much in the past, but also between the lines, under them, around them, over them, beyond them. I hope that we name our search a search for depth and breadth and substance, and I hope that we accept this quest with the confidence that indeed there are such riches to be found and generated.

I hope that the spirit of change is a generous one which seeks and expects to find strength and to give credit in ways that affirm, push to new limits, and empower. I hope that we have the courage and the compassion to work through with our students their discontent and discomfort as they face realities that they may not choose to face by their own volition. I hope that we can operate with the courage of our convictions despite the knowledge that the task is complex, the pathways are often rough, and the struggle to traverse them is inevitably intense and infinite.

One Small Step at a Time

In giving myself the same challenge that I give to others, I have tried to act as a teacher-researcher in my own classes. The effort is twofold. One part is to imagine ways of approaching the complex task of re-visioning what a course might be like and experimenting in small ways to determine how I can compress the distance between the ideals that I hold as teacher, writer, scholar and the realities that I recognize in teaching, learning, and living. The second part is to be as consistent as I can about holding my own feet to the fire, forcing myself to be vigilant about *conscious teaching*.

In essence, in recent years I have forced myself to turn each classroom into an open inquiry. By doing so, I have gained more comfort with being straightforward with students about what I see myself trying to do in the courses and why. I am much more consistent than I used to be about taking the time to let them in on my picture of things; to invite them to share their pictures—if they have any; to invite them to respond, to be straightforward about what is happening to them in the course in terms of its impact or not on their thoughts, beliefs, knowledge, or understanding; and to invite them to make their own sense of the experience. In other words, I spend much more time than I used to talking with students about teaching, learning, knowledge, and understanding.

Basically, I have learned two lessons. The first is that "sometimes I win, sometimes I lose, sometimes the game gets called for rain," but always I remind myself of the bidirectional path between theory and practice, the interchangeable space of what it means to be teacher and what it means to be learner, and the never-ending nature of the educational endeavor.

The second lesson is that I get more satisfaction as a teacher having to make decisions in a complex world by letting questions, rather than answers, be my guide. The questions that I have found to be most useful from course to course are:

1. How should I construct my students' field of vision so that they have the chance to see the boundaries of the texts that I have chosen and perhaps even their own limitations as thinkers and readers who have or have not been prepared to operate in certain ways?

2. How have I defined the terms of their reading experience? What counts? What does not count?

3. What is the purpose of the "literature" / the sources of information and insight that I am using? How will these sources help to do what I value most fundamentally, i.e., to develop in my students a passion for language, an understanding of language well-used, an understanding of analytical frames as constructed tools, and an understanding of the limitations of one's knowledge?

I find that these three basic questions significantly affect the specific choices that I make in a given course. My answers about focus—the carved out space of inquiry—and the sources of information and insight

vary. I have discovered that "pairings" are extremely useful for thought
and discussion. For example, I teach a course called "The Essayist Tradition among African American Women." I distribute across our classroom conversation several contrasts from which we discuss resonance,
consonance, and harmony:

1. I pair the voices of African American women in novels, poems,
   and/or song ("creative" writing) with their voices in essays (nonfiction prose).

2. I pair the voices of men who established our sense of what it means
   "to essay" (e.g., Montaigne, Emerson, Thoreau) with the voices of
   nineteenth-century African American women as they created a
   space within such a conversation for their own manner of "essay-
   ing."

3. I pair the voices of the African American women who laid a foundation in this genre with those who, in our contemporary context,
   are remaking that foundation.

4. I pair the "reading experience" of written texts (essays) with visual
   texts (photographs, films, videotapes) and/or oral presentations.

The point for me is not in choosing a particular set of texts (there are so
very many from which to choose) or in having the "contrasts" be of a
particular kind (difference and similarity can emerge from all kinds of
sources). It is, rather, to keep in focus how I answer my three basic questions while establishing, course by course, the guidelines for how I make
such decisions regarding which texts and what classroom activities. I find
this type of decision making liberating since, regardless of how I define
the "core" reading experience, I am free to draw boundary lines of one
sort or another so that my students and I can have the joy of crossing
them.

The Refrain

I believe that whatever we do with theory and practice in our classrooms,
it should not leave us, as the Ghanaian-born poet, Abena Busia, says
within the context of talking about what it means to live in exile:
"stranded on the shores of Saxon seas" (5).

Our mission is not to preserve Western authority at all costs. It is to
preserve humanity. If we can hold in our sights the notion that the imperative is to preserve the richness of our human selves and the universe
on which we depend, then we just might be able to envision, perhaps,
that diversity, flexibility, and change need not always give notice of

colliding worlds. Community can grow out of the dialectic. We can be different and still be valuable. We can have different points of focus, different points of departure, and still be engaged quite substantively in the same noble enterprise. Sometimes, if given the opportunity, the community that emerges from a multiplicity of perspectives can chronicle the coming of worlds in which we actually make room for difference without death.

What's more, I believe that if we can convince ourselves of these possibilities, then we might just be able to hold our students' attention to the task long enough to convince them of these possibilities as well. A more wide-ranging view of educational processes over time can enable us, teachers and students, to imagine that our feelings of disintegration and chaos are at once an illusion and an ever-present reality. I believe that the collective of these things can help us make sense of this never-ending task that we call education, not just for ourselves, but for our students. These approaches push us to see that learning is dynamic and that its systems and structures should also be part of a process in which we are never finished but forever becoming.

The warning is to move with care, recognizing as Busia says, that "this razor's edge of human choice is all we have ever had" (74). On our shoulders is the responsibility of deciding well, not just in good faith but in good conscience, with good information and considerable thought. We must now go beyond access. We must go beyond intent. We must even think beyond the singularity of the teaching of literature, or developing literacy, or making curricula. We must act with the courage of our well-deliberated convictions, with a compassion that underscores a recognition of our interconnectedness with others, with the desire to talk and to listen well, with an understanding that survival is a cooperative venture. After all, it seems to me that our very lives depend on it.

Works Cited

Busia, Abena P.A. *Testimonies of Exile*. Accra, Ghana: Woeli, 1990.

Cooper, Anna Julia. *A Voice from the South*. New York: Oxford, 1988.

Lloyd-Jones, Richard, and Andrea A. Lunsford, eds. *The English Coalition Conference: Democracy through Language*. Urbana, IL: NCTE, 1989.

Marshall, Paule. *Brown Girl, Brownstones*. New York, Random, 1959.

Morrison, Toni. *Playing in the Dark: Whiteness and the Literary Imagination*. Cambridge, MA: Harvard UP, 1992.

10 Cultural Institutions: Reading(s) (of) Zora Neale Hurston, Leslie Marmon Silko, and Maxine Hong Kingston

Anne Ruggles Gere
University of Michigan

Morris Young
University of Michigan

As new texts have entered the literary canon and the university curriculum in recent years, they have been accompanied by/defined by readings or interpretations and discussions that have acted to signify their cultural value and to legitimize the presence of these texts in the larger public as well as within the more critical arbiter of culture, the academy. Readings of texts and subsequently of their writers become almost as important as the texts themselves because they act to locate the text/ writer within the culture. Recent discussions of critical theory raise questions about the nature of these readings. Michael Bérubé, for example, asks "whether academization is the life or death of 'culture.' Is institutional literary study a means to the preservation of culture(s), or does it mark the death-by-assimilation of vibrant, challenging writers, movements, and modes of thought?" (18). Posing the issue in these terms opens the way for consideration of the interrelations between public and academic receptions of texts, between professionalism and antiprofessionalism in English studies, between genres of writing, between critical theory and pedagogical practice. Such considerations highlight the processes of and the complexities inherent in incorporating certain texts into the canon, but they leave unaddressed the institutionalization of particular readings of texts. How do interactions of literary theory, professionalism, textual features, public reception, and conventions of publishing shape the kinds of readings we teach in our classrooms? And in the case of historically marginalized writers, how do we negotiate these readings of texts with our readings of cultures?

We propose to explore these questions by considering institutionalized readings of three recently canonized texts, Zora Neale Hurston's *Their Eyes Were Watching God*, Leslie Marmon Silko's *Ceremony*, and

Maxine Hong Kingston's *The Woman Warrior*. By institutionalized readings we mean those interpretations promoted by individuals possess-
ing "cultural authority"; such readings frequently appear in classrooms
as part of the (re)production of culture. Institutions, as Mary Douglas
reminds us, "do the classifying," and institutionalized readings, drawn
from the discourses of those with cultural authority, classify the ways
we come to regard texts and, often, the writers who produce them. Here
we focus on the readings institutionalized by publications and / or pedagogy.

Written by women from historically marginalized groups, each of
these three texts includes features that raise questions about genre and
publishing conventions. While the first two are categorized as novels and
the third as autobiography / nonfiction, each defies easy categorization.
Their Eyes includes features that some readers call folklore (see Jackson;
Byrd; and Gloster) or, in more recently fashionable terms, "the illusion
of oral narrative" (Gates 196). *Ceremony* eschews chapter divisions and
blends poetry with prose in its seamless narrative. The generic status of
The Woman Warrior has been contested since its publication, with critics
arguing that it does not conform to conventional definitions of autobiography (see Wong).

Institutionalized readings, by nature provisional, receive authority by
fulfilling purposes specific to given contexts. Accordingly, the readings
applied to these texts do not remain constant but shift with time and cir-
cumstance, as the multiple readings of *Their Eyes* over nearly six decades
demonstrate. The earliest readings, in the form of reviews by Richard
Wright, Alain Locke, and Ralph Ellison, conceptualized *Their Eyes* as a
romance, concentrating on Janie's relationship with the three men in her
life. More important, these early reviewers constructed *Their Eyes* in
terms of absences or what it lacked. Wright, the harshest critic, excori-
ated the novel for having "no theme, no message, no thought" and
Hurston for having "no desire whatever to move in the direction of serious fiction" (25). In similar vein, Alain Locke faulted *Their Eyes* for its
failure to dive "down deep either to the inner psychology of characterization or to sharp analysis of the social background" (10). Wright, Locke,
and Ellison, who served as cultural arbiters of the Harlem Renaissance,
sought to create a unique cultural aesthetic and found Hurston's text
wanting because it failed to conform to their definition of black creativity. By framing Hurston's novel in these terms, her critics could turn her
acknowledged gift with language into a fault, claiming that it enabled
her to pander to a white audience. However, white critics, both academic
and journalistic, gave *Their Eyes* no attention. This combination of neglect and a reading of absences plunged *Their Eyes* into obscurity.

Few critics attended to *Their Eyes* for over three decades, and the few who did described it as folklore, highlighting Hurston's training as an ethnographer and drawing connections with her more anthropological texts, such as *Mules and Men*. James Byrd, for example, comments that the novel contains "competent handling of folk material, especially the peculiar idiom of folk speech and the 'big old lies' of Negro folk characters" (37). This reading constructs Hurston as a collector and purveyor of folklore, and it makes a case for the verisimilitude of the novel's language rather than looking to any aesthetic features. Details of Hurston's life, particularly her Southern roots and her ability to represent the culture of "her people," lent credibility to these folklorist readings of *Their Eyes*. In concluding his account of Hurston's "genuinely authentic" novel, Byrd asks "how this Northern-educated author came to know the Black and white folk of the South so well" and responds with a quote from Hurston's autobiography that she "was born a Southerner and had the map of Dixie on my tongue" (41). Such readings simultaneously exoticize Hurston and reinforce the Wright/Locke/Ellison view that *Their Eyes* lacks artistic seriousness. Positioning Hurston as one of "them" and from that distant place while at the same time claiming her as one of "us" (with a Northern education) suggests that *Their Eyes* represents history, not a unique cultural aesthetic and "artistic" cultural product. As we will explain shortly, *The Woman Warrior* received a similar reading.

Conventions of publication supported this folklorist reading of *Their Eyes*. The single page of unsigned prose that serves as an "introduction" to the first edition asserts that "This is the story of Miss Hurston's *own people*, but it is also a story of all peoples—of man and of woman, and of the mystery that the world holds" (our emphasis). This sentence, the last on the page, instructs the reader to approach *Their Eyes* as an introduction to (an)other culture, and holds out the possibility of universalizing the difference of "all peoples." The second sentence of the introduction—"Her writing is of the essence of poetry, deeply communicative, possessed of a *primitive rhythm* that speaks truly to the consciousness even before thought can form" (our emphasis)—lends further support to the folklorist reading by suggesting that the language, which operates at a preconscious level, does not represent aesthetic choice and sensibility but a kind of automatic reproduction of patterns derived from an alien population. The major portion of this introduction traces the plot outline of Janie's interactions with the three men in her life, thus highlighting the novel's romantic aspect. Critic Evelyn Helmick, who interweaves details of Hurston's life ("a stormy love affair that threatened to overwhelm her") with commentary on the novel, emphasized this reading as she declared, "And the story is, from beginning to end, a love story of Janie, a romantic, sixteen-year-old quadroon, who dreams of marriage" (8).

Neither the folklorist nor the romance reading generated great critical interest, and, having failed to attract what Bérubé calls an "ongoing research program," one that generates a reliable number of "entries in each year's MLA bibliography" (60), *Their Eyes* dropped out of print until 1965, when it was reissued by Negro Universities Press. This edition included the same one-page introduction, but the novel entered a different social context than it had thirty years earlier. Social and political movements of the 1960s focused new attention on the work of African Americans. Journals such as *Phylon* and *The Crisis*, which had long published criticism of African American writers, were joined by others that addressed a broader audience; MLA convention programs began to include sessions on African American authors. Darwin Turner's *In a Minor Chord* included *Their Eyes* in its survey of black literature, and critics began to focus on different angles, such as the significance of time and the racial self-hatred evidenced by the Mrs. Turner character (see Giles; Rayson).

While this increased and varied critical attention shifted its status somewhat, a more significant transition in readings of *Their Eyes* was effected by three African American women: Mary Helen Washington, June Jordan, and Alice Walker. In 1972, the same year that the short-lived Fawcett edition of *Their Eyes* was issued, Washington published an essay entitled "The Black Woman's Search for Identity," which considered *Their Eyes* in terms of its meaning for African American women rather than its ability to represent folklore competently or its entertainment value as a romance. By so doing, Washington initiated a new way of reading *Their Eyes*. June Jordan followed in 1974 with an article that, at long last, undercut Richard Wright's critical objections to *Their Eyes*. Arguing that white media manipulation insists on one artist to represent the black aesthetic, Jordan offered a more pluralistic alternative. While acknowledging Wright's power in inscribing protest and hatred, she asserted the importance of Hurston's affirmation of community and love of African Americans in *Their Eyes*. This combination of suggesting new possibilities for interpretation and releasing *Their Eyes* from its bondage to Wright's negative view opened the way for many new readings.

Walker's 1975 article furthered Jordan's project of reading *Their Eyes* as "the prototypical Black novel of affirmation [as] . . . the most successful, convincing, and exemplary novel of Blacklove that we have. Period" (6). Walker's account of her 1973 search for Hurston's grave, before Walker herself had gained the cultural authority she now enjoys, includes high praise for *Their Eyes* and declarations of its significance to Walker and other African American women writers. Walker constructs Hurston, as Henry Louis Gates, Jr. later phrased it, "to establish a maternal literary ancestry" (186) and prepares the way for her later assertion regarding *Their Eyes:* "There is no book more important to me than this one" (86). Placing "In Search of Zora Neale Hurston" in *Ms* magazine probably contributed as much to new readings of *Their Eyes* as what Walker said about the novel. Ever since the 1937 reviews, which appeared in *New Masses, The Nation,* and *Saturday Review,* everything written about *Their Eyes* had appeared in small-circulation academic folklore journals or journals intended primarily for African American audiences (both Washington and Jordan published their articles in *Black World,* for example). By publishing the article in *Ms,* Walker (re)introduced Hurston to a wider—and relatively highly educated—public and accomplished the cultural work of initiating a dialogue between academic and public audiences. Walker performed this dialogue in her article by including excerpts from Robert Hemenway's about-to-be published biography of Hurston along with quotations from Langston Hughes and both a librarian and student familiar with the Hurston collection in Yale's Bienecke Library. These multiple voices, along with two photographs (one occupying an entire page) of Hurston, a picture of Hurston's gravestone, a chronology of her life, a list of Hurston's books in print at the time, and Walker's parenthetical note after *Their Eyes*—"Originally published in 1937, this novel is Hurston's masterpiece" (89)—brought *Their Eyes* to the public while simultaneously opening the way for new readings of it within the academy.

Later in 1975, the MLA convention program included a session on Hurston which included these titles: "Discoveries in the Hurston Biography" by Robert Hemenway; "The Fiction of Zora Neale Hurston" by Barbara Smith; and "Zora Neale Hurston, Folklorist" by Trudier Harris. While this last title indicates the continuing vitality of folklorist readings of *Their Eyes,* the very existence of this session, coupled with Mary Helen Washington's report that participants in this session circulated a petition to get *Their Eyes* back into print (x), shows readings of this novel taking new directions. The petition, the growing number of articles, and the regular (beginning in 1975) Hurston sessions in the MLA program were supported by and helped to generate a new edition of *Their Eyes.* Published in 1978 by the University of Illinois Press, this edition, with a cover design featuring "the porch" and the pear tree, invited a more complicated reading of the novel. In her foreword to this edition, Sherley Anne Williams laments that Hurston was "remembered more as a *character* of the Renaissance than as one of the most serious and gifted artists to emerge during this period" and credits Hurston with "the literary skill to convey the power and the beauty of . . . heard speech and lived experience on the printed page" (ix). In summarizing / forecasting the plot, Williams gives prominence to Janie's relationships with Killicks, Starks, and Tea Cake but also suggests readings that position *Their Eyes* in relation to more prominent texts. In discussing Janie's experience on the muck, Williams writes: "Janie has come *down*, that paradoxical place in Afro-American literature that is both a physical bottom and the set-ting for the character's attainment of a penultimate self-knowledge (think of Ellison's Invisible Man in his basement room or the hero of Baraka's *The System of Dante's Hell* in the Bottoms)" (xiv–xv). No longer simply the record of an exotic culture, *Their Eyes* is thus read as an aesthetic cre-ation worthy of comparison to that of prominent African American male artists.

Nine years later, the University of Illinois edition advertised itself in a banner superimposed on the cover—"1987/50th ANNIVERSARY / STILL A BESTSELLER"—suggesting that *Their Eyes* was and had always been a popular success. As Philip Fisher reminds us, cultural work of-ten involves forgetting as much as remembering—"a last step, the for-getting of its own strenuous work so that what are newly learned habits are only remembered as facts" (4)—and this advertisement performed part of the cultural work necessary to establish *Their Eyes* as a popular as well as an academic success by erasing the history of its critical ne-glect. This edition also encouraged mediation between academic and popular readings with its back cover blurbs from Doris Grumbach of *Saturday Review* and Susan Blake of *American Book Review*. While *Their Eyes* gained in popular appeal, it continued to generate an increasing number of variant readings. Issues such as female quests, sexual poli-tics, authority and authorization, metaphor and voice, violence and or-ganic consciousness, and structures of address joined folklore, romance, community, and self-realization as points of departure for readings of this novel. A Hurston biography, collections of essays, and book-length studies also appeared, lending authority to Hurston's status as author and, thereby, to *Their Eyes*.

The 1990 Harper Perennial edition of *Their Eyes*, which framed Hurston's text with a foreword by Mary Helen Washington and an afterword by Henry Louis Gates, Jr., along with bibliographies of works by and about Zora Neale Hurston and a chronology of her life, further institutionalized emergent readings. While Washington affirms that "this is a rich and complicated text and that each generation of readers will bring something new to our understanding of it" (xiii), she highlights a feminist reading that focuses on the issue of voice. Gates offers a more pluralistic reading, claiming for *Their Eyes* a "multiple canonization in the black, the American, and the feminist traditions" (190), but he defines it as "a bold feminist novel, the first to be explicitly so in the Afro-American tradition" (187). The attractive (expensive), multicolored cover design featuring Janie beneath the pear tree reinforces a more metaphorical reading of *Their Eyes* and enhances its cultural authority by displaying its capitalistic value.

As this account shows, complicated interactions of public and academic receptions of the text, the presentations of various editions, convergences with feminist theory and postmodern views of language, multiple constructions of Hurston, sociopolitical circumstances, and the visible professionalization of a significant number of African American scholars all played a role in creating multiple readings of *Their Eyes*. The dramatic shift from reading this novel as "having no theme, no message, no thought" to reading it as multiply canonized "in the black, the American, and the feminist traditions" (Gates 190) demonstrates the provisional and shifting nature of all institutionalized readings.

Leslie Marmon Silko's *Ceremony* represents another kind of institutionalized reading. Published in 1977, this novel received immediate critical approval. The *New York Review of Books* asserted, "Without question Leslie Silko is the most accomplished Native American writer of her generation. . . . A splendid achievement," and this sentence has adorned all subsequent paperback editions of *Ceremony*. N. Scott Momaday's Pulitzer Prize-winning *House Made of Dawn* (1968) prepared both public and academic readers for novels by Native Americans, so *Ceremony* found a ready audience. A number of reviewers reminded readers of *Ceremony*'s (and Silko's) exotic appeal. *Kirkus* described it as "an emotionally convincing picture of a culture unfamiliar to most" (18). *Choice* affirmed that Silko "has confidence in her genre and confidence in her people—the characters and people she lives among" (684). Barbara Jacobs, in a less flattering review, asserted that "though the plot is sometimes as confused as Tayo's thoughts, the rhythmic chants and simple prose are compelling" (1147). Despite this generally positive response, Silko's novel has never achieved the kind of celebrity status accorded to Hurston's *Their Eyes*. A small number of articles on *Ceremony* appear in the MLA bibliography each year, but the number does not approach those on *Their Eyes*. During the period between 1982 and 1992, for example, Hurston had 143 entries while Silko had only 61. By themselves, these numbers indicate little, but the journals and readings they represent fill out the picture. Articles on Silko have appeared in journals such as *MELUS*, *The Journal of Ethnic Studies*, *American Indian Quarterly*, and *Critique*. With relatively small circulations, these journals do not reach the broad audiences available to the *PMLA* articles on Hurston. There has been no celebratory edition equivalent to the 1990 Harper Perennial edition of *Their Eyes*, although the Penguin edition of *Ceremony*, issued after Silko's *Almanac of the Dead* appeared, looks more thoughtfully produced (expensive) than earlier editions, and it contains the addition (on page 179) of a full-page rendition of Old Betoni's stars. The places where work about *Ceremony* has appeared, and the terms in which it has been represented by publishers, indicate that it has not yet become, at least in the terms that *Their Eyes* has, a book on which public-academic dialogue focuses, a book for all readers.

Yet readings of *Ceremony* have been institutionalized. In 1983, the MLA issued *Studies in American Indian Literature: Critical Essays and Course Designs*, the second volume in a series initiated by its Commission on Languages and Literatures of America. Edited by Paula Gunn Allen, this volume includes suggested designs for courses that include Native American literature, critical articles on novels such as *Ceremony*, lists of resources, and discussions of oral literature and autobiography. *Ceremony* receives prominent attention in the introduction as one of the few novels by a Native American woman, and Allen also comments on the need for those teaching *Ceremony* to attend to "Laguna traditions, history and present conditions" (x). Among the critical essays included is Allen's "The Feminine Landscape of Leslie Marmon Silko's *Ceremony*," which emphasizes the significance of the land in Silko's novel: "We are the land. To the best of my understanding, that is the fundamental idea that permeates American Indian life; the land (Mother) and the people (Mothers) are the same" (127). Allen explains Tayo's illness as a "result of separation from the ancient unity of person, ceremony and land" (128) and asserts that his cure derives from reuniting Tayo and the land. No doubt Allen's cultural authority, both as an academic and as a representative of the Laguna people, helped institutionalize this reading of landscape in *Ceremony:* a number of other critical articles followed suit by considering Silko's portrayal of the land (see, for example, Garcia; Nelson; Smith; and Swan).

Allen also helped generate another of the institutionalized readings of *Ceremony* by describing Tayo's ability to carry out the ceremony as deriving from "his status as an outcast who, at the same time is one of the Laguna people in his heart" (131). This reading of *Ceremony* as the story of Tayo the half-breed, as a narrative of liminality, has been developed by Diane Cousineau and Gretchen Ronnow among others. Cousineau reads the half-breed as a rejection of hierarchy and dualistic opposition. Ronnow does a Lacanian reading of *Ceremony* that takes pleasure in Tayo's lack of a totally cohesive, unified self. She concludes that Tayo learns by the end of the novel "that Otherness contains the fullest possibilities of Presence" (88). In its various forms, this reading of *Ceremony* plays upon Silko's personal condition as being biculturally Native American and Anglo by connecting Tayo with the author's own Laguna-European roots. Nearly all the readings that emphasize the half-breed issue make a connection with the status of the author.

Other institutionalized readings emphasize textual features, particularly orality/oral traditions. Questions of genre become prominent in such readings, as critics look at Silko's representations of traditional poems and stories. Konrad Gross, for example, describes Silko as attempting to "subdue the novel to the conditions of orality and to indianize it by assigning to it a ritual pattern. . . . [I]t [*Ceremony*] goes against the widespread contemporary belief that the purpose of novel writing is to play with various realities, not to master reality" (99). By framing the innovative qualities of *Ceremony* in terms of deviation from contemporary critical fashion, Gross does not encourage additional readings of this novel. Although it would be possible to interpret the language of *Ceremony*—as Barbara Johnson, Elizabeth Meese, and others have done with *Their Eyes*—in terms of its creativity, its poetic figures, and its postmodern qualities, the readings of its orality have emphasized difference and exoticism.

Mythical/spiritual dimensions of *Ceremony* take prominence in other readings. Apparently taking seriously Paula Gunn Allen's admonition to develop appropriate background in Laguna history and tradition, critics who set forth readings of the spiritual/mythical lard their accounts with footnotes from ethnographers. Typical of these, Edith Swan's "Healing via the Sunwise Cycle in Silko's *Ceremony*" includes quotations from anthropologists Franz Boaz, Elise Parsons, and Leslie White, among others. Swan argues that "Ghostway, the ceremony conducted on Tayo's behalf by the Navajo medicine man Betoni," (313) constitutes the center of the novel. Sketching the details of his ceremony, complete with charts that trace Laguna cycles of time and space, Swan concludes that "Tayo's becoming is complete, a new balance achieved, and he has forged his place in the schematic order of Spider Woman's metaphysics" (326). Whatever the motivations behind this and similar readings of *Ceremony*, it evoked a highly negative response from Paula Gunn Allen. In a 1990 article, she writes,"I believe I could no more do (or sanction) the kind of investigation of *Ceremony* done by some researchers than I could slit my mother's throat. Even seeing some of it published makes my skin crawl. I have yet to read one of these articles all the way through, my physical reaction is so pronounced" (383). This visceral reaction from a critic with Allen's cultural authority casts all mythical/spiritual readings of *Ceremony* in a negative light. Allen's reaction includes a warning against those who pursue such readings. Even as she acknowledges her own previous injunction that instructors ground themselves in historical and ethnographic material relevant to the novel, she writes: "But to use the oral tradition directly is to run afoul of native ethics, which is itself a considerable part of the tradition. Using the tradition while contravening it is to do violence to it. The ethical issue is both political and metaphysical, and to violate the traditional ethos is to run risks that no university professor signed up for in any case" (379). Allen's critique extends beyond these readings and readers to Silko herself: "[T]he story she lays alongside the novel is a clan story and is not to be told outside of the clan. I have long wondered why she did so. Certainly, being raised in greater proximity to Laguna village than I, she must have been told what I was, that we don't tell these things outside" (384). By questioning Silko's motives and ethics, Allen undercuts the authority of *Ceremony* as well as its author. If Silko betrays her people by telling a clan story to outsiders, does she deserve her readers' trust?

As was true for *Their Eyes*, readings of *Ceremony* have evolved from complex interactions of textual features, multiple constructions of the author, sociopolitical circumstances, and public and academic receptions. While recent criticism of *Their Eyes* has been generative and led to additional readings, the reductive readings of *Ceremony*'s oral features combined with Allen's powerful objections to mythical/spiritual readings have prevented a similar burgeoning of critical attention to *Ceremony*. Furthermore, *Ceremony* has lacked serious and sustained extra-academic attention, and the resulting lack of dialogue between public and academic readers may also have limited its readings. Whatever the reasons, this novel appears to be, for the moment, receding from both public and academic view. Nearly all the articles published on *Ceremony* in the past three years have embedded this novel in discussions of thematic issues or of other novels by Native Americans, and none of these articles positions *Ceremony* in the center of the current critical discussions as Gates's and Washington's articles do *Their Eyes*.

The appearance of Maxine Hong Kingston's *The Woman Warrior* in 1976 spawned a set of institutionalized readings that helped constitute Asian American literary studies. Of course, Asian American literature existed before 1976, and Frank Chin, Jeffery Chan, Lawson Inada, and Shawn Wong led the project of recovering Asian American literary texts by editing one of the first collections of Asian American writing, *Aiiieeeee! An Anthology of Asian-American Writers* (see Chin et al.). However, it is Kingston's *The Woman Warrior* which has had a dramatic impact on American literary studies, becoming, in the view of many, the exemplary Asian American text and one of the multicultural texts that has contributed to expanding the canon. Kingston herself has secured a place in the contemporary American literary scene, bolstered early on by critical acclaim in the popular media and public sphere as evidenced by prestigious book awards like the National Book Critics Circle Award for *The Woman Warrior* (1976) and the American Book Award for *China Men* (1980), as well as by being the recipient of NEA and Guggenheim fellowships (see Li; and Wong).

The institutionalized readings of *The Woman Warrior* have taken shape with the steady increase of publications since this work first appeared. Selections from *The Woman Warrior* (most often excerpts from "No Name Woman") appear with regularity in the leading anthologies of American literature and college readers. At least 88 critical essays on *The Woman Warrior* have appeared in the MLA bibliography since 1982, and the Modern Language Association recently published a guide to teaching *The Woman Warrior* as part of its "Approaches to Teaching World Literature" series (see Lim), placing Kingston in the company of such canonical figures as Chaucer, Shakespeare, Melville, and Whitman.

Unlike Hurston and Silko, then, Kingston garnered almost contemporaneous popular and academic recognition within a relatively short period of time. Perhaps this unusual reception results from *The Woman Warrior*'s ability to fulfill the expectations, requirements, and desires of both the larger public market and a more specialized critical industry of literary studies. Kingston's text appeared at a time when the United States was engaged in discussions about women's rights and "minority" rights. The literary canon was under fire for its narrow view of "American literature," and the MLA's Commission on the Language and Literatures of America (which brought out the 1983 volume on teaching Native American literature) actively sought to foster institutional recognition of minority literatures.

Market forces and a receptive audience, whether public or academic, play an important role in the institutionalization of a reading, particularly when that reading fulfills the audience's expectations of the text. The public reception of *The Woman Warrior* was filled with desire for the exotic and the oriental as exemplified by Jane Kramer's *New York Times* review:

> Chinese-Americans must find it even more bizarre that we have dismissed the mystery of China for the mystique of the Chinese revolution. Ten years ago they bewildered us and we ignored them. Now we peer at them in their American Chinatowns, desperate to discover if they belong to Peking or Taiwan—as if the answer to that one question were all we needed to complete our understanding. Ten years ago they were the clichés of immigrant America. They were the Chinese waiter, the Chinese laundryman. Now they are part of our new rhetoric, and they are still anonymous. (1)

Kramer's review describes an enthusiasm for things Chinese (during this time of the opening up of the People's Republic of China) that echoes with consumer desire for cultural products. Kramer does make the distinction between Chinese and "Chinese-Americans" (hyphenated as if to suggest a duality), but she has constructed a particular type of Chinese American. She has in mind the Chinese immigrant who has only recently found a life in America, ignoring the fact that five or six generations of Chinese had already been living in America, had been citizens for some time, and had not been confined by the imagined boundaries of Chinatowns. Thus, Kingston and her book are reduced to representing things Chinese, thereby fulfilling the expectations of a public looking for the exotic and oriental. The public was eager to institutionalize Kingston and *The Woman Warrior* because, in many ways, it fed their expectations and confirmed their beliefs about this "foreign" culture which has remained mysterious even on America's own shores.

The *New York Times* was not alone in producing such a review (similar reviews appeared in mainstream national publications like *Time* and *Newsweek*). Kingston herself believed that two-thirds of the reviews of *The Woman Warrior* were in some way praising the stereotypes that she aimed to bring into question, remarking "What I did not foresee was the critics measuring the book and me against the stereotype of the exotic, inscrutable, mysterious oriental" ("Cultural" 55). Kingston also recognized early on that there would be "institutionalized" readings of her text: "The women's lib angle and the Third World angle, the *Roots* angle" ("Cultural" 55). However, what she did not count on was being located outside of America, or perhaps, inside but not *of* America. The production or reproduction of the oriental in these reviews acts in many ways to maintain a certain cultural hegemony. On the one hand, America enthusiastically and genuinely expresses its interest in Chinese culture; on the other hand, by constructing an essentialist Chinese culture, these reviews ignore the existence of something called "Chinese American," the production of a "new" culture within the intersections of the Chinese and the American. The public is willing to accept only limited representation of a "minority," and what it does accept must fit the cultural representations that have already been assigned to it.

Perhaps even more disturbing is the reduction of a diverse culture to the writings of a single person. Kingston herself is frustrated when she is expected to be the single representative of her race and is more disturbed when she hears non-Chinese people saying to a Chinese person, "Well now I know about you because I have read Maxine Hong Kingston's books" (Islas 11). Kingston sees this problem only being addressed with the emergence of more Chinese American writers, following the example of African American writers who have, in her eyes, "already surmounted the problem" (Islas 11). Kingston's acknowledgment of African American writers and her hope for Chinese American writers echo June Jordan's assertion that there can be diverse interests and multiple projects in a community. Just as Hurston was criticized early on by Richard Wright and others for pandering to whites, Kingston has been charged by writers like Frank Chin with playing to a "white" audience (and marketplace) and perpetuating stereotypes. Chin has been right to the extent that the public has accepted a certain construction of Kingston and Chinese America while ignoring the possibility of a diverse community. But Kingston's huge presence has contributed to the production of new Asian American literature which, in turn, creates a more "literate" audience, more critical readers, and more readings.

While the public reception of *The Woman Warrior* has been problematic, the equally problematic academic reception has been generative for the relatively young field of Asian American literary studies. Despite the criticism by Chin that she does not represent "real" Asian American art, Kingston in many ways becomes the lone canonical figure to at least provide the field some force with which to establish itself in literary studies. However, there is also a tension between Asian American literary studies and the larger institution of the academy. Asian American literary studies often finds itself offering correctives and challenging oriental and exotic representations that make their way into the curriculum under the guise of cultural pluralism. Just as the reviewers fed a public market hungry for a text like *The Woman Warrior*, so academic critics who create readings of Kingston feed a critical industry that allows and supports their existence. The construction and institutionalization of readings is in many ways not a gatekeeping function but one of survival as material must be recovered or produced in order to maintain an economy of literary criticism and instruction. Thus, while there is much debate about the ethics involved in interpretation (especially when considering "marginal" writers), it often comes down to material interests, cultural capital, and the sustaining of a critical industry.

The appearance of a study guide, then, might suggest that Asian American literature has found a place in the academy. The MLA guide, *Approaches to Teaching Kingston's* The Woman Warrior, suggests that Kingston's text can be used in a variety of disciplines: English and American literature, American studies, ethnic studies, women's studies. However, each of these disciplines has different interests and in pursuing them will often emphasize aspects of the text to the point where there can be only a single reading, a single meaning in the book. And while Kingston recognized that her book would be read from certain "angles," the reification of the text in the academy concerns her:

> Young women on campuses carry *The Norton Anthology of Literature by Women* like a talisman, like a shield. Just so, they carry *The Woman Warrior;* they call it "the book." "We're studying the book in class." "Will you discuss the book with us?" I don't like all this overpraising of my daughter and rudeness toward my sons—especially since my writing has gotten better—wiser and more skillful—as I've gone along. ("Personal" 24)

In some ways the production of a study guide only acts to further reify the text. While its purpose is to aid in the instruction of material that may be unfamiliar, there is a danger that the guide itself will act in the reproduction of racist representations as those who use it may not consider fully the range of readings not included. The guide can offer diverse readings of "the book," but no matter what disclaimer is made (perhaps even by Kingston), there will be a desire to see the guide itself as a "talisman," as a "shield," as the authoritative and authenticating text.

The guide is divided into two parts. Part One is concerned with materials, discussing the history of the actual text, providing suggestions for critical and background studies, and other work which can aid in the classroom. Part Two is called "Approaches" and is divided into three sections: "Cultural and Historical Contexts," "Pedagogical Contexts," and "Critical Contexts: Genre, Themes, Form." While the entire section provides approaches to teaching *The Woman Warrior*, the division into three smaller sections clearly defines particular readings. The section on "Cultural and Historical Contexts" is concerned primarily with addressing the cultural issues in the text, acting to counter the "misreadings" that so often accompany it. The section "Critical Contexts" discusses textual and theoretical features, emphasizing the aesthetic and rhetoric of the text rather than reading it as strict ethnographic study.

However, the section on "Pedagogical Contexts" is perhaps the most revealing example of institutionalized reading as we see how the text is introduced and received in particular classroom situations. For example, the essay by Judith Melton, "*The Woman Warrior* in the Women's Studies Classroom," reduces the discussion to issues of Chinese patriarchy and the struggle for female identity in a bicultural environment. The context of a women's studies class makes this understandably the focus, but this can also be harmful if such a focus acts only to reinforce stereotypes of Chinese culture and emphasize certain cruel practices, such as footbinding, as being an essential Chinese characteristic. Another essay, Paul McBride's "*The Woman Warrior* in the History Classroom, " reads the text as "microhistory," as though it is the personal experience of Kingston which becomes a representative experience for Chinese American women. Although Kingston tells her own individual story, McBride sees Kingston's text as "usher[ing] us into the otherwise inaccessible domain where micro[-] and macrohistory met, where the individual understands and reacts to the relentless forces of history" (98). In other words, her experience can be translated into the experiences of others in a larger historical context.

While Melton and McBride are only offering two readings in a guide offering a variety of readings, their inclusion in a section called "Pedagogical Contexts" warrants some concern. First, their presence suggests that they present exemplary pedagogical strategies for the teaching of the text. But second, and reflective of the hegemonic force of American culture, these readings signal a still pervasive reduction of things oriental. Granted, the disciplines Melton and McBride are reading for (women's studies and history) have different interests than literary studies or ethnic studies, but they allow their desire to fulfill particular expectations which preclude them from a more critical engagement with the larger cultural text that accompanies *The Woman Warrior*. As a result, readings of *The Woman Warrior*, both orientalist and corrective, have been institutionalized. The irony is, of course, that without this institutionalization, without the critical debate fueled by such readings, a critical industry of literary studies and a public market would both cease to exist.

As this examination of institutionalized readings of *Their Eyes, Ceremony*, and *The Woman Warrior* indicates, many forces and circumstances interact to produce readings, and these readings continually shift and change. While academics play an important part in institutionalizing readings, they do not operate unilaterally. As the cases of *Their Eyes* and *The Woman Warrior* show, the conventions and economics of publishing, along with the interplay of public and academic readings, contribute to the way texts are read. As the instance of *Ceremony* suggests, absence of the public-academic dialogue may contribute to a decrease in readings of all sorts. John Rodden asserts that we are all "institutional readers" because the reading process does not occur in a vacuum: "our responses to literature, as to everything else, are influenced by our historical-institutional affiliations" (70). This does not mean that all readers enjoy equal status or that there is no conflict among classes of readers. Much of the current hostility expressed by the public press toward the academy can be seen as a reaction to professors who construct themselves as professional readers. As Michael Bérubé observes, the general public sees the notion of a professional class of "readers" as suspicious because it is a "disenfranchisement of their rights as readers of English" (22). Lawrence

Levine, Shelley Rubin, Karen Halttunen, and other students of American culture have shown that anxiety frequently energizes the (middlebrow) public's attention to readings institutionalized by the academy, but that hostility often underlies that anxiety. Furthermore, even though it remains largely unacknowledged and untheorized, anxiety also shapes academics. A clear line of anxiety runs from graduate school orals through pretenure evaluations to professorial concerns about the status of the critical industry, creating a link between what Jonathan Freedman calls "those unlikely twins, the middlebrow and the academic" (21). Recognizing, implicitly or explicitly, their similarity to, even as they declare their difference from, the middle-brow public, academics struggle to create viable identities for themselves. Their authority as professional readers comes into question when the public resists or undercuts their declarations. As the cases of Hurston and Kingston demonstrate, institutionalized readings do not always emerge in the heights of the academy to be handed on to a passive but receptive public. Our investigation shows that the institutionalization of readings frequently involves complex transactions between public and academic constituencies, transactions in which the role of the public (middlebrow) reader cannot be described as trivial.

The complex interactions between public and academic spheres become even more complicated with texts marked by racial and gender marginality. In considering each writer, we have noted a theme of construction and contestation of identities. Though the public and academy often seem posed against each other, they do seem to share a project of constructing writers to fulfill the expectations and desires that they have already placed upon them. We see in Hurston, Silko, and Kingston writers who have constructed identities in their works, either "fictional" or personal, but in many ways unique and not representative of whatever group claims them as representative. An anxiety drives both the middlebrow public and the academic when they confront subjects that are not easily classified and understandable until they construct them as such and can then incorporate them into their own projects. Institutionalization, then, becomes a process of transforming complex identities into texts that can be processed and disseminated more easily into larger public and academic spheres.

These interactions between public and academic spheres bear political implications. Just as we cannot afford to ignore the concerns of the public whom we educate and who, in turn, supports the critical industry upon which our very livelihoods depend, so we cannot overlook the complicated dialogues between public and academic readings that help constitute the institutionalized readings we (re)produce in our classrooms. Rather than presuming that our cultural authority confers un-limited power, we would do well to consider how and where the power signified by institutionalized readings circulates. Our students can of-fer help in this consideration. Occupying as they do a liminal position between public and academic spheres, they simultaneously enrich our understanding of the public worlds from which they arrive as they be-come (in varying degrees) part of the academy.

Works Cited

Allen, Paula Gunn. "Special Problems in Teaching Leslie Marmon Silko's *Ceremony*." American Indian Quarterly 14 (Fall 1990): 379–86.

———, ed. *Studies in American Indian Literature: Critical Essays and Course Designs*. New York: MLA, 1983.

Bérubé, Michael. *Marginal Forces/Cultural Centers: Tolson, Pynchon, and the Politics of the Canon*. Ithaca: Cornell UP, 1992.

Byrd, James W. "Zora Neale Hurston: A Novel Folklorist." *Tennessee Folklore Society Bulletin* 19 (December 1955): 103–7.

Chin, Frank et al. eds. *Aiiieeeee! An Anthology of Asian-American Writers*. Washington, D.C.: Harvard UP, 1974.

Cousineau, Diane. "Leslie Silko's *Ceremony*: The Spiderweb as Text." *Revue Française d'Etudes Américaines* 15.43 (February 1990): 19–31.

Douglas, Mary. *How Institutions Think*. Syracuse: Syracuse UP, 1986.

Ellison, Ralph. "Recent Fiction" *New Masses* 3 (July 1941): 22–26.

Fisher, Philip. *Hard Facts: Setting and Form in the American Novel*. New York: Oxford UP, 1985.

Freedman, Jonathan. "Beyond the Usual Suspects: Theorizing the Middlebrow." Colloquium Paper, University of Michigan. April 1993.

Garcia, Alesia. "Politics and Indigenous Theory in Leslie Marmon Silko's 'Yellow Woman' and Sandra Cisnero's 'Woman Hollering Creek.'" Paper, MLA Convention. 28 December 1992.

Gates, Henry Louis, Jr. Afterword to *Their Eyes Were Watching God: A Novel*, by Zora Neale Hurston. New York: Harper, 1990.

Giles, James R. "The Significance of Time in Zora Neale Hurston's *Their Eyes Were Watching God*." *Negro American Literature Forum* 6 (Summer 1972): 52–53, 60.

Gloster, Hugh M. "Zora Neale Hurston: Novelist and Folklorist." *Phylon* 4 (1943): 153–59.

Gross, Konrad. "Survival of Orality in Literate Culture: Leslie Silko's Novel *Ceremony*." *Modes of Narrative: Approaches to American, Canadian, and British Fiction: Presented to Helmut Bonheim*. Ed. Reingard M. Nischik and Barbara Korte. Wurzburg: Konigshausen & Neumann, 1990. 88–99.

Halttunen, Karen. *Confidence Men and Painted Women: A Study of Middle-Class Culture In America, 1830–1870*. New Haven: Yale UP, 1982.

Harris, Trudier. "Zora Neale Hurston, Folklorist." Paper, MLA Convention. December 1975.

Helmick, Evelyn T. "Zora Neale Hurston." *The Carrell* 2 (June–December 1970): 1–19.

Hemenway, Robert E. "Discoveries in the Hurston Biography." Paper, MLA Convention. December 1975.

———. *Zora Neale Hurston: A Literacy Biography.* Urbana: U of Illinois P, 1977.

Hurston, Zora Neale. *Mules and Men.* Philadelphia: Lippincott, 1935.

———. *Their Eyes Were Watching God: A Novel.* Philadelphia: Lippincott, 1937.

Islas, Arturo. Interview with Maxine Hong Kingston. *Women Writers of the West Coast: Speaking of Their Lives and Careers.* Ed. Marilyn Yalom. Santa Barbara, CA: Capra, 1983. 11–19.

Jackson, Blyden. "Some Negroes in the Land of Goshen." *Tennessee Folklore Society Bulletin* 21 (1955): 37–41.

Jacobs, Barbara. "New Books from Franklin Watts." *Booklist* 73 (Spring 1977): 1147.

Johnson, Barbara. "Metaphor, Metonymy, and Voice in *Their Eyes.*" Black Literature and Literary Theory. Ed. Henry Louis Gates, Jr. New York: Methuen, 1984. 205–21.

Jordan, June. "On Richard Wright and Zora Neale Hurston: Notes toward a Balancing of Love and Hatred." *Black World* 23 (August 1974): 4–8.

Kingston, Maxine Hong. *China Men.* New York: Knopf, 1980.

———. "Cultural Mis-readings by American Reviewers." *Asian and Western Writers in Dialogue: New Critical Identities.* Ed. Guy Amirthanayagam. London: Macmillan, 1982. 55–65.

———. "Personal Statement." *Approaches to Teaching Kingston's The Woman Warrior.* Ed. Shirley Geok-lin Lim. New York: MLA, 1991. 23–25.

———. *The Woman Warrior: Memoirs of a Girlhood among Ghosts.* New York: Knopf, 1976.

Review of *Ceremony,* by Leslie Marmon Silko. *Kirkus Reviews* 45 (January 1977): 18.

Review of *Ceremony,* by Leslie Marmon Silko. Choice 14 (July / August 1977): 684.

Kramer, Jane. "On Being Chinese in China and America." *New York Times Book Review* 7 Nov. 1976: 1, 18.

Levine, Lawrence W. *Highbrow/Lowbrow: The Emergence of Cultural Hierarchy in America.* Cambridge, MA: Harvard UP, 1988.

Li, David Leiwei. "The Naming of a Chinese American 'I': Cross-Cultural Sign / ifications in *The Woman Warrior.*" *Criticism* 30.4 (Fall 1988): 497–515.

Lim, Shirley Geok-lin, ed. *Approaches to Teaching Kingston's The Woman Warrior.* New York: MLA, 1991.

Locke, Alain. "Jingo, Counter-Jingo and Us." *Opportunity Journal of Negro Life* 16.1 (January 1938): 8–11, 27.

McBride, Paul W. "*The Woman Warrior* in the History Classroom." *Approaches to Teaching Kingston's* The Woman Warrior. Ed. Shirley Geok-lin Lim. New York: MLA, 1991. 93–100.

Meese, Elizabeth. "Orality and Textuality in Zora Neale Hurston's *Their Eyes.*" *Crossing the Double Cross: The Practice of Feminist Criticism.* Ed. Elizabeth Meese. Chapel Hill: U of North Carolina P, 1986.

Melton, Judith M. "*The Woman Warrior* in the Women's Studies Classroom." *Approaches to Teaching Kingston's The Woman Warrior.* Ed. Shirley Geok-lin Lim. New York: MLA, 1991. 74–79.

Momaday, N. Scott. *House Made of Dawn.* New York: Harper, 1968.

Nelson, Robert M. "Place and Vision: The Function of Landscape in *Ceremony.*" *Journal of the Southwest* 30.3 (Autumn 1988): 281–316.

Rayson, Anne. "The Novels of Zora Neale Hurston." *Studies in Black Literature* 5 (Winter 1974): 1–10.

Rodden, John. *The Politics of Literary Reputation: The Making and Claiming of "St. George" Orwell.* New York: Oxford UP, 1989.

Ronnow, Gretchen. "Tayo, Death, and Desire: A Lacanian Reading of *Ceremony.*" In *Narrative Chance: Postmodern Discourse on Native American Literatures.* Ed. Gerald Vizenor. Albuquerque: U of New Mexico P, 1989. 69–89.

Rubin, Joan Shelley. *The Making of Middlebrow Culture.* Chapel Hill: U of North Carolina P, 1992.

Silko, Leslie Marmon. *Almanac of the Dead: A Novel.* New York: Simon, 1991.

———. *Ceremony.* New York: Viking, 1977.

Smith, Barbara. "The Fiction of Zora Neale Hurston." Paper, MLA Convention. December 1975.

Swan, Edith. "Healing via the Sunwise Cycle in Silko's *Ceremony.*" *The American Indian Quarterly: Journal of American Indian Studies* 12.4 (Fall 1988): 313–28.

Turner, Darwin T. *In a Minor Chord: Three Afro-American Writers and Their Search for Identity.* Carbondale: Southern Illinois UP, 1971.

Walker, Alice. "In Search of Zora Neale Hurston." *Ms* (March 1975): 74–79, 85–89.

Washington, Mary Helen. "The Black Woman's Search for Identity: Zora Neale Hurston's Work." *Black World* 10 (1972): 68–75.

———. Foreword to *Their Eyes Were Watching God: A Novel,* by Zora Neale Hurston. New York: Harper, 1990.

Williams, Sherley Anne. Foreword to *Their Eyes Were Watching God: A Novel,* by Zora Neale Hurston. Urbana: U of Illinois P, 1978.

Wong, Sau-ling Cynthia. "Autobiography as Guided Chinatown Tour? Maxine Hong Kingston's *The Woman Warrior* and the Chinese American Autobiographical Controversy." *Multicultural Autobiography: American Lives.* Ed. James Robert Payne. Knoxville: U of Tennessee P, 1992. 248–79.

Wright, Richard. "Between Laughter and Tears." *New Masses* 25 (October 5, 1937): 22, 25.

11 A Flock of Cultures— A Trivial Proposal

Robert Scholes
Brown University

French printer's first attempt to set Mr. Williams' "The Great American Novel." 3 Mountains Press.

The pigs were ranged on one side, the dogs on another, and then from a third a flock of cultures crept up from time to time. (Anderson et al. 50)

It is tempting to read the French printer's creative typography as an allegory of contemporary education: pigs on the right, dogs on the left, and a flock of cultures timidly trying to find a place among them. Are all those creatures perhaps feeding on the rotting carcass of Western Civilization? Other interpretations may well occur to you. Feel free— this is not a classic text; it lacks authority and intentionality. My own reading of it, however, reminds me of what a contested field education is today, how polarized and politicized it has become, how difficult it is to speak reasonably and effectively about a coherent core of study for college students. Nevertheless, this is just what I propose to undertake. Specifically, I hope to explain just why such concepts as "Great Books" and "Western Civ" cannot really solve the problem of our "flock of cultures," and then I shall go on to make a "trivial proposal" for a different core of humanistic study for college students. The arrogance of such a gesture is all too apparent. In my own defense I can only say that it is accompanied by a comparable amount of humility. I do not expect to solve our problems here, only to advance our discussion of them beyond the point of mutual accusations and recriminations.

Our problem as I see it—that is, the problem of college instruction in general and any humanistic core for such studies in particular—can be

This essay originally appeared in *College English* 53.7 (November 1991): 759–72. Used with permission.

put in the form of two questions. It is my hope that those concerned about education, whether they are on the "Right" or the "Left," might agree that it is reasonable to see our problems in this manner. One question is how we can put students in touch with a usable cultural past. The other is how we can help students attain an active relationship with their cultural present. These two questions are intimately related, of course. We cannot answer one without taking a position on the other. Therefore, I shall try to consider them both, though my "trivial" proposal is concerned mainly with the second. To approach the matter of usable cultural past, I shall have to begin with questions of canonicity. This may at first seem like just another assault on "Western Civ" and the "Great Books," but I ask for your patience. This is a different kind of critique, I believe, and it will have a different outcome than is usual. To begin with, however, we will need to have a clear understanding of the cultural role of canons.

Without going into a full etymological investigation (which I have undertaken elsewhere), let me note briefly that our words *cane, canon,* and *cannon* are derived from the same Greek root, which had a primary reference to a type of reed or cane—and that most of their variations in meaning can be seen as metaphorical or metonymical extensions of the properties and uses of the reed and the palm. It seems reasonable to speculate that the straight and segmented form of certain canes led to their use in making lines and measurements. The first measuring sticks or rulers were probably canes. Certainly the meanings associated with the word *canon* in its Greek forms show clearly enough how measurement extends to control, criticism, and even taxation. Our English word *ruler,* though not connected etymologically with *cane* or *canon,* will serve to illustrate how measurement and governing always seem to go together, since the word means both measuring stick and one who governs.

The tubular inner shape of canes has also been extended to cover all sorts of similar objects, as the meanings of the French and Latin word *canon* clearly demonstrate. Our English restriction of the spelling *cannon* (with two n's) to distinguish the guns from other sorts of canons is a very recent development in the history of a very old world. These are different spellings only, not different words. Guns and ruling are associated in more ways than one. The English, of course, seem particularly responsible for institutionalizing the cane as the instrument for beating docility into subject peoples and Greek into schoolboys. The *OED* illustrates the use of *cane* as a verb with a quotation from a Victorian newspaper: "I had a little Greek caned into me." Many a native in India had Shakespeare as well as other canonical texts caned into him by the curricular arm of the British Raj. The Empire was based on its cannon, canon, and canes—to a startling degree.

The use of the word *canon* to mean a body of sacred texts comes to us from Latin rather than Greek, and specifically from the Latin of the Roman Church, where it is an extension of the notion of a *canon* as rule or law. The most common extension of this sense of the word in literary studies has until very recently been in reference to the works written by a single author. In the bibliographies of *PMLA*, articles with the word *canon* in their titles most frequently have used the word in just this sense. We speak of the Shakespeare canon or the Defoe canon, meaning no more than the works really written by these authors as opposed to those that might be erroneously attributed to them. Inevitably, however, some of the religious connotations of canonicity flow into this secular use. Where there is a canon, there is both power and sanctity. Above all, however, there is discipline. A textual canon is always a disciplinary function. A canon is in every sense a phallocratic object.

First the law, then the sacred text. As religious practices and beliefs are institutionalized in a church, the canonical texts are separated from the apocrypha, or the angelic from the satanic verses, as matters are put in the Islamic canon. Canonical texts are held to be fully authorized, in the sense of ultimately attributable to God. They are, therefore, not only sacred but authoritative, truthful. What is excluded from the religious canon turns into mere literature—a principle that we should note, for it says much about literature as a discipline, or as a field of study that, for good or ill, is not quite disciplined. Perhaps I should at this point make my own position clearer. I have no case to make against either canons or disciplines. They are the essentials of academic life, and I am an academician. I only want to emphasize that canons and disciplines need one another. They go together. And discipline, like canon, is a word that scarcely conceals its potential for abuses of power. We need disciplines in order to think productively. We also need to challenge them in order to think creatively.

The tightening of thought that constitutes a discipline inevitably is accompanied by a tightening of control over some canon of texts or methods. For example, as Plato tried to move Greek thought closer to monotheism, he found it necessary to turn Homer into an apocryphal text, a text that tells lies about God. It is clear that Plato and Socrates admired Homer and knew the Homeric texts the way some Christians know their Bible, but Homer was exposed as literature rather than scripture in Plato's *Republic*—and suffered the consequences. Plato, of course, did not share our concept of literature, which is itself a product of the consolidation of literary study as a branch of aesthetics in the late eighteenth and nineteenth centuries. What his example illustrates is that the tendency to canonize and apocryphize is a feature of monotheistic or totalizing forms of thought. In particular, as disciplines constitute themselves, they institutionalize discourses, regulating not only admission to canonicity but also the right to produce texts with authority, the right to interpret, and, in this manner, they often control the permitted kinds of interpretation as well. Not only is this a feature of churches as institutions, it is also a feature of sciences and other belief systems that emerge out of monotheistic religious practice. Excessive rigidity, however, is dangerous for disciplines and institutions, which often forget the roots of canonicity are in a flexible plant.

While we are thinking of the emergence of canons and disciplines, we should remember that sciences as well as religions are subject to this pattern of development. We sometimes forget that our empirical sciences emerged dialectically out of Thomistic Christianity, substituting authorized observation of nature for authorized interpretation of scripture, but requiring the same assumption of a universe governed by a single set of rules. These sciences ultimately came to challenge certain religious dogmas, of course, but they did so by constituting themselves around a discourse of authority, as Kuhn and Foucault have helped us to understand. The attempts by practitioners of "creation science" to have their views recognized as scientific have so far foundered on this very dialectical rock. Marxism, too, which in its early days repeatedly claimed the status of a science, has never justified those claims and now hovers between religion and literature. In the physical and biological sciences, of course, there is little reverence for texts as such. These are disciplines that center themselves around a method or canon of rules rather than a canon of sacred texts.

We can distinguish science and religion, then, as institutions that share a need for authoritative control of textuality, but differ importantly over whether this authority resides in a canon of methods or a canon of texts. This formal study of literature as a branch of the arts emerges only after the rise of science has demonstrated the way a discipline can coalesce around certain carefully defined objects and methods of study. The study of literature as discipline (as opposed to the study of Greek and Latin grammar and a mixed bag of classical texts) began with English works like Lord Kames's *Elements of Criticism* but was really consolidated by the German Romantics in texts like Schiller's letters *On the Aesthetic Education of Man*, Schelling's *Philosophy of Art* (especially the last section on "The Verbal Arts"), and the section on poetry that closes Hegel's *Lectures on Fine Art*. In these texts, and in their less systematic English counterparts by Coleridge, Shelley, and others, the notion of literature as a branch of the fine arts, characterized by "Imagination"—the absolutely critical word—became sufficiently clear and stable to support a field of study.

Literary study, however, has never quite defined its objects as neatly as the sciences have defined theirs. It has hovered between the forms of canonicity proper to science and those proper to religion, sometimes regarding its objects of study as specimens, but more often giving them the status of quasi-religious texts, not grounded in the Word of God exactly, but in the Imagination, which, as Coleridge so explicitly argues, is analogous to and partakes of the creativity of God the Creator. In making this move, the Romantics and followers like Arnold were actually reversing the Platonic process, putting Literature at the center of culture by claiming that Imagination enabled literary Artists to shape in language or plastic matter versions of Absolute Truth. This Romantic move also resulted in the establishment of canons oriented to a single language and culture, because such canons were felt to embody the Spirit of a particular nation or people. In this manner, English, or French, or German literature could be seen as a body of material that needed sorting out into canonical and noncanonical texts; those that embodied the proper Spirit and those that did not. This sorting, and the exegesis of the chosen texts, accordingly became the projects of a quasi-priestly caste, gradually organized around their national literary canons into academic disciplines. Our present English departments are, among other things, the inheritors of a discipline partly organized by this cultural history. They are also partly organized by an older tradition of rhetorical study, which they acquired when they sublated the rhetoric departments in many American universities about a century ago. Rhetoric has been organized around a canon of methods, with texts used merely as examples. English literature organized itself around a canon of texts, relegating the methods of rhetoric to a minor role. The stir and struggle we are presently experiencing may indicate that this traditional hierarchy is beginning to become unstable.

In drawing out the connections between canons and forms of institutionalized power, I may have seemed to be headed toward some quasi-Foucauldian critique of power itself, along with a plea for the elimination of all canons. Nothing could be further from my intent, however, since I am persuaded that the connection between institutions and canons is inevitable. Furthermore, our awareness of the existence of canons and our understanding of the process by which they are maintained and altered makes it possible for us to influence canons through the institutions that support them and to change the institutions through their canons. What I am opposed to is the pretense that there may be some cosmic canon that transcends all institutions because it is based on an unexaminable and unchallengeable Absolute. This, I contend, is the case with notions like "Great Books" and "Western Civ," in which a flock of cultures march under the banner of a canonical eagle. I also want to suggest that some shifting between canons of text and canons of methods has been a regular part of cultural history, so that we should regard it as a normal feature of our lives. I want to suggest that we are at a point in cultural and textual studies where a realignment between these two types of canonicity may be pedagogically sound and helpful. At this moment, however, my main point is that there has never been a canon of "Great Books."

There is no canon of "Great Books," in my view, because there is no intellectual core to the notion of "Great Books" in the first place. Literary study, though far from being a quantifying science, obtained a degree of coherence by organizing itself around Romantic concepts of Art, Imagination, and Spirit. Other textual studies organize themselves by time, by genre, or by other systems of connection among their objects, just as biology has organized itself around the concept of life, the cell, and so on. But such notions as those of "Great Books" and "Western Civ" have no disciplinary focus, and hence, no academic core. There is, just to consider the most basic matters, absolutely no notion of bookish Greatness that has any coherence whatsoever. Allan Bloom would tell us, I suppose, that all the Great Books exhibit something called Greatness of Soul, but the concept of Great Souls is just as vague—in both adjective and noun—as what it is supposed to define. Nor is the notion of Western Civilization much of an improvement. There can be no notion of textual greatness, I am arguing, apart from a set of texts organized by a discipline. Of course, there have been great philosophers—but only since philosophy has been a discipline could we perceive them as such. Nor is their "greatness" of the same kind as that of Mozart, Shakespeare, or Tintoretto. All these are "great" only in contexts, partly narrative ones, that allow them to be perceived as such.

Western Civ, I maintain, lacks the coherence for pedagogically sound instruction. Such coherence as it might have, I would add, comes from a philosophy that even its adherents no longer claim to accept. One of the things we need to remember when considering concepts such as "Western Civ" is that they originated in the Eurocentric thinking of German philosophers. The greatest of these, of course, was Hegel, who systematized the notion of cultural progress from East to West in ways that still haunt most of our thinking on these subjects:

> The History of the World travels from East to West, for Europe is
> absolutely the end of History, Asia the beginning. . . . [A]lthough the
> earth forms a sphere, History forms no circle around it, but has on
> the contrary a determinate East viz., Asia. Here rises the outward
> physical sun, and in the West it sinks down; here consentaneously
> rises the sun of self-consciousness, which diffuses a nobler brilliance.
> The History of the World is the *discipline* [emphasis added] of the
> uncontrolled natural will, bringing it into obedience to a Universal
> principle and conferring subjective freedom. The East knew and to
> the present day knows only that *One* is Free: the Greek and Roman
> world, that *some* are free: the German World knows that *All* are free.
> (*Philosophy of History* 103–4)

What Hegel meant by the German world, in this instance, was Europe
after the fall of Rome, a Europe that had been overrun by Germanic tribes
moving from east to west: the Angles, the Saxons, the Franks, the Goths,
the Lombards. He also meant a Europe in which ultimately Protestant-
ism would come to elevate the materialism of the Roman Catholic
Church to a more spiritual level, finally realizing Christ's message that
every human soul is free and worthy of development. He describes this
process, in a memorable passage, as subjecting Christianity to "the terrible discipline of culture":

> Secularity appears now [he was writing of the sixteenth century] as
> gaining a consciousness of its intrinsic worth—becomes aware of its
> having a value of its own in the morality, rectitude, probity and
> activity of man. The consciousness of independent validity is
> aroused through the restoration of Christian freedom. The Christian
> principle now passed through the terrible discipline of culture, and
> it first attains truth and reality through the Reformation. This third
> period of the German World extends from the Reformation to our
> own times. (334)

I am introducing Hegel into this discussion of Western Civ and Great
Books for a number of reasons, which I must now try to explain and
clarify. As I have already partly indicated, I believe that our tendency to
speak in terms of Western Civ is derived from the degeneration of
Hegelian ideas into the repertory of "common sense." I call this degeneration because, in this passage from systematic thought to folk wisdom,
Hegel's ideas have been separated from the rationale that drove them.
By putting them back in their Hegelian context, I hope to show both what
they have lost in this transition and how we shall have to adapt and
modify them to make them useful again for curricular purposes. Let me
begin this complex process by pointing out that for Hegel the idea of
studying the West without the East would be ludicrous. The basic principle involved here is Hegel's view of history as a dialectical process, in
which the new always results from the negation and sublation of the old,

in which certain elements of the old are retained within the new synthesis. By seeing the West as the dialectical heir to the East, Hegel incorporates understanding of the East as a necessary part of the study of Germanic (or Western) culture. Here is a typical passage in which he specifies the sort of exchange involved in this process:

> In the struggle with the Saracens [the Crusades], European valor had idealized itself to a fair and noble chivalry. Science and knowledge, especially that of philosophy came from the Arabs into the West. A noble poetry and free imagination were kindled among the Germans by the East—a fact which directed Goethe's attention to the Orient and occasioned the composition of a string of lyric pearls, in his "Divan," which in warmth and felicity of fancy cannot be surpassed. But the East itself, when by degrees enthusiasm had vanished, sank into the grossest vice. (360)

The East had its time of spiritual flourishing, and sank, as every culture in history is doomed to do, in Hegel's view, until history comes to an end—an end he hoped and believed was being attained in his own time. The fact that history did not end in his time, and that it has taken some surprising turns since then, constitutes part of our problem in putting Hegelian ideas to work today. In terms of Western Civ, however, there are two other aspects of Hegel's thought that we should remember. In recognizing the enduring achievements of the great literary figures of the past, Hegel also insisted on their pastness. In this view the continually increasing distance of the literary past from the present makes the need for a properly modern literature more acute:

> No Homer, Sophocles, etc., no Dante, Ariosto, or Shakespeare can appear in our day; what was so magnificently sung, what was so freely expressed, has been expressed: these are materials, ways of looking at them and treating them which have been sung once and for all. Only the present is fresh, the rest is paler and paler. (*Aesthetics* 605)

For Hegel the whole of "Western Civ," the "discipline" of Western culture, is almost unbearable to contemplate. The only thing that redeems this spectacle is the sense that it has a purpose, that it is progressive, because it is the history of Spirit realizing itself through the rise of human consciousness. But we need to catch some echo of his own voice on this matter:

> Without rhetorical exaggeration, a simply truthful combination of the miseries that have overwhelmed the noblest of nations and polities, and the finest exemplars of private virtue—forms a picture of most fearful aspect, and excites emotions of the profoundest and most hopeless sadness, counterbalanced by no consolatory result. We endure in beholding it a mental torture, allowing no defence or

escape but the consideration that what has happened could not be otherwise: that it is a fatality which no intervention could alter. And at least we draw back from the intolerable disgust with which these sorrowful reflections threaten us, into the more agreeable environment of our individual life—the Present formed by our private aims and interests. In short we retreat into the selfishness that stands on the quiet shore, and thence enjoy in safety the distant spectacle of "wrecks confusedly hurled." But even regarding History as the slaughter-bench at which the happiness of peoples, the wisdom of States, and the virtue of individuals has been victimized—the question involuntarily arises—to what principle, to what final aim these enormous sacrifices have been offered. (*Philosophy of History* 21)

Without that final aim, which in Hegel's case is a theological one—that of the Absolute realizing itself through humanity's increasing understanding of the world and the role of the Spirit in it—the spectacle of Western Civ is quite simply unbearable. What is wrong with our present adaptations of this notion of Western Civ, I am arguing, is that, on the one hand, they do not acknowledge the horror of the spectacle but present it as a series of glorious achievements, and on the other hand, that they finesse the question of history and of historicism in particular. The past two centuries of historical events have certainly demonstrated that history did not end with Hegel. And surely, philosophical thought during those years has combined with political and social events to make it virtually impossible for us to sustain a Hegelian belief in the direction of history by a providential Absolute.

It will be useful in this context to compare Hegel's view of cultural history as a "slaughter-bench," redeemed only by the progressive domination of Spirit over matter, with Walter Benjamin's view of the same terrain, which is consciously set against the historicism and idealism of Hegel's followers. Benjamin asks "with whom the adherents of historicism actually empathize":

> The answer is inevitable: with the victor. And all rulers are the heirs of those who conquered before them. Hence, empathy with the victor invariably benefits the rulers. Historical materialists know what that means. Whoever has emerged victorious participates to this day in the triumphal procession in which present rulers step over those who are lying prostrate. According to traditional practice, the spoils are carried along in the procession. They are called cultural treasures, and a historical materialist views them with cautious detachment. For without exception the cultural treasures he surveys have an origin which he cannot contemplate without horror. They owe their existence not only to the efforts of the great minds and talents who have created them, but also to the anonymous toil of their contemporaries. There is no document of civilization which is

> not at the same time a document of barbarism. And just as such a document is not free of barbarism, barbarism taints also the manner in which it was transmitted from one owner to another. A historical materialist therefore disassociates himself from it as far as possible. He regards it as his task to brush history against the grain. (256–57)

Benjamin, it should be noted, does not deny the greatness of the minds that have created cultural treasures. Even when trying to speak as a "historical materialist," he must acknowledge the flashes of Spirit that animate the treasures of Western Civ—and so, I believe, must we. But such flashes are not intelligible, not even perceptible, without a context. Hegel's own "greatness"—and I would be the last to deny it—can only be comprehended, measured, and criticized in a context of other systematic thinkers. Without the threads of filiation that bind him to Plato and Aristotle, to Fichte and Schelling, to Marx and Freud, and above all, without a sense of what dialectic or systematic thought actually may be, Hegel may only seem, as he did to Goethe's daughter when he came to dinner, to be "an unclear thinker."

The point I am trying so laboriously to make is that any presentation of Europe's cultural past must itself be laboriously thought out and carefully presented. When disconnected texts are presented in surveys of Great Books, one of the first things lost is history itself. When texts that speak to one another—that address the same problems, that work in the same medium or genre—are studied, then such courses can make sense. They will make the greatest sense, however, if they take a narrative structure that finally connects them to the present. To return to the example I have been working with, Hegel is important to us because our thought is still shaped by ideas he formulated so powerfully—and because we need to reject some of those ideas in order to understand our own situation.

In my view, every discipline should offer courses in its own history, or in some coherent segment of that history ending with the present time. But there can be no coherent overview of the historical whole, no single historical core of Great Books embodying something called "Western Civilization." And if any single discipline's history were to be privileged as the best embodiment of the ideal Western Civ fails to reach, that would certainly be the "History of Art from Egypt to America"—which is regularly ignored in courses called "Western Civ." I would privilege sculpture and painting because they are so palpable, so representable, so suited to a generation attuned to visual texts. In the history of art, what my teacher George Kubler called so beautifully "the shape of time" can be grasped as a structure to which other historical events and texts can be attached. However—and here my discourse will take its final turn toward the specific and practical—I also want to argue that historical studies themselves should be preceded or accompanied by another core, designated to help students situate themselves in their own culture, and, in particular, designed to make the basic processes of language itself intelligible and fully available for use. Toward the establishment of such a core, I now wish to make the "trivial proposal" mentioned in my title.

This proposal will be trivial, perhaps, in the sense that it will make a much smaller claim than that made by Great Books or Western Civ curricula. It will be trivial, however, in another sense: trivial in that it is an attempt to rethink in modern terms the trivium that was the core of medieval education. This will also be a radical proposal, in the sense that I propose to go back to the roots of our liberal arts tradition and reinstate rhetoric, grammar, and dialectic at the core of college education. These three subjects—grammar, dialectic, and rhetoric—you remember, constituted the preliminary studies to the medieval quadrivium of arithmetic, geometry, astronomy, and music. Our culture is too complicated for education to be quadrivial, now, but not for a trivial core. To envision such a thing, we need only rethink what grammar, dialectic, and rhetoric might mean in modern terms. My own rethinking of these terms has taken the form of seeing all three of the trivial arts as matters of textuality, with the English language at the center of them, but noting their extension into media that are only partly linguistic. I offer the results here, with a certain humility, as trivial in yet another sense. This is crude, provisional thinking, meant to stimulate refinements and alternatives rather than to lay down any curricular law.

This modern trivium, like its ancestors, would be organized around a canon of concepts, precepts, and practices rather than a canon of texts. In particular, each trivial study would encourage textual production by students in appropriate modes. Since this is a modern trivium, such production would include, where appropriate, not only speaking and writing, but work in other media as well. Similarly, texts for reading, interpretation, and criticism would be drawn from a range of media, ancient and modern. I will present my trivial proposal in the form of a set of courses, each of which would be based not on a canon of sacred texts but on certain crucial concepts to be understood not simply in a theoretical way but in their application to the analysis of specific cultural or textual situations. This means that the specific texts selected could have considerable variety from course to course and place to place, though it may well be that certain texts should prove so useful that they would be widely adopted for use in textual curricula. In some cases, even "classic" texts from philosophy and literature will present themselves as the most useful things available—which may tell us something about why they have become "classics" in the first place. At any rate, the specific titles given in the following descriptions are meant to be illustrative rather than prescriptive.

My first trivial topic is grammar, traditionally the driest and narrowest of academic subjects. I propose to change all that, however, by means of a course of study that follows the implications of the grammar of the pronouns all the way to the subject and object positions of discourse. I see "grammar," conceived in this generous manner, as an alternative to traditional composition courses, taking perhaps two semesters of work, the first of which might be called "Language and Human Subjectivity." The basis of this course would be the way that their mother tongue presents human beings with a set of words and grammatical rules in which they may attain subjectivity at the cost of being subjected. The very heart of such a course would be the grammar of the pronouns, beginning with *I* and *you,* as opposed to *he, she,* and *it.* But this grammar must be connected to the philosophical questions of the subject and object and the ethical relationship of *I* and *thou.* The virtual loss of *thou* in English, except in certain religious contexts, would make one point of discussion. In designing such a course I would be careful to use a mixture of theoretical texts and illustrative embodiments of the problems of subjectivity. For instance, the necessary theory is conveniently embodied in such discussions as those of the linguist Emile Benveniste on "The Nature of Pronouns" and "Subjectivity in Language" in *Problems in General Linguistics;* in Hegel's dialectic of Master and Servant in the *Phenomenology of Spirit;* in Freud's *Das Ich und das Es,* which is usually translated as *The Ego and the Id,* but which is just as properly translated as *The I and the It;* and in other works by Piaget, Vygotsky, and Lacan, for example.

Some of this is not easy reading, I will grant you, but basic college work in the sciences is not easy either. There is no reason why we should not ask students to make an effort in the study of human textuality that is comparable to what they would make in economics, biology, or any other discipline. On the other hand, we have the opportunity—and the necessity, I would say—of also presenting our topic through texts that embody the charms of specificity and narrativity. In the present instance, my colleagues and I have found that the cases of "wild" children—such as the boy found in Aveyron in the eighteenth century, whose case is available in print and in François Truffaut's excellent film on the subject—make these issues concrete and emotionally engaging (see Malson's *Wolf Children and the Problem of Human Nature,* which includes a full translation of Itard's *The Wild Boy of Aveyron;* Shattuck, *The Forbidden Experiment*). Another extremely useful narrative approach to these matters is embodied in Samuel Delany's *Babel-17,* a work of science fiction focused on a language that is dehumanizing precisely because it lacks the pronouns *I* and *you*.

Other matters that properly belong to a course on "Language and Human Subjectivity" would include the problem of human alienation (Hegel and Marx) and the very specific problems of feminine subjectivity in language, especially those relating to the loss of women's family names in history through the adoption of husbands' names by wives, and the use of the male pronoun as the general pronoun for males and females. This topic is clearly presented in Dale Spender's *Man Made Language* and many other works. The whole question of style and personal voice in writing can also be properly deployed under this rubric, along with the study of the essay and the lyric poem as literary forms that have for several centuries enacted the problems of attaining subjectivity in language. Here, also, is the place for students to experiment as writers with the subjective modes of textuality. Many traditional dimensions of the English curriculum can find their places in such a course as this, and they will be energized in the process by their functioning in a course with the specific conceptual goal of developing students' awareness of the relationship between language and human subjectivity.

The second semester of "grammatical" study in my new trivium would treat the topic of "Representation and Objectivity." Representation is an activity in which a textual subject positions someone or something else as a textual object. The growth of the sciences in modern Europe and America is a process elaborately connected to the development of "objective" discourses. One could almost define science as an objective discourse about a certain body of material. Because of the importance and power of such discourses, it is essential for students to learn how they work and what their strengths, costs, and limitations may be. The problems of representation and objectification become especially important in those disciplines involving objects of study that have a strong claim to a subjectivity that may be suppressed (even violently) in order to represent them as objects. It is in the human or social sciences, then, that we will find the most suitable textual material for a course such as this one: sociology, anthropology, and history will offer us topics that are at least accessible to our competencies if not within them.

A semester's work in "Representation and Objectivity" should share theory with the study of subjectivity in language, but it should also have a base of its own in theories of representation and narrativity, whether semiotic or new historicist. It should also draw upon the self-reflective metadiscourse of whatever field is selected for emphasis in a particular version of the course. That is, if the course takes anthropological writing as its focus, it should include both samples of unreflective anthropologizing and works that stand in a metadiscursive relation to such unreflective work, such as selections from Lévi-Strauss's *Tristes-Tropiques* and writing on the problems of anthropological discourse by Clifford Geertz and James Clifford. If a historical topic is to be the center of the course, metahistorical work by Charles Collingwood, E. H. Carr, and, of course, Hayden White might compose part of the theoretical basis of the investigation. It is also easy to imagine a course focused on European representation of its Oriental Other, which takes Edward Said's *Orientalism* as a point of departure. No metatext should take a position of unquestioned validity, of course, but should be used to open up the questions of objectivity and representation so that students can enter them as writers. I think best results will come in courses with a clear focus, such as the anthropologizing of Native Americans, or the historicizing of a specific event in American life, or the sociologizing of a specific American class or culture. In studying such a topic, a range of objective, frankly subjective, and metadiscourses would function as ways of learning both about the specific topic and about the larger processes of representation and objectification that enable scientific discourses to function.

The second trivial topic in the core curriculum I am proposing would be dialectic. In its modern dress, and because the word "dialectic" has drifted far from its earlier usage, a course in this trivial topic might be called "System and Dialectic." Such a course would have as its object of study discourses that work at a high level of abstraction and systematization, in which texts are constructed not so much by representing objects as by abstracting from them their essential qualities or their principles of composition. This is preeminently the domain of philosophy itself, and especially of the tradition of Continental philosophy from the pre-Socratics to Derrida. It may well be that literature departments would need help from our friends in philosophy to mount courses that approach this topic effectively, but several decades of literary theory ought to have made us readier to undertake such a project ourselves than we were some years ago.

The intent of such study would be, in part, to make available to students the tradition of clear and systematic thinking that has been so crucial to the history of what Richard Rorty has called "the rich North Atlantic nations"—so that such students may learn to employ the resources of logic and dialectic in their own thinking and writing. A further intent, however, would be to introduce students to those countertrends, arising mainly within philosophy itself, that seek to criticize or even undo that very tradition. Put more specifically, absolutely essential philosophers such as Plato, Aristotle, Kant, and Hegel might

be read and discussed in speech and writing, along with such antitheti-
cal writers as Nietzsche, Wittgenstein, Heidegger, Derrida, Rorty, and
Davidson. Such a course might have a particular theme, such as philoso-
phies of science, which would bring Aristotle, Bacon, Locke, Kuhn, and
Feyerabend into prominence, or government, which would make Plato,
Machiavelli, Hobbes, Montesquieu, and others important—or education,
or language, or justice, or freedom. The point would be for students to
learn both how to use and how to criticize discourse that takes reason,
system, and logical coherence as its principles of articulation.

The last of the trivial topics I am proposing might well be taught first
in any sequence of core courses, because it deals with more familiar
matters and perhaps even with more immediately accessible material.
But I am not offering a rigid order or sequence of courses here, in any
case, but trying to suggest how one might go about revitalizing the old
trivium, the third division of which was rhetoric. I would be inclined to
call a modern course in rhetoric something like "Persuasion and Mediation." Such a course would obviously include the traditional arts of
manipulation of audiences but would also point toward the capacities
and limits of the newer media, especially those that mix verbal and visual textuality to generate effects of unprecedented power. Such a course
would embrace the traditional topics of rhetoric but would extend them
in certain specific directions. For instance, one might well wish to begin
with Aristotle's *Rhetoric,* but in this kind of course the *Poetics* would also
have a place as a discussion of both another type of manipulation and a
specific medium (tragic drama) that mediates human experience in a
particular way, incorporating the hegemonic codes of a particular cultural situation. From here one might go on to such texts as Nietzsche's
Birth of Tragedy and Brecht on "Epic Theatre." In this connection it would
be especially effective to move from the rhetoric of theatre to the rhetoric of film and visual spectatorship in general, in which the gendering
of subjects and objects of viewing could be considered (as in Laura
Mulvey, Teresa de Lauretis, and John Berger, for instance), along with
other ideological analyses of the rhetoric of the mass media in both direct (overt) and indirect (covert) manipulation of viewers. Plays, films,
and television texts would be the objects of rhetorical analysis in such a
course, along with such more overtly persuasive tests as political
speeches and advertisements.

In such a curricular core of study, students might well encounter as
many "classic" texts as in more traditional core curricula, but these texts
would not be studied simply "because they are there," but as the means
to an end of greater mastery of cultural processes by the students themselves. By putting language and textuality at the center of education, we

would not be making some gesture of piety toward the medieval roots of education, but we would certainly be acknowledging the cultural past of our institutions. More importantly, however, we would be responding to the "linguistic turn" of so much of modern thought and to the media saturation that is the condition of our students' lives as well as of our own. Already, in such a trivium, the cultural past will have begun to be presented as a body of texts that can help students to understand their current cultural situation—just as they help their teachers (who also, of course, continue to be students). This trivium should also serve to whet the appetite for other courses that attend more specifically to the historical narratives of one or another mode of cultural activity. If the pigs and the dogs learn to communicate and negotiate with one another, perhaps they can turn this flock of cultures into a nest of singing birds, and make such music as will stir the corrupting carcass of Western Civilization itself. That, at least, is my hope.

Works Cited

Anderson, Margaret, Jane Heap, and Ezra Pound, eds. *The Little Review* 9.3 (1923): 3–51.

Benjamin, Walter. *Illumination.* Trans. Harry Zohn. New York: Schocken, 1969.

Benveniste, Emile. *Problems in General Linguistics.* Trans. Mary Elizabeth Meek. Coral Gables, FL: U of Miami P, 1971.

Berger, John. *Ways of Seeing.* New York: Penguin, 1977.

Brecht, Bertolt. *Brecht on Theatre.* Trans. John Willett. New York: Hill, 1964.

Carr, Edward Hallett. *What Is History?* New York: Vintage, 1961.

Collingwood, R. G. *The Idea of History.* New York: Oxford UP, 1956.

Delany, Samuel. *Babel-17.* New York: Gregg, 1976.

de Lauretis, Teresa. *Alice Doesn't: Feminism, Semiotics, Cinema.* Bloomington: Indiana UP, 1984.

Freud, Sigmund. *Das Ich und das Es.* Wien: Internationaler Psychoanalytischer Verlag, 1923.

Geertz, Clifford. *The Intrepretation of Cultures: Selected Essays.* New York: Basic, 1973.

Hegel, G.W.F. *Aesthetics: Lectures on Fine Art.* Trans. T. M. Knox. New York: Oxford UP, 1975. 2 vols.

———. *Lectures on the Philosophy of History.* Trans. J. Sibree. New York: Dover, 1956.

———. *Phenomenology of Spirit.* Trans. A. V. Miller and J. N. Findlay. New York: Oxford UP, 1977.

Kames, Henry Home, Lord. *Elements of Criticism.* 1762. New York: Johnson Reprint Corp. 1967.

Lévi-Strauss, Claude. *Tristes Tropiques.* New York: Atheneum, 1970.

Malson, Lucien. *Wolf Children and the Problem of Human Nature: With the Complete Text of* The Wild Boy of Aveyron. New York: Monthly Review, 1972.

Mulvey, Laura. "Visual Pleasure and Narrative Cinema." *Screen* 16.3 (1975): 6–18.

Nietzsche, Friedrich. *The Birth of Tragedy: And the Case of Wagner.* Trans. Walter Kaufmann. New York: Vintage, 1967.

Said, Edward. *Orientalism.* New York: Pantheon, 1978.

Schelling, F.W.J. *The Philosophy of Art.* Ed. and trans. Douglas W. Scott. Minneapolis: U of Minnesota P, 1989.

Schiller, Friedrich. *On the Aesthetic Education of Man.* Ed. and trans. Elizabeth M. Wilkinson and L. A. Willoughby. Oxford: Clarendon, 1967.

Shattuck, Roger. *The Forbidden Experiment: The Story of the Wild Boy of Aveyron.* New York: Washington Square, 1980.

Spender, Dale. *Man Made Language.* London: Routledge, 1980.

White, Hayden. *Tropics of Discourse: Essays in Cultural Criticism.* Baltimore: Johns Hopkins UP, 1978.

12 Polylogue: Ways of Teaching and Structuring the Conflicts

Gary Waller
University of Hartford

I

In his recent book, *Beyond the Culture Wars,* Gerald Graff very kindly singles out for praise some of the curricular developments in the Carnegie Mellon English department I directed from 1983–1989. In Graff's view, what I have elsewhere termed "polylogue" (Waller, "Knowing the Subject"; "Theory, R.I.P.") exemplified his much-discussed concept of "teaching the conflicts"; certainly, it informed the curricular and pedagogical connections my colleagues and I carried out in the English department and had important implications for restructuring not only English but other humanities departmental structures. Like the curricular developments at Syracuse, which have been recounted by Steven Mailloux and others, the story of the Carnegie Mellon English department's theory-centered undergraduate curriculum has been told from a variety of viewpoints (Waller, "Paradigm Shift"; *Lexington;* "Theory, R.I.P"; McCormick, "Using Cultural Theory"; *Culture of Reading*). It was commented upon in the *Chronicle of Higher Education* as well as at ADE, NCTE, and other disciplinary conferences; it was the occasion for two textbooks (Waller et al., *Lexington;* McCormick et al., *Reading Texts*) that have been given an unusual amount of attention (for instance, substantial reviews and articles in *College English, Genre,* and the *MMLA Bulletin*); its principles also influenced the recommendations on the English major at the 1987 English Coalition Conference; and, in 1988, an outside committee evaluating the department said the core courses of its curriculum could and should become a model for other universities and colleges. In retrospect, what we achieved during those years now seems less roseate, characterized by not a little smoke and mirrors and not a trivial dose of grandiose self-persuasion, but the experiment certainly taught those of us caught up in it much about the politics, not to mention the pedagogy, of curricular reform. Some of us have moved on, and I, for one, now see many of the principles that we were exploring as having a more general application, most notably in the area of an interdisciplinary approach to general education and (as I increasingly learn about the work done in the Coalition of Essential Schools) even at the secondary level.

In this essay, I will focus less on the details of what we achieved at Carnegie Mellon and more on issues and questions that could apply to other situations and to the general issue of institutionalizing and teaching critical theory. After a brief description of the core courses in the curriculum, I will address some of the wider theoretical and pedagogical issues currently under discussion in the discipline at large which these courses attempted to address, and also some of the administrative and organizational problems that may occur when instituting reforms within traditionally structured departments. Adapting a phrase of Freud's, I want to stress the "pleasures" we encountered in introducing a level of metacritical theorizing into curriculum and pedagogy, while acknowledging that there are also potential "unpleasures" that deserve to be given some mention and which have caused some of us involved in the curriculum's development to rethink, debate, and reformulate our ideas.

At Carnegie Mellon in 1983–84, we instituted a group of literary and cultural studies courses that were required of all undergraduate English majors—those majoring in creative, technical, and professional writing as well as literature. What we termed "the English core" consisted of three sophomore courses, "Discursive Practices," "Discourse and Historical Change," and "Reading Twentieth-Century Culture." They were organized around the theoretical issue of reading as both an individually (or "cognitively") and a collectively (or "culturally") produced activity. "Reading," after all, is not a "natural" process but rather a culturally produced one; its assumptions vary according to different reading formations and with readers' (often very different) immediate purposes. We therefore made the issues of interpretation, of "reading texts," the central theoretical focus of the core. As a further principle of organization, we had our first-year course anticipate the three organizing concepts of the sophomore courses: *language* (which incorporated some study of cultural semiotics and the interplay of cultural production and discourse as well as the function of literary and nonliterary uses of language); *history* (which considered questions of historical difference and appropriation—how, in short, we described ourselves, through texts of the past, as historically constituted beings); and *culture* (which focused on cultural diversity and cultural theories, including the relations between literary and nonliterary cultural artifacts).

These three core courses, built around *language, history,* and *culture,* were designed neither to present students with accounts of contemporary theory nor to encourage them to take up any kind of party line on any theoretical or political issues. Rather, through the study of carefully selected readings, including literary texts, they were designed to help students participate in discussions of (and to write about) some of the most important debates raised by contemporary theory. Above all, the courses encouraged students to develop a knowledge of a number of different positions in these debates—to feel and think their way into Graff's "conflicts." Perhaps we were, in effect, restating Graff's terms: instead of our "teaching" the conflicts, our students were "learning" them and matching (or recognizing) what they learned with what they already possessed or had experienced. No particular theoretical approach to texts was to be privileged, but the power and interest of a variety of approaches, even in a relatively simplified form, were to be made part of the dialogues—or, since there were many voices, the "polylogues"—in which students were invited to participate and encouraged to bring their own reactions and views. A careful balance was to be maintained: between a degree of overlap among the three courses, which would ensure continuity and reinforcement, and acknowledging that there would be, necessarily and appropriately, contradictions of approach and material. Early planning meetings of the faculty were, therefore, replete with pie charts and discussions of shared (and differing) concepts, approaches, and texts. Polylogue must also be played out in faculty as well as student interactions and collaborative learning.

Even to speak of learning "theory" is a slight misnomer. Rather, language, history, and culture provided opportunities for *theorizing;* they were presented to students as sites of interest, sometimes as intense struggles, that have generated diverse and often contradictory critical practices in past as well as recent theory. Subsequently, I have become less happy with the dominant metaphors of struggle, conflict, and Graff's culture "wars." We hoped at the time that the "conflicts" our students learned would not turn into agonistic struggles, with triumphantly "correct" and defeated, "incorrect" positions; we hoped rather that what would develop was a shared awareness that such debates were intensely interesting, complex, and important—and not just for academic studies but for our understanding of and actions in the broader society.

The textbooks that Kathleen McCormick and I developed from these core courses and the preparatory, first-year reading and writing course are eventually to go into second editions, suggesting that there is a not an inconsiderable audience beyond Carnegie Mellon. The textbooks gave us pedagogical tools to carry out these developments, and our students emerged from the program (even following their first-year, preparatory course) very different from the way I did from my own traditional grounding in English, philosophy, and history. Our students were able (naturally, at various levels of ability and appropriateness—in this the new pedagogy is somewhat like the old) to foreground their literary and ideological assumptions, to speak of meanings as constructed by both reader and text and of criticism as historically situated and culturally produced, and to see the human subject (whether while reading texts or at other times) as a construct, not as an objective point of origin.

The relationship with "traditional" conceptions of English is worth pursuing in detail because even in the 1990s, most attempts to translate into English curriculum and pedagogy something of the new theory will take place in departments only cautiously interested in it—perhaps only to the extent of hiring a young theorist or two, maybe even tenuring him or her—but which, in practice if not explicitly, will keep such activities visible but on the margins of traditional activities. First of all, then, I want to acknowledge that this brave new model of curriculum and pedagogy, as we all gleefully—even a little masochistically—recognized, was not part of the world in which most of us had grown up (and prospered). Those of us who embraced it (or were embraced by it) have done so while wrestling with assumptions that made the once dominant view of English seem less aggressive, less political, less confrontational, less concerned with pedagogical strategies, let alone with "theory." We had, for the most part, learned a subject called "English literature." It was (to use a common humanist metaphor drawn, as so often is the case, from the seemingly value-free, "natural" world of the pastoral) a field in which to wander, a large field with often difficult terrain, which could, with effort, afford us a variety of rural pleasures. It seemed—and this was sometimes intimidating but sometimes part of its pleasure—to belong to someone else, to a conglomerate, perhaps, to tradition, or to what we were told was our common culture. We could admire the scenery, the cultivated flower, the ha-ha, the towering pines, the ancient oaks, and (of course) the daffodils, roses, or lesser columbines. We could measure it (after a proper apprenticeship in measurement) from side to side, and find, indeed, that it is hundreds of miles long and at least forty leagues wide. We could cultivate a few native flowers in a corner or two. We could even, though somewhat reluctantly, teach some of our younger companions to pen a line or two about the delights of wandering and gazing at the sights.

I won't push the metaphor further, however tempted I am. That was what English was. It allowed us, therefore, the achievements of continual exploration and, eventually, areas of mastery. Those are not unimportant achievements. But the new approach to English that we at Carnegie Mellon were developing (and we may not want even to call it "English") claimed to offer more. The difference was summed up for me in two comments on the bottom of the ubiquitous course evaluation sheets. (We all know the situation: At the end of a semester, when three novels still have to be read in two weeks, and there are three quizzes and two statistics assignments due tomorrow, and Waller is still going on about how every performance of *The Winter's Tale* makes him cry [or as he puts it, "weep"] and now you have to fill out these fifteen pointless, overlapping questions, and there's a two-inch space at the bottom for comments, and you feel like scrawling, with Mr. Kurtz, "exterminate all the brutes. . . .") One comment was: "I learned an enormous amount about the subject in this course." The other was: "This course changed the way I look at myself as a subject." The first we can unpack to mean—and, again, these are not inconsiderable matters—I read poems and plays I didn't know about, I learned what *terza rima* is, I discovered something of Victorian England or American writers in Rome, or I learned how to recognize or even write heroic couplets. The second involves becoming more aware of how language has manipulated my life, how many of my assumptions about politics, religion, or capitalism no longer seem "natural" or, sometimes, even desirable. It involves asking how I am constructed contradictorily by socially produced, even unconscious drives. It involves questions about how my gender and class and race have given me certain assumptions, not just about my reading and writing of literature, but about my readings of and my writings about our society, my history, my participation in a complex and always changing culture. It puts "literary" study out in the world and connects it in very public ways to the social and cultural forces that impinge upon my life. It connects it to an examination and theorization of the basic fundamentals of communication—reading and writing.

Anyone involved in trying to find structures and pedagogies by which to mediate the "new" English will be asking today: What business does English literature, once the province of dusty, tweedy, largely male professors, have in claiming so much? And what educational benefits does all this "stuff" (a term used by advocates and detractors alike to describe theory and the practices that grow from it) produce? These are not illegitimate questions, and we must formulate clear and persuasive answers.

There is, first, a relatively easy, institutional answer. It is that every discipline, however changeable, constitutes itself historically and, therefore, ought to be permitted to work through its own defined questions and problems. From that perspective, many of the developments in the discipline, including the development of separate rhetoric programs, the integration within or banishment of film, communication, or theory from the study of literature, are all necessary stages in the breaking down and reformulation of paradigms for study and learning. If we take the province of our discipline today as—in the words of Jonathan Culler and James Kinneavy in their very moving debate on the Ph.D. in English at the MLA's Wayzata conference in 1987 (see Lunsford et al., "Doctoral Studies")—the study of reading and writing in their discursive and historical contexts, then literary studies is inevitably going to raise questions that take "English" out into the world and into different configurations according to the demands of that world—and, indeed, raise questions which historians, political and social scientists, and psychologists have traditionally taken as "theirs." Traditionally, in English, we have asked these questions in relation to literary texts themselves, but not always, for we are interested as well in raising questions about textuality and the multiple and contradictory ways languages unravel, overflow, and contain or repress meanings, the ways texts articulate absences as well as presences, the ways language brings experiences into being by providing discursive structures by which "subjects"—note, not simply "individuals"—find themselves "written" and "read." We are interested in how our discoveries overflow from our reading of "mere" literary texts into our possibilities and responsibilities as subjects, with different as well as shared histories within our complex and ever-changing culture. We are interested in reading and writing, both as fundamental competencies and as subjects for theoretical understanding of and investigation into their place and value in the world.

The world-directness of the new English—and, I would argue, of what is emerging as the New Humanities in general—is crucial. Whatever else we are doing in wrestling with developing curricular structures and pedagogical practices by which the new approaches can be introduced to students—and I certainly wanted my Carnegie Mellon students to read no less Chaucer, Shakespeare, Austen, Brontë (though I would hope that all of us, as a strange and contradictory people called Americans, would equally read the writings of African and Hispanic Americans and minorities of different sexual orientations, races, and classes)—we are helping students to make differences within their individual lives and, beyond that, to make informed interventions in the changes and chances of our society. Our job is not just to give them texts to admire but to give them language to use—options, issues, choices, lexicons—by which they might ask questions of whatever texts they encounter. We are not only teaching a "subject"—a supposedly objective body of knowledge that has been constituted by agreement, whether it is called "literature" or, even more narrowly, the "aesthetic" dimension of literature—or good writing habits, or how to write a pleasing story or poem. We are teaching—our students and ourselves—through the medium of textuality, in its discursive and historically constituted structures, to explore and study themselves as "subjects." Our goal is not the subjection of a neophyte reader to a masterwork—even though there are times when we all, even the most experienced readers, certainly do and should feel like neophytes. Our goal is rather to develop the skills and confidence (and some understanding of the epistemological underpinnings) to become strong readers of texts—"masterworks" and others—to be able to analyze the ideological dimensions of writing, of our own and others' readings, to raise questions of class, gender, race, and agency in relation not only to texts that seem explicitly to demand such questions, but also to those that don't and for whose writers such questions might have seemed unnatural or pointless. In short, we are teaching our students not only a "subject"—English or literature—but also the ways through which they might know themselves as "subjects." Inseparable from the literary texts we read are the texts of our own histories, the text of the present, and the text of our historically and culturally constructed selves.

I will move to concrete examples. In spring 1988, I was teaching one of our core courses at Carnegie Mellon, "Discourse and Historical Change." That semester I was using a number of essays—by Terry Eagleton, Raymond Williams, Louis Althusser—to raise questions about reading historically remote texts; the course focused on two detailed examples: the representation of gender in early modern poetry and drama, and the development of a sense of American "identity" from the Puritans to Hawthorne. At the end of the semester, we were studying *The Scarlet Letter*. As late-twentieth-century readers, we were reading Hawthorne's reading of the Puritans, who were in turn reading the inscrutable ways of the Almighty. As well, we were reading—and, not incidentally, reading as educated and, therefore, distinctly privileged men or women within a society gradually becoming more sensitive to gender construction—a nineteenth-century male's reading of the struggles of being a woman in the seventeenth century. These multiple perspectives provided the basis of a final theoretical paper on reading texts in what was termed "their" time and in "ours." But *we* (and now that word "we" has a less certain tone today, doesn't it?) gave the perspectival nature of reading historically a further dimension: we were reading a white male's reading of the ways a white female was being constructed within the distinctive ideological pressures of European American history. For what gave our study not only an interest in the interrelations of reading and gender but also in reading and race and class was that, alongside *The Scarlet Letter,* we were reading Frederick Douglass's autobiography. It was one of my African American students who raised the question of where she fitted into the unfolding drama of the historical construction of the American subject that our study of Hawthorne had presented. She had felt disempowered, silenced, marginalized by the Puritans we had read, and now we had come to a text (Douglass's) through which she could enter the critical discourse. Her repertoire at last matched that of a text she was being required to study. It was not that she now had a way of ignoring or not reading *The Scarlet Letter;* on the contrary, Douglass was helping to add another perspective to her paper on Hawthorne—one that reflected her history and personal repertoire as a twentieth-century African American woman. She also, incidentally, read a poem (which I had written the summer before while at the English Coalition, held near the Wye Plantation where Douglass had lived) about reading, as a white man, Douglass's life story and writings. It had just been published in the *New Virginia Review* (see Braunton 13–14) and so provided her with another perspective: what right had a white, middle-class (and foreign-born) male to comment on "her" history? She wrote a passionate, well-documented paper; she displayed both her knowledge of the subject and her sense of herself as a subject. She became, in her paper, a deconstructor of the canon, of traditional literary criticism, and of "English" as both a harmless and alien field of study. But the "field," to revert to my earlier metaphor, was found to contain undergrowth and native plants that she could recognize, cultivate, and gain nourishment from. She was, in short, discovering how to discover and critique both the *subject* of English and the subject of *English.*

These discoveries were made in a sophomore/junior course. My second example of polylogue in the classroom comes from a largely first-year class, and this time from my teaching at the University of Hartford. As a dean, I am not required to teach; as a teacher and a theoretician and practitioner of pedagogy, I still feel impelled to do so. So in spring 1993, I was teaching a general education course in Hartford's well-known "All University Curriculum" to a class in which a variety of students from different schools and colleges were studying what I, somewhat uncomfortably, had to refer to in the course title as "Western Heritage." I constructed part of the syllabus as a polylogue around the question of religious experience in the West, using a variety of texts from Saint Augustine to Freud to Persig as well as a bunch of religious poems and lyrics. Inevitably, students learned something of the "subject": they were, for instance, appalled generally by the fervency of Saint Augustine's self-lacerations and his linking of religious and sexual experiences, and generally convinced but depressed by Freud's explanations of similar phenomena. They were also encouraged to bring their own, strikingly varied experiences of religious experience—Jewish, Roman Catholic, various Protestant denominations, indifference, New Age—to bear on the subject. Above all, they learned how they were constructed as subjects of a powerful and, to a large extent, taken-for-granted aspect of their own positioning within late-twentieth-century Western society—how, in short, they were constructed as "subjects." We were not simply studying the texts for the students' own sakes; or, equally simply, to encourage their "subjective" responses. We were constructing an analysis of how "Western Heritage" constructed us all as complex subjects of a complex inheritance—and perhaps of ways by which we could assert ourselves as agents, constructed, but yet not absolutely determined by, our pasts. And we were integrating, theoretically and experientially, what we were discovering into the very pressing world around us. As one of my students put it, thinking aloud: "This religion stuff: I been thinking about it. Like, it's been around for a long time: maybe even longer than AIDS." Of course, he may be wrong.

I want to mention now the important question of the appropriate level in a curriculum at which theoretical material should be used. My suggestion is that at the first-year level, theoretical essays should be discussed alongside literary and media texts, but sparingly, and only after intense preparation by the instructor. Teachers need to be aware of and to make clear to their students what issues might be at stake, and they should encourage self-conscious and detailed discussion of them, but they should not rush directly to a sophisticated level of theoretical discussion. Textbooks like *Reading Texts* (McCormick et al.) or *Text Book* (Scholes et al.) can be of great help in alerting relatively inexperienced teachers to some of the relevant theoretical issues. At Florida State University, for instance, in the summer before they start teaching the first-year course, graduate teachers are introduced to how theoretical issues may arise in the classroom by studying *Reading Texts*. Our "Theories of Reading" course for our graduate teachers sometimes includes a critique of *Reading Texts*, Robert Scholes's *Textual Power*, and other innovative texts that are trickling onto the market with an eye to helping graduate instructors discover ways they might mediate complicated theoretical issues for their first-year students.

If, at the first-year level, some caution ought to be exercised over the introduction of theoretical essays, at the sophomore or junior levels, such essays can certainly be introduced, discussed, and read along with other literary or cultural texts—not to establish an orthodox "line" on a text or theoretical issue, but to open up discussion and allow students to both deepen and problematize their own developing perspectives. In "Discourse and Historical Change," along with a selection of literary and related texts from past periods, I use such essays as Tony Bennett's "Literature in History," which speaks to the ways texts are read differently in different historical formations; or Raymond Williams's "Dominant, Residual, and Emergent," which discusses patterns of historical change and struggle; and extracts from as broad a spectrum of theorists as Eliot to Althusser. On occasion, I also use Williams's *Keywords*, in which case one of the course assignments requires students to construct the history of a "key word" not found in Williams. This has been a very successful exercise. Students like the idea of extending (and in a sense correcting) an authoritative textbook. I typically have students nominate the words for which they wish to construct a history ("gay" is one that Williams does not include, and there has been a perfectly understandable curiosity about its history, which is in fact very interesting) and briefly justify their choices. I then direct them to the *OED* and some other resources and invite them to add sources they discover on their own. Sometimes the results have been summaries of the sources; at other times, somewhat subjective responses to what they discovered. The best results have been essays on the history, not just of the changing meanings of words but of the ways in which our history has used certain, "key" words to embody its ideological contradictions and debates—or, indeed, its polylogues. Words like class, sex, gender, individual, literature, city, country, and myriad others made not only fascinating subjects in themselves but reveal the ways by which we are constructed as subjects.

Courses devoted primarily or exclusively to particular theories, theoretical movements, or theorists are, in my view, certainly appropriate for juniors and seniors, as are those that read literary or media texts in conjunction with theoretical texts and issues. Thus, I have often structured a recent course on the sixteenth-century lyric around the issue of the interconnections of gender, reading, and writing. My teaching of early modern poetry at Carnegie Mellon was informed by this principle. Typically, we would read poems by the canonical, male Petrarchists, along with popular lyrics and lyrics by (until recently) neglected women poets, along with essays by Freud, Kristeva, Mulvey, Barthes, and others on gender and language. As well, we would have a three-week-long segment discussing Theweleit's *Male Fantasies*, a psychocultural study of the *Freikorps*, the German fascist mercenaries of the 1920s, asking questions about both particular insights Theweleit offers into gender construction and his methodology. All the students contributed to a collective project, what we termed "The Book of Stuff," an assemblage of theoretical and historical writings that they all could use for their readings and research papers. The result was, I think, a highly successful combination of reading, theorizing, and multiple pleasures.

These instances from the classroom may convey something of our practices during years in which our program was taking shape. They are meant to reinforce a very necessary warning, however, if the evident "pleasures" of theorizing the undergraduate curriculum are not to turn into "unpleasures." It is that the theories and theorizings of the teachers cannot remain immune from the same self-scrutiny that we wish our students to undergo in relation to their reading and writing experiences. "Theory" has currently acquired such prestige in the discipline that there are all-too-evident signs that it will engender an all-too-familiar elitism and a lack of concern for curriculum, classroom practices, and the students themselves. But given not just committed and rigorous theoretical thinkers but, more particularly, enthusiastic and flexible teachers, the pleasures of teaching theories and theorizing to undergraduates in an atmosphere of generosity will, I believe, far outweigh the unpleasures.

II

I turn now to more general observations about how instituting such a curriculum as that which we indulged in at Carnegie Mellon—and exploring its pedagogical implications—opened up various organizational and intellectual problems and challenges that may be of interest to others who are wrestling with the place of critical theory in the learning experience. Such matters include whether, as an increasingly powerful minority of our colleagues maintain, "theory" is an autonomous discipline, replacing "literature," and whether it can even be "applied" to literary or other "nontheoretical" texts; whether (as some of our detractors maintain) giving theoretical issues such a high priority degenerates into a kind of pseudo- or shadow philosophy; whether raising questions of race, gender, and class (as most of us do) predetermines a certain range of answers; how to stop the "conflicts" from degenerating into simply another kind of agonistic (and, some would say, masculinist) struggle for hegemony among theoretical factions; the place of "classics" in theoretically oriented courses; the much-overlooked issue of pedagogy; and the problem of establishing new curricular structures and pedagogical practices in a traditional institution. These are all vital issues in the humanities and some of the social sciences today, and I will touch on some of these matters in my following remarks.

Given the current ferment over the theory and practice of English, there is clearly no one, correct way of instituting either curricular structures or pedagogies. There are, as McCormick has argued, three ways in which theory is currently being brought into the undergraduate curriculum (McCormick, "Always Already Theorists"). One is by substituting the study of "theoretical" texts for "literary" texts, thus constituting something like a new canon and transforming the study of English from the study of one body of texts to the study of another. The second approach to introducing theory into the curriculum is to add a course or two in theory to an existing traditional, canonical curriculum. This gradualist approach—or what I once termed the "park bench" approach (Waller, "Paradigm Shift")—is probably the most widespread, although, as Graff argues, without actually staging within the structure and rationale of the curriculum the theoretical debates that such theoretical courses should raise about the rest of the curriculum, the debates are likely to produce students who are puzzled, intellectually schizophrenic, and cynical, and the opportunity for polylogue may never develop. The third approach, which is close to what we did at Carnegie Mellon and is also incorporated in the University of Hartford's "All University Curriculum," is to develop some theoretically structured courses like those I have described, make them the intellectual focus of the curriculum, and encourage the multiplicity of issues they raise to become part of the discussions and debates in other classes. For the first few years of the program, all teachers of the core courses at Carnegie Mellon shared their syllabi and met regularly to discuss issues and pedagogy (and by doing so, of course, were able to demonstrate how a theoretical issue like intertextuality operates in the most apparently mundane material practices!). I cannot stress too strongly my belief that such interchanges are an essential part of successfully introducing theory and theorizing into the curriculum. Teamwork and commitment are crucial—not to establish a party line but to emphasize the importance of the issues being enacted and the right of all participants, faculty and students alike, to enter into the "polylogue."

A number of people—including some of our colleagues—criticized the goals of our curriculum for settling for a liberal pluralism (I was struck by the fact that we were, in the space of a few months, attacked in print by members of both the ultra-Right, for betraying Western Civilization, and the ultra-Left, for maintaining bourgeois liberalism under a gloss of poststructuralism). As my discussion, I hope, makes clear, "polylogue" is not simply a valorization of relativism, any more than, in the classroom, it is a simplistic recommendation of a pedagogy based on discussion. It is rather the encouragement and empowerment of a multiplicity of positions, combined with the willingness to examine and critique the assumptions underlying those positions. A healthy curriculum, however the particular details within it may change, should be built not just upon the recognition of pluralism, but upon carefully structured ways of making that pluralism work intellectually and educationally. If we can find creative ways of bringing together the variety of theories, methodologies, and conceptions of what "English" is—not just for administrative convenience, but as a means, as Graff argues, of actually staging or teaching the conflicts—then we may find ways not merely of making our curriculum appear innovative but, far more important, of preparing students for a fuller entry into a genuinely participatory democracy. I believe that such an educational goal acknowledges that college gives students an opportunity not simply to "bank" knowledge and methods, but to develop some perspectives on, some metawareness about, them—and also to act upon that awareness.

Such a goal has undeniable practical consequences. The paradigmatic shift the language disciplines are undergoing is not just theoretical but pedagogical. Departments need to find not only curricular structures but classroom practices that will help their students to stage the contradictions in which our society and history have placed us and to which the texts of our culture, including those we valorize as "literature," articulate. The questions we all need to ask as administrators and teachers include: How creatively are the overlappings and conflicts being used in the education of our students? How well, for instance, are we involving our students in the debates over that group of key words that are crucial not just in current educational debate but for our whole society—gender, race, ethnicity, and class? These key words are, of course, the focus of major challenges to our future as a society, and they are not easy challenges to meet. To these, I would add another, which our curriculum attempted to enact, and that is agency—those areas of action, choice, knowledge, and commitment we struggle to claim for ourselves on the basis of our understanding of how we are constructed by our societies and our histories. In my view, the major goal of a curriculum built on polylogue is to enable students to become agents in this sense—to become aware of how they are constructed, in their different histories, by society, culture, ethnicity, and gender, by scientific or religious paradigms of thought and material practices—but, in doing so, to become aware of the possibilities of choice and action and the principles by which they articulate those choices and actions. And, of course, such discoveries should affect those of us who teach.

Beyond the classroom, and the department, a further challenge that has not been met is that of allowing the development of (and a reward for) these activities and commitments within traditionally structured institutions. At Carnegie Mellon, we were lucky to have institutional backing for our work. We were able, by accidents of place and history, to institutionalize cross-disciplinary perspectives and innovative pedagogies within one department. Hartford's "All University Curriculum" serves a similar function as the basis of a remarkable general education structure. It has been given an educationally central place by administration and faculty. But, at many other institutions, cross-disciplinary teaching and curricular development are often stifled by the current, predominantly one-directional, organizational structure, which gives few incentives and, as a consequence, little permanent support for faculty activities outside the traditional channels. Recent studies of university organization have suggested that establishing and justifying the development of curriculum and pedagogy that follow from critical theory have fallen disproportionately on individual faculty members. That the breakthroughs in knowledge—and, increasingly in pedagogy— occur on the boundaries of received or conventional organizations of knowledge is well known, of course, to the sciences, to many of the social sciences, and, increasingly (though at a distance), to the humanities. But what we need to look for is a set of structures, practices, and assumptions that would provide increased support and rewards for the many faculty activities that transcend traditional departmental and disciplinary boundaries, that would encourage us all to see interdisciplinary educational activities on a par with, and in some contexts even more significant than, traditional "disciplinary" activities.

It is not that departmental or disciplinary needs of organizing knowledge are wrong and should be abandoned. As Ernest Lynton puts it,

> [T]he organization of the university should retain enough flexibility to allow not only the formation but also the termination of multidisciplinary programs and projects. In these cases, it is not a question of replacing one quasi-permanent organization by another; that would simply be substituting one rigid set of structures and assumptions with another. (Lynton and Elman 174).

So it is not a matter of eliminating departments and disciplines (though, inevitably, over time, these will change and indeed may fade, merge, or even disappear); it is a matter of finding harmonious structures through which disciplines can, separately and together, take up pressing educational issues as they arise. It is evident, however, that implementing some of the most crucial missions of the university in the coming decades means overcoming the inertia that a rigid and often moribund set of departmental priorities may all too easily instill. Most importantly, to quote Lynton again,

> [I]mplementing the new missions of the university faces serious barriers as long as the allocation of resources, not to speak of the evaluation and rewards system for faculty, places much greater priority on disciplinary than on interdisciplinary activities. (Lynton and Elman 187)

How is this problem to be overcome? The fundamental challenge is to find ways of rewarding and developing faculty activities that cut across disciplinary and departmental lines while retaining the most vital parts of the dominant, one-dimensional structure that links department to college to university. Maybe, as Lynton argues, the basic resources for the instructional activities of an administrative unit—the university as a whole is the focus of his analysis, but the principle is applicable at the college or departmental level—should be divided into two unequal portions. The larger one would be allocated, in the traditional manner, to deans of colleges, and through them, to the academic departments. These funds could be used for the department's traditional disciplinary courses and programs. The rest would be directed into a second stream of resources that could be made available to the college (or department) only for interdepartmental and intercollegiate instructional activities—for what I term courses involving polylogue or for what Graff sees as staging the conflicts.

As we realized at Carnegie Mellon, what is at stake here is not territory or jurisdiction but a whole conception of education. The national swing back to the value of general education courses—not as a necessary step nor a frustrating barrier to reaching a specialized major but, rather, as the core of an undergraduate education—is starting to be given more than just lip service. We are all general educators: "service" teaching is what we are all primarily concerned with. An adequate education is one in which the issues and problems of our individual and communal lives are contextualized in the contradictions of the contemporary world, in its multiple histories, and in its epistemologies. This trio of contexts (the contemporary, the historical, the ways to knowledge and power) should not be seen as add-ons to a specialized education but as integral parts of it. But such a principle needs to be articulated in more than theory; it needs to be embodied in the concrete, material practices and structures by which we organize the university and its constituent units.

Finally, I want to stress a further lesson that we learned at Carnegie Mellon: that teaching in relation to interdisciplinary, "polylogous" demands must not become another indulgence in elitist superiority. We are teaching for students who will go out into the world. There is a moment—one of the most poignant, I think, in the canon (at least for those

of us who want occasionally to beat up on the canon while also exploring and, admittedly, revering it)—at the end of *The Tempest*, when
Prospero, the poet-magician-scientist-politician-patriarch-teacher-dra-
matist-poet-interdisciplinarian, steps, in part, out of Shakespeare's play
and addresses the audience, asking its members (in a moving version of
an old trope) for applause. But he is also asking for something different.
He acknowledges that the play the audience has just witnessed will be
"confined," trapped, nullified, unless its impact is taken out of the theater into the lives, as well as the words, of its audience. But how the
audience will do that is not up to the actor who, in any performance,
speaks the lines; nor is it even up to the dramatist who wrote the lines.
It is up to the members of the audience themselves to break the confines
of the theater, of art, of "texts" and "canon," and go into the world, to
become aware of themselves as "subjects," to become aware of having
been manipulated, whether by the two hours of traffic on the stage they
have witnessed, by the multiple languages of our society, by politics, by
advertising, by Hollywood, by fundamentalism, or by their educational,
ethnic, gender, or class constructions. What the audience will do is certainly not predictable, any more than what a reader will do with a text
is enforceable. Meanings are not manageable nor controllable. The "subject" our students are learning is not "The Meaning of *The Tempest*" nor
"Shakespeare's Farewell to the Stage," although these are not insignificant topics for discussion. It is that they themselves are constructed
within the multiple reading and writing situations in which they will
find themselves, both in the study of literature and in the study of their
society.

This is not always a comforting discovery. English was, for many of
us, once a more comforting study, before a time when we had to teach
reading and writing to illiterate students, before that mythical time when
we could take for granted that "every schoolboy" knew Wordsworth and
Austen and James. . . . Once, somewhere—to indulge myself one final
time in my pastoral metaphor—we could rest beneath the trees, warble
on an antique pile, watch damsels bathe in purling streams, bewail the
loss of youth and beauty. It is sometimes tiring to discover oneself as
constructed, dislocated, uncertain, uncomfortably self-conscious, caught
in the contradictions of history and ideology. Polylogue may be an exciting challenge to us—as teachers, developers of curricula, and administrators. But it is more exhausting and certainly less simple than the
straightforward mastery of a subject—just as we are learning that teaching is easier to promote and assess than learning. But, as Prospero implies, this sense of learning what it is to be a subject need not be
imprisonment. Caliban gets his island back, Ariel his freedom, Miranda

and Ferdinand each other (with all the dangers that may involve). And Prospero? Prospero—let us say—is the authoritarian teacher, the professor who has lived by the book and by asserting the authority of his office. It is he who has created a version of the pastoral—a mode that, as Raymond Williams and others have pointed out, is designed to comfort the consciences of the ruling class. Prospero knows—for he controls Ariel with its promise—that we desire release, freedom, liberty, what I have termed "agency." But he finally learns that it comes at some risk and unpredictability and by acknowledging others' voices and others' claims to truth. It is, he discovers, the only way to be truly human—not an essentialist statement but one that acknowledges that our humanity and our knowledge about it are always in the world, always changing and challenging. That is why Prospero breaks with the pastoral world and why those of us in the language disciplines, including English, must break with it—at least as a representation of our reality. To be, in the words of the oracle in *The Winter's Tale*, a "true subject," Prospero knows he must drown his book, break his staff, and then announce his own powerlessness. "Welcome, sir," he announces, "This cell's my court. Here have I few attendants, / And subjects none. . ." (*The Tempest* V.i. 165–67). To know the subject, we must also know ourselves as subjects.

Works Cited

Bennett, Tony. "Texts in History." *Journal of the Midwest Modern Language Association* 18.1 (1985): 1–18.

Braunton, Devon. *Other Flights, Always.* Merlin, 1990.

Douglass, Frederick. *Narrative of the Life of Frederick Douglass, an American Slave. Written by Himself.* Boston: Published at the Anti-Slavery Office, 1845.

Elbow, Peter. *What Is English?* New York: MLA, 1990.

Graff, Gerald. *Beyond the Culture Wars: How Teaching the Conflicts Can Revitalize American Education.* New York: Norton, 1992.

———. *Professing Literature: An Institutional History.* Chicago: U of Chicago P, 1987.

Hawthorne, Nathaniel. *The Scarlet Letter: An Authoritative Text, Essays in Criticism and Scholarship.* 3rd ed. Ed. Seymour Gross et al. New York: Norton, 1988.

Lloyd-Jones, Richard, and Andrea A. Lunsford, eds. *The English Coalition Conference: Democracy through Language.* Urbana, IL: NCTE, 1989.

Lunsford, Andrea, Helene Moglen, and James F. Slevin, eds. *The Future of Doctoral Studies in English.* New York: MLA, 1989.

Lynton, Ernest A., and Sandra E. Elman. *New Priorities for the University: Meeting Society's Needs for Applied Knowledge and Competent Individuals.* San Francisco: Jossey-Bass, 1987.

McCormick, Kathleen. "Always Already Theorists: Literary Theory in the Undergraduate Curriculum." *Pedagogy Is Politics: Literary Theory and Critical Teaching.* Ed. Maria Regina Kecht. Urbana: U of Illinois P, 1991. 111–31.

———. *The Culture of Reading and the Teaching of English.* Manchester, UK: Manchester UP, 1994.

———. "Using Cultural Theory to Critique and Reconceptualize the Research Paper." *Cultural Studies in the English Classroom.* Ed. James A. Berlin and Michael J. Vivion. Portsmouth,NH: Boynton/Cook-Heinemann, 1992. 211–30.

McCormick, Kathleen, and Gary Waller, with Linda Flower. *Reading Texts: Reading, Responding, Writing.* Lexington, MA: Heath, 1987.

Scholes, Robert. *Textual Power: Literary Theory and the Teaching of English.* New Haven: Yale UP, 1985.

Scholes, Robert, Nancy R. Comley, and Gregory L. Ulmer. *Text Book: An Introduction to Literary Language.* New York: St. Martin's, 1988.

Shakespeare, William. *The Tempest* and *The Winter's Tale. The Riverside Shakespeare.* 6th prnt. Ed. G. Blakemore Evans. Boston: Houghton, 1976.

Sinfield, Alan. "Give an Account of Shakespeare and Education. . . ." *Political Shakespeare: New Essays in Cultural Materialism.* Ed. Jonathan Dollimore and Alan Sinfield. Manchester, UK: Manchester UP, 1985. 134–57.

Theweleit, Klaus. *Male Fantasies.* Trans. Stephen Conway with Erica Carter and Chris Turner. Minneapolis: U of Minnesota P, 1987. 2 vols.

Waller, Gary. "Knowing the Subject: Critiquing the Self, Critiquing the Culture." *ADE Bulletin* 90 (Spring 1990): 7–11.

———. "Theory, R.I.P.? Relax: Introduce Polylogue." *ADE Bulletin* 102 (Spring 1993): 22–25.

———. "Working within the Paradigm Shift: Poststructuralism and the College Curriculum." *ADE Bulletin* 81 (Spring 1985): 6–12.

Waller, Gary, Kathleen McCormick, and Lois Josephs Fowler, eds. *The Lexington Introduction to Literature: Reading and Responding to Texts.* Lexington, MA: Heath, 1986.

Williams, Raymond, "Dominant, Residual, and Emergent." *Marxism and Literature.* Oxford: Oxford UP, 1976. 120–27.

———. *Keywords: A Vocabulary of Culture and Society.* New York: Oxford UP, 1976.

13 Attitudes and Expectations: How Theory in the Graduate Student (Teacher) Complicates the English Curriculum

Wendy Bishop
Florida State University

College and university English departments are attempting curricular change in response to institutional critiques and analyses like those by Robert Scholes and Gerald Graff. The work of both of these scholars helps us understand how English departments have developed. In *Textual Power*, Scholes outlines the pitfalls of current English department stratification, showing how most departments overvalue the consumption of literary texts and undervalue nonliterary and pseudo-nonliterary texts, particularly student compositions. In examining this hierarchy, he claims:

> For me the ultimate hell at the end of all our good New Critical intentions is textualized in the image of a brilliant instructor explicating a poem before a class of stupefied students. . . . Our job is not to intimidate students with our own superior textual production; it is to show them the codes upon which all textual production depends, and to encourage their own textual practice. (25)

According to Scholes, we need to begin sharing our complicated textual practices with all students, examining these practices together, making them more comprehensible and more democratic.

In *Professing Literature*, Gerald Graff traces the history of "English" from a course of undergraduate study in the nineteenth century, focused on classical texts, to the development at the century's turn of graduate programs, modeled on European universities with their philological and linguistic emphases (22–23, 57). Through periods of intense change, English departments survived—in fact, they grew—because they remained flexible. Over time, however, this flexibility would prove problematic. In his more recent work, *Beyond the Culture Wars*, Graff again points out the self-serving benefits of English studies' "amiable rule of laissez-faire" and then focuses on the problems this rule has created. In essence, the still-dominant "field-coverage" model allows departments to create new categories for every challenge to existing categories, absorbing and defusing the interests of alien constituencies. By doing this, English departments have "enabled the American curriculum to relieve the increasingly conflicting pressures placed on it by painlessly expanding its frontiers, adding new subjects, courses, and programs without asking those in control of the already established ones to change their ways" (7).

Field coverage allows English to keep the lid on a simmering pot. Recently, though, the heat has been turned up—in response to changes in American academic culture—and the pot has started to boil over: feminists, compositionists, new historicists, poststructuralists are all claiming "voice" in English department matters and challenging the status quo that field coverage supports. Graff urges us to avoid the pitfall of developing a false consensus *yet again*. He believes we should teach the conflicts of our positions through various forums that support a new vision of department integration, airing perspectives and discussing conflicts within all classrooms and through the development of department-held conferences and symposia.

Many English departments are paying serious attention to these institutional critiques even as our solutions fall short of accomplishing what is being suggested.[1] For instance, in my department we have debated the usefulness of an undergraduate course in critical theory. We have instituted theory and multicultural course requirements in our graduate curriculum, reviewed graduate degree requirements, and renamed some of our graduate courses. However, it is very easy for well-intentioned programs like ours to compromise their own larger vision in the elusive search for department unity. If teaching the conflicts is relegated to a few courses and if requirements are changed but content is not, field coverage has prevailed. It can only be hoped that departments currently able to institute multiple-course reconfigurations will eventually become departments willing to consider more radical *and integrative* curricular reform, reform that will take place vertically—within graduate and undergraduate programs simultaneously—as well as horizontally—reconceptualizing fields and periods of study.

As a profession, we have changed the way we talk more than we have changed our daily practices. In these discussions, postmodern theory offers several lenses for our discipline, and the language of critical theory may prove to be a lingua franca among subdisciplines. However, while a rhetorician and a literature scholar can attempt to find common ground regarding curricular reform, most of us have failed to consider how the "theory" in our graduate student (teacher)s complicates any changes we hope to introduce into the culture of English studies. New graduate students in English—including those who track into degree programs in literature, rhetoric, *and* creative writing—are constituted by the theories of learning that they bring with them. In the rest of this essay, I'll illustrate the degree to which our students are sites of conflicting theories and suggest that we need to "read" them better if we truly aim to improve our programs. Overall, it is necessary to ask our graduate student (teacher)s to share their attitudes and expectations, to articulate their tacit theories, for tacit theories rapidly come into conflict with the explicitly new theories being introduced into many programs, whether through coursework or dialogue or both.

I come to this discussion from my position as a teacher-educator. Each summer I introduce current research and pedagogy in composition and rhetoric to a diverse set of graduate teaching assistants, studying at the M.A. and Ph.D. levels. In the summer course, "Teaching Writing in College," I reverse the usual English department hierarchy and privilege writing over reading, composition over literature, at least temporarily, in order to ask new teachers to consider seriously the learning needs of their prospective first-year writing students. Through ethnographic study and informal observation, I know such reversals cause resistance and conversion—temporary to enduring—and are part of this educational process; new teachers must try on personas as well as explore practices as they include *first-year writing instructor* as one of their graduate program identities (see Bishop; Brooke). However, "trying on" an identity is not the simple shrugging into a new coat that the metaphor predicts; teachers aren't always aware (nor are their teacher-educators or graduate professors) of the firm theories they have and upon which they often base their attitudes toward classrooms, graduate school, and professors (see Welch). I use theory here in the largest sense—a reasoned prediction, often based on observation, about how things work—and often these tacit theories combine to form an individual's worldview.

New teachers are obviously influenced by their chosen area of study. Those tracking into the literature program, for instance, predictably resist the deemphasis of literature that can occur in a writing teacher education course, and those on the creative writing track may embrace the elements of writing process pedagogy that are most congruent with the creative writing workshop model of instruction. What is less clear is the degree to which field coverage and traditions of compartmentalization in English studies—majors and minors, strands or tracks—have produced a compartmentalization of GTA thought, and to what degree GTAs' theories of learning lead them into particular educational choices even as their professors attempt to mold these seemingly "blank-slate" new students to the professors' professed fields of study or critical approaches.

I have experienced the impermeability of the boundaries between tracks. I am often surprised at the lack of transference between teacher education at one level (first-year classrooms) to GTA teachers' practices at other levels (second- and third-year classrooms). I attended a workshop at my university composed entirely of experienced first-year writing teachers. In designing the workshop, we intended to brainstorm ways to use writing more often in 2000- and 3000-level introduction to short story and literature courses, courses often taught by senior GTAs. As the workshop leader asked each table to report back on strategies for using writing in the literature classroom, I heard a disappointing litany of exercises where writing was still used primarily to test knowledge: pop quizzes, short essays, research papers. Drafting, response groups, student-led discussion from journals, question making, and ungraded free writings—writing to learn activities—were all left in the dust of the first-year sequence.

Last summer, a GTA—one of a group of promising students deeply immersed in the study of critical theory—sent me a letter and a draft version of the common first-year curriculum that he hoped to teach. In this proposal, he derived his teaching theory from poststructural theory, choosing a ten-year-old, fifth edition of a well-known language reader and selections from Orwell and other classic essayists. I read this student as well versed in critical theory but poorly versed in composition theory, research, and practice. He planned for extensive discussions using technical, theoretical language and provided less support for writers in the process of constructing texts. Since this teacher entered our program with credit for previous teaching, exempting him from our summer teacher education courses, it was impossible to tell what composition texts he had read, but it felt like not very many. Clearly, theory was already in the student.

I can most clearly illustrate how filled by theory or theories our graduate students are by sharing excerpts from a year-long research study. These excerpts show how one Ph.D. student entering the literature track, without previous training but with strong attitudes and expectations about English studies and the value of literary texts, tested a new theory of learning against the strong one he already had. Again, while this student—whom I'll call Dennis—represents a literature student incorporating and resisting instruction in writing theory, he proved just as resistant to—because unacquainted with—the postmodern critical theories that are beginning to undergird our literature track.[2]

As we'll see in the case of this student, departments can mandate program requirements for theory, but they can't put theory into their faculty nor into their students. By "reading" Dennis, we can see that "theory" in the largest sense develops within the complicated territory of a GTA's experiential theories of learning and of school. For instance, Dennis relied on degrees held: always pay more attention to a graduate student than an undergraduate, to the M.A. than the B.A., to the Ph.D. than the M.A., and so on. Equally, Dennis expected his students to learn from him based on a similar premise: they should pay attention and believe him because he was a graduate student and they were first-year students, because he was an experienced academic writer and they weren't yet experienced, and so on.

I want to annotate very brief portions of a much more extensive set of taped interviews that I conducted with Dennis over a twelve-month period when he was training to be a teacher and I was participant-observer in his teacher education class (the summer before I was to begin teaching that class myself). Dennis was enrolled in two three-credit teacher education courses and mentions the teachers of those courses— Bonnie and Rick—in the transcripts below. After the summer 1990 courses, I continued to interview Dennis as he began doctoral work in English literature and taught his first two semesters of first-year writing. I need to emphasize the illustrative nature of my readings and excerpts. The quotes I've chosen to use are representative, although, of necessity, they are extracted from the rich context of the ethnographic study (which includes data collection with twenty-eight other new teachers as well as case studies of seven other teachers besides Dennis).

I also want to mention Dennis's successful negotiation of the English program. During the month I composed this draft, Dennis was preparing his dissertation prospectus. In his third year of teaching for the first-year writing program, he was in good standing as a teacher and as a student. During the previous three years, some of his strongly held theories of learning and classrooms had modified, while others had proved resilient, since changes in the graduate curriculum—undertaken to emphasize multicultural perspectives and incorporate contemporary critical theory—had been instituted within this English department. As I mentioned above, this was mainly accomplished by adding more course requirements in those subjects. The movement toward theory and multiculturalism has been less clearly instituted across the English department curriculum because an equal transformation within the *teaching* of all department professors has not been evidenced. Graduate students, naturally, gravitate toward faculty members who teach in familiar ways, say, by offering the familiar rewards of "A" grades for New Critical, literary-analysis essays. Due to undergraduate literature course class sizes of forty-five or more students, due to a large number of linked 4000/5000 literature courses of comparable size and graduate courses of twenty or more, due to unfamiliarity with contemporary writing theory, and due to preference, most professors continue to teach by the lecture/exam or lecture/literary analysis and research essay method at both the undergraduate and graduate levels (see Sullivan).

My reading of Dennis illuminates the degree to which our graduate students are already fully-formed, tacit theorists—about to mix and match the theories that they are presented with by an English department which itself is driven by multiple and conflicting theories—and are a functional graduate student outfit.

Professors as (Male) Authorities

Dennis found composition theory particularly difficult to accept because it conflicted with his theory about teachers, particularly college professors. Professors were authorities, usually right about issues by virtue of their degrees and long experience:

> **7/12/90**
>
> *Wendy:* There's something that prompted you to feel that you should consider this [composition theory] at least?
>
> *Dennis:* Yeah, I mean, the basic fact is that Rick's a Ph.D. These guys [Rick and Bonnie] are Ph.D.s and I'm not. You've been doing this for a hell of a lot longer than I have.
>
> **7/17/90**
>
> *Dennis:* Doesn't a teacher have to trust his knowledge and instincts? And what else do I have to give the student if not the sum of my knowledge and understanding?
>
> **7/30/90**
>
> *Dennis:* I mean, on the one hand, these people are Ph.Ds and they've been teaching for thirty years so they have, I mean roughly thirty years, so they have a system of thought. Like I've never been uncomfortable with the fact that a classroom isn't a democracy. It really bugs some students, I've never really been bothered with it. Because, that's a professor, he has a certain point of view, learn it! . . . Now if you want other points of view, take another class . . . You're guaranteed that you're going to get another point of view, because it's a different person teaching it.

Dennis did know that professors were contradictory creatures—not all professors agreed with each other—but, as a group, he vested them with wisdom because they had achieved a place in the English department hierarchy that Dennis himself wished to achieve. If they contradicted each other, so be it; the student's job then is to endure, engage (Dennis often chose battle metaphors) with each professor, and go on to the next until he gains the needed status from which to assert his own authority. The authoritative professor evoked by Dennis is a male; his female professor, Bonnie, is grouped into "you guys," for professors are always designated in his speech with the pronoun *he*. This is not surprising given that Dennis appeared to enroll in (or recall) only those courses from his M.A. program taught by men, and the first fall courses in his Ph.D. program were also taught by men. Senior women professors in his academic life were as scarce as they are in the profession in general, and those he encountered in the summer of 1990 taught composition and women's studies.

In Bonnie's class, Dennis was asked to write on first-year student tasks, which he resented (I explore this attitude in more detail below). As important as the task, though, was the course context: Dennis was writing here for a female professor whose opinion he doubted since she praised him for texts he himself could not value:

> *Dennis:* And she loved it [his last paper], I don't know why?
>
> *Wendy:* You thought for sure this is writing with a small *w* and she's saying, hey, for me, this is writing with a large *W*. And go back to your argument of "She's been doing this a long time, she's in the system, she has a Ph.D." Does that shake things up a little?
>
> *Dennis:* Hum, no, then I would probably be tempted to say that she's just being nice. I don't know.
>
> *Wendy:* Because she's a woman?
>
> *Dennis:* I didn't say that!
>
> *Wendy:* I asked it. I'm a woman, I can ask that.
>
> *Dennis:* I didn't say that. I refuse to get into an argument. I just read the articles on sexual discrimination. . . .

Dennis is normally eager for an argument—relishing the academic war of words that I discuss below—but here he denies his female professor a normal academic's authority when her advocacy for informal, exploratory writing threatens to undermine his trained preference for literary essay writing. For Dennis, professors are authorities, but some professors have more authority than others, based on gender. In this, he reflects the values of English studies during the last hundred years, for only slow changes have occurred in the gender makeup of English departments over the last twenty years.

Teaching and Learning as Battle

Because knowledge, in Dennis's theory, is developed through personal authority, wresting such authority from a classroom turns learning into a battle. I am not the first to point out that the battle metaphor often signals an interest in hierarchy and a degree of comfort with confrontational argumentation. Although composition scholars, feminist scholars, and many other academics who identify themselves as part of marginalized subdisciplines in English studies tend to challenge such seemingly masculinist tropes, the tropes are still prevalent. As a student of literature, still the dominant group within English studies, Dennis could be expected to partake of this contentious metaphoric tradition:

> 7/30/90
>
> [regarding writing his papers for professors]
>
> *Dennis:* It was always a "me versus you" type of mentality . . . I went and looked up their [the professors] articles and books. I could tell, so I had these strategies. If you know where the enemy is, you know how to fire upon him.
>
> [regarding a particular professor]
>
> *Dennis:* He ran the class, basically, like 1930s Germany. It was strictly lecture. He could come in, we did three books, *Scarlet Letter, Moby Dick, Huckleberry Finn,* and he basically would come in and would read the book to you. And every sentence, he would interpret every other sentence.

In this battle, the experienced, (male) degreed professor has the edge and students push the limits of his authority at their own risk:

> 7/30/90
>
> *Dennis:* He didn't want anyone else's opinion. . . . Out of class, I argued with him and I didn't agree. . . . basically, I learned after the first exam, after *The Scarlet Letter,* the type of symbolism that he wanted . . . and the same with another professor. I wrote basically the same essay on an exam roughly four times, almost word for word, I think. Or at least, types of sentences were the same. "Man's a creature in possession of language. . . ." All I had to say for this one professor is that "Keats celebrates language as an event through this particular device." Then the next time: "Virginia Woolf celebrates language in this way. . . ." I have yet to find a professor that doesn't want in some shape or pattern his own opinions. No matter how much [they] say, "I want to see original thinking" . . . that's a lie.

Given Dennis's theory of learning as a battleground with the tables turned in the favor of the professor, it's no surprise that he has trouble with the collaborative, student-centered, feminist instructional model advocated in his teacher education classes. Even as he is being instructed to consider classrooms as something other than academic battlegrounds, Dennis's most prized day of the summer occurred when he took over his GTA mentor's writing class:

7/12/90

> *Dennis:* . . . What I thought was the best day . . . there were so many people talking and I was firing questions off. I really enjoyed that. That was good. That's the way I'd like to run the class, an hour and a half battle.

Dennis has re-created his own educational past: he's at the helm, captain of the ship, the officer calling the charge, firing off questions in the heat of the battle and the center of the action. However, during his training, he is asked to give up his hard-won superiority and advantage. And it is not that Dennis is unaware of other theories of learning; before he began his summer teacher education courses, he predicted this problem on a questionnaire. In response to "What do you need to learn about teaching writing?" Dennis answered: "I know how to teach effectively. I know how not to hurt the feelings of others. I do not know how to do both." For Dennis, in the necessary classroom war, someone is bound to be wounded, and teachers do not dare become too sensitive on the battlefield of knowledge. Dennis feels he needs no other teacher preparation than his careful observations of his own previous classrooms from which he has abstracted this functional theory of learning. School is a bracing battle that unfortunately often hurts.

Conflicting Theories

Dennis's theory of learning, attitudes toward professors, and expectations for his classrooms, based on his observations of literature courses he had enrolled in, immediately set him in opposition to both composition *and* reception theory:

7/16/90

> *Dennis:* How can students, who by definition lack specific knowledge, simply stumble upon knowledge? No, I am not underestimating their capabilities. But I am questioning the students' ability to teach themselves to write. It seems to me to be the blind leading the blind. I thought the provision of guidance was our function. I thought that's what a teacher did. Current thought reduces my role to absurd tour guide, a man with a dim flashlight waving at tourists wandering aimlessly in the dark. It's not only wishful thinking, but it's a disservice to the students themselves. When I enter a classroom, I expect to be offered something that I did not have before. But that offering comes from the instructor; what he knows becomes part of me.

Dennis's opposition is based, of course, on his experiences with the transmission and banking models of the teacher-centered instruction he has experienced. His role with former professors was to profess their way of reading. His role with his students, since he's senior to them, should be to show them the way, to offer them something. Student-centered learning represents the blind leading the blind, since knowledge—in Dennis's theory—is something transmitted from master to novice. Yet, in his education courses, he has been strongly introduced to an alien model of learning.

7/17/90

> *Dennis:* Students find it difficult enough to communicate effectively without worrying about their membership in an interpretive community. And if we hold to the postmodern premise that reading and meaning are relative, then I can never read the student paper "correctly," can never give the "right" response. I'm defeated before I begin. I can't accept that. I have to "go" with what I think is right and hope the students *are* learning to write— even if they are only conforming to the standards of my own interpretive community.

Certainly Dennis is able to understand the premises of poststructural theory. But he is unable to inhabit those positions because, by accepting multiple readings and teachers as senior learners, he might risk losing the classroom war; he would do this by being untrue to his past school experiences and the theories he had abstracted from his Master's-level literature studies.

Theories of Writing

Dennis knows how to write papers to please his professors. He's a successful graduate student. Here's how he goes about it:

7/30/90

> *Dennis:* You have the due date looming over you... by the time I finish [reading the assigned] text, there'll usually be a few things that have stuck out that I'll have noticed, so I'll drop some notes, and we'll raise questions in class.... Then, when we're approaching the paper, I usually have a general idea in mind. And then I start systematically, "Okay this is the point I'm going to prove." I'll have a thesis... and then I'll go into the text and see if I'm right, before I start taking real notes, because I'll specifically quote. "This quote matches what I want to say, this quote doesn't." Once I get a body of quotes and notes, then I usually start making an outline. So I'll take every quote that I want to use out of the text, put it on a couple of sheets of paper and then dismiss the text....

> *Wendy:* Do you go much to outside critical work?

> *Dennis:* I kind of rely more on my own critical theory. I don't see the purpose of rehashing what everyone else has written. . . . Usually what I'll do is I'll find a nice set of quotes from the research that I've done and then have that as a "set of quotes #2"—there's a set of quotes from the text and a set from the [critical] literature. And then I'll stick them in where I want them, where I think they'll look good.

Dennis has developed an effective method for writing traditional, academic literary essays. When he enrolls in a teacher education course intended to teach him current process theories of writing instruction, there is an immediate mismatch. He hates writing the class assignments which require him to do the same type of papers he'll be assigning in first-year writing: "Now those papers I turned in for Bonnie—the last one, I should have had my M.A. rescinded. It was that bad. And she loved it; I don't know why." Dennis has trouble appreciating the informal, exploratory, multidraft essay; in his view, more elementary types of writing will take place in first-year writing. Equally, he feels he is wasting his time writing such prose, for his standards have been molded around literary analysis and research essays with their sets of references and techniques of close reading:

7/30/90

> *Wendy:* So even within formal academic style, you don't like informal academic style. . . ?
>
> *Dennis:* Even if I'm writing a letter, it's always big W [writing]—I mean, it's always I'm just in this big W set. I've just been taught, I have to "do something" that's better than it was before. Sometimes it's just like I don't want to do it [write]. That's why I don't write as much as I used to, because it's like climbing the big W.
>
> *Wendy:* You have really high standards, but you also agree with those standards?
>
> *Dennis:* Yeah. Hey, it just hit me. I think in the class [teacher education], maybe I want big W and Rick is willing to settle for the little *w?*

Dennis, like many new writing teachers, wrestles with issues of response and the difficulties of grading student texts. He has always preferred literary text to *all* other texts, including those by students and by theorists:

8/1/90

> *Dennis:* Finally, after nearly six weeks of abstractions, of rhetoric and composition duckspeak, I finally was able to get to my first love: literature. Now I understand that the ENC1102 class is structured as Writing *through* Literature. But, nevertheless, I was quite

pleased to hear the names Faulkner and Kafka, rather than Elbow and Murray.

Dennis is fighting some new battles here as he enters an English department that gives at least minimal acknowledgment to the value of different types of text and new types of academic writing. Dennis is a graduate student proficient in the thesis-statement literary paper. Even when convinced that he should use certain writing invention strategies in the first-year classroom, making the move to *believing* in those strategies or in a new view of the writing process is very difficult. Dennis is pained at having to write writing with a lowercase *w* and chooses to teach invention strategies not on the basis of how effective they might be for student writers, but instead on the basis of how they strike him personally:

9/12/90

Dennis: Well, it's a struggle because I don't use them [invention strategies]. I know how to do this stuff already. It's more internalized, so it's hard for me to distance myself from it and not come off saying—and I found myself doing it at first—that may have been why I had so much trouble doing it [teaching invention strategies] at first—I may have come off saying "Well, this is stupid but we're doing it anyway." And I can see the problems resulting from that. . . . And, in some respect, I do think these things are stupid, but that may just be because I don't need them anymore. Like, I, I absolutely refuse to do the house thing [draw a floor plan of a former home]. I thought it was utterly a waste of time, so I haven't done it.

What I find interesting when I read across this year of interviews with Dennis is not only his resistance but also his successful adaptation. Changes did occur in his attitudes toward teaching, in the shape of his classrooms, and even in his theory of learning (at least for first-year writing). However, Dennis overall remained much the same in his expectations about graduate school learning, simply because the new theories offered to him did not prove more compelling than the old ones he held.

Dennis's original theories proved profitable; his first-semester graduate literature professors rewarded him for his already developed, literary-analysis writing skills and did nothing to reinforce the writing and learning theories raised in his summer education courses. In one of his two American literature courses, Dennis received a grade of 95 for a paper on "Who is the Catcher in the Rye?" which began: "One does not always have to read a novel to enjoy a finely crafted and highly symbolic work of fiction" and received a professor's comments of:

"Excellent paper, intelligent, clearly argued, written with grace and precision. Parallel is exact—and your analysis leaves little doubt as to the cogency of your argument. Hey, you write good!" Dennis had brought off another capital *W* production.

Another paper he shared with me was from the second American literature course. "The Split Reality of the Puritan Sensibility" as a title suggests a course lecture phrase, and the essay opens with this thesis statement: "Any consideration of the seventeenth and early eighteenth century American—specifically Puritan—sensibility must proceed from the assertion that Puritan culture was theocentric in its focus, revolving around a constant attention to the relationship between God and man." This paper received the response: "A+. Well-organized and clear exposition. Good explanation." More notable are the drafts from this paper. On five separate pages, Dennis hones the opening thesis paragraph, a sentence at a time, adding one more sentence each page. The last several draft pages represent the single hand-written draft of the full paper which proves his carefully wrought thesis. Both literature course essays capitalize on the skills and process Dennis was able to articulate the summer before he enrolled in those Ph.D. courses and bear scant resemblance to the forms or process of writing required in the first-year classes he was teaching.

The year-long study of Dennis's teaching, of course, illuminates the complicated play of old and newly encroaching theories and suggests the resiliency of field divisions. To some degree, Dennis changed his attitudes toward process instruction and his first-year writing classes (changed them particularly from the more current-traditional model he *thought* he would institute before being trained that summer), but his life in the newly theorized English department curriculum remained compartmentalized for many reasons: he enrolled in the courses of professors who themselves were not engaged in theoretical and curricular debates, and when he was introduced to theory, it was in the education or critical theory course, cordoned off from his daily practice.

Having spent one year with Dennis as a participant-observer and another two years as a department friend who continued to undertake good-natured verbal "battles" concerning the value of composition theory, the problem of subjectivity in grading, the shape and direction of English studies, and the value of literary and student texts, among many other topics, I believe Dennis to be the perfect example of a student who would benefit from Gerald Graff's proposal that we teach the conflicts in the curriculum, for clearly they are being played out every day when his attitudes and expectations intersect with those of his professors and students in the halls and classrooms of the English building. However, his case also reminds us that the situation is far too complicated to be resolved by *structural* curricular change. Dennis needs to see his literature and composition teachers in dialogue—co-teaching, participating in department conferences and colloquia, negotiating in a lingua franca—making it harder for Dennis to claim total allegiance to one discourse and deny credibility for another. This means, of course, that the professors under whom Dennis studies would need to learn about and respect each other's work. It means that departments would need to regularly promote meritorious women to the rank of full professor, eliminating the associate professor-level "glass ceiling" that can develop as a larger number of women enter departments, many of whom are completing exemplary but often nontraditional work. And this means that departments will have to pay attention to the hierarchy of texts identified by Robert Scholes in order to examine their own valorization of certain academic genres during times of curricular revision and during annual and tenure reviews. If a department doesn't value composition textbook writing equally with the writing of critical essays and "creative" prose, drama, and poetry, and allow those texts to count toward tenure, faculty will play out the department's value system in the classroom and in department interactions. And Dennis will be watching and learning.

The issues that I've outlined here as being at play in a typical research university also play out in two- and four-year colleges. Graduate students like Dennis will mostly take up teaching positions within our two- and four-year colleges, replicating the habits they developed in their graduate teaching and imitating the practices of professors they studied under, including those in their undergraduate pasts. If their professors taught writing and reading quite differently or taught writing as if it were a course in reading, these graduate student (teacher)s would be influenced in the same direction. If graduate students at my institution teach first-year writing and junior- and senior-level literature based on different theories of learning, they are likely to continue to do the same as they teach undergraduates at other institutions.

Important questions remain to be answered: Is the move to theory only another battle and, if so, in what type of war? How do we shape change when professors, students, and curricula are informed by tacit and explicit theories, many of which directly contradict the others? Even as Dennis wanted and needed to change his attitudes towards first-year writing instruction, he noted that such change was incredibly difficult:

12/5/90

Wendy: So, in a way, you thought they [first-year writers] would be fully formed writers with just bad habits . . . ?

Dennis: . . . Maybe I was thinking they should all be like me type of thing, you know, because I considered myself a decent writer when I got into college.

Wendy: You have an in-the-head criteria of great freshman writing?

Dennis: I don't know great. I don't like the word great.

Wendy: Your criteria of freshman writing . . . ?

Dennis: Uh huh.

Wendy: It's not your rankings of literary writing?

Dennis: No. No. No. That's one thing I have managed to separate.

Wendy: I've been advocating viewing students' writing as literature. . . .

Dennis: Their grades would sink. Their grades would sink. Don't make me do that.

Wendy: No, I'd rather have you reconsider literature, but we'll talk about that another time.

Dennis: Okay (laughter). Seems like an argument there.

Wendy: Literature with a regular, healthy, small *l.*

Dennis: Oh no. We talked about that before with a *w.* (Laughter) I don't want to get into that again.

Wendy: Okay.

Reading Dennis, we find that learned theories of reading and writing are always foregrounded against a backdrop of tacit theories of learning, classrooms, and teaching roles that have been built up through a student's astute observation of professors and English studies as an institution. Such a complicated matrix of interactions suggests that we can't just talk theory talk and ask our students to do the same. Instead, we have to examine the roles graduate student (teacher)s are asked to assume in our classrooms, in their own classrooms, as writers and as readers, in every course in the English curriculum. Equally, we have to make explicit our own tacit assumptions about these issues as we discuss the future and directions of programs. At the least, we may have to give up some autonomy to develop curricular comprehensibility—some of us trying to do some of the same things, more or less, some of the time—for this will encourage dialogue. I'm not suggesting that we all teach the same way—that's an impossible and unappealing solution—but I do believe we should agree to talk about how our theory exists in practice as we recalibrate curricula. We need to learn from all our fields, that is, from each other. For even when we think we are conducting the decision-making process in the private forum of department faculty meetings, Dennis's case shows that our students are internalizing our conflicting theories and creating strategies for survival in every English course that they take, and those strategies will affect an enormous number of students in undergraduate English classrooms in the future.

Notes

1. The textual stratification that Scholes points to marks such a great division between different strands of English studies that Graff himself, according to Christy Friend, problematically ignores one of the largest department level issues—the relationship of literature and composition.

2. Dennis's case-study data is part of a book-length manuscript in progress, *Composing the New Teacher of College Writing: Ethnographic Readings and Reflections,* and was funded, in part, by a grant from the Research Foundation of the National Council of Teachers of English.

Works Cited

Bishop, Wendy. *Something Old, Something New: College Writing Teachers and Classroom Change.* Carbondale: Southern Illinois UP, 1990.

Brooke, Robert. *Writing and Sense of Self: Identity Negotiation in Writing Workshops.* Urbana, IL: NCTE, 1991.

Friend, Christy. "The Excluded Conflict: The Marginalization of Composition and Rhetoric Studies in Graff's *Professing Literature." College English* 54.3 (March 1992): 276–86.

Graff, Gerald. *Beyond the Culture Wars: How Teaching the Conflicts Can Revitalize American Education.* New York: Norton, 1992.

———. *Professing Literature: An Institutional History.* Chicago: U of Chicago P, 1987.

Scholes, Robert. *Textual Power: Literary Theory and the Teaching of English.* New Haven: Yale UP, 1985.

Sullivan, Patricia A. "Writing in the Graduate Cirrocumuli: Literary Criticism as Composition." *Journal of Advanced Composition* 11.2 (Fall 1992): 283–99.

Welch, Nancy. "Resisting the Faith: Conversion, Resistance, and the Training of Teachers." *College English* 55.4 (April 1993): 387–401.

14 Teaching Theorizing / Theorizing Teaching

James Phelan
Ohio State University

Genre Considerations

I always have trouble reading essays about teaching theory. "Too prescriptive," I find myself saying, or "too general," "too simplistic," "too mechanical," "too condescending." In the natural course of teaching, we all think about why some things work and some things don't. Because the chemistry between teacher and student varies so much from class to class, my knowing that something works for you doesn't give me confidence that it will work for me. The recommendations in such essays typically become additional options on my list of "Things To Try" rather than a set of compelling ideas that make the "Must Do" list. All in all, I'd rather read theory than read about how to teach it.

So, in writing this piece, I have had a particularly nagging reader-over-my-shoulder repeatedly whispering, "Stop kidding yourself and your readers; we both know that the best—and most honest—advice you can give them is, 'There are lots of good—and bad—ways to teach theory; do what works for you, but never be completely satisfied with what you do. Stop reading this and go read Foucault.'" I haven't succeeded in silencing that voice—and haven't been sure that I should want to. In listening to the reader's voice, I became convinced that my essay could not simply ignore the diversity of productive solutions to any problem I might address, even as I also wanted to recommend something that my readers might move to the top of their lists of "Things to Try." Consequently, I have written a dialogue among several speakers, a dialogue that attempts both to present my particular recommendation and to exemplify the theoretical position underlying that recommendation. If the dialogue succeeds, there's no need for me to name that position.

From Theory to Theorizing

[A group of faculty are gathered in the English department commons room. As people go about getting coffee, leafing through The New York Times, *and chatting in twos, one of them suddenly addresses the group.]*

Betty: I could use some advice. I'm doing the undergraduate theory course for the first time next semester, and I'm trying to decide what I want to teach and how I want to teach it. I've been asking myself, "What should the students know by the end of the semester?" and can't seem to settle on an answer.

Katie: Well, if you want to reflect where the profession is right now, then you should probably teach feminism, poststructuralism, and New Historicism. To do those well you'd have to get into Marxism, psychoanalysis, and linguistics too. That'd give you plenty to do in one course.

Mike: Too much, I'd say. If you feed your students a strict diet of Derrida, Lacan, Irigaray, and Foucault, they won't digest any of it. It'll come back to you in papers and on exams in mushy blocks of unintelligibility. Before they can read Derrida, they need to know something about the history of criticism. Plato and Aristotle, though founding fathers of the Western phallogocentric tradition, are raising issues in ancient Greece that we're still grappling with today. What are the canon wars, if not fights over the role and influence of poetry in the state? What is deconstruction, if not a quarrel with Aristotle's notion of tragedy—and by extension other literature—as an imitation of an action that is whole and complete? But even if you find Plato and Aristotle too ancient for your postmodern students, I'd think you'd want to give your students some historical overview of twentieth-century criticism, starting maybe with T. S. Eliot and I. A. Richards, going through Wellek and Warren, Brooks, Wimsatt and Beardsley, Crane, Hirsch, and then on down through the explosion of theory in the '70s, ending up perhaps with the intersections of multiculturalism and theory. If you don't historicize the movements Katie wants you to teach, the students will think that those movements are theory *tout court.* And that's something I definitely wouldn't want them thinking by the end of the course.

Jim: Katie and Mike's ideas each have some merit, but I think they're both advocating something that I hope you won't do—namely, treat theory as if it's separate from what we usually do, a field to cover in the same way that the Renaissance is something to cover in the curriculum. The whole point of the so-called theory revolution is that theory is inescapable, that every one of our courses rests on an implicit theory, that the whole curriculum itself reflects a theory. I think you should teach exactly the same poetry, fiction, or drama that you're teaching in your other course next quarter but spend your time examining the theory underlying the interpretations you're teaching in the other course.

Bill: I hear what you're saying about not divorcing theory from the rest of what we do, but the trouble with your recommendation is that the students will be exposed to only one kind of theory. As Graff says, teach the conflicts. Don't just teach your interpretations and their underlying theoretical principles, but show how those interpretations and the theory are subject to questioning, challenge, and contradiction by other perspectives.

Betty: Why am I not surprised that the four of you give four different answers? But, if Bill doesn't object, I'd like to avoid the conflicts among you for a minute and suggest that maybe there's something even more fundamental to get at in this course. If we accept for now Jim's point that a major lesson of the theory revolution is that theory is inescapable, then might it not be worth shifting attention away from *theories,* i.e., the doctrines of particular critics or schools, and toward *theorizing,* i.e., the activities of theory, primarily asking questions about first principles, about methods, about what is generalizable and what isn't and why?

Katie: Sounds to me as if you could be creating a form / content split. I used to be a great believer in the "develop-thinking-skills-now-and-learn-content-later" approach to literature and criticism, but the longer I've been around, the more limits I see to that approach. I hated the elitism of Hirsch's initial lists of cultural literacy as much as anyone, but I find what he says about the crucial role of background knowledge in understanding discourse to be persuasive. If you want to build the course around the idea that theory is asking certain kinds of questions, I don't think it will work unless you're also doing a substantial amount of traditional coverage of content. So I still say focus on feminism, poststructuralism, and New Historicism—plenty of theoretical questions there.

Mike: Remember, too, that these days students take theory because they want to be able to associate clear signifieds with the signifiers they hear us tossing around—they want to know stuff like what deconstruction is, who Derrida is, and what Freud has to do with criticism. Many of them feel that theory is a big secret that only the faculty know—and they want to be let in on it. Some of the students are scared by it, and some who initially aren't become fearful a few weeks into the course—"Professor Mike," they say, "reading this stuff is not like reading Mark

Twain." Other students are excited and stay excited throughout the course—"Professor Mike," they say with a different inflection, "reading this stuff is not like reading Mark Twain." Fearful or excited, our students want *information* that will let them in on our alleged secrets. You can teach them about asking questions, but make sure you tell them the secrets. Give them a historical narrative of theory in the twentieth century and you'll give them what they want and what they need.

Jim: Well, I can see where this is going. I could say that my idea of foregrounding the theory of your other course is a great way to teach theory and theorizing, and Bill could say that the "teach the conflicts" approach is an even better way to do it. Right, Bill?

Bill: Yup. Teaching the conflicts means not only teaching conflicting questions, but it also generates questions about the conflicts. Sounds to me like it's ideally suited to an emphasis on theorizing rather than theories.

Jim: But I take it, Betty, that you have something else in mind when you talk about emphasizing theorizing rather than theories.

Betty: Well, I think I do, though I'm not sure I can articulate it yet. Let's try something and see what happens. Would each of you describe your critical identity for me? [*Much nervous laughter, then finally murmurs of willingness.*]

Katie: Well, I tend to treat texts as sites where a culture's gender ideologies get played out, sometimes in ways that the text—or other critics— try hard not to acknowledge. If I had to pigeonhole myself, I'd guess I'd say I'm a poststructuralist feminist. In the classroom, though, I do all kinds of things: teach New Critical techniques of close reading, discuss relations between biography and literature, do some psychoanalytical stuff, some deconstruction. I'm not sure I have a stable critical identity— though I suppose that's appropriate for a poststructuralist.

Mike: Well, some people call me a New Historicist, but I'm not sure that's how I'd describe myself. Like mainline New Historicists, I'm interested in the ways literature interacts with other texts to reflect and transform a larger Culture Text. But like Old Historicists, I'm interested in assessing the quality of individual texts, and I've been sufficiently influenced by my earlier formalist training to think that verbal and structural complexity are among the significant marks of aesthetic quality. So I don't know whether to declare allegiance to the Old Historicism or the New.

Bill: I suppose I'm a cultural critic, but my orientation is different from Mike's. I'm less interested in "the text" and in any monolithic notion of

History than I am in how readers' and critics' assumptions about texts reveal aspects of their culture. In other words, I'm interested in such things as what the apparent shift from regarding literary texts as verbal icons to regarding them as nodes in a web of intertextuality says about our shifting cultural values. I've gravitated toward Graff's proposals because, in my view, they tap into something very significant about our current literary-critical culture: we carry on quite diverse activities without ever asking our students—and sometimes even ourselves—to confront that diversity. Those people who think that literary critics are parasites living off the creativity of others would call me a metaparasite, so I prefer the label cultural critic, even if it's a tad uncomfortable.

Jim: Call me wishy-washy. I'm interested in lots of things, and I work in different ways at different times. Would it mess up your experiment if I opted out and refused to identify myself according to my allegiances?

Betty: Not at all. In fact, it helps make my point—that there is a huge gap between what critics and theorists do and the way we teach theory. Jim was most explicit about how uncomfortable the labeling made him, but all of you built wiggle-room into your answers. Why? Maybe you've all been rereading *Hamlet.* Maybe you're all afraid of commitment. Or maybe your own critical activity doesn't neatly fit into the set of available identities offered through affiliation with current critical schools. And as beautifully unique as each one of you is, I'd suggest that in feeling this gap you're typical of most critics.

Mike: And your point is?

Betty: My point is that our usual ways of teaching theory, especially introducing it to students, are misleading. We teach students about schools and movements, about critical doctrines, beliefs, and positions, but it's hard to find large numbers of flesh and blood theorists whose identities conform to the possibilities outlined by those positions. We need a way to tighten the fit between the way individual critics and theorists think of themselves and the way we teach students about the field of theory.

Katie: If I'm following the logic of your objection, then you're on the verge of suggesting that we should survey the 33,000 members of the MLA about their critical identities, analyze the results into 33,000 critical profiles, and then teach those. Are you about to waylay us into collaborating with you on an NCTE grant proposal?

Seriously, though, I still don't see what you're getting at. Feminists, after all, are always reminding their detractors that there is no one feminist position that all who call themselves feminist subscribe to. But that doesn't stop anyone from teaching capital F, capital T, Feminist Theory, or, indeed, from teaching about the schools and movements within feminist theory; certainly it's helpful to talk about differences among American feminists, British feminists, French feminists or to differentiate, as Elaine Showalter did over a decade ago, among the movements she called feminist critique, gynocriticism, and écriture féminine. Though Showalter's categories no longer do justice to current work in feminism, they remain useful to anyone who, like Mike, would want to think about the history of feminist criticism. Of course you don't want anyone to think that such sorting is the endpoint of learning about feminist theory, but, as a way to begin, it has a lot to recommend it. And so does the schools-and-movements approach to theory, more generally. Where are your thoughts leading you?

Betty: As I said, I'm still not sure. I'll readily grant that the schools-and-movements approach has the huge advantage of organizing what might otherwise appear to be an utterly messy field; by giving students a map, the approach allows them to get oriented and to think about where they'd like to locate themselves in that field. I think that what I'm starting to feel uneasy about are the metaphors of map and field. Their power to provide orientation comes at the price of encouraging us to think of discrete locations and relative fixity or stasis. I'd like to try some metaphors that characterize theory not as a position but as an action, or, better, a series of actions that begin with the asking of a certain kind of question and that end only at provisional stopping points. "Theory as a Perpetual Motion Machine."

Bill: OK, I'm beginning to see what's behind this. We build the wiggle-room into our self-descriptions because we don't envision ourselves as embodiments of a pure position but as people who are *doing* criticism and theory in a way that makes sense for our particular projects. But the notion of theory as a machine frets me. Just as you're becoming uneasy with the schools-and-movements approach, I'm becoming increasingly unhappy with the "approaches" approach because it tends to turn each approach into a machine for reading. Feed the text into this end of the Marxist machine and get a Marxist reading out that end. I very much admire Steven Lynn's essay demonstrating several approaches to the passage from Brendan Gill's *Here at The New Yorker,* but I hesitate to give it to my students. I'm afraid that they'll take it as more evidence that theory is a set of text mulchers—figure out the kind of mulch you want and then select the appropriate theory. Because Lynn's purpose is to illustrate the workings of different approaches, he can't help it that his fine readings are hothouse tomatoes rather than bushes occurring in the wild, but they still have a somewhat artificial quality. Another positive feature of teaching the conflicts is that all the texts I work with are primarily intended not for students in a theory class but for some other audience immediately concerned with the ongoing conflict.

A Course on Theorizing

Betty: Okay, makes good sense. Maybe we should talk some more about the activities of theory and then come back to the question of the appropriate metaphor. Katie, how did you come to write your last article?

Katie: Well, as I was teaching *Beloved,* I kept thinking about who Morrison's primary audience was and kept wondering about the ways that my experience as a white, middle-class, thirty-five-year-old woman in the academy was influencing the way I was interpreting her text. I wanted to question not the validity of my reading but the kinds of claims I could make for it in relation to claims that might be made for readings by white male critics, black male critics, black female critics, white academics of both sexes, black nonacademic critics. The essay was more about the whole issue of subjectivity and group identity in reading than about *Beloved.* I feel as if I just scratched the surface of the problems entailed in taking the issue seriously, so I'd like to do more with it, but at the moment I feel stuck about where to go next.

Betty: Suppose I were to teach your essay as an example of reader-response criticism. Would you feel I was (mis)appropriating it?

Katie: Well, I don't have any objection to the label, but it doesn't seem to say a whole lot about the essay. I guess how I'd feel would depend on what else you did with the essay besides locate it in the reader-response field.

Jim: I think I'm starting to catch on. Betty, I see the difference between Katie's idea for your course—theory's hottest hits—and her activity in her last essay. But you can't teach different critics' composition processes, even if that's what you wanted to do. So what are you getting at?

Betty: Well, if I can shift the students' expectations early in the quarter, then I won't need to know how many drafts, say, Scholes took the first chapter of *Protocols of Reading* through. Instead, I can show students that the text on the page itself contains a dynamics that we might call "theorizing." Scholes's chapter isn't just a set of theses about how reading works. It's an effort to answer a *question,* or perhaps better, to address a *problem* about the relation between readers' desires to find the center of a text's interest and their desires to use the text as a springboard for exploring their own interests. Scholes goes about answering the question according to a particular *method;* and the whole procedure is built on certain *principles and assumptions* about language, texts, reading, culture, semiotic codes, intertextuality, and other things. All of these elements—question, answer, method, principles—come together in the service of a larger *purpose,* which can be discerned in the essay's *dialogic relation* to theorists who argue for the value of respecting authorial intention, to reader-response critics who want to liberate the reader, and to cultural critics more generally: Scholes wants to offer a new model of reading that synthesizes three key principles from these different traditions: (1) attention to the formal features of the text, which produces what he calls centripetal reading; (2) recognition of different readers' rights to respond more powerfully to some parts of the text than others; and (3) attention to the way that both kinds of reading depend on intertextuality and especially the common cultural codes shared by intertexts. I'd try to show how Scholes's overall purpose animates the activity of the whole essay—and show students that they can come to recognize these dynamics working in a slightly different way when we think about chapter 1's role in the whole book. Furthermore, in emphasizing the notion of Scholes's chapter as a kind of action, I'd also invite reflection on the kind of action we're performing in doing this analysis. I'd try to get the students to see that from Scholes's point of view, the analysis would be both centripetal and intertextual, and I'd invite them to discuss whether he'd find our treatment congenial, and if he didn't, whether we'd want to change it or not.

Bill: And if at the end of all that, what do you gain beyond helping them understand Scholes?

Katie: Let me see if I can answer. You gain the same kinds of things that writing teachers gain when they bring so-called "real world writing" into their classrooms. You move the teaching of theory out of what we were calling the hothouse and into the world of work that most theorists know. And by getting them to approach the theory texts as actions, you might help the students regard them as work (or action) always in progress, and thus open to objection and revision as well as acceptance and appropriation. Furthermore, by turning Scholes back on your method of reading him, you remind the students that your way of analyzing is itself an action-in-progress. Right?

Betty: Right; in fact, you've articulated better than I could when I walked in here this morning. Thanks.

Jim: I don't especially want to disrupt sisterly solidarity, but what about Katie's earlier worry that you're going to be reintroducing a form-content split? If the schools-and-movements approach goes wrong in emphasizing content at the expense of form, you seem to be running the risk of overcompensating. Does your goal of emphasizing real-world theory help you decide what to put on your reading list?

Betty: Well, as I think about it, I want to say that it makes all the difference and absolutely no difference at all. My first step would have to be to theorize my course. What are my purpose and my central question? So far, I've been talking about a very general purpose—to shift emphasis from theory to theorizing—so I need to move down the ladder of generality. I need to think about my audience of advanced undergraduates, most of whom have never formally studied theory before. Keeping in my mind the suggestions you four made at the beginning of this conversation, and Mike's particular point about what students often want from a theory course, I think my first need is a reading list that represents more than one theoretical perspective. Jim, your idea to teach the theory underlying my other course is, I think, better served by my actually doing that in that course. But keeping in mind my desire to get away from schools and movements, I don't want to do a survey or even a version of Mike's history. What I want is to take a recurring problem or issue and have the students read a sampling of work that addresses that issue—sometimes directly, sometimes indirectly. The approach would borrow from Graff's "teach the conflicts" model, Bill, but it's not identical with it. Exploring conflict would get subsumed by the larger purpose of tracing the activities each theorist performs as she addresses the recurring problem in her own way. And I wouldn't want to select only readings that are in conflict. Instead, I'd want to examine for any two cases the question of whether their apparently different views are conflicting, complementary, or just different.

   Given all that, I think my question would have something like the following form: "What can we learn about contemporary theory and theorizing by studying a significant body of work on X?" where X is the issue or problem—the author, history, language, ideology, intention, the reader, gender, and difference are just a few of the possible candidates.

Jim: In some ways, it sounds very good to me. But I'm still troubled by a few things. It seems to me that you're going to end up with a syllabus that will look a lot like one kind of standard syllabus for a theory course. And in that respect, you're going to be reinforcing the split between theory and everything else that I was trying to combat with my initial idea of teaching the theory underlying the practice of your other course.

Betty: I think on that issue we may just disagree. I worry less about isolating theory, because I think it's an important curricular statement for us to say, "In some of our courses, we will focus not on our discipline's usual objects of study (literary texts) but rather on some texts that are the products of our discipline." I think it is very valuable to offer our students the opportunity to devote a course to thinking about the activities that go into producing the work of our discipline. In that connection, I would argue that the activities of theory are not fundamentally different from the activities of practical criticism. The main difference is in the kind of question that the theorist asks; rather than inquiring into the specifics of a given text, the theorist asks about the conditions and grounds of critical activity or about more generalizable properties of literature and criticism.

Bill: Come back to earth and tell us more about your reading list for next quarter.

Betty: I'm thinking that the course's question will be, "What can we learn about contemporary theory and theorizing by studying a significant body of work on the reader?" The reading list would mix some mainline reader-response essays with work that indirectly treats the reader but whose assumptions about reading powerfully affect its direction. The syllabus might look something like this:

> *Week 1:* "The Reader under the Power of the Text": Wimsatt and Beardsley's "The Affective Fallacy"; Booth's chapter on "The Control of Distance in *Emma*" from *The Rhetoric of Fiction*.

> *Week 2:* "Breaking Away from the Text": selections from Bloom's *The Anxiety of Influence* and Holland's *5 Readers Reading*.

> *Weeks 3 and 4:* "The Virtual Text and Interpretive Communities": Iser's "The Reading Process: A Phenomenological Approach"; Fish's "Affective Stylistics" and "Interpreting the *Variorum*"; Fish's "Why No One's Afraid of Wolfgang Iser" and Iser's response.

> *Weeks 4 and 5:* "The Question of Competence": Culler's chapter on "Literary Competence" from *Structuralist Poetics* and selections from Rabinowitz's *Before Reading*.

> *Week 6:* "The Poststructuralist Reader": de Man, "Semiology and Rhetoric"; D. A. Miller, selections from *The Novel and the Police*.

> *Week 7:* "The Difference Gender Makes": selections from *The Resisting Reader* and Flynn and Schweickart's *Gender and Reading*.

> *Weeks 8 and 9:* "The Ethics of Reading": selections from J. Hillis Miller, *The Ethics of Reading;* Nussbaum's *Love's Knowledge;* and Booth's *The Company We Keep*.

> *Week 10:* "Future Directions": Robert Scholes, *Protocols of Reading,*
> Chapter 1, and Robert Scholes and Nancy Comley, "Responsible
> Extravagance: Reading after Post-Structuralism".

I'd also select a small number of literary works to use in connection
with this reading. I'd ask the students to write essays that emphasize
the activities of theorizing: at least one paper devoted to reconstructing
the question, answer, method, principles, and purpose of one of these
pieces; at least one paper that took issue with one or more of the pieces;
and at least one longer essay that involved the students in developing
their own questions about the reader in interpretation.

I'd like to return to Jim's point that this syllabus will look like a standard kind of theory course. In one respect that is true, but I'm not bothered by that. I'm not trying to reinvent the theory syllabus as much as I
am trying to reorient our activities with the syllabus.

Practical Pedagogy

Katie: I don't know about Jim, but I think you should be more bothered.
If you only reorient the activities within your version of the standard
syllabus, you haven't gone far enough, because you haven't really paid
any attention to the political dimension of your course, especially to the
political consequences of that reading list. The list shows how the theoretical canon reflects the literary canon: it's dominated by white men,
though you find room for a few white women. Whatever else you might
be teaching the students about theory, you're implicitly teaching them
that it's mostly an activity for the pale and male among them.

Bill: I'm not sure I buy that. If Betty's emphasis is on the dynamics of
theory, on understanding what it means to ask a fruitful question and
on how a theoretical conclusion is always nested within a set of principles and assumptions, then unless she does something in her pedagogy
to discourage women or students of color from engaging in these activities, she's sending the message that theory is for everyone in the class. If
she gives different treatment to the texts by women or different treatment to women and minority students, then I'd worry about the politics of the course. But as it is, it seems to me that she is equipping all her
students with ways of reading that will help them with any more explicitly political work they might want to take up.

Betty: Thanks for the defense, Bill, but if I understand Katie correctly,
then she is saying that, by selecting this male-dominated reading list,

I've already given texts by women—and by people of color—a different treatment. And I have to say that she has a very good point.

Katie: In effect, the point is an extension of the caution against creating a form-content split. You're so focused on the matters of form—on teaching theorizing underlying theory, on equipping the students with useful ways of reading theory—that you neglect the messages—some of them very powerful—you send with your reading list.

Mike: I can see all that, but the set of prominent reader-response theorists isn't exactly a multiculturalist's dream. And I can't help but think that text selection will become a pretty dreary process if it eventually boils down to the task of selecting works by members of all relevant— that is politically active—minority groups.

Betty: Indeed, it would be, and I'm not about to make that my main principle of selection. But not to pay any attention to the kinds of issues that Katie is raising is only to perpetuate the institutional politics that has given us a white male-dominated canon of theory. At the very least, I'll incorporate the work of African American critics and theorists such as Henry Louis Gates, Jr., Houston Baker, Hortense Spillers, and Barbara Christian; I could sacrifice the Fish-Iser debate, or save it for one of the paper assignments. I'm open to suggestions for other revisions.

Mike: Are you open to suggestions from your students? More generally, how will you handle your authority in the course? Many people are now emphasizing the importance of having a student-centered classroom, of decentralizing the teacher's authority, of moving away from a unidirectional flow of information from teacher to student. It's my experience that in theory classes, the students actually want the teacher to be the fount of wisdom from whom they can drink—or to go back to my earlier metaphor, they want us to tell them the secrets of theory.

Betty: I know what you mean. Any suggestions?

Katie: I think I'd try to get the students to take responsibility for the course as much as possible, as soon as possible, even though most of them won't have had theory before. If you want to get them thinking about theory as action, then you should get them acting even in the matter of text selection. Your course outline makes a lot of sense, but I wonder whether you might want to present the students with something less complete on the first day and get them involved in completing it. Even before you showed them any part of it, you might have a discussion about reading some particular short text that you could pass out and see what kinds of issues emerged, and then refer back to the discussion in negotiating the final reading list as a group. Of course, you'd have to be supplying information about the possible options on the reading list, but you could do your best to avoid rigging the outcome of the vote.

Bill: It won't surprise you to hear me say this, but I think it would be important later on when you're working with the texts, first, to encourage disagreement, to let the students know that you don't have a party line you're going to be asking them to follow, that theorists themselves disagree a lot about the quality of all these essays, and that some disagreements must, at this juncture, be left unresolved.

Jim: I like these ideas, but I think that in the regular class sessions, you're going to have to run the show. If you want to teach them about the activities of theory, if you want to show the dynamics of arguments, you're going to have to do some old-fashioned, teacher-centered pedagogy. You could do it Socratically; indeed, that's the way I'd suggest you try it, but you're going to have to be both Socrates and Plato; that is, you're going to have to engage in the question-answer, give-and-take with the idea that you'll go wherever it leads—as long as it leads to the destination that you've planned in advance.

Betty: I'm not quite sure if I can balance Bill's advice—to let the conflicts emerge and let some remain unresolved—with Jim's advice to keep a strong hand on the tiller. But I think that together you give me something to aim at: a way to conduct the course so that by the end of it, they learn enough not just about reader theory but also about theorizing so that I become obsolete. My goal would be to move from a teacher-centered to a student-centered pedagogy over the course of the quarter. If that succeeds, I might even be able to dispel the notion that we have the secrets of theory and that their job is to get us to tell them those secrets. Easier said than done, I'm sure. But that's where the challenge will lie.

Bill: We said we'd get back to the issue of developing new metaphors. Any suggestions?

Jim: We need something organic, obviously; how about theory as a rain forest?

Katie: Intriguing, but perhaps too complicated. Who's going to be the plants, who, the animals? More particularly, who's going to be the toucans, who, the slugs? You get the idea, I'm sure.

Mike: Okay. Then how about theory as endlessly growing vines?

Bill: That might work. What do you other people think?

Betty: That I'm too tired to think hard about it right now. Maybe we could meet here again tomorrow and talk about the metaphor—unless someone has another idea.

Katie: Well, how about the ways in which your course fits in with the rest of the curriculum.

Betty: Now I'm really tired. But okay, metaphors and connections for next time.

Jim [*deadpan*]: I think we should talk about all the things wrong with everything we said today.

Betty [*matching Jim's tone*]: Fair enough; that would give us about fifty-nine minutes for metaphors and connections.

Works Cited

Baker, Houston A., Jr. *Afro-American Poetics: Revisions of Harlem and the Black Aesthetic.* Madison: U of Wisconsin P, 1988.

Bloom, Harold. *The Anxiety of Influence: A Theory of Poetry.* New York: Oxford UP, 1973.

Booth, Wayne C. *The Company We Keep: An Ethics of Fiction.* Berkeley: U of California P, 1988.

———. "The Control of Distance in Jane Austen's *Emma.*" *The Rhetoric of Fiction.* 2nd ed. Chicago: U of Chicago P, 1983. 243–71.

Christian, Barbara. *Black Feminist Criticism: Perspectives on Black Women Writers.* New York: Pergamon, 1985.

Culler, Jonathan. "Literary Competence." *Structuralist Poetics: Structuralism, Linguistics, and the Study of Literature.* Ithaca: Cornell UP, 1975. 113–31.

de Man, Paul. "Semiology and Rhetoric." *Allegories of Reading: Figural Language in Rousseau, Nietzsche, Rilke, and Proust.* New Haven: Yale UP, 1979. 3–19.

Fetterley, Judith. *The Resisting Reader: A Feminist Approach to American Fiction.* Bloomington: Indiana UP, 1978.

Fish, Stanley. "Affective Stylistics" and "Interpreting the *Variorum.*" *Is There a Text in This Class? The Authority of Interpretive Communities.* Cambridge, MA: Harvard UP, 1980. 303–22, 147–74.

———. "Why No One's Afraid of Wolfgang Iser." *Diacritics* 11:1 (1981): 2–13.

Flynn, Elizabeth A., and Patrocinio P. Schweickart, eds. *Gender and Reading: Essays on Readers, Texts, Contexts.* Baltimore: Johns Hopkins UP, 1986.

Gates, Henry Louis, Jr. *The Signifying Monkey: A Theory of Afro-American Literary Criticism.* New York: Oxford UP, 1988.

Hirsch, E. D., Jr. *Cultural Literacy: What Every American Needs to Know.* Boston: Houghton, 1987.

Holland, Norman. *5 Readers Reading.* New Haven: Yale UP, 1975.

Iser, Wolfgang. "The Reading Process: A Phenomenological Approach." *The Implied Reader: Patterns of Communication in Prose from Bunyan to Beckett.* Baltimore: Johns Hopkins UP, 1974. 274–95.

——. "Talk like Whales: A Reply to Stanley Fish." *Diacritics* 11:3 (1981): 82–7.

Lynn, Steven. "A Passage into Critical Theory." *Conversations: Contemporary Critical Theory and the Teaching of Literature.* Ed. Charles Moran and Elizabeth F. Penfield. Urbana, IL: NCTE, 1990. 99–113.

Miller, D. A. *The Novel and the Police.* Berkeley: U of California P, 1988.

Miller, J. Hillis. *The Ethics of Reading: Kant, de Man, Eliot, Trollope, James, and Benjamin.* New York: Columbia UP, 1987.

Morrison, Toni. *Beloved: A Novel.* New York: Knopf, 1987.

Nussbaum, Martha C. *Love's Knowledge: Essays on Philosophy and Literature.* New York: Oxford UP, 1990.

Pryse, Marjorie, and Hortense J. Spillers, eds. *Conjuring: Black Women, Fiction, and Literary Tradition.* Bloomington: Indiana UP, 1985.

Rabinowitz, Peter J. *Before Reading: Narrative Conventions and the Politics of Interpretation.* Ithaca: Cornell UP, 1987.

Scholes, Robert. *Protocols of Reading.* New Haven: Yale UP, 1989.

Scholes, Robert, and Nancy R. Comley. "Responsible Extravagance: Reading after Post-Structuralism." *Narrative* 1:1 (1993): 3–12.

Showalter, Elaine. "Feminist Criticism in the Wilderness." *Critical Inquiry* 8 (1981): 179–205.

Wimsatt, William K., Jr. *The Verbal Icon: Studies in the Meaning of Poetry.* Lexington: U of Kentucky P, 1954.

III Pedagogy

15 Does Theory Play Well in the Classroom?

Barbara T. Christian
University of Califorinia–Berkeley

I

The title of my presentation that I gave to the organizers of this conference is "Does Theory Play Well in the Classroom?" I'm going to deconstruct that title for a minute so that I can go on and talk about what I really want to talk about. And actually, it does move me into that because, as I looked at the title later on, I realized that by theory, we now mean a particular theory; of course, there have always been theories; we just didn't call them theories before. That is, we are always theorizing, and the reason why we are now using that word, rather than some other word, is something that we might reflect upon perhaps twenty-five years from now. Someone will ask the question, "Why is it that, in literary studies, the word theory, which was so often associated with science, is now being used?" It may have something to do with our sense of inferiority in this technological age. But in any case, if I were to rewrite that title, theory would have an "s" after it, or I probably would use the verb "theorizing," which I prefer to the concept of an artifact, such as a theory. And, of course, "the Classroom" does not exist. There are classrooms. Many different kinds of classrooms, different kinds of institutions; even in Berkeley, in my own department, I have many kinds of classrooms from year to year. So, as I looked at the title again, the only word that I really still agree with is "play." I hope we're going to do a little bit of that today.

There are two different kinds of things I want to do, although they're related. The first is to conceptualize for you, a bit, the essay that you read,

Editors' note: Barbara Christian's essay is taken from her longer presentation at the Summer Institute in 1991. It deals in part with an earlier essay she wrote, "The Race for Theory" (*Cultural Critique* 6 [Spring 1987]: 51–63) and with passages from Toni Morrison's *Beloved*, particularly pages 86–88. Though shortened for inclusion in this volume, the essay highlights the salient points and retains much of the personal tone of her remarkable presentation.

"The Race for Theory," for which I have become notorious. And the second part, which is what I generally like to do, is to contextualize, or at least talk a little bit about, the way I teach Toni Morrison's *Beloved*. I think both are actually related, as I recall what it is I wanted to say in "The Race for Theory." And in the tradition of feminists (I consider myself to be one), I want to begin by giving a kind of a personal context as to why it is that this essay might have, in fact, been written.

Well, it takes me all the way back to where I come from, which is the Caribbean. I grew up in a culture, a society, in which there is a split of cultures which I often call "the highs" and "the lows" (I have written a piece with that title, in fact), where language and the way one approached knowledge differed from the school and the church to the street and what we called "the yard." And I think it was growing up in that society, where there was such a contrast between the languages that were acceptable in these two places, and which were really different, that made me so aware of how values are vested in the kind of language that one uses. So, for example, if you were in the yard in the street, what you do is, you "long talk" in the Caribbean, or you "lie." That's the kind of word you use. Or as some African Americans might say, you do a lot of "signifying." Of course, in the church and in the school, we spoke a kind of British English that was the only way in which you could be heard at the time. We see some of that occurring now in literary criticism where "signifying" has become "signification," and "long talk" has become the "vernacular."

The kind of literature that I read when I was going to school was primarily that which was imposed by the colonials, not necessarily a bad thing. But there was no recognition of the fact that there was a very strong oral, vital tradition of storytelling which focused a great deal on the sound of language—not only on what was said, but how it sounded. I gave you an excerpt from *Beloved* precisely because the neglect of sound is one of the major problems I have with the theoretical language that so many of us are being forced to use if we are to be promoted. Now, one of the reasons why that concerned me when I was growing up had to do with the contradictions involved in what was valued. That is, we all knew we wanted to get by and that the way in which we were weeded out of the system had very much to do with whether or not we sounded British or whether or not we sounded Caribbean.

So, of course, we learned to sound two ways. But even those who expected us to sound British would not allow us to sound that way if we were in the marketplace. Somebody who didn't know how to long talk was not going to make it in the society—even if they became the finest speaker of British English and knew all of the literature. Now this brings me to another point that I want to stress—that was important in my upbringing. It's interesting that "Dover Beach" is a poem that you all received to read because, in fact, it was one of the poems that we not only read but had to memorize. And I must say that even though there were many, many critiques that we did of "Dover Beach" without our knowing at the time that we were deconstructing it, the fact that it sounded the way it sounded was also important because it meant that we remembered it, and we related to it in some way. One of the things that I do regularly in my classroom is to look at literature from the point of view of its muscularity—that is, to read it aloud so you hear it.

I think that is one of the problems that I find with theoretical frameworks dealing with literature today. Even as we talk about the vernacular, we do not see literature as the *embodiment* of principles, but rather a *statement* of principles. That literature is, in fact, sensual-erotic as well as intellectual; from my point of view, that is what intelligence means. So that's one of the first conceptualizations for the essay that I was to write many, many years later.

A second would be that when I finally did move into the academic world, it was not into literature but into literacy. I taught in a program called SEEK in City College, and the idea of that program was to teach apparently "uneducable" blacks and Puerto Ricans so that they could enter the city colleges. It was thought that they could not, in fact, do that, but one of the things we found, which of course makes perfect sense when you think about it, was that if we chose literature to which they could relate, to use a '60s term, they began to learn to read. They wanted to read. And again, this had not only to do with the content of the literature but the way it sounded; it was through that process that I got into African American literature. The excavating of texts that were no longer available was not only about the meaning but about the fact that the students became involved in the sound that was being made, and many of them, in fact, went on to learn to read and write and to become scholars and many other things. This experience, of course, would turn me around in terms of what I felt literature was about.

I realize that a third very important influence on "The Race for Theory"—and this I reflected on just in the last couple of weeks—was an essay that was written by Alice Walker called "In Search of Our Mothers' Gardens," in which I think that Walker really proposes a critical theory. I think that writers, very often traditionally, are the ones who are good theorizers. Walker asks the question, "From whence does my tradition come?" since, in fact, African American women, until recently, have not had the privilege of writing. "What is my legacy of creativity?"

At first she looks at "the written tradition" in which writers like Nella Larson participated; she found them, of course, in a state of what she calls "contrary instincts" (wonderful phrase, sounds good too), and what she means by that is that they are caught between the dominant society's definition of what literature is and the folk tradition from which they're coming. That was not satisfactory, really, in terms of a legacy, the ground that she needed to stand on, or what she felt she needed as a contemporary writer. Walker said she "finally . . . realized that instead of looking high, she ought to look low," and on that low ground she found the many black women who had expressed their creativity in forms such as quilting, storytelling—in all of the various forms that they had access to. For me, this is a completely different definition of art as well as literature. It is on the low ground, where the folk express their creativity, that Walker later on would be able to tap as a basis for her own literary creativity. Therefore, the whole question of whether one has "a room of one's own" shifts, doesn't it? That is a third consideration in terms of the essay that I wrote.

And then the fourth, and perhaps the most important recently, is that I am situated in an African American Studies department at Berkeley that is twenty years old, and we have been trying to put together a coherent curriculum that deals with conflict as well as points of sameness in terms of relating to our students. I have classes in which students come from a variety of disciplines, large classes of people who come from all over the campus to study African American literature because they feel that it means something to their existence now and that these classes can help to explain where they are right now. I'm not just talking about African American students. In most of my classes, the majority of the students are not African American. Many, many of them are Euramerican, Chicano/a, Native American, all kinds of folk. The fact is that they come into the classroom because literature means something to them. That's partially because I am teaching a subject that has been fortunate enough to be graced by writers like Walker and Morrison and Marshall and Wideman and writers of that sort during the last twenty years, so students are interested in reading that literature.

What I am primarily interested in, in relation to my students, is how we get into a dialogue about the way that literature opens them up. The writer is really very much involved in a dialogue with the reader, and I see myself in relation to that dialogue between the writer and the reader, who is not likely going to become a literary critic. I also work extensively, though, with graduate students who are interested in African American literature, women of color literature, or whatever we want to call it. In fact, right now, I have marvelous graduate students. I do find, however, and I want to emphasize this point, that although many of them are acquainted with critical texts, the majority of them have not read the literature. I'm stunned sometimes, as I speak with students who are studying African American literature, that they have never read Frederick Douglass nor approached Ralph Ellison. It seems to me that there is something wrong there in terms of that kind of imbalance. It has partially something to do with the kind of undergraduate training that many of them are receiving right now, where critical texts have become so much of what they read that they are no longer reading the actual literature itself.

That's extremely important to me, the literature, not because I'm a naive romantic, but because, at least in the African American tradition, the creative writers are often the ones who have had the opportunity to theorize about the worldview of African Americans. African Americans, until recently, have not had access to what we call the academic institutions of the West. So their primary domain, in terms of writing for African Americans and their explanation of the world, has been in their literature. I think that the literature not only allows writers to express or, as many of the women writers feel, heal themselves, but it also allows them to relate to different audiences, what we sometimes call "double voice." This has been problematic for the African American writer in the sense that one has to write to "the dominant group" and also one's own group. Writing, therefore, that is very sensual and erotic, that is double-voiced and quoted, that includes chants and proverbs, that uses sound, is extremely important in order to relate to different audiences. It is much, much more difficult to appropriate that kind of literature than the abstract intellectual logic that one might get in some of the Western forms that we think of as theory.

Now I believe that theorizing takes many forms, that it can be, in fact, culturally specific. The idea that theory only takes the form of the analytical, abstract, logical essay is precisely the reason why I ran from philosophy to literature when I was in high school. I felt that when we studied heavy philosophy, something was missing there: there was a split between the head and the body. What I needed, for myself anyway, was a coming together, an interrelatedness of the fact that the body and the soul are one, to put it in the phrase of one of our writers, and I felt that this was what literature actually did, what philosophy could not do.

So, that is one of the reasons I was profoundly disturbed at the conference at which "The Race for Theory" was written and given. For two days, most of us "minority scholars," as we were then called (a term I hate), got together and talked to each other, but not about the literature. I'm not sure exactly what we were talking about, but it was clearly very boring, alienating, and had very little to do with what I thought we were there for; it had something to do with mimicking what was thought to be the way in which one ought to talk about literature if one were to be validated or respected today.

The essay then became for me a riff. "The Race for Theory" not only says that we *are* a race for theory, but also that there *is* a race for theory. There are many such riffs in it, so sensual, playing with words to break up the kind of absolute deadening of atmosphere I felt we had fallen into at that conference.

I have to tell you the truth; I'm absolutely amazed at how "significant" this essay has become, since I wrote it in three hours, pretty much as a way of alleviating the boredom that I happened to be situated in. But, of course, it is serious play. I am willing to discuss, contest, and argue about this essay, partially because many black women critics who have agreed with me are now being characterized as "reactionary abolitionists" by some of our brothers, precisely because we are not into "theoretical criticism."

The language of theory is part of the process of making you feel uncomfortable enough to have to think another way. I can see some of what that language is about, except that I think it lacks the surprise and sensuality that I find in literary writers who also sometimes make you struggle. I mean, Toni Morrison makes you struggle, but you're loving it; there's a kind of a pleasure involved which I think is missing in theory, and I find this to be absolutely unacceptable. I think there are a lot of new and important insights that have come from "the new contemporary theory." But the way in which it is written, I think, indicates something about it that is problematic, and it has a great deal to do with a kind of puritanism, which may be because so much of it is French, but that may be my own bias! But, in other words, it doesn't have a kind of sensuality, and so I think it is very hard to play with it in the classroom.

I want to tell a story about that in relation to writers. There was another conference of African American writings, critics, and writers, and one of the writers, a very important writer, called me up in tears from the conference. She had been at a couple of sessions on her work, and she said "I didn't understand one word . . . what's happening to my work?" And she was absolutely serious. She had taken all this time to craft it, and she went to sessions where she felt that her work was completely miscommunicated, not only in terms of the content, but in the way it was spoken about. I thought about that, and I came to feel very strongly about writers and about readers; perhaps I don't feel strongly enough about critics.

Many people interpret "The Race for Theory" as antitheory, which it is not. What it is, is against theory that is not related to literature. But, of course, it is a theoretical essay. My problem with high theory today is not with it in itself but with what I see happening in the way people are hired, appreciated, and seen in the academic community. In other words, if you are not doing theory, high theory, at least where I am at (at Berkeley), people do not think of you as doing very much, and you're not getting hired. People are promoted on the basis of high theory and so on, and so what I would like to see is something more democratic. That is partially what this piece is about.

I wonder if, in fact, there are different functions. Let me put it this way: some of us are interested in literature, and some of us are interested in theory, and some of us are interested in the relationship between these two and in whether or not it is possible to do all those things. I mean, I think these functions are all valuable. For a very long time in the African American tradition as well as in the West, the literary critics were often the artists. I think that there are certain kinds of tasks that we perform—one of which is that we study; we continue to focus on the contextualization of the literature. That is, we are looking at it continuously from another perspective. We are also looking at the way in which language is used in particular traditions and bodies of literature that writers themselves are not necessarily looking at because they are much more focused on what they are trying to express. We're very much involved, I think, in a dialogue between the reader and the writer, but most important, I think that our writing is one of the ways in which their writing lasts. If writing is not written about, it disappears. So I see that as being one of the major roles of the critic. My daughter is always saying to me, "Well, you're a critic, that means you judge." That is one of the reasons the word "critic" is also problematic for me. Because when you say you're a critic, most people in the world think, "Oh, you're a critic. You say this book is good, and this book is bad, and this book is in between, and this book is. . . ." I don't think this is what critics do most of the time. I think they ought to be illuminating the works. That is a word I tend to use, "illumination." A very old-fashioned word, I know.

My problem concerns what is going on in terms of academic currency. Another way of putting it is that theory is a new and trendy thing. This has become what every university rushes out to get right now. Theory is on the cutting edge, and the question as to whether or not these theorists can teach literature in the classroom doesn't come up during the hiring process. I have been involved in feminist theory classes, and I'm very interested in that, and I'm very interested in what African American theory should be. But I actually think that African American theory comes out of the literature and the folk tradition, which is what I want to stress. I think that there are various ways to go about it. The problem is that, even though theorists are saying that they are the ones on the top, the hierarchy is developed, and so part of theory ought to be a deconstructing of the theorists themselves. That's also what I wanted to do in "The Race for Theory." It's a deconstructionist piece, contributing my perspective to the academic community.

I'm wondering what we mean by an academic community? The best conversations I have had about literature, I will tell you, have been in my kitchen, with women who had to read the works they were reading. In fact, they don't even call these readers by their last names; they call them Toni and June and so on, because they need it for their lives. They are part of an intellectual community we don't acknowledge. When I go get my hair cut, the women talk about Audré Lorde. I'm serious; this is actually happening. I think we have an erroneous idea, at least in the community I come from, that the only people who read these books are critics and students who are forced to read them in classrooms. Now I find that I'm not just talking about contemporary literature. We can talk about Toni Morrison's *Beloved,* and a lot of my friends who are not in the "academic world" have then gone back and read *Incidents in the Life of a Slave Girl* because they now know it. So I don't know what we mean by an intellectual community, and I wonder about this split between the real world and the academic world.

The academic world is *in* the world. I mean, that's the problem. One of the things I'm concerned about my students knowing is what I call the "literary geography": the way literature gets produced, what writers really do, the power of reviews, what goes on in the background. In other words, I want my students to know that there is not only the text, but that there is also a context out of which this text is arising. This discussion going on among writers is about what I call the "literary geography," and it is related to the social and political geography of what is going on now. In this way, the text that they're reading from the nineteenth century is looked at in a completely different way because of what we're dealing with right now. In other words, one of my roles is to show them that the division between "the real world" and the world of the academy is not really there. The university exists precisely in the world; it is in it.

II

There are a few things I wanted to mention about Toni Morrison's *Beloved,* and it does relate to what we are talking about now. I've been doing an essay on the way in which Morrison's *Beloved* is being written about at present [Editors' note: see Christian 1993]. I find out that it is being written about very well—in fact, from a psychoanalytic point of view, a Marxist point of view, a poststructuralist point of view, and so on. But one of the ways it is *not* being written about, which is very much at the core of the novel, is from what I would call an African point of view. The novel itself, it seems to me as I read it, and teach it, and talk with people who have read it, is generated by the phrase "ancestral worship." The reason it is called *Beloved*—the beloved that it is dedicated to, the "Sixty Million and more" that it is dedicated to—has to do with a philosophical concept about ancestral worship that comes from Africa, which many African Americans, at least until lately, have believed. Now, many of us don't know what that (nor what the "middle passage") is, so we miss that completely in the novel. Even though Morrison has said this many times in her interviews, it's what I do not see coming up in the criticism.

What concerns me is why the African American perspective, which is central to the novel, is not being dealt with. Probably because most of us are not trained in this, are we? I want to spend the rest of my time this morning talking about how we might bring that perspective to bear on the novel so that we might better grasp this literature in its own cultural terms.

The novel is, without question, from an African American perspective, a revisioning of the narratives of the nineteenth century. Morrison was able to use an entire tradition that precedes her, revisioning slave narratives (particularly female slave narratives) as well as nineteenth-century African American novels. If you read enough of the tradition, you can see that this novel is the other side of *Clotel,* which was the first novel to be published by an African American man, William Wells Brown. In *Clotel,* the mother kills herself for her child. She does escape slavery, the escape is successful, but she does not have her child. She goes back to get her child, and, in the process of going back to get her child, she is recaptured, and so she drowns herself. Morrison reverses that process and retells that story from a different perspective. In one of her essays, Morrison talks about how the novels of the nineteenth century and the historical novels that precede her all the way up to the 1970s focused primarily on the institutions of slavery rather than on the psyches of the slaves themselves. Now one of the reasons for that, of course, had to do with the goal of the novels of the nineteenth century, which was the abolition of slavery. Therefore, there was a strong indictment of the institution. Another reason for this focus on the institution of slavery stemmed from the fact that, as we moved into the twentieth century, most Americans, black and white, did not know enough about or want to remember the institution of slavery so that you could focus on the slaves as "individuals in communities."

So we can see Morrison, in her revisioning of the literary tradition preceding her, is filling in the silences, the spaces of the narrators who were not able to say or could not speak in that way, for multiple reasons. First, the narrators of the nineteenth century very often fell silent out of modesty (that is the word Morrison uses); because they were trying to persuade whites to abolish slavery, there were certain things they should not speak of because it would not help their case. Also, the scholarship on African American slavery from an African American historical perspective didn't come out until the 1960s; writers attempting to write historical novels before that period were confronted by the problem of ignorance. Many people didn't know, were not aware of, how the slave community existed; for a very long time, there was an assumption that there was not a slave community. Only through historical scholarship were writers like Morrison able to free themselves into imagining the psyches of their characters, rather than having to lay out a historical base. Finally, so many of the nineteenth-century African American writers did not write about these things because they did not want to remember them, because, if they did, they could not go on. So Morrison, upon hearing that and going back to where it is that they did not want to go, asks, "Why didn't they pass it on? What didn't they pass on?"

African Americans have sung many songs about slavery, but the one area (and Morrison looked and looked and looked) that they are virtually silent on is the "middle passage." The middle passage is the horrifying journey of the slave ships from the West Coast of Africa to the Caribbean and to the U.S.; in that passage across the Atlantic, there are different estimates about the millions and millions of Africans who died from disease or killed themselves or whatever. It was a tremendous and horrendous passage; people were packed in ships like cargo. Much of the historical data comes from slave traders, the captains of ships who repented because of how terrifying a situation it was. They wrote what we might call "exposés" of the process. So that section in the novel, where you have Beloved, Sethe, Denver, and the voices intermingling, is, among other things, about the middle passage. Beloved, when she talks about the man with the pointed teeth and his hot thing and so on, could be talking about being in the hull of the ship and coming out of the water; it's both a death and a birth and a horrendous memory.

In writing *Beloved,* Morrison was asking a simple question: "Why? Why are they silent about that?" Her sense was that the process of healing involves remembering; healing can only begin when you remember that which you don't want to remember. I was talking about this to a group in Hawaii a year or so ago; they were all Japanese Americans whose families had never told them that they had been in internment camps, and, therefore, they did not understand why, in fact, they were doing what they were doing. For Jews, with their history of the concentration camps, the situation is just the same. In other words, the process of remembering is part of the process of healing. That's one of the reasons why I think Morrison wrote this novel, and why there are so many historical novels being written right now by African Americans.

The historical event that forms the basis for this novel is the true story of Margaret Garner, a slave woman in Ohio who attempted to escape across the Ohio River; as she was being recaptured, she killed two of her children. Morrison discovered this story, which, by the way, was a very well-known event that the abolitionists made much of. Morrison, one of the most influential black editors of the last twenty years, came upon this story in the process of researching *The Black Book,* a scrapbook of African American history. What really happened to the factual Margaret Garner is that she was recaptured and tried, not for the crime of killing her children, but for stealing herself, a crime of property that resulted in her return to slavery.

Now, for many reasons, it's important to note the difference between the event, the historical, factual event, and what Morrison does with it. African American literature is often turned primarily into a history lesson and is not looked at as literature. Morrison looks at this event from a writer's point of view which is specifically her own and, as she does in all her work, she deals with the paradox of the event. What Morrison does is to try and move into the issue of how you claim your own freedom. That is, how does one claim one's own freedom? It is one thing to be legally free; it's another thing to *claim* that freedom. For Morrison, in *Beloved,* part of the process must be reconciliation and healing. That is, remembering that which you don't want to remember in order to be healed is part of the process to freedom. So the novel focuses on characters who were born slaves and who are attempting to free themselves.

The question Morrison asks is, while one can understand why Sethe kills her child, does she have a right to do it? Beloved, who actually embodies the past, gives flesh to that experience. The senses, the sounds, the words do that. By bringing Beloved into the picture, the child coming back, Morrison explores one way of reconciling oneself in a physical way with the past, so that one can move forward into the future. So Morrison actually changes the Garner story; the event signals to the writer the possibility of the story.

Teaching the differences between the story of Margaret Garner and this novel is one of the ways I often move into the teaching of the novel itself. The core of the novel is about the claiming of freedom, a central question for African Americans from the time of slavery to the present. For Morrison, a great deal of that claiming of freedom has to do with remembering, collective remembering, and the process of going through that remembering to the point of healing. In changing the Garner story, Morrison introduces important philosophical dilemmas that still remain contemporary issues for African Americans. It is not just a story of a re-claiming of history; it has very much to do with a palpitating, pulsating dilemma for African Americans. When I teach classes in which there are many African Americans, this novel is the most moving for them of any novel that I think I've ever taught, even if they cannot articulate precisely how. In writing from an African American perspective, in writing about an African American experience, Morrison writes them through the healing process.

Morrison sees this healing process as having something to do with the crux of mothering itself, so one of the ways I also approach teaching *Beloved* is to explore the fact that none of the major characters in the novel had been mothered. This novel questions the concepts of mother and motherland—Africa. But this theme is also embodied within the story of Sethe. We have the whole issue of mother love; does she have the right to kill her child for love? For Morrison, there is a learning process in becoming free to mother; one reason Sethe's response is so extreme is that she knows what it is "to be without the milk that belongs to you." She is overly possessive in relationship to her children, some people might say, because she was not mothered. This is true of all the major characters.

I heard from Morrison while she was working on this novel, and I remember one time I asked her, "What are you doing? What are you writing?" and she said, "Girl, I'm writing an opera." That is, whether you've read it or you've listened to a program about it on television, you already know what the event is: Sethe kills her child. That's not the issue. Most of the time when you go to the opera, you know the plot. Then you have monologues, duets—as in the Paul D and Sethe scene when they make love—and the three women forming a kind of tableau very often, a gesture, a chorus, the voices that come on and out and speak at the same time or sing at the same time, and, of course, in this section, we have a space in the clearing, if you can imagine it that way. I think it helps students really get into it. We are going to read the following passage because it includes so many of the voices that Morrison uses so much throughout the novel, beginning with the very first line: "It was time to lay it all down."

> It was time to lay it all down. Before Paul D came and sat on her porch steps, words whispered in the keeping room had kept her going. Helped her endure the chastising ghost; refurbished the baby faces of Howard and Buglar and kept them whole in the world because in her dreams she saw only their parts in trees; and kept her husband shadowy but *there*—somewhere. Now Halle's face between the butter press and the churn swelled larger and larger, crowding her eyes and making her head hurt. She wished for Baby Suggs' fingers molding her nape, reshaping it, saying, "Lay em down, Sethe. Sword and shield. Down. Down. Both of em down. Down by the riverside. Sword and shield. Don't study war no more. Lay all that mess down. Sword and shield." And under the pressing fingers and the quiet instructive voice, she would. Her heavy knives of defense against misery, regret, gall and hurt, she placed one by one on a bank where clear water rushed on below. (86)

Now, I know where that line "It was time to lay it all down" comes from, because it's a part of my tradition. Where does it come from? From the spiritual, "Down by the Riverside." In other words, it comes right out of the African American spiritual tradition. It was time to lay it all down. Of course, within the line, even if you didn't know that, the issue of time is crucial, central to this novel. Time, in fact, is continuously disrupted or, we might say, informed by memory. The ideal time to "lay it all down," the meaning of that phrase, has something to do with precisely the work of the novel. What does she mean by "It was time to lay it all down?" Notice the way Morrison puts these next lines together: "Before Paul D came and sat on her porch steps, words whispered in the keeping room had kept her going." Of course, the alliteration moves into a kind of healing process, and then the words helped her endure the "chastising" and "refurbished the baby faces of Howard and Buglar and kept them whole in the world." We really have the novel again in those four or five lines. The verb, taking control, helped her keep going.

Now, since we don't have time to discuss the whole novel, at this point, when I use this excerpt (pages 86–89) in class, I usually ask students, "Well, who is Paul D in the novel?" The name Paul, of course, reminds us of the Biblical Paul. His name before was Saul. One of the suggestions I have for people who are really interested in Morrison and what I always tell my students is that it's absolutely necessary to have your Bible by your side. The Bible is central to African American culture since it was the only book that one was often allowed to have access to during slavery. Many people could not read; they memorized whole sections of the Bible. That is, of course, the African American tradition; the oral tradition uses the literary text. Morrison sees the Bible, a written tradition, as one that has been transformed by the oral tradition in the African American culture. In fact, one of the goals of contemporary African American writers is the negotiation between oral and literary traditions. I don't know if negotiating is the correct word, but the way in which they interrelate them.

Morrison is also very much involved in myth, from Greece, from Africa, Native American myth, and, of course, African American myth, which she views as being intersections from the world of African Americans as it evolved. Some scholars argue, in fact, that Greece got much of what it got from Africa, and that's part of the point that Morrison is making. Now in her work, there are always, in the center of the novel, three-women households. Three women-headed households. Three. Three women representing the trinity, but also the cycle of life. The three-women households serve almost as a signature in her novels. Most of us are used to the Christian concept of the male trinity. But, of course, preceding Christianity, there was a female trinity: after all, it's women who give life, and, for Morrison, that is a much more natural situation than a male trinity. I think it's also her way of saying that African Americans have been criticized for women-centered families (what we call matrilineal and matrifocal but not matriarchal), families that take a different form from your nuclear Western family, where the father is the head. In her households, it is women-centered, and then you spiral out to the men.

For example, through the character of Denver, Morrison comments on the existence of women-centered relationships, even across lines of race, space, and personal freedom; Denver is the transitional figure from slavery to freedom. She is the one who is born on the way from slavery to freedom, and, interestingly, Morrison brings in the whole dilemma of sistering through sisterhood with Amy Denver. Morrison treats the issue of sisterhood across races because Aimée means, in French, "beloved." Denver not only represents a geographical space; she comes out of these two women who do something very good together on the Ohio, which is giving birth to her. On the other hand, even though Amy is a young girl, she sees herself as a daughter of an indentured servant, bringing up that whole history in relation to whites. She does feel superior to Sethe. Nonetheless, Sethe, in naming Denver, recognizes the role of Amy Denver in bringing Denver into the world and thereby investigates all of these issues of kinship.

Related to these concerns is Morrison's exploration of women preachers. Baby Suggs is similar to another character in African American literature, but shown from a very different perspective. Baby Suggs is a preacher, a female preacher. Those of us who have studied African American literature and history know there were many, many women preachers, black women preachers, in the nineteenth century (Sojourner Truth, for example). In fact, Margaret Garner's mother-in-law was a preacher. The fact that there were many itinerant women, black women preachers, is often repressed; in our telling of this, we usually focus on the men and think of this as a male prerogative. But, in fact, this was one of the ways in which women could free themselves from the dictates of what black women were supposed to do. Women, too, could say: "God called me. I transcend the laws of man because God called me to do this work, so I can go out traveling on the road because this is something that God has given me to do." And there is a whole tradition of these preachers within which Baby Suggs falls, and they often preached not in churches, but in the African way, in clearings. That is, they preached in the space of nature itself, which partially has to do with being able to allow the spirit to come in, to be in the context of nature, nature and the spirit being interrelated. So Morrison, then, is able to use this character, Baby Suggs, again partially because historical data has freed her to tell that such women existed and also because they were called upon to do, of course, what Baby Suggs was doing.

One could consider why it is that the female preachers have dropped out of our histories and that the male preachers are the ones which remain. And very often, it is because women preached in the clearings and the natural settings, rather than in the institutional churches, partly because they couldn't enter them. Morrison is recalling an African orientation, because in many African orientations, churches are in nature; you stand under a tree, you're in a clearing space, and so on, because you must be in touch with that natural environment in order to get into yourself. In Morrison, it is consistent in all of her novels: she uses nature as the context for healing.

Morrison is revising tradition and looking at the way in which women are central. She's also turning traditional understandings around because the character who is really raped sexually in this novel is Paul D. In most of the literature and criticism that's being written, rape has been the central symbol of African American women's condition in slavery. This is the first novel in which a writer has willingly, consciously, looked at what we've known all along from studying about slavery: the sexual violation of men. One of the questions we talk about in classes is why it is that we're so much more willing to discuss the sexual violation of women than of men. This is because men are then put in a "female position." Now it's being written about in Charles Johnson's *Oxherding Tale*. He has just won the National Book Award for *Middle Passage. Oxherding Tale* is one of the first novels written by a black man in which he looks at the slave man as concubine, if you can put it that way. In *Dessa Rose*, Sherley Anne Williams looks at the relationship between Nathan and Miz Rufel, who was a slave mistress in a somewhat different way. But this is the only novel I know of that looks at it from the point of homosexual violation, rather than heterosexual.

In this context, I would suggest that African American literature has tended to get a bad rap in relation to men. If you really look at the novels, if you really read them, the fact that they're female-centered seems to generate a kind of anxiety, but, in fact, the men do quite well in most of these novels. Paul D, for example, has to go through a different kind of healing process, which is what you hear about from Sethe's perspective. One of the processes of healing is to be able to tell her that he wore that bit, that he had got that neck collar around him, and that Sethe would look at him and still regard him as a man. What black men have had to go through is that their women have seen them "powerless." That is the limit, and that's what keeps Paul D on the run. He's running; he can't stay anywhere. His own fear is that he is not all that he is, so when she returns that look, that's partially what he needs.

Sethe needs something else. She needs to reenact the ritual of killing the baby, and she needs to turn the pick or the saw in the right direction. Instead of turning it in on herself and her children, she turns it out. That is healing. I taught this whole book for a long while in a hospital in San Francisco with emotionally disturbed black people, and it was wonderful because the problem these people were having was that they didn't want to remember. They remembered in fragments because they didn't want to remember the terrible things that had happened to them and the terrible things they had done to others. The novel seemed to them to be quite normal, the way it's written. It is about their pattern of remembering and what they need to do to heal, to go through, that is partially what this novel is all about.

Let me just conclude with some reflections on how gender issues are worked out in this novel. Consider this passage:

> After situating herself on a huge flat-sided rock, Baby Suggs bowed her head and prayed silently. The Company watched her from the trees. They knew she was ready when she put her stick down. Then she shouted, "Let the children come!" and they ran from the trees toward her.
>
> "Let your mothers hear you laugh," she told them, and the woods rang. The adults looked on and could not help smiling.
>
> Then "Let the grown men come," she shouted. They stepped out one by one from among the ringing trees.

> "Let your wives and your children see you dance," she told them,
> and groundlife shuddered under their feet.
> Finally she called the women to her. "Cry," she told them. "For
> the living and the dead. Just cry." And without covering their eyes
> the women let loose.
> It started that way: laughing children, dancing men, crying
> women and then it got mixed up. Women stopped crying and
> danced; men sat down and cried; children danced, women laughed,
> children cried until, exhausted and riven, all and each lay about the
> Clearing damp and gasping for breath. In the silence that followed,
> Baby Suggs, holy, offered up to them her great big heart. (87–88)

Note what happens to these categories: "laughing children, dancing men, crying women." In the process of going through this ritual, they also intersect with one another and interact so that they begin to change. Everyone begins to do what everyone else is usually associated with; black women are often associated with crying, black men with dancing, and so on, and then they begin to change. The movement into this life is what African American literature is about:

> She told them that the only grace they would have was the grace
> they could imagine. That if they could not see it, they would not have
> it. (88)

Morrison here, herself, is working an intersection of the physical and the spiritual in the language, in the way in which it's written. And it is this that is central to the African American literary tradition: the intersection here of the erotic and sensual, of the body and the spirit. For me, it is these things that lie at the core of literature.

Works Cited

Brown, William Wells. *Clotel; or The President's Daughter: A Narrative of Slave Life in the United States.* London: Partridge & Oakey, 1853.

Christian, Barbara T. "Fixing Methodologies: *Beloved.*" *Cultural Critique* 24 (Spring 1993): 5–15.

———. "The Race for Theory." *Cultural Critique* 6 (Spring 1987): 51–63.

Harris, Middleton A., comp. *The Black Book.* New York: Random, 1974.

Jacobs, Harriet A. *Incidents in the Life of a Slave Girl. Written by Herself.* Ed. L. Maria Child. Boston: Published for the Author, 1861.

Johnson, Charles. *Middle Passage.* New York: Atheneum, 1990.

———. *Oxherding Tale.* Bloomington: Indiana UP, 1982.

Morrison, Toni. *Beloved: A Novel.* New York: Plume, 1988.

Walker, Alice. *In Search of Our Mothers' Gardens: Womanist Prose.* New York: Harcourt, 1983.

Williams, Sherley Anne. *Dessa Rose.* New York: Morrow, 1986.

16 Mr. Eliot Meet Miss Lowell and, ah, Mr. Brown

Paul Lauter
Trinity College

> Heritage. How have we come from our savage past, how no longer to be savages—this to teach. To look back and learn what humanizes—this to teach. To smash all ghettos that divide us—not to go back, not to go back—this to teach. Learned books in the house, will humankind live or die, and she gives to her boys—superstition.
>
> —Tillie Olsen ("Tell Me a Riddle" 81)

"What counts for theory?" This is a weighty question in academic circles nowadays. Its implications carry us beyond the academic gates—particularly in this historical moment. For the debates which have recently dominated public discourse about the humanities, like those over "political correctness," seem suddenly as archaic as Warren Gamaliel Harding, a rearguard fungus, so to say, rapidly deliquescing. The issue, I want to suggest, is no longer the value of multiculturalism, for it is here to stay. Rather, the problem is translating multiculturalism into effective classroom practice, and the need, therefore, to understand its historical and theoretical roots.

Toward that end, I want to look back at the youth of our profession, the 1920s—a troubling, contentious time, not unlike our own. It began with what appeared to be a feminist triumph and a significant socialist victory, but also with overt and widespread racial assaults. It continued through an orgy of commodity fetishism and ended with economic disaster that only war would finally alleviate. It was marked by a fundamentalist revival and, not surprisingly, loud public conflicts over dirty books (like *Ulysses*), "declining" morals, evolution, and "what do they learn in the schools."

In the post–World War I decade, American literary culture was one site of such conflicts. But that, we have largely forgotten. Indeed, as Cary Nelson has so strikingly remarked in *Repression and Recovery*, we have "forgotten that we have forgotten." Nelson is referring here to the varied poetic practices largely buried by the triumph of experimental modernism. But the same comment could well be made about the contemporaneous debates over theory. We have forgotten that we have forgotten the range of alternatives to "The Metaphysical Poets," Mr. Eliot's canonical service, which I will use here as a representative icon of our profession. To represent some of the alternatives, I shall introduce Amy Lowell—a name familiar by its absence—and Sterling Brown—a key figure in African American culture for over four decades, but who is as absent as Lowell from other discourses.

The processes by which these alternatives were marginalized and functionally erased from academic discussion, I want to suggest, derive in large part from the deep stake two or three generations of our profession have had in "The Metaphysical Poets" and in the constellation of theory and practice established by Eliot, Pound, and their New Critical successors. These reigned for over half a century and continue, in my view, to constitute what might be called the "pedagogical canon." By "pedagogical canon" I do not mean the "primary texts"—as we used to call them—selected for classroom study, for this canon has indeed, especially in American literature, been significantly modified. I refer, rather, to the still-dominant modes for reading and analyzing literary works, especially in the schools, and to the critical texts of the Eliotic/ New Critical tradition—like Cleanth Brooks and Robert Penn Warren's *Understanding Poetry*—that lie behind and validate these practices.

The commitment of literary academics to such predecessors *feels* rather like the stake of the child in its determinative parent, for it is hard otherwise to explain the slightly hysterical attachment to the Eliotic "sensibility" evident among many colleagues of middle years. And Eliot is a hard parent: he exacts cultural homage not only in his display of learning, in the authoritative voice that can speak of "our civilization" without stuttering, but in the very structure of his discourse, which leaves little room for disagreement with its *ex cathedra* judgments. Few essays as Eliot's "The Metaphysical Poets" demonstrate so explicitly the process of canon formation, critical to consolidating cultural or social power in a contested terrain. Here Eliot invokes the authority of a particular set of texts—those predominantly of the Elizabethan dramatists and the metaphysical poets—which he presents as constituting the main "current of [English] poetry." He maps the deviations from that mainstream in Milton and Dryden, the lost meanderings of that current in Romantic and Victorian England, and its implicit reemergence in the complex texts of high modernism. He offers a supposedly historical rationale—the "dissociation of sensibility" that mysteriously afflicted seventeenth-century intellectuals—for relegating writers like Shelley and Tennyson to the literary Apocrypha. And he provides a set of standards with which to judge contemporary aspirants for inclusion in that main tradition: the poet, he insists, is no "ordinary man" (247), but a person whose refined "sensibility" (247), marked by "a direct sensuous apprehension of thought, or a recreation of thought into feeling" (246), enables him to amalgamate "disparate experience" (247). Eliot's terms here are remarkably *psychological* rather than aesthetic: "sensibility" as distinct from "sentiment," associative in thought rather than merely proficient in "literary" technique, personal "maturity" as the final measure of *poetic* value.

I have rehearsed these familiar details because I wish to foreground the critical correlation of a particular artistic style—the rapid association of disparate experience, the maintenance of contradictions in tension—with a particular idea of psychological maturity.[1] This correlation helps to explain the persistence of the forms of teaching that the Eliotic tradition generated, even as the textual canon which he helped establish has increasingly been problematized. If one accepts this linkage, what we teach is not merely a form of analyzing literary art, but the path to maturity—a view, I should add, held by critics as different as Cleanth Brooks and Lionel Trilling—not to speak of current generations of formalists.

Once such pedagogical paradigms are established, the strong momentum of educational and publishing institutions as well as of our own investments in what we know how to do tend to keep them in place long after their usefulness—as with our health-care and adversarial legal systems—has been fatally compromised. The Eliotic "pedagogical canon" remains surprisingly powerful. One result, I think, is how my students, almost uniformly, regard poetry as a code for which another, observably more "mature" person—the teacher—has the only correct key. They're right, of course: if the close analysis of well-known texts constitutes the central task of the literature classroom, then students at virtually any level will feel powerless before the skills and intertextual knowledge of the instructor. In fact, I would argue that the "theoretical correctness"—if I may coin such a phrase—of traditionalists from William J. Bennett to Lynne Cheney stands in the way of opening up literature to students. What theoretical correctness communicates is this: the universe of cultural knowledge is fixed, a strand of pearls of wisdom, extracted from more or less resistant texts and displayed in an intellectual grouping denominated "Western Civilization." Such pearls need only be transmitted from apostle to novice, as a preacher hands down gospel lessons. I cannot imagine a more crippling pedagogical stance, and yet it continues—in large measure because, as the old political adage has it, "you can't beat somethin' with nothin.'" Multiculturalists have not yet produced distinctive, consistent pedagogies corresponding to new canonical changes. There are beginnings: student-response teaching strategies (for example, at South Windsor High School in Connecticut), an interrogation of students' and instructors' "subject positions" (as in some USC and Cornell classrooms), various efforts to shift to students responsibility over historical contexts and even syllabi (as in essays collected in a new book edited by John Alberti). But, as yet, the challenges to the Eliotic pedagogical canon remain somewhat scattered.

Which is why I want to return to Amy Lowell and Sterling Brown. I do not wish to overstate certain similarities: the long neglect of their large bodies of critical writing, for example, their interest in the commonplace and the concrete, their commitment to poetry as performance, and the utter marginalization of their verse. Especially, I should add, of Lowell's, for Brown's poems are at least available in a paperback volume issued by a small Chicago-area press, whereas Lowell's are nowhere in print. For me, their theories of poetry—embedded *in* poetic texts—contest Eliot's. Their theories, likewise, lead to distinctive reading strategies and therefore, potentially, to differing classroom practices.

Much of Lowell's critical prose was devoted to establishing Imagism as a literary movement which would contest with *fin de siècle* conventionality for American public approval. In her essay on "The Imagists: 'H.D.' and John Gould Fletcher," she reproduces the manifesto which served as preface to *Some Imagist Poets,* the first of the anthologies which she edited. It emphasizes using "the language of common speech," "new cadences" to express new ideas, "freedom in the choice of subject," and, above all, a "hard," "clear," concentrated poetry which "renders particulars exactly" through the presentation of images (240–41) which produce definable "effects." Imagism, she insists, "is presentation, not representation." Her emphasis upon "conveying" "the writer's impression" or mood "to the reader" stands in sharp and, I think, quite conscious contrast to Eliot's focus upon tradition and on the necessary depersonalization of verse.

Lowell's application of her Imagist theory is illustrated by the opening of "Madonna of the Evening Flowers,"* from her 1919 volume, *Pictures of the Floating World:*

> All day long I have been working,
> Now I am tired.

---

*"Madonna of the Evening Flowers," "Venus Transiens," and "The Sisters" from *The Complete Poetical Works of Amy Lowell.* Copyright © 1955 by Houghton Mifflin Company. Copyright © reviewed 1983 by Houghton Mifflin Company, Brinton P. Roberts, and G. D'Andelot Belin, Esquire. Reprinted by permission of Houghton Mifflin Co. All rights reserved.

I call: "Where are you?"
But there is only the oak-tree rustling in the wind.
The house is very quiet,
The sun shines in on your books,
On your scissors and thimble just put down,
But you are not there.

The poem moves from these conversational cadences and from within the house to the garden with its variety of flora, and the increasing intensity of feeling is represented by the rush of floral detail and the lengthening of lines:

You tell me that the peonies need spraying,
That the columbines have overrun all bounds,
That the pyrus japonica should be cut back and rounded.
You tell me these things.
But I look at you, heart of silver,
White heart-flame of polished silver,
Burning beneath the blue steeples of the larkspur,
And I long to kneel instantly at your feet,
While all about us peal the loud, sweet *Te Deums* of the Canterbury
    bells.

While the poem works, I think, within Lowell's Imagist paradigm, it raises interesting questions about gender—especially of the ambiguous speaker—and power in relationships.

As significant, perhaps, is that "Madonna of the Evening Flowers" is in effect paired in the book with the poem which immediately precedes it, "Venus Transiens":

Tell me,
Was Venus more beautiful
Than you are,
When she topped
The crinkled waves,
Drifting shoreward
On her plaited shell?
Was Botticelli's vision
Fairer than mine;
And were the painted rosebuds
He tossed his lady,
Of better worth
Than the words I blow about you
To cover your too great loveliness
As with a gauze
Of misted silver?

For me,
You stand poised

> In the blue and buoyant air,
> Cinctured by bright winds,
> Treading the sunlight.
> And the waves which precede you
> Ripple and stir
> The sands at my feet.

I have to attribute some degree of intent to Lowell in the placement of these poems: "Venus" with "Madonna," a poem which depends upon knowing classical myth and Renaissance painting, with one asking only that the reader appreciate garden flowers, a form of worship defined by "the words I blow about you" (and the reciprocal "ripple and stir" of waves of passion) against that of the lover whose imagined kneeling is sanctioned by the *"Te Deums* of the Canterbury bells." If "Madonna" can be taken to exemplify Lowell's Imagist theory, "Venus" seems to me to embody a rather different theoretical design, the design of the closet. For the poet's words here are by no means hard or clear, and what they "present" is, perversely, a veiling: the words at once literally reveal and are said to "cover" the "too great loveliness" of the lover's naked body.

Lowell's deployment of language to flaunt and to veil and her use of imagery of denuding to represent intense converse are consistent with her practice in the better known poem, "The Sisters," a work about the "queer lot . . . [of] women who write poetry." There, Lowell raises the question of "flinging" "reticences" into the wind in the speaker's initial encounter with Sappho (why, one might ask students, Sappho; what do you know of her?):

> This tossing off of garments
> Which cloud the soul is none too easy doing
> With us to-day. But still I think with Sappho
> One might accomplish it, were she in the mood
> To bare her loveliness of words and tell
> The reasons, as she possibly conceived them,
> Of why they are so lovely.

Lowell constituted her public persona by claiming to "bare" her words and tell all her "reasons": smoking cigars, turning night into day, flaunting eccentricity, and asserting that poetry claimed everything in the world for its subjects. Well, everything that's in "good taste," as she says properly somewhere. Beyond "good taste," and beyond Imagism, too, are the passions one must, as in "Venus Transiens," veil and yet embrace. Further, this "closet theory" opens ways for reading other closely linked poems, like "The Weather-Cock Points South," in which the speaker tells how "I put your leaves aside, / One by one" until she reaches a "bud," which is "more than the calyx."

But my central point about "Venus Transiens" is less to unpack its closet than to suggest how the poem promotes distinctive pedagogical strategies. We might begin with the observation that the closet door, like Lowell's language in the poem, always has, as it were, inner and outer surfaces: the speaker within speaking "out," the reader without trying to "listen" in. Seen thus, the poem can offer more than a clever manipulation of language. While it is a resistant text and thus usefully subject to the explicatory power of close reading, it also presents an opportunity for raising with students their roles as audience, listening to the speaker within. Especially in comparison with "Madonna," "Venus" enables us to ask: in what ways do these texts open themselves to readers and in what ways do they hold readers at a distance? What does one need to know to read either poem? Does it construct you as part of its reading community or not? Does Lowell employ classical allusions in "Venus" in the same ways as Eliot, say, or Pound? And moving beyond the issue of audience toward the New Critical shibboleth of "Intention," if Lowell seems in some degree to hide behind her words, why might she be motivated to do so? With this question we may place our students and ourselves in the crossroads of private life, so called, and public values: just what bids us to conceal that which, with every fibre of our being, we would flaunt—precisely, perhaps, in proportion to the degree we are forbidden.

Here, the correlation of how one speaks and what one wears (or bares), so central to "The Sisters," can provide students with the opportunity to focus on the poem's relatively unthreatening dimensions of their own experience. For the linking of conventions of dress and of language are commonplaces of youthful discourse (though the relationship of such knowledge to poetry is probably not often insisted upon). Just as clothing reveals, it hides; as words display, they cover—in no arena so forcefully as that of gender definitions. The epistemology of the closet, as Eve Kosofsky Sedgwick has pointed out, is not a remote outlook of the sexually marginalized, but centrally implicated in all sexual—among other—definitions in our culture (see Sedgwick, "Epistemology"). Pedagogically, the poem seems to me to open a response strategy by situating readers as observers at a small drama of passion, some of whose critical moves are unfamiliar or, at best, ambiguous.

Nowhere does that ambiguity more clearly arise than in connection with how one reads the line "For me." Deliberately recollecting the opening "Tell me," the line is emphasized by the stanza break, which immediately precedes it. In the first stanza the poem has raised a series of aesthetic questions: "Was Venus more beautiful / Than you are"? "Was Botticelli's vision / Fairer than mine"? Were his "painted rosebuds" "Of better worth" than my words? In one sense, these questions are dismissed by the line "For me." "For *me*," that is, the point is that "you stand" there "treading the sunlight"; the aesthetic questions disappear. Read as "*For* me," however, the answers to the questions about beauty turn implicitly on the sexual passion which the poem's words proclaim and, at once, encode. In this respect, "Venus Transiens" hinges on how one speaks the words *for* and *me* and on how a member of the audience "reads" the drama unfolding before her. It thus insists upon pedagogies which foreground audience, response, the aural and the public dimensions of verse.

Sterling Brown likewise wishes us to "hear" texts, though the voices he orchestrates differ sharply from the *sotto voce* of "Venus Transiens." Brown is concerned with performance, the speaking or singing voice—and thus vernacular—and audience. His critical essays continually return to these issues: the small size and divided outlook of the black writer's primary audience (*Negro Poetry and Drama* 80; "Introduction" 10–11); the capacity of "dialect, or the speech of the people," to express "whatever the people are" (*Negro Poetry and Drama* 43); the power of oral folk expression to inspire and direct written art. But to state his concerns in this abstract and generalized way is, I think, to miss the historical embeddedness of Brown's criticism. From his 1929 review of "unhistoric" histories by Allen Tate, Robert Penn Warren, and Claude Bowers, among others ("Unhistoric History" 134–61), to his 1953 comments on the transplantation of African American folk art to the city ("Negro Folk Expression" 60–61), Brown's objective is not to pose a transcendent theory of art but to use criticism to gain visibility and cultural space for black people in changing historical contexts. For as he and the other editors of *The Negro Caravan* comment, "creative literature has often been a handmaiden to social policy" ("Introduction" 3).

His poem celebrating "Ma Rainey"[**] embodies much of his theoretical stance:

I

When Ma Rainey
Comes to town,
Folks from anyplace
Miles aroun',
From Cape Girardeau,

[**]All lines from "Ma Rainey" from the *Collected Poems of Sterling A. Brown*. Ed. Michael S. Harper. Copyright © 1932 by Harcourt Brace & Co. Copyright © reviewed 1960 by Sterling A. Brown. Reprinted by permission of HarperCollins Publishers, Inc.

Poplar Bluff,
Flocks in to hear
Ma do her stuff;
Comes flivverin' in,
Or ridin' mules,
Or packed in trains,
Picknickin' fools. . . .
That's what it's like,
Fo' miles on down,
To New Orleans Delta
An' Mobile town,
When Ma hits
Anywheres aroun'.

II

Dey comes to hear Ma Rainey from de little river settlements,
From blackbottom cornrows and from lumber camps;
Dey stumble in de hall, jes a-laughin' an' a-cacklin',
Cheerin' lak roarin' water, lak wind in river swamps.
An' some jokers keeps deir laughs a-goin' in de crowded aisles,
An' some folks sits dere waitin' wid deir aches an' miseries,
Till Ma comes out before dem, a-smilin' gold-toofed smiles
An' Long Boy ripples minors on de black an' yellow keys.

III

O Ma Rainey,
Sing yo' song;
Now you's back
Whah you belong,
Git way inside us,
Keep us strong. . . .

O Ma Rainey,
Li'l an' low;
Sing us 'bout de hard luck
Roun' our do';
Sing us 'bout de lonesome road
We mus' go. . . .

IV

I talked to a fellow, an' the fellow say,
"She jes' catch hold of us, somekindaway.
She sang Backwater Blues one day:

> *'It rained fo' days an' de skies was dark as night,*
> *Trouble taken place in de lowlands at night.*

> *'Thundered an' lightened an' the storm begin to roll*
> *Thousan's of people ain't got no place to go.*

> *'Den I went an' stood upon some high ol' lonesome hill,*
> *An' looked down on the place where I used to live.'*

> An' den de folks, dey natchally bowed dey heads an' cried,
> Bowed dey heavy heads, shet dey moufs up tight an' cried,
> An' Ma lef' de stage, an' followed some de folks outside."
>
> Dere wasn't much more de fellow say:
> She jes' gits hold of us dataway.

The poem begins by describing Ma Rainey's audience by geography (Cape Girardeau, Poplar Bluff), class ("blackbottom cornrows," "lumber camps"), and range of feelings. That is, its initial move is to establish the particular reception community in which this artist works. Furthermore, the poem ends by focusing on the transformed social relationships *in* the reception of the artwork: in the beginning, Ma "comes out before dem" as performer; at the end, she "lef' de stage, an' followed some de folks outside" as one who shares their lives. Between these moments, Ma sings a historically rooted song, "Backwater Blues," based on a particularly devastating Mississippi River flood. The poem literally embodies verses from this song: it thus suggests one way in which peoples' art and written verse are related. As Amiri Baraka points out, Ma Rainey was herself a transitional figure, "perhaps the one who can be called the *link* between the earlier, less polished blues styles and the smoother theatrical style of most of the later urban blues singers" (Jones 89). But more, the poem also suggests a critical connection between peoples' experience and the cultural work of poetry.

These relationships are not at all simple, however, as the variety of voices *within* the poem indicate: we hear a narrator, a fellow from Ma's audience to whom the narrator talks, and Ma Rainey herself, singing. The common coin among them is, first of all, a way of speaking: vernacular—black, Southern, mainly rural dialect. And second, a set of experiences embodied not only in "Backwater Blues," but also by "de hard luck / Roun' our do'" and "de lonesome road." Paradoxically, and in accord with how Brown understands not only the blues but his own art, while the subject matter may be devastation and displacement, the *function* has to do with "git[tin] way inside us, [to] Keep us strong."[2] That is, against the terrors thematized by flood and famine and the road, the artist plays a shared music and voice and, as in "Strong Men," a laughter that proves a weapon of struggle and survival.

This poem, in short, presents a theory about the origins and functions in a crucial historical moment of African American expressive art and about the continuity—rather than Eliot's romanticized discrepancy—between the artist and the people she speaks of and with. It is thus necessarily about audience and the material conditions of cultural production—theoretical categories distant from those of "The Metaphysical Poets." But what I want to emphasize are the very different *pedagogical* directions in which Brown's ideas lead. Like Lowell, interestingly, the theory exemplified in "Ma Rainey" works to take poetry from the silent study to the platform, from the discipline of the footnote to that of the Method. Unlike Lowell, it opens issues about the relationships of "popular" and "high" cultures, blues and written poetry, rap and formal criticism—issues of more than abstract concern to many students.

Most of all, this theory problematizes the usually assumed "normality" of studying poetry *in* a classroom. It allows a set of questions, usually foreclosed, to be raised in class: When is poetry useful? Toward what ends? Do you use it? Why? How do the venues for its use compare with that of the classroom? How do the forms of verse encountered outside the classroom differ from or match those engaged within? In what ways have they intermixed? The objective here is first to denaturalize the classroom as the site for the consumption or even discussion of poetry and thus to legitimize a variety of poetic "situations." By so doing, I think one also opens the core questions of the canon: what art is "legitimate" to study, toward what ends, and in what circumstances? To be sure, such discussions will bring us to that other crossroads, the one Lionel Trilling designated as "bloody," where art and politics meet. But it does so in a way that arises not so much from the instructor's insistence on the "politics of the canon"—a dominantly professional imperative—but from the students' real experience of disjunction between forms of art that function in their daily lives and the forms (and forms of study) legitimized within academe.

At the beginning of these remarks, I raised the question: "What counts for theory?" That question, in turn, led me to the issue of teaching: what needs to change in classroom practice to bring the new broadened textual canon alive for all our students? In sketching some ways in which poems by Amy Lowell and Sterling Brown can be understood as theoretical texts, I am proposing not only that answers lie in the poems themselves, but that the poems radically question the formalist assumptions that continue to underwrite yesterday's dying pedagogical canon. The poems help foreground some of today's key pedagogical issues: the classroom not as a neutral site of recondite learning, but as a conflicted public space; the roles of the different people in the classroom in creating knowledge; the functions of terms of analysis and identity formation, like gender, in the construction (and denial) of knowledge. In short, I think these poems help us shift attention from the formal properties of language to the cultural work of art, a process which moves us—to return to my epigraph—from the worship of icons, however bright, to the study of what humanizes, however painful.

Notes

1. It is also true, of course, as Richard Ohmann has pointed out, that the mode of *explication de texte* fit the needs of the literary profession in the post–World War II period both for what then seemed a politically neutral stance toward texts and for a technical strategy that could distinguish "English" from other, potentially competitive, academic departments.

2. Cf. Ralph Ellison. "Richard Wright's Blues":

> The blues is an impulse to keep the painful details and episodes of a brutal experience alive in one's aching consciousness, to finger its jagged grain and to transcend it, not by the consolation of philosophy but by squeezing from it a near-tragic, near-comic lyricism. (78)

Works Cited

Brooks, Cleanth, and Robert Penn Warren. *Understanding Poetry.* 3rd. ed. New York: Holt, 1960.

Brown, Sterling A. "Ma Rainey." *The Collected Poems of Sterling A. Brown.* Ed. Michael S. Harper. New York: Harper, 1980. 62–63.

———. "Negro Folk Expression." *Phylon* 11 (Autumn 1950): 60–61.

———. "Unhistoric History." *Journal of Negro History* 15 (April 1930): 134–61.

———, ed. *Negro Poetry and Drama.* Washington, D.C.: Associates in Negro Folk Education, 1937. Rpt. New York: Atheneum, 1969.

Brown, Sterling A., Arthur P. Davis, and Ulysses Lee. "Introduction." *The Negro Caravan.* New York: Dryden, 1941. 10–11.

Eliot, T. S. "The Metaphysical Poets." *Selected Essays.* 1950. New York: Harcourt, 1964. 241–50.

Ellison, Ralph. "Richard Wright's Blues." 1945. *Shadow and Act.* New York: Random, 1964. 77–94.

Jones, LeRoi. *Blues People: Negro Music in White America.* New York: Morrow, 1963.

Lowell, Amy. "The Imagists: 'H.D.' and John Gould Fletcher." *Tendencies in Modern American Poetry.* New York: Macmillan, 1917. 235–343.

———. "Madonna of the Evening Flowers," "Venus Transiens," "The Sisters," "The Weather-Cock Points South." *The Complete Poetical Works of Amy Lowell.* Boston, Houghton, 1955. 210, 210, 459–61, 211.

———. *Pictures of the Floating World.* New York: Macmillan, 1919.

Nelson, Cary. *Repression and Recovery: Modern American Poetry and the Politics of Cultural Memory, 1910–1945.* Madison: University of Wisconsin Press, 1989.

Olsen, Tillie. "Tell Me a Riddle." *Tell Me a Riddle: A Collection.* 1961. New York: Dell, 1971. 63–116.

Sedgwick, Eve Kosofsky. "Epistemology of the Closet." *The Lesbian and Gay Studies Reader.* Ed. Henry Abelove, Michele Aina Barale, and David M. Halperin. New York: Routledge, 1993. 47–48.

Some Imagist Poets: An Anthology. Boston: Houghton, 1915.

17 The War between Reading and Writing— and How to End It

Peter Elbow
University of Massachusetts at Amherst

We tend to assume that reading and writing fit naturally together: love and marriage, horse and carriage. It is a commonplace that the very best thing for writing is to read a great deal—and it seems as though those students who write best are readers. But when we see things in binary pairs, one side usually ends up on top—privileged or dominant: love and marriage, man and woman. I will argue that this is true here too and that reading has dominance over writing in the academic or school culture. But my main point in this essay is that the imbalance is unnecessary. Reading and writing can work productively together as equals to benefit each other and the profession. Both parties can be on top. We can create a better balance and relationship between reading and writing. To do so we will need to give more emphasis to writing in our teaching and our curricular structures and use writing in more imaginative ways. When we achieve this productive balance, even reading will benefit.

There are four sections here: (1) Sites of conflict between reading and writing; (2) How reading is privileged over writing; (3) Benefits of ending this privilege; (4) Ways to end the war and create a more productive interaction between reading and writing.

Sites of Conflict between Reading and Writing

Gerald Graff wrote a whole book about the conflicts in the English profession and never focused on the most striking and problematic conflict of all: that between reading and writing—between literature and composition (Friend).

This essay first appeared in *Rhetoric Review* 12.1 (Fall 1993): 5–24 and is reprinted by permission of *Rhetoric Review*.

The conflict of interest between reading and writing shows itself most clearly perhaps in the question of authority. From ancient times on, authors were the source of 'author'-ity—and it was the reader's job to find out what the author intended to say. Someone who could establish himself as "writer" or "author" (and it was usually "he") was felt to be special—even as seer or oracle. Thus people often sought out authors or writers in order to hear their pronouncements on all sorts of matters (thus the phenomenon of "table talk").

In recent times, readers have battled back successfully to take authority for themselves. The New Critics convinced much of the profession that the author's intention didn't matter. Deconstructive theorists convinced much of the profession that even the concept of meaning in a text is problematic. Roland Barthes speaks of the death of the author giving rise to the birth of the reader; he characterizes the reader as alive and sexy and full of energy, and the "scriptor" as pallid and lacking in juice.

The most specific focus of contention is over who gets authority over the meaning of a text. Take my own text here as an example. I get to decide what I *intended to say.* You get to decide what you *understand me to say.* But as for what I actually *did say*—what meanings are "in" my text—that is a site of contention between us. We see this fight everywhere, from the law courts to literary criticism to the bedrooms: "But I said . . ." / "No you didn't, you said. . . ."

So the interests of the contending parties are clear. It's in the interest of readers to say that writers' intentions don't matter or are unfindable, to say that meaning is never determinate, always fluid and sliding, to say that there is no presence or voice behind a text—and finally to kill off the author. This leaves the reader in complete control of the text.

It's in the interest of writers, on the other hand, to say that their intentions are central—to have readers actually interested in what was on writers' minds, what they intended to say. As writers we often fail to be clear, but it helps us if readers have some faith that our authorial meanings and intentions can be found. If I am lost in the woods, you have a better chance of finding me if you think I am actually there. And it goes without saying that writers are interested in not being killed off. (Even critics who celebrate the death of the author are likely to get irritated when readers completely misread what they have written.)

Writers also have interest in *ownership* of the text—and, as with "killing," I want to take this metaphor literally. Writers have an interest in monetary payment for their labor. But of course the figurative psychological meaning is more pervasive. Writers *feel* ownership. People sometimes like to say now that the sense of individual ownership over words is only a recent, modern phenomenon, but even Chaucer in the fourteenth century wrote into his poem a plea to copyists to please not "miswrite" his words in copying the text.

Listen to the dismay of Toni Morrison on this point:

> Whole schools of criticism have dispossessed the writer of any place whatever in the critical value of his work. Ideas, craft, vision, meaning—all of them are just so much baggage in these critical systems. . . . The political consequences for minority writers, dissident writers and writers committed to social change are devastating. For it means that there is no way to talk about what we mean, because to mean anything is not in vogue (Sanders 25).

Here is Scott Russell Sanders commenting on her statement:

> Rightly or wrongly, many of us who make novels and stories and poems feel that the net effect of recent theorizing has been to turn the writer into a puppet, one whose strings are jerked by some higher power—by ideology or the unconscious, by ethnic allegiance, by sexual proclivities, by gender, by language itself. We may wade through Derrida and Adorno and de Man, we may read Harold Bloom and J. Hillis Miller and Stanley Fish, or we may simply hear rumors of what they and their innumerable followers are up to; whether at first or second hand, we learn that to regard ourselves as conscious, purposeful, responsible artists is a delusion; we learn that material conditions or neuroses control us; we learn that our efforts at making sense are doomed to failure; we learn that our words, like Zeno's forlorn rabbit, will never reach their destination (25).

Am I only telling a story of readers privileging themselves over writers? No, writers privileged themselves over readers long before the intentional fallacy was a gleam in the eye of Wimsatt and Beardsley. Writers often say, "What do readers know? My toughest audience—sometimes my main audience—is me. For some pieces, I don't even *care* whether readers understand or appreciate my efforts." So perhaps it's not surprising that readers have finally retaliated with a modern doctrine that says, "What do writers know? We can read the text better than they can. Intention is a will o' the wisp. Never trust the teller, trust the tale." In short, where writers are tempted to think they are the most important party in the transaction, readers and academics are tempted to think they are the most important party (Wallace).

Just as children think their parents should always have them in mind, many modern readers think that writers should always have them in mind. When readers are teachers (and most teachers think of themselves more as readers than as writers), they tell students, "You must always keep us in mind as you write." And if student writing is weak, they diagnose "writer-based prose!" and assume that the student stopped thinking about them—when in fact the problem was probably that the student was *too* preoccupied with the teacher-reader. When readers are theorists (and most theorists also think of themselves more as readers than as writers), they often completely contradict that teacherly advice and declare, "There is no such thing as writing without readers in mind— no such thing as private writing. If you *thought* you were not thinking about us and just writing privately in your journal for yourself alone, you were fooling yourself. You are never not thinking about us" (see, for example, Harris 66).

But writers, like parents, tend to insist on time away from the imperious demands of readers. Writers know they need some time when they can just forget about readers and think about themselves. Yes, writers must finally acknowledge the humbling truth that, in the end, readers get to decide whether their words will be *read* or *bought*—just as parents have to accept that, in the end, the child's interests must come first. But smart writers and parents know that they do a better job of serving these demanding creatures if they take some time for themselves.

I hope it's clear that this reader/writer conflict isn't just theoretical. I feel it quite concretely in my teaching—especially in a writing course for first-year students. Yes, ideally I want my students to feel themselves as both writers and readers. But my pressing hunger to help them feel themselves as writers makes me notice the conflict. That is, I want my students to have some of that uppitiness of writers toward readers—to be able to talk back—to say, "I'm not just writing for readers or teachers; I'm writing as much for me—sometimes even *more* for me." I want them to fight back a bit against readers.

Let me point to another conflict of interests between writers and readers: a conflict over the relationship between *language* and *knowledge*. Writers frequently testify to the experience of knowing more than they can say, of knowing things that they haven't yet been able to get into words. Readers on the other hand (especially when they are also teachers or academics), being mostly on the receiving end of texts, are often tempted to put forth the doctrine that all knowledge is linguistic, that there is nothing we can know outside of language: "If you cannot talk about an experience, at least to yourself, you did not have it" (Emerson 252).

Again, this isn't just theoretical. Paying better attention to the *in*articulate—having more respect for the nonverbal—often leads writers to the articulate. Most of my own progress in learning to write has come from my gradually learning to listen more carefully to what I haven't yet managed to get into words—waiting and trying to feel better my nonverbal feelings and intentions—and respecting the idea that I know more than I can say. This stance helps me be willing to find time and energy to tease into language what the phenomenolist Eugene Gendlin calls my "felt bodily sense." The most unhelpful thing I've had said to me as a student and writer is, "If you can't say it, you don't know it." Not surprisingly, painters, musicians and dancers are more than a little amused at the odd dogma that all knowledge is linguistic—that if you can't say it in language you don't know it and it doesn't count as knowledge.

I want to call attention to some very central pedagogical implications of this point about language and meaning—a point that writers often understand and readers and academics and teachers often do not. The main thing that helps writers is to be *understood.* Pointing out what we don't understand is only the second need. In my teaching, I find it helpful to assume that I often *can* hear intentions that are not really articulated. Yes, I'll point out where these intentions are badly realized, but if my goal is to make students feel like writers, my highest priority is to show that I've understood what they're saying. It's only my second priority to show them where I had to struggle.

I see a third conflict between readers and writers these days: over whether to trust language. Again let me describe the conflict in terms of my own teaching. If my goal is to get my first-year students to take on the role of reader, I should constantly try to get them to distrust language. For it is a central tenet of intellectual and academic thinking in this century that words are not a clear and neutral window through which we can see undistorted nonlinguistic things.

Of course, I acknowledge the merit in this skeptical view of language. Nevertheless, if I want to help my students experience themselves as *writers,* I find I must help them *trust* language—not question it—or at least not question it for long stretches of the writing process till they have managed to generate large structures of language and thinking. Some people say this is good advice only for inexperienced and blocked writers, but I think I see it as enormously helpful to myself and to other adult, skilled, and professional writers. Too much distrust often stops people from coming up with interesting hypotheses and from getting things written. Striking benefits usually result when people learn that decidedly unacademic capacity to turn off distrust of language and instead not to *see* it, to look through it as through a clear window, and focus all attention on the objects or experiences one is trying to articulate. Let me quote a distinguished poet and writer, William Stafford, about the need to trust language and one's experience:

> Just as any reasonable person who looks at water, and passes a hand through it, can see that it would not hold a person up; so it is the judgment of common sense people that reliance on the weak material of students' experiences cannot possibly sustain a work of literature. But swimmers know that if they relax on the water it will prove to be miraculously buoyant; and writers know that a succession of little strokes on the material nearest them—without any prejudgments about the specific gravity of the topic or the reasonableness of their expectations—will result in creative progress. Writers are persons who write; swimmers are (and from teaching a child I know how hard it is to persuade a reasonable person of this)—swimmers are persons who relax in the water, let their heads go down, and reach out with ease and confidence." . . .
> . . . [M]y main plea is for the value of an unafraid, face-down, flailing, and speedy process in using the language (22–23).

For the last site of conflict between reading and writing (and an intriguing one), let's look at what's called "invisible writing." A couple of decades ago, James Britton and colleagues (35*ff*) were interested in how important it is for writers to get that literal, short-term feedback of simply *seeing* what they are writing. They demonstrated this by artificially taking it away. That is, they tried writing with spent ballpoint pens so they couldn't see what they were writing (but putting carbon paper and another sheet underneath the page they were writing on). Sure enough, they felt stymied and their writing fell apart. But then Sheridan Blau replicated the experiment many times—and showed in virtually every case that students and professionals were *not* significantly harmed by ten- and twenty-minute stretches of what he called "invisible writing" (despite some initial frustration). Indeed, students often produced better pieces in various modes or genres under these conditions (Blau). His explanation of the phenomenon seems right to me from my own trials of invisible writing: when you can't see what you are writing you are almost automatically forced into a much greater focus of attention and energy on what you are trying to say—on the meaning and intention in your mind. And you can't stop and worry; you must forge on.

What these experiments show is the odd fact that normal writing is really both-writing-*and*-reading. Invisible writing stamps out the reading we normally do as we write and forces us to engage in nothing-*but*-writing—with a consequent boost of concentration and intensity of mind. Thus invisible writing is strikingly helpful with a common problem: finding ourselves stalled in our writing and spending most of our so-called *writing* time sitting and reading back over what we have already written. Word processors make invisible writing very easy: just turn down the screen.

How Reading Is Privileged over Writing

Most schools and colleges emphasize reading and neglect writing. An investigation of English classes in secondary schools has found that students spend less than 3 percent of their class and homework time devoted to writing a paragraph or more—and most of the "writing" time in class consists of writing short-answer exercises (Applebee).

In most school and college courses, reading is more central than writing. Even in English departments there is usually only *one* writing course—some kind of "freshman writing." Sometimes there is a sprinkling of creative writing or other advanced writing courses—but even when these are given, they are available to comparatively few students. Other departments (except for journalism) typically have no writing courses.

Of course, writing is *assigned* in a fair number of courses (though some students in large universities learn to avoid much writing for their whole college career). But when writing is assigned, it is traditionally meant to *serve* reading: to summarize, interpret, explain, or make integrations and comparisons among readings. In the last couple of years there has even been a widespread move to change the first-year writing course into a reading-and-writing course, even though it is usually the *only* writing course—the only place in the entire curriculum where writing is emphasized more than reading. In every other course in the university, reading is privileged and writing, when used at all, is used to serve reading.

I won't try to analyze here the complicated historical and cultural reasons why we have this imbalance, but I can't resist mentioning one interesting hypothesis (Laurence). If we assign much writing, we find ourselves positively awash in what is admittedly discouraging or depressing: our students' thinking and feeling—with all its naiveté, its appearance of reflecting nothing but brainwashing by the shallowest pop culture. We can spare ourselves from any real immersion in extensive student thinking and feeling about our topic if we assign mostly reading, if we use carefully focused topics on the few occasions when we do assign writing, and if we fill up our classes with lectures or carefully controlled discussions. Howard Gardner points out in one of his most recent books that good teaching and learning seldom happen unless we understand and acknowledge and learn to deal with what is really happening in students' minds.

The dominance of reading has produced some powerful political and economic consequences for higher education. It is fairly common for English departments to "live off" writing teachers—paying them poorly, denying them the possibility of tenure, and providing poor working conditions, in order to give tenure, much better pay, and a lighter teaching load to teachers of reading or literature. People who teach writing are apt to be TAs or nontenure track lecturers or adjunct part-timers who must piece together jobs at two or three institutions, and they are often paid less than $1,000 per course—with no benefits. They often don't know if they'll be hired till a month or a week before the term begins—sometimes, in fact, only after the semester has started. (James Slevin lays out these conditions in more detail and makes an interesting argument about the reasons for the imbalance.)

Let me turn from the outward material conditions of employment to the inward premises of our thinking. That is, the relationship between reading and writing in most school and college courses enacts a kind of root metaphor or originary story of our culture: that we hear and read before we speak and write—that input precedes output. This seems a natural story: babies and children seem to hear before they can speak—to listen before they answer. But it's not so simple. Yes, children wouldn't speak unless they grew up in the presence of other speakers, and of course babies and children usually answer when spoken to. But careful observation of children suggests that it works the other way round too: the reason why children *get* input—*hear* language—is often that they *initiate* the "conversation." Even when a baby gives as little as a gurgle or a coo, parents often take it as the initiation of discourse (which it sometimes is), and respond. Babies don't just read the textbook and listen to lectures and then answer questions; sometimes they start the conversation. Babies often "write" before they "read."

I suspect that the child's initiation of speech is as important or more so in learning to talk than the initiation by others. That is, the adult's enabling act is as much listening and understanding and answering as it is starting a conversation. The most productive and generative act by a teacher or parent is often to listen. In short, most parents instinctively know that their job is to get children to start with output, not input—start with writing, not reading.

But the relationship between reading and writing in schools and universities belies this instinctive wisdom of parents. Our very conception of what it is to learn privileges reading over writing because that concept has been shaped by the same root metaphor: *learning is input*—"taking things in"—putting things inside us. People think of the root activities in school as listening and reading, not talking and writing. Of course, when we stop and think about it, we realize that students learn from output—talking and writing—but we don't naturally think of learning as talking and writing. Notice, for example, how many teachers think of testing as measuring input, not output. Tests tend to ask, in effect,

"How well have you learned the ideas of others?" not "What new ideas of your own do you have?"

Even if we grant that, more often than not, input precedes output, and that we usually speak and write in response to what we hear and read, we must still beware a claim that some people make today: that *all* writing is in response to text or textuality. This is not a fair translation of Bakhtin's insight about the ubiquity of voices. When people fixate on a theoretical dictum that all writing is in response to texts, they paper over a concrete and indeed political distinction: the distinction between asking students to write in response to our texts and lectures vs. asking them to write in response to their own ideas and experience (even if their ideas and experience are made up of texts and voices already inside their heads). Even if we were to take it as our main goal to show students that what they experience as their own ideas and voices are really ideas and voices from outside them, our best strategy would be to get them to write extensively about something *before* reading any new texts about it. That is the best way to make visible all the voices that are already jampacked inside their heads.

Why is it that our profession stresses so much the *reading* of imaginative writing—fiction and poetry and drama—while neglecting the writing of it? Most of us got into the field not only because we loved to read imaginative writing but also because we liked to write it—often harboring wishes to be writers. But as adult professionals, we tend to run away from it. We seldom write it or ask our students to write it. Can we really say we understand something we never try to engage in? We should surely require Ph.D. candidates at least to *try their hand* at the kind of writing they profess to understand and hope to teach.

I've had an interesting glimpse into the archaeology of this fear of writing in literature professors. Whenever I teach any graduate course in writing, I ask students to write case studies of themselves as writers: to look back through their lives at what they've written and to figure out as much as they can about how they went about writing and what was going on—to try to see all the forces at play. I've noticed a striking feature that is common in literature students that I don't much see in graduate students from other disciplines: a wry and sometimes witty but always condescending tone they take toward their younger selves who were usually excited with writing and eager to be great writers. Behind this urbanity I often see a good deal of disappointment and even pain at not being able to keep on writing those stories and poems that were so exciting to write. But instead of acknowledging this disappointment, these students tend to betray a frightening lack of kindness or charity— most of all a lack of *understanding*—toward that younger self who wanted to grow up to be Yeats or Emily Dickinson. Instead, I see either amused condescension or downright ridicule at their former idealism and visionary zeal. My point is that no one can continue to engage in writing without granting herself some vision and idealism and even naive grandstanding. Yet these literature students, now that they see themselves on the path to being professors of literature—that is professors of reading—seem to need to squelch any sense of themselves as writers.

Even in M.F.A. programs, which are devoted to writing and which are sometimes even guilty of neglecting reading, we see an odd but powerful ritual that privileges readers over writers: the so-called "gag rule." It is standard in workshops that writers must be silent and only readers may speak. That is, writers must refrain from the most natural thing that they might want to do, namely to specify the kinds of response they need from readers or the issues they want readers to explore. (This pervasive custom seems to derive from the early Iowa workshops, and perhaps has definite gender associations of writers as "tough guys who can take it.")

Notice how the dominance of reading over writing is embedded in our language. The word *literacy* really means power over letters, i.e., reading and writing. But as literacy is used casually and even in government policy and legislation, it tends to mean *reading*, not writing. Similarly, the word *learning* tends to connote reading and input—not writing and output. Finally, the very words *academic* or *professor* or even *teacher* tend to connote a reader and critic, not a writer. Thus deeply has the dominance of reading infected our ways of thinking.

I can conclude this section by making it clear that I am not arguing *against* reading—against the importance and special value of reading and listening—only against privileging them over writing and speaking. Reading and listening are precious for the very ways they are different from writing and speaking. They are precious because they ask us to step outside our own preoccupations and to hear what others have to say, to think in the language of others, to recognize authority of others without letting it overwhelm us, and above all to relinquish some control. I hope that my long advocacy of the believing game or methodological belief will show that I don't slight this side of our intellectual life (see Elbow, "Game"; "Methodological").

Nor am I trying to imply that students are already good at reading and listening. Far from it. Yes, learning means getting inside someone else's language and thinking, taking in ideas, indeed taking in lists of brute facts—and getting them right. But I suspect that part of students' difficulty with reading stems from the ingrained educational pattern I'm pointing to here: It's always, "Read first and then write to see if you've got it right. What *they* have to say is more important than what *you* have to say." Reading and listening might go better if we sometimes said, "Let's start with what *you* have to say. Then we'll see if the reading can respond to it and serve it." I find it common for people to be more interested in a subject and be able to take in more new material about it if they first work out their own thinking about it.

Benefits of Ending This Privilege

What if we undid the imbalance? The benefits would be considerable. If we gave more centrality to writing, it would help out with an important and vexing problem in the teaching of reading itself. That is, we often have difficulty getting students to see how the meaning of a text is actively created and negotiated—not just found as an inert right answer sitting there hidden in the text or in the teacher's mind or in a work of authoritative criticism. "Yes," we say to our students, "the text puts some constraints on our reading. Not any interpretation is acceptable. Nevertheless the resulting meaning is something that readers have to build and negotiate." This lesson is all the harder to teach because students sometimes flop over into the opposite misunderstanding of reading: "Well this is what *I* think the poem means, and nothing you can say will change my mind. Literature is just a matter of *personal opinion*."

Reading can learn from writing here. Writing involves physical actions that are much more outward and visible than reading does. As a result, it is easier to see how meaning is slowly constructed, negotiated, and changed in writing than it is in reading. The erasing, crossing out, and changing of words as we write is much more visible than the erasing, crossing out, and changing of words that do in fact go on as we read—but more quickly and subliminally. Students can see evidence of the same process in the messy manuscripts and revisions even of famous published authors. And we usually *experience* the construction of meaning more vividly, even painfully, when we write than when we read. Most writing teachers now try to set up their classes so that students can experience how written meaning is constructed through a process of thinking, generating trial text, revision, and social negotiation with peers and teachers. It seems to me then that writing is the most helpful paradigm we have for teaching what may be the central process in our profession and what we most want to convey to students: the way meaning in both reading and writing is constructed and negotiated.

By the way, because the reading process is so quick and hidden, it seems less fraught with struggle for people who are skilled. Therefore, literature teachers often fail to experience themselves in the same boat or engaged in the same process as their unskilled students. When it comes to writing, however, almost all teachers experience the common bond of struggle or even anxiety, no matter how good they are. Writing is a leveler.

But students *could* come to see reading as a "process" of cognitive and social construction if only there were a tradition in literature, as there is in writing, of teachers and researchers sharing what we might call "rough drafts of reading": showing or talking about their actual reading process *from the beginning*—for example, by working with colleagues or students on texts they have not seen before; giving an honest protocol or an accurate account of the mental events that go on in one's mind while engaged in creating meaning from a text. I like to call this giving "movies of the reader's mind." If there were more widespread attention to this sharing of our own reading processes, we'd spend more time talking to our colleagues and to our students about how of course we misread and misunderstand an enormous number of words and phrases and sections of a text as we engage in even the most skilled reading. That is, the mysterious innerness of reading isn't just because good readers "revise" and correct themselves so quickly and often subliminally; it's also because there's no tradition of revealing misreadings and wrong takes (like sharing early drafts). Where the writing tradition of the last two decades shows teachers how to write with students and share what they produce in its raw crummy state, the literary tradition tells literature teachers that it would be wrong to teach a class on a text that they have not carefully studied and mastered beforehand, and that it would be odd to have a discussion with colleagues about a text they've never seen before. Reading becomes vivid and alive in classes where everyone, even the teacher, reveals early rough "readings" in process, and shows how these are adjusted and transformed over time and by means of negotiation through comparison with readings by others.

One of the virtues of reader-response criticism is that if people really engage in it honestly and empirically, it tends to make them braver about the kind of exploring I've just described. It promotes professionalism in the good sense (nondefensive thinking together) and undermines professionalism in the bad sense (trying to hide your struggles and to erase bonds with the unwashed). I'm suspicious of the fact that reader-response criticism has gone so deeply out of fashion in literary criticism. I know there are lots of culturally sophisticated reasons, but frankly, I think a lot of it can be explained this way: critics began to stumble onto a critical method that required giving naked accounts of what was actually happening inside them as they read—and decided to back away from the process.

If writing were more central, we would see a similar gain to literary study in the realm of evaluation or testing. The field of composition has managed to convince schools and colleges that testing means testing a practice or a performance, not a content: that if we want to find out how well students write, we've got to get them to write—despite budgetary pressures and the blandishments of cheaper tests of grammar and usage from ETS and ACT. In the case of literature, however, virtually every school, college, and university in the country accedes to ETS and ACT testing of literature and reading by means of multiple-choice, machine-graded tests—many of them tests of correct information. (Of course colleges have mostly gone along with the ETS decision to omit required writing in SAT II, but that wasn't a decision to trust multiple-choice tests of writing ability; it was a decision to forego trustworthy knowledge of writing ability. Indeed, this decision was deeply influenced by an argument in the other direction: "minority students' writing ability will not be measured fairly if there is only a 20 minute writing sample—with the attendant overdetermination by dialect cues.) We see some of the same difference between writing and reading if we look at teachers' course exams: it has come to feel peculiar if the final exam in a writing course asks mostly for recall of ideas and information—whereas that does not seem peculiar in many literature courses.

Another benefit of emphasizing writing: it will yield us a better model not just for reading but for learning itself. The dominance of reading at all levels of education reinforces the problematic banking metaphor of learning: the assumption that students are vessels to be filled. But when we give equal emphasis to writing, we are more likely to assume the contrasting metaphor: *learning is the making of meaning*. This metaphor helps explain much that is otherwise paradoxical about the learning process:

- The more we write and talk, the more we have left to write and say. The greater the number of words that come out of us, the greater the number of words we find left inside.

- When students feel empty ("I have nothing to say, nothing on my mind") the cause is not insufficient input but insufficient output. What gets more words in their heads is more talking and writing.

- Of course teachers and politicians love to talk: the more people talk the more they want to talk.

When we see learning not as input but as the making of meaning and connections, these phenomena become natural, not paradoxical.

Notice too that when we stop privileging reading over writing, we stop privileging passivity over activity. Yes, I grant the usefulness of the currently fashionable paradoxes: that the reading is really "writing" (actively creating meaning), and writing is really "reading" (passively finding what culture and history have inscribed in our heads). But in the end I would insist that writing simply does promote more activity and agency than reading:

- Reading tends to imply "Sit still and pay attention," while writing tends to imply "Get in there and do something."

- Reading asks, "What did they have to say?" while writing asks, "What do you have to say?" In normal speech, listeners usually want to know what the speaker was actually intending to say, and this reinforces the impulse to "look for the right answer" in reading. Similarly, speakers usually have the impulse to say what's on their mind, and this reinforces the impulse for writers to take authority over their own meaning.

- Reading tends to be a matter of the teacher and author choosing the words; writing tends to be a matter of the student choosing the words.

- Reading means consumption; writing means production. Part of the stale passivity of students comes from their being cast always in the role of consumer.

- I would point even to the purely physical dimension. Writing involves more physical movement than reading. Try this experiment: on an occasion when a discussion class goes listless or dead, have everyone stop talking and silently read a helpful piece of text; on another occasion have everyone stop and write something. You'll find that students tend to be more awake and involved after they write—even displaying more tonus in their bodies—than after they read. (Notice also how the physical act of reading out loud—especially with any gesturing—helps the cognitive dimension of reading.)

In short, when we make writing as important as reading, we help students break out of their characteristically passive stance for school and learning. The primacy of reading in the reading/writing dichotomy is an act of locating authority away from the student and keeping it entirely in the teacher or institution or great figure. The privileging of reading over writing has locked schools into sending a pervasive, deep-level message: "Don't speak until spoken to; don't write your own ideas till you prove that you can reproduce correctly the ideas and information of others; writing *means* responding to authority outside the self; as a student you should be a consumer of knowledge, not a producer!"

If we made writing as important as reading, we might begin to feel ourselves as writers too, not just readers. At present, when we take on the role of "academic," we tend to take on the role of reader and critic— and not writer. To make this large change, we'd have to foster and nour- ish creative risk taking in ourselves and in the profession. We celebrate the imagination in the authors we study; we would grow as a profes- sion if we celebrated and cultivated it in ourselves too. Just as society or individual relationships lose vitality and intelligence if women or mi- norities are suppressed, so English is losing vitality and intelligence be- cause writing is suppressed.

Let me end this section by answering a possible objection: "We have to keep writing in its secondary role—as the medium for responding to reading—or else we will invite romantic solipsism. If you invite students to write out of their own experience rather than in response to texts, you will increase the rampant individualism our culture suffers from—per- mitting students to disappear into cocoons of solipsistic isolation." This fear rests on a misguided model of individual development—a kind of parody of Freud and Piaget that says children start out as egocentric monads dominated by selfish desires to stay separate and egocentric; and that they cannot become "decentered" or social without a terrible struggle. It's as though we fear that our students are each in their own little bathroom and we must beat on the door and say, "What are you *doing* in there? Why have you been in there so long with the door locked? Come on out and have some wholesome fun with us."

But a very different course of development now seems more believ- able and generally accepted—a model that derives from thinkers like George Herbert Meade, Bakhtin, and Vygotsky: our children *start out* very social and intertwined. Their little selves are not hermetically sealed atoms but are rather deeply enmeshed or rooted in the important fig- ures in their lives. We don't have to struggle to make children want to connect with others—they are naturally already connected. We don't have to bang on the bathroom door to make them listen, feel part of, and collaborate with the various people and cultural forces around them. They may not want to listen to us but that doesn't make them private and solipsistic. (In fact it's usually the private and solipsistic kids that listen best to us teachers.) What this picture of human development shows us is that separateness and autonomy are not qualities that chil- dren start out with but rather qualities they only gradually achieve— often with struggle and setbacks throughout adolescence and young adulthood. It can be a slow and difficult process for individuals to achieve a certain autonomous sense of self such that they can think and do things that are *disapproved* of by the community they feel part of. And it is writing, by the way, which is particularly powerful as a medium to help adolescents begin to learn to become a bit more reflective; able to converse with themselves; not be so prey to cultural messages and peer standards and pressures.

I can give a concrete illustration of this psychological model: I find that when I work with adults, college students, and high school students, they are usually grateful when I show them various ways to use *private* writing—when I clear a lot of time and space and almost force them to do writing that they will not show to me or anyone else. If they are not already accustomed to using writing this way, they tend to experience it as a release or even as empowering. But when I work with first graders, they are uninterested and unimpressed. They tend to want to share everything they write. That is, as we get older, we tend to work at separating ourselves and sorting out what we choose as our own—and where we choose to fit in. It's a life task. The point of my digression into developmental psychology, then, is this: if we move toward giving as much importance to writing as to reading—for example by sometimes inviting initiatory autonomous writing from the student's own experience rather than always having writing respond to reading—we can nevertheless trust that students will come to us with a strong social connectedness that we couldn't stamp out if we tried.

Ways to End the War and Create a More Productive Interaction between Reading and Writing

There are some specific practices that will help reading and writing reinforce each other better—in both curriculum and teaching.

In curriculum, the important steps are obvious and can be quickly described. First, we need more writing courses. When students are polled, they usually ask for more writing courses. Second, we need more of what are called "fifty-fifty courses": half reading and half writing. Here are some good examples in the curriculum at the University of Vermont: "Writing Literary Criticism"; "Reading and Writing Nonfiction"; "Reading and Writing Autobiography"; "Personal Voice"; "Writing *The New Yorker.*" Some campuses have junior-level courses in the disciplines ("Writing in Physics" or "Writing in Anthropology") that are really fifty-fifty courses. Such courses are probably the most natural and fruitful place for reading and writing to mutually enhance each other: courses where we go back and forth constantly between reading and writing and neither activity is felt as simply a handmaiden to the other one.

In teaching, there are various ways that reading and writing can learn from each other. Let me look more concretely now at some teaching practices to see interesting ways in which we can give more emphasis to writing.

The obvious step is to assign more writing, but this leads to an obvious problem: it causes so much more work for us as teachers with all those papers to grade and respond to. But we can largely avoid this problem if we learn to use writing in the varied and flexible ways we use reading. For example, in most courses we have both required reading and supplementary or suggested reading: texts we feel all students must read and texts we expect diligent or interested students to read. We don't ask or expect them all to do it. Yet we seldom take this approach with writing.

In other words, whereas we usually have a spectrum of reading from high stakes to low stakes, most teachers fall unthinkingly into the habit of treating all writing as obligatory, high-stakes work. Writing is usually handled in such a way as to make it an unpleasant ordeal, even a punishment—for the students *and* the teacher. The flexible and varied uses of reading is a mark of the respect and sophistication with which we treat reading. We need to respect writing with similar flexibility— by also having low-stakes, supplementary, and experimental writing instead of being so rigid and one-dimensional about it.

Notice, above all, that we don't *evaluate* or *grade* all the reading we assign. It feels perfectly normal to assign lots of reading and only test or evaluate or grade some of it. For the rest, we assume that if students don't do it, they'll be less successful at the activities we do grade and evaluate. But somehow teachers tend to assume they have to evaluate and comment on every piece of writing they assign. Many breakthroughs in our relation to writing occur when we learn to have a whole spectrum of writing—from high stakes to low stakes:

> A few pieces (as now) that we evaluate and count as important.
>
> Some more informal pieces that we collect but only grade with a check—or with check-plus and check-minus. Some of these might function as drafts for evaluated pieces.
>
> Some pieces that we collect but just read or even just glance over— and that's all.
>
> Some pieces that are purely private to help students think to themselves about the reading or discussion or lectures. Sometimes we devote some class time to this writing; sometimes we make it a journal assignment to be done as homework and just check periodically to make sure students are keeping them up.

Some nonrequired pieces that are "supplementary" or "suggested": we read and give a brief comment to those pieces that are done. Even if relatively few students do these pieces, there are striking benefits not only to those students but in fact to the quality of the class as a whole. There is a richer mix of voices in the conversation—some of them much more invested and authoritative.

More and more teachers are helping students learn more by getting them to share their writing with each other, for example, in pairs or small groups. It takes very little time for just sharing—and a great deal is learned. (It takes more time if we want students to give each other feedback, but that is not crucial. The greatest learning comes from the sharing itself.) In addition, many teachers get students to contribute (say) weekly to a computer conversation about the course material—if only in a low-tech way where students simply go to the computer lab once a week and add a few screens full to a class-conversation disk.

Similarly, teachers are learning flexible ways to publish student writing. We can use a lab fee to pay for class publications; can ask students to bring in twenty or so copies of something they have written. If I ask for two pages, single-spaced, back-to-back on a single sheet, this is very easy to manage, and therefore I can do it a number of times in a semester. Even in a class of one hundred students, we can ask them to bring in just twenty copies of their piece in order to make publications of a more manageable size.

Publication of student writing flushes out some interesting assumptions about reading and writing: we take it for granted that students should shell out money for reading, but some teachers are startled at the thought of asking them to do the same for writing. But such money is well spent, and students usually appreciate the result. And when we realize that students will have to pay for the publication of their writing, we tend to adjust our assignments in a helpful way: "Let's see. How can I frame an assignment that will lead to pieces of writing that other students would actually want to read and benefit from?" This is a question that cuts right to the heart of good pedagogy: how to connect our material to their lives. The publication of student writing helps us here because when students write for publication, *they* find connections we'd never dream of.

If we brought to the evaluation of student writing the critical sophistication we take for granted in literary work, we wouldn't do so much rigid and thoughtless *ranking* or *grading*. That is, in literary study we realize that there is no single, correct interpretation of a text, that even the best critics cannot agree, and that it would be laughable to assign a quantitative grade to a text (and certainly not one based on one quick reading late at night). Thus literary consciousness would help us get away from assuming that we can immediately grade student writing with quantitative scores of A, B, C, and so forth. Grades of "strong," "medium," and "weak" would suffice. And by the end of the semester, these crude grades, along with a portfolio, would "add up" or at least point clearly to a final grade.

Writing as springboard. The conventional practice is almost always to start with reading and then write in response—making the writing serve the reading. But we can turn that around and write first and make reading serve writing. Certain teachers at all levels are slowly learning this approach. For example, teachers get students to write about an intense mental experience and what it feels like inside their heads. They use this as a springboard for reading some poems by Emily Dickinson. The goal is not just to read and appreciate Dickinson better—though of course that happens too—but to take student writing more seriously. Students come at Dickinson more as peers, saying things like, "She used a metaphor in this way, but I decided to do it that way." When I had trouble getting students to connect with Shakespeare—putting him "under glass" as it were—for example, in reading *The Tempest,* where Prospero seems both hallowed yet unattractive—I started off by asking my students to write informally about their most longstanding, unresolved grudge (fun in itself). When we turned to Shakespeare, students were more invested and skilled in dealing with this difficult Prospero and his grudge and the play. One of the main emphases in the powerful "Writing-Across-the-Curriculum" movement is on helping students use writing not just for demonstrating what they have learned but also for the process of learning itself. Indeed many people call this the "Writing-to-Learn" movement.

Reading as springboard. But writing doesn't have to come first to be important. We can have *reading* come first—and still serve writing. That is, we can use the reading as something to reply to, bounce off of, or borrow from. In this practice we are not trying to make the writing "do justice" to the reading or "get it right." We are inviting students to use the reading as a springboard to their own writing: to use the theme or structure or spirit or energy of the text to spur their own writing. This, after all, is standard practice by writers (as Harold Bloom and others show): to misread or misuse or distort the works of others as a way to enable your own writing.

This approach is particularly important in getting students to try out imaginative pieces like those they are reading. Students are often nervous about writing poems, stories, or dramatic scenes/dialogues. We can help them by borrowing themes or structures from the reading. For example a few key words or phrases from a poem can serve as a helpful springboard or scaffold that will help students find a way to write a poem or story of their own. Of course students need to be invited to treat imaginative writing as an experiment—not necessarily to finish or revise. I don't feel I can grade these pieces, but I can require that they be done.

Making writing more central in what was formerly just a "reading" or literature course causes a major change in the way students come at the reading. They are braver, more lively, and more thoughtful. We read differently when we read like a writer (see Charles Moran's classic article, "Reading Like a Writer"). Students come at purely analytic discussions of texts in a much more shrewd and energetic way when they have had a chance to try out some of the same kinds of writing in an experimental, playful, nongraded way.

Rough drafts of reading. Students and colleagues would benefit enormously from the kind of workshop activity I described earlier: where students and teacher work together on texts that neither has seen before—periodically pausing during the process of reading to write out how they are perceiving and reacting to the text. This process helps everyone see vividly how reading creates meaning by a process of gradual and often collaborative and transformative negotiation.

None of these teaching practices can be called wild or visionary any more. All are being used by teachers at all levels with all kinds of students. And if we use them more, we will think of more ways to bring reading and writing into a relationship of mutual support.

To close, I'll evoke an image—a corrective paradigm for the relations between reading and writing. Teachers of kindergarten and first grade all around the country are demonstrating that writing is easier and more natural than reading, and that writing is more useful than reading for entrance into literacy. Their practice is based on a fact that is startling but obvious, once demonstrated. Tiny children can write before they can read, can write more than they can read, and can write more easily than they can read. For small children can write *anything they can say*—once they know the alphabet and are shown the rudimentary trick of using invented spelling. In fact the process works even with younger children who don't know the alphabet. Even they can "write" *anything* by just making scribbles. Often they don't need to be taught; just ask them what writing is and they'll do purposeful and meaningful scribbling. They'll call it writing and they'll be able to read back to you what they "wrote" (Harste, Woodward, and Burke).

In many classrooms around the country, kindergarteners and first graders are not just writing stories but "publishing" their own books.

Teachers and helpers type up their writing in conventional spelling to go with the pictures that the children drew with their writing, and then these books are bound with cloth covers and become texts for reading. We tend to have been brainwashed into thinking that reading comes first and that reading is easier than writing, but the reverse is true. It has been demonstrated over and over that children get quicker understanding and control of literacy—language and texts—through writing than through reading. Thus output precedes input—and prepares the way for input. (People have done research comparing the stories that children in these classrooms write and read. The stories they write are at a higher level of development and sophistication than the stories they read.)

Of course, the effects of this approach were obvious once people like Don Graves had the sense to figure it out: it vastly improves students' skill and involvement in *reading*. Students are much more excited and competent when they read what they and their classmates have written than when they read published books from the outside (especially basal readers). They learn reading faster; they have a healthier stance toward reading—a stance that recognizes, "Hey, these things called books are what we write. Let's read books to see what other people like us have written." No longer do children think of books as something written by a corporate, faceless "they"—like arithmetic workbooks.

There is a much-told story of a reporter visiting one of these class-rooms where the first graders eagerly offer to show him some of their books. "Have you really written a book?" the reporter asks one child with a tone of condescending surprise. "Haven't you?" replies the child.

Just think how it would be if we and our students were more like these first graders. They are so eager to read and to write; they are the happiest and most invested in their literacy of any students in the whole educational world. We can move decisively in that direction by ending the priority of reading and giving more serious and playful priority to writing—through bringing to writing some of the flexible sophistication we use in reading—so that both processes reinforce each other as equals.

Works Cited

Applebee, Arthur N. *Writing in the Secondary School: English and the Content Areas*. Research Report No. 21. Urbana, IL: NCTE, 1981.

Blau, Sheridan. "Invisible Writing: Investigating Cognitive Processes in Composition." *College Composition and Communication* 34.3 (October 1983): 297–312.

Britton, James, Tony Burgess, Nancy Martin, Alex McLeod, and Harold Rosen. *The Development of Writing Abilities (11–18)*. London: Macmillan Education, 1975.

Elbow, Peter. "The Doubting Game and the Believing Game." *Writing without Teachers.* New York: Oxford UP, 1973. 147–91.

———. "Methodological Doubting and Believing." *Embracing Contraries: Explorations in Learning and Teaching.* New York: Oxford UP, 1986. 254–300.

Emerson, Caryl. "The Outer Word, Inner Speech: Bakhtin, Vygotsky and the Internalization of Language." *Critical Inquiry* 10 (1983): 245–64.

Friend, Christie. "The Excluded Conflict: The Marginalization of Composition and Rhetoric Studies in Graff's *Professing Literature.*" College English 54.3 (March 1992): 276–86.

Gardner, Howard. *The Unschooled Mind: How Children Think and How Schools Should Teach.* New York: Basic, 1991.

Gendlin, Eugene. *Focusing.* New York: Bantam, 1979.

Harris, Jeanette. *Expressive Discourse.* Dallas: Southern Methodist UP, 1990.

Harste, Jerome C., Virginia A. Woodward, and Carolyn L. Burke. *Language Stories and Literacy Lessons.* Portsmouth, NH: Heinemann Educational, 1984.

Laurence, David. Personal communication.

Moran, Charles. "Reading Like a Writer." *Vital Signs.* Ed. James. L. Collins. Portsmouth NH: Boynton/Cook, 1989.

Sanders, Scott Russell. "The Writer in the University." *ADE Bulletin* 99 (Fall 1991): 22–28.

Slevin, James. "Depoliticizing and Politicizing Composition Studies." *The Politics of Writing Instruction: Postsecondary.* Ed. Richard H. Bullock and John Trimbur. Portsmouth, NH: Boynton/Cook, 1991. 1–21.

Stafford, William. *Writing the Australian Crawl: Views on the Writer's Vocation.* Ann Arbor: U of Michigan P, 1978.

Wallace, Elizabeth. Unpublished mss. Department of Humanities, Western Oregon State College.

18 Reading Lessons and Then Some: Toward Developing Dialogues between Critical Theory and Reading Theory

Kathleen McCormick
University of Hartford

In *Criticism and Ideology*, Terry Eagleton writes that "any particular act of reading is conducted within a general set of assumptions as to the ideological signification of reading itself within a social formation" (62). While Carl Kaestle argues that there is "no way to summarize for a whole society the significance of so commonplace and pervasive an activity as reading" ("History of Literacy" 125), this essay attempts to articulate and to bring into dialogue some of the dominant contemporary significations of reading within the academy and to connect those significations to larger relationships of power and knowledge within the culture. In developing such connections, I will try to unravel the "ideological significances" of which Eagleton speaks, probing beneath the apparently banal, everyday skill or practice of reading. It is, as Foucault and others have taught us, precisely in the details of the commonplace where the ideological glue of a culture is to be found.

It has been widely noted that ways of conceiving reading within the research community and ways of teaching reading have changed quite dramatically over the last two decades.[1] No longer is reading thought to be simply a passive taking in of information; rather, it is now regarded by most researchers—and from a variety of disciplines and perspectives—as a complex, active process.[2]

Repeatedly, one hears from teachers and researchers from both the political Left and Right that reading is not simply an abstract skill, but a social action which occurs in specific social circumstances. As Graff writes, "there is . . . no trouble-free zone of reading" (56). Readers are no longer thought to be mere blank slates but social beings who approach texts with rich and varied backgrounds. Similarly, texts are not so widely depicted as static containers of meaning but rather as capable of being read differently, depending on the reading context and the reader's background. As Anthony Easthope and John Thompson note in a discussion of literary theory: "The past two decades have witnessed what in the natural sciences would be termed . . . a paradigm shift. . . . The new paradigm denies that the text exists 'in itself' apart from the way it is read in a context of interpretation" (vii).[3]

And yet, despite the increasing emphasis on the reader's background, on varying contexts of reading, and on reading as a process, the "commonsensical," objectivist model which assumes that reading is a skill and that texts "contain" information which skilled readers should simply take in and "comprehend" correctly still dominates much teaching and research. How often, for example, is a student told, in virtually any course on any subject, to first "read" a textbook, a novel, a historical document, a scientific study and then to go on to do something else— be it to write, answer questions, do problem sets—as if "reading" were simply the taking in of information transparently coded inside a text? Allan Bloom, in *The Closing of the American Mind,* adopts this position when he argues that "a liberal education means reading certain generally recognized classic texts, *just reading them* . . . not forcing them into categories we make up" (344; emphasis mine), as if it were possible to read from a neutral, category-free perspective. Even the genteel British idiom that one goes up to university (or, at least, to one of the two older universities) to "read" a particular subject suggests a strong sense of gaining knowledge and power by means of the simple accumulation of particular information contained within culturally sanctioned texts and institutions. As Sharon Crowley argues:

> The practice of reading pedagogy (called "teaching literature" in English departments) is generally "occulted" . . . at least after students leave elementary school. The practice of teaching people to read difficult and culturally influential texts is carried on, for the most part, as though it were innocent of theory, as though it were a knack that anyone could pick up by practicing it. (26)

There are at least three reasons why an alternative, more self-consciously theoretical, and institutionally contextualized model of reading has had such difficulty taking hold. First, the discourse communities that dominate reading instruction and research have not adequately retheorized the reader as a social subject and the text as a social production. They have, instead, fallen back on an objectivist model that privileges the text or, at the other extreme, embraces a subjective or expressivist model which privileges the reader's personal response. Both of these approaches—often unwittingly, as I will argue throughout this essay—take the reader and text out of the social context even while attempting to argue for their placement within it. As Alan Sinfield argues

> [T]he twin manoeuvers of bourgeois ideology construct two
> dichotomies: universal versus historical and individual versus social.
> In each case the first term is privileged, and so meaning is sucked
> into the universal/individual polarity, draining it away from the
> historical and the social—which is where meaning is made by people
> together in determinate conditions, and where it might be contested.
> (141)

Second, those who work in the areas where such retheorization of the
reader and text has been most fully undertaken—and I will argue that
this is primarily in the areas of literacy research in the United States and
in the predominantly British tradition of literary and cultural studies—
have not yet developed a detailed translation of this retheorizing into
pedagogical practice.

And third, the diverse disciplines that contribute to reading research
and pedagogy have not yet engaged in the dialogue that is necessary to
interrogate critically the implications of their very different definitions
of readers and texts. They are simply, in one sense, not "reading" each
other. In the absence of such dialogue, work in reading remains fragmented, and its transformative capacities, limited.

Whether or not they are conscious of it, however, teachers at all levels are always teaching their students how to read. The different ways
students are asked to read imply particular values and beliefs about the
nature of texts, the nature of readers as subjects of texts and as subjects
in the world, and about meaning and language itself. Yet, the dominant
ideological signification of reading often works against students' developing the capacity to think "critically" about what they read, as many
national assessments have demonstrated.[4] As one possible solution to
this apparent absence of "critical reading," students need to learn to locate the texts they read as well as themselves as reading subjects within
larger social contexts; in short, they need to be able to inquire into and
understand the interconnectedness of social conditions and the reading
and writing practices of a culture.[5]

To translate such goals into the classroom, however, one needs first
to have a clearly articulated theory of readers as social subjects. Men and
women are neither fully determined by the culture of which they are a
part nor simply individuals who can become "free" of the dominant
ideologies of that culture; rather, we are all, as Graeme Turner puts it,
balanced between social determination and autonomy (132). From such
a perspective, one needs to recognize and communicate to students that
they are both *interdiscourses*, the product of the various competing and
often contradictory discourses that permeate their culture (Morley,

"Texts, Readers, Subjects" 164), and also *agents,* capable not of transcending these discourses, but of negotiating, resisting, and taking action within them. Second, one needs to have a well-articulated theory of textuality that sees a text not as a container of truth or universal significance, but as something produced under specific material conditions and repeatedly reproduced by different readers—including students—in different conditions. In short, texts need to be seen as what Tony Bennett and Janet Woollacott call "texts-in-use" (265)—that is, products of "the concrete and varying, historically specific functions and effects which accrue to 'the text' as a result of the different determinations to which it is subjected during the history of its appropriation" (*Formalism and Marxism* 148). And those different textual "functions and effects" need to be regarded not simply as the result of individual, personal interpretive acts; rather, like texts and readers themselves, they need to be placed within larger cultural contexts so that their particular consequences and alliances can be analyzed. Finally, once such retheorizing has been established, one has to develop new pedagogical practices.

During the past two decades, work in literary and cultural studies—most particularly in Britain and more recently in America—has accomplished such retheorizing of the reading subject and the text, but such work has only just begun to be translated into concrete pedagogies. By entering into more active dialogue with other areas of reading that focus more specifically on pedagogy, literary and cultural studies can begin to locate reading within the complex cultural contexts in which it actually occurs.

The goal of this essay, therefore, is to begin to develop more active dialogue among reading teachers and researchers and, particularly, to encourage more of those in contemporary literary and cultural studies to enter into the conversation about reading. In what follows, I will develop a map of models of reading, grouping statements and positions about the interactive nature of reading on the basis of the three distinctive aspects of the reading situation that can be privileged: the text, the reader, and the cultural context. There, too, I will identify participants in this conversation as following either a *cognitive, expressivist,* or *social-cultural* model.[6] I will argue that these three approaches are not diametrically opposed to each other, but may usefully be seen in dialectical relationship. Each acknowledges the importance of the reader, the text, and the larger social context in the reading situation, but each assigns quite different significations to the terms. After developing this map, I will return to discuss literary and cultural theory and pedagogy.

The Cognitive Model

Since the development in the 1960s of the "mind's new science" of cognitive psychology,[7] the cognitive model of the reading process has been
the most influential in reading research and pedagogy, despite being,
in many ways, the most conflicted.[8] While it is rooted in an objectivist
tradition, the insights of cognitive psychology over the past decade or
so, particularly in work done in "schema theory," repeatedly go beyond
the limits of "clean" empirical work. Schema theory argues that readers
comprehend new information by relating it to structures of information—or schemata—that already exist in their memories. It emphasizes
the interactive nature of reading—the relationship between the reading
experience of a "real" reader and a text—and, in particular, the importance of a reader's prior knowledge in making sense of texts (Anderson,
"Notion of Schemata"; "Schema-Directed Processes"; Rumelhart, "Building Blocks"; "Interactive Model"; Bransford and McCarrell; Spivey). As
Anderson notes, "the schema that will be brought to bear on a text depends upon the reader's age, sex, race, religion, nationality, occupation—
in short, it depends upon the reader's culture" ("Role" 374–75). Schema
theory, therefore, can help to locate the reader as a subject-in-history and
the text as a "text-in-use," and it is at these points—developing a
historicized theory of the reader and the text—that a potential for dialogue exists between schema theory and contemporary cultural studies.
    Despite this potential, however, the objectivist convictions of cogni-
tive psychology that language is a transparent means of communicat-
ing facts about the world and that knowledge is directly embodied in
texts repeatedly redirect the focus of schema theory away from broader
cultural analysis and toward a study of the "appropriate" schemata necessary for readers to possess in order to "comprehend" a text "correctly."
Thus, while schema theory, at least theoretically, understands the complexity and richness of schemata, it repeatedly oversimplifies them in
its experimental analyses, thus diminishing its potential for significantly
changing the dominant ways in which reading is taught. On the surface,
schema theory should, as Willinsky suggests, help to develop "more
active roles" for readers in the classroom (77). In fact, however, it tends
rather to reproduce traditional roles in students who must passively
accept from their teachers the "appropriate" background knowledge so
that they can understand texts "correctly." Let us look, for example, at
some recent revisions of basal readers which are informed by schema
theory.
    Using research done in schema theory on the importance of readers'
background knowledge, Isabel Beck and Margaret McKeown revised the

questions and information surrounding the story "The Raccoon and Mrs. McGinnis," a story in a basal reader designed for seven-year-olds. Although this story is taught in the primary grades, the reading lessons it teaches students are relevant to college teachers because these lessons continue to impinge on students' reading habits. The story is about a woman, Mrs. McGinnis, who one night wishes on a star for a barn for her animals. That night, bandits come to steal her animals, but they are frightened by a raccoon (presumably because of its mask) that comes to her doorstep each night looking for food. In their haste to get away, they release the animals and drop a bag of money. The raccoon picks the bag up and drops it on Mrs. McGinnis's doorstep while searching for food. Mrs. McGinnis finds the money, assumes that her wish has been granted, and builds the barn for her animals.

Beck and McKeown's goal was to "activate" or "establish" "relevant background knowledge prior to reading" and to "highlight . . . events that were most important to the development of the story" in order to "facilitate comprehension" (67). They argue that the "key" background knowledge necessary to have when reading this story is an understanding of the concepts of "coincidence" and "habit." Thus, they emphasized these two concepts to students to try to prevent students from developing a "faulty interpretation" (70) of the story which would ascribe intentionality to the raccoon (69–70).

What definitions of reading, "background knowledge," and textuality inform this pedagogy? Beck and McKeown clearly regard reading as the "correct" comprehension of a text, and their primary teaching objective is to facilitate correct comprehension. This objectivist definition of reading overrides their attempt to make reading more "interactive" and to draw on students' prior knowledge. Since they conceive of reading as a difficult skill, students are assumed to need continual, intrusive prompts to get them through a story. Further, although they talk about the importance of students' background knowledge and although this knowledge is central to schema theory, Beck and McKeown do not actually ever allow students to use what might possibly be their *own* very varied background knowledge to read the story because, to do so, they would have to acknowledge that the story could be read in multiple ways. The objectivist model, which they take up more unilaterally than the schema theory from which their work derives, cannot admit this possibility.

Yet one can also imagine a pedagogical context in which a diversity of schemata could be brought to bear on Beck and McKeown's students' reading of "The Raccoon and Mrs. McGinnis." Let us assume that many of the students reading the story have read a fair amount of children's literature and are used to reading (or listening to) stories in which tank engines talk, rabbits wear clothes and regularly steal vegetables from their neighbors' gardens, and animals in general are presented as sentient beings. From this perspective, it would not only be perfectly plausible to imagine that the raccoon intentionally left the money on the woman's doorstep, but it would probably be difficult not to assume this. Nonetheless, as the study demonstrates, students by the age of seven can understand that raccoons are simply creatures of habit, and, in fact, they may differentiate between the raccoons that come to their doorsteps and those they read about in books.

A teacher might attempt to draw on this rich background knowledge involving the children's familiarity with story conventions and their general understanding of animal behavior. For example, rather than trying to inundate students before their reading with enough "prior" information to prevent them from seeing the raccoon as a sentient being, teachers could let students develop different readings of the raccoon and the story in general, introducing, in the context of the discussion, the concepts of habit and coincidence, not to get students to an "enhanced comprehension" of the "correct meaning" of the text, but to discuss with them how the story changes if the raccoon is or is not seen as intentional. This kind of discussion would both draw on and enrich students' schemata.

Another schema that this story employs that might well be activated in students, but which is not acknowledged by Beck and McKeown, is poverty. For the story is "about" Mrs. McGinnis's lack of money as much as it is about coincidence. Surely, many children who live in poverty—and a sizable number in the middle class—will have heard their parents "wish upon a star" to have money to buy food, winter clothing, toys, a car, a house. For students with this background knowledge, the key point that Beck and McKeown are trying to emphasize—that Mrs. McGinnis's bag of money appeared completely by chance—may represent much more than an abstract lesson in learning about coincidence. Reading the raccoon as intentional may suggest that some cosmic (or social) force for good exists which takes care of people when they need help, and this reading might, therefore, be comforting for a child who hopes that his or her own family might be left a bag of money. In contrast, the reading of the raccoon as merely a creature of habit rather than a force for good might suggest the unlikelihood of anyone's wishes upon stars actually coming true.

I do not bring up these two examples to suggest that a "better" reading of the story would see the raccoon as intentional, but to illustrate the ways in which Beck and McKeown's pedagogy limits what it is supposedly trying to enhance—students' active participation by the activation and development of schemata. To develop any reading of a text, one puts the text in particular contexts. Yet, surely, the children's literature schema and the poverty schema might be seen as being important to this story, at least as important as the coincidence schema. By assuming that the context in which they set the story leads to the "correct" reading of it, Beck and McKeown are presenting a view of texts as complete in themselves and as containing one meaning which the reader needs to get "right." Further, they are discounting—in fact, they do not even allow for—the possibility of students bringing in any background information that could support an alternative reading of the story. Thus, far from leading to more active participation, Beck and McKeown's revisions of the basal reading questions further delimit the range of students' possible reactions to the story.

This kind of reading lesson, which follows what Paulo Freire calls the "banking system" of education, is a part of most students' history, and these lessons often persist well into college in courses in which students are expected to stare at the page—whether it is a physics textbook or a Wordsworth poem—and get it right. In part, pedagogies slide back into an objectivist model because that model is so powerful, and it is the one that has dominated perspectives on reading. The entry of more radically alternative perspectives that can fill in the more complex aspects of schema theory, however, has the potential to take reading pedagogies in quite different directions, and it is to one of these perspectives, one that privileges the reader, that I now turn.

The Expressive Model

"Expressivist" theories emphasize the richness and uniqueness of students' backgrounds and encourage them to develop their own "individual" and "authentic" responses to texts. Expressivist models of reading are also widely seen as an alternative to objectivist, especially cognitively based, models because, since they focus primarily on the role of the reader, they motivate the development of innovative, student-centered pedagogies that encourage "active" learning.

It was not until the reader-response movement of the 1970s—when Louise Rosenblatt's pioneering work of the 1930s finally received the recognition it deserved—that the study of reading in the United States was brought actively into the area of university and high school literature teaching. Reader-response criticism manifested itself as a powerful alternative to the more objectivist model of reading established by New Criticism (see Fish 42–43). Rosenblatt emphasized the active and

individual nature of reading, when she wrote: "Every time a reader experiences a work of art, it is in a sense created anew. Fundamentally,
the process of understanding a work implies a re-creation of it" (*Literature as Exploration* 113; see also Fish 28; Holland 340; Iser 119; Bleich, *Subjective Criticism* 18).

Reader-response critics recognized that a theory which argues for the
active nature of the reader necessarily problematizes the objective status of the text. But while these critics were able to say what the text was
not—an objective container of meaning—they were never able to articulate what it *was*, other than a projection of the reader. Fish, for example,
poses this question: If one contends that "formal units are always a function of the interpretative model one brings to bear, they are not 'in' the
text . . . [then] what is that act [of reading] an interpretation *of*?" (164–
65). He acknowledges that he is unable to answer this question but argues
that "neither . . . can anyone else" (165). And, within reader-response
criticism, at least, he was correct (see, for example, Holland 40; Iser ix;
Rosenblatt, "Transactional" 39). Such speculations about the text are
unable to supplant the objectivist model of reading, however, not only
because they are vague, but also because they are seen as applying primarily to literary reading rather than to the reading of texts in general.

Nonetheless, the willingness of reader-response critics to challenge
the status of the text—even in the absence of a clear reconception of it—
did lead to the development of new teaching practices in which literature was no longer seen as a body of privileged texts whose meanings
students must "understand correctly" but rather as what Langer calls
"a horizon of possibilities" (*Literature Instruction* 37) in which students
are free to respond personally and emotionally. The importance of the
reader-response movement in democratizing the teaching of literature
cannot be overestimated. By asking students "Is there a text in this class?"
as Stanley Fish did, reader-response teachers were seemingly able to give
students the authority to create their own texts. David Bleich's development of a pedagogy centered on the "response statement"—an informal
essay in which students record "the perception of a reading experience
and its natural, spontaneous consequences, among which are feelings,
or affects, and peremptory memories of thoughts, or free associations"
(*Subjective Criticism* 147)—was perhaps the single, most innovative methodology for literary reading and writing in the last two decades. In the
United States, most approaches to teaching literature in the schools and
in many colleges and universities use some adaptation of Bleich's response statement. And yet, while response pedagogy appears to give
students a voice, it can also leave them unaware of the determinants of
that voice and, therefore, powerless either to develop or interrogate it.

Over the last two decades, critics and teachers have attempted to develop a somewhat fuller sense of the socially constructed nature of both the reader and the text in order to help students begin to understand and interrogate the determinants of their voices.[9] These modifications of "subjective criticism" (to use the title of one of Bleich's early books) are only partially successful, however, because they are working from an inadequately developed theory of the reader and the text in history. To illustrate this inadequate accommodation of expressivist views between reading and social constructivism, let us look at an example which attempts, but ultimately seems to fail, to develop within students a sense of their own social construction: Sylvia White and Ruie Pritchard's account of teaching *Huckleberry Finn* to students in the American South.

White and Pritchard attempt to encourage their students to see not only that readings of texts change over time but that their own beliefs and values—which, as they learned in the first lesson, are culturally produced—should help them in determining which particular reading they will take up. However, since they neither introduce students to discourses that would enable them to examine the social and cultural factors that helped to determine their reading of the book—nor to a theory of the reader and text in history—their students seem unable to perform the kind of analyses White and Pritchard ask of them. In the end, the contradictory combination of an expressive theory of the reader and an objectivist theory of the text appeared to win out, at least in the student whose essay White and Pritchard quote as exemplary:

> The book Huck Finn shouldn't be causing so much trouble I mean the man is dead that wrote it. I'm black myself and it don't bother me because I know it all happened I mean he was writing a novel and his intention was to be realistic and so therefore he had to write it as it is. . . . Even if Mark Twain was being prejudiced what difference would it make now the man is dead. It couldn't have bothered people back in those days because most slaves didn't know any better. The same stuff that was in it 100 years ago is in it now so why all of a sudden they want to do something like this. . . . I don't see nothing wrong with teaching it to children as a matter of fact I feel like they should know how their ancestors lived. (210)

This student's view of the text is clearly objectivist: "the same stuff that was in it 100 years ago is in it now"; he does not seem to be aware that texts can be read differently in different historical formations (the point of this assignment); nor does he question *why* one might read it differently in the 1980s than when it was first written. Further, he does not appear consciously to recognize that readers will reproduce texts differently in different historical circumstances, although he implies this by suggesting that the novel today can teach students about how their ancestors lived. But why does he think Twain's "prejudice" would not matter today, particularly when many people—black and white—assume that it does matter? White and Pritchard argue that this student is an example of "self-dependent learner[s]" in whom "the ideas emerge from the students' personal knowledge of their own beliefs and values, as well as from the information the novel is presenting to them" (210). However, because this student has been given no explicit guidance on how to interrogate or even understand his own beliefs and values, the opinions he offers on the book's reception are not contextualized. While this assignment attempts to establish broader social contexts for response, like most reader-response approaches, it finally appeals to students' native capabilities, assuming that it is enough if students have "personal knowledge of their own beliefs and values" (210). But as Willinsky writes of the expressive tradition:

> The question that remains is whether students are prepared for handling the difference between the literacy they have begun to work with, in which they pursue their own meaning, and the reading expected of them outside the classroom, in which they are sent hunting for the meanings of others. (87).

The capacity of the expressivist model of reading to challenge the objective-cognitive model, therefore, is limited for three reasons. First, it has not developed a theory of the text that is powerful enough to replace the dominant, commonsensical objectivist notion of a text as a container of meaning. Second, while this model claims to focus on the reader and while it does, in practice, allow readers to respond "freely" to texts, because it conceives of readers primarily as "individuals" rather than social subjects, it does not investigate or require students to investigate the social conditions underlying their responses to texts any more than the cognitive model. Third, the impact of this model on the reconception of reading is limited because it is relegated primarily to the realm of literary reading and does not generalize well to reading other kinds of texts.

The Social-Cultural Model

I turn now to the social-cultural model of reading. While various reading theorists contend that the reader's social context is important, contemporary literacy researchers—historians, educational specialists, anthropologists who study reading in the contexts of broader issues of literacy and education—are the only group of explicitly defined "reading researchers" who seriously study social context.[10] They have argued that even to grasp what literacy is "inevitably involves social analysis" because one needs to explore "the functions that the society in question has invented for literacy and their distribution throughout the populace" (Scribner 72). Far from being an abstract skill, in this model, literacy is "a social process" (Willinsky 6; Barnes and Barnes 34; Heath 355), "a complex of actions that take place inside a web of social relationships and social assumptions" (Resnick and Resnick, "Varieties" 192). In such a view, the "essence" of reading is "reconstructing a text on the basis of a reader's cultural resources" (Barnes and Barnes 48).[11]

Reading, from this perspective, is seen not as a narrow task performed primarily in school to "comprehend" or learn, but as something done all the time and in all kinds of rich contexts. Often drawing on the tradition of semiotics, literacy researchers are beginning to study the reading of all kinds of texts—from price labels to stop signs, recipes, newspapers, and junk mail (see Heath 352–56; Barnes and Barnes 43). Further, many, such as Shirley Brice Heath, inquire specifically into readers' motivations for reading, asking such questions as "Where, when, how, for whom, and with what results are individuals in different social groups of today's highly industrialized society using reading and writing skills?" and "How have the potentialities of the literacy skills learned in school developed in the lives of today's adults?" (350).

While Scribner points out that literacy is not necessarily "the primary impetus for significant and lasting economic or social change" (75), many literacy researchers advocate the development of a reading capacity in which readers are not only functionally or culturally literate, but are what Henry Giroux calls "critically literate" (*Theory and Resistance* 226). This approach marks a distinctive break with the impoverished sense of social context found in both cognitive and expressivist models of reading. Critical literacy consists not only of being able to comprehend the texts one reads or to link them with one's own personal worlds. Rather, to be a critically literate reader is to have the knowledge and ability to perceive the interconnectedness of social conditions and the reading and writing practices of a culture, to be able to analyze those conditions and practices, and to possess the critical and political awareness to take action within and against them. Suzanne de Castell and Allan Luke, for example, argue that

> In liberal-democratic societies, participation in the political process implies not only the ability to operate effectively within existing social and economic systems, but also to make rational and informed judgements about the desirability of those systems themselves. ("Defining 'Literacy'" 173; see also Shor 37; Liston 144–64).

The capacity to make rational and informed judgements about the world is largely a *reading* capacity, and, while it can be taught to students in a variety of forums, the primary one should be in their reading lessons. For, if students are to learn how to read the world critically, they must be given access to discourses that can allow them to analyze that world, discourses that can enable them to explore the ways in which their own reading acts, as well as the texts of their culture, are embedded in complex social and historical relations.

But what form of pedagogy is to follow from this third model? I, of course, recognize that teaching practices are not necessarily directly connected to a particular theoretical orientation. As Knoblauch notes, the relationship between the two is "properly dialectical, each term conditioning and reshaping the other" (126), and yet certain practices can be privileged by a particular theoretical perspective. Understandably, virtually all who work within the social-cultural model are critical of any model of reading that regards reading simply as a skill or of textbooks that seek to decontextualize texts from the particular conditions of their use (Resnick and Resnick, "Varieties" 192; Barnes and Barnes 43–50; de Castell and Luke, "Models" 100–5). But the expressivist model is also inadequate. For, while the development of "subjective" readings of texts is important, personal engagement is not enough if students are to learn to read and negotiate the diversity of texts of the culture.

Freire argues that one needs to develop "problem-posing" practices in which "the teacher is no longer merely the-one-who-teaches, but one who is himself taught in dialogue with the students, who in turn while being taught also teach" (*Pedagogy* 67), and he prefers this way of teaching to the "banking method" of education in which the teacher simply "deposits" information into students (*Pedagogy* 58). This dichotomy, however, is somewhat less helpful than it initially appears. As Kathleen Weiler argues:

> While Freire's work is based on a deep respect for students and teachers as readers of the world, the conscientization he describes takes place in a relatively unproblematic relationship between an unidentified liberatory teacher and the equally abstractly oppressed. The tensions of the lived subjectivities of teachers and students located in a particular society and defined by existing meanings of race, gender, sexual orientation, class, and other social identities are not addressed by Freire. (329)

In the absence of clearly defined theories of the subjectivities of teachers and students, it is possible for the social-cultural model to result in pedagogies that follow either an authoritarianism similar to that developed by the objectivist model or a valorization of the individual that is characteristic of the expressivist model. There is, however, another tradition to consider. It is the work done on theories of the subject and theories of the text within cultural studies. Like all the voices heard thus far, it has multiple registers, and yet there are distinct aspects of it that can contribute significantly to the development not only of a theory of reading, but of practical pedagogies on all levels of reading education that can effectively challenge the objectivist model and that can truly represent reading to students as a deeply imbedded cultural act.

The "Reader" in Cultural Studies

Cultural studies has grown out of the varied strands of British and European Marxism which stress the constructed or determined nature of social practice. Raymond Williams argues that determination needs to be construed as the "setting of limits" and the "exertion of pressures," mediating carefully between primitive deterministic models often associated with Marxism and liberal models of autonomous human behavior. Within cultural studies, there has been a reaction against determinist positions that regard audiences as powerless subjects merely "spoken" by the cultural discourses that traverse them. Arguing against the textual determinism made most popular by "screen theory" (MacCabe), Stuart Hall, Paul Willemen, and David Morley, among others, have contended that readers are not simply the "subject of the text," but also "social subjects" who live in a particular social formation and who are immersed in a variety of complex cultural systems, of which a text is only a single component (Hall 136–38; Willemen 48; Morley, "Texts" 170–71). While texts are thought to encourage readers to construct a "preferred" meaning, it has been argued that most readers will, to some extent, create a "negotiated" version of a text which contains both "adaptive" and "oppositional" elements (Hall 137). Recognizing that readers are balanced between determination and autonomy and that they will construct meaning differently depending on their particular knowledge and background has led within cultural studies to significant developments in theories of subjectivity, particularly in the areas of television and film spectatorship, as the reader/viewer has come to be regarded as an active, potentially resistant agent.[12]

A number of these developments have recently begun to be extended to various classroom situations and pedagogical practices. Many teachers are currently arguing that, if students are to become active makers of meaning of texts, they must also be given access to discourses that can help them experience their own readings of texts—as they make the text address their contemporary historical condition—as a process of production in dialectical relation to other readings in the past.[13] Yet, frequently, teachers working from a social-cultural perspective do not necessarily imagine that they are primarily teaching students *reading* capabilities, and, consequently, it is possible that the reading lessons they give students will seem (both to the students and perhaps to the academy at large) to be particular to certain "special interests," rather than crucial for all forms of reading. Let us look at two examples—from a cross-cultural perspective and a social-psychoanalytic perspective—which, despite their differences, converge in their positions that (1) to "read" texts or the world, one must attempt to situate them within the complex cultural and historical contexts in which they have been produced and received, that neither texts nor readers are static entities but, rather, are produced and reproduced in different social contexts; and that (2) different readings of texts have consequences. In these two examples, I want to focus primarily on the ways in which teachers develop new pedagogies to help translate theoretical insights into particular practices that students themselves can enact and from which they can learn.

Greg Sarris has developed a pedagogy for his American Indian literature class in which, in one class period, he tells his predominantly white, middle-class students a story that was originally told to him by his Pomo elders and, in the next class period, asks them to retell the story. The assignment is meant both to "engage the life experiences of the students" (174) and to "enable students to scrutinize their experiences or what constitutes their assumptions" (174). In asking students to become conscious of how they retold the story—what omissions they made, what they emphasized, etc.—the assignment is set up from the start so that students do not see reading as either a task in which a reader "faithfully" reproduces a text or simply responds subjectively. This assignment, in many ways, bears striking similarity to cognitive experiments; unlike most of the cognitive researchers, however, Sarris is truly interested in pursuing the cultural underpinnings of differences between student readings of the story and those readings that would have been preferred in the story's original Indian community.

The differences between a student's story and the original do not indicate "wrong" readings, but readings from a different cultural perspective. Reading, in this context, is seen by students as a social act. In scrutinizing their reproductions of the story, students begin to recognize and analyze some of the ways in which their own subjectivities are constructed by middle-class American culture (175). They also become conscious of the differences between the conditions in which the text was written and those in which it was reproduced by them: "What began as a dialogue across white middle-class American culture and that of Kashaya Pomo culture became a larger dialogue across other texts and American Indian cultures associated with those texts" (175). Thus they see that they, as readers, are socially constructed subjects, that texts are also constructed in particular social contexts—which may be quite different from their own and which they may need to study—and that different ways of telling stories have consequences.[14]

From an apparently very different perspective—psychoanalytic theory—Patricia Donahue and Ellen Quandahl also develop a culturally situated reading pedagogy. They use Freud's case study of Dora as both a model of the reading process and as the text students read and write about.[15] Although the reading lessons they provide to their students occur in a different context from that described by Sarris—with "basic studies" students, most of whom are African American, Hispanic, and Filipino, and with a very different kind of text—like Sarris, their pedagogy also introduces students to the notion that, as readers, they are socially constructed, but that they have agency, that texts are produced in determinate conditions and reproduced by readers under other determinate conditions, and that ways of reproducing texts have consequences.

As the students read and reread the case history, first to try to put it in chronological order, then to explore the "insights and blindnesses" of the text, and then to rewrite a conversation between Freud and Dora from Dora's perspective, they learned that "to interpret is to look from a point of view" and that "no reading"—whether Freud's or their own—"is comprehensive, identical with the original" (645, 646). So, while they learn that it was impossible to be completely "faithful" to the text, these students do not simply revel in the subjective capacity of readers to interpret texts differently. They, like Sarris's students, begin to examine the conditions of the text's production, considering "Freud's point of view as a product of his training as a psychoanalyst, his experience as a nineteenth-century male, husband, and father, and his commitment to certain perspectives" (646). The students, as Donahue and Quandahl write, "had to situate Freud's text . . . in contexts of history, gender, and discipline, and see it as a construct that is cultural as well as personal" (646). While these students did not have to develop in detail their own interpretations of Dora,[16] the assignments are clearly organized to help students recognize that their readings, no less than Freud's, must also be situated in broader cultural contexts. And, when the students rewrote a "session" from Dora's point of view, they examined the consequences of certain ways of reading over others: "[M]any of their Doras were critical and angry with Freud" (646). Finally, the assignments were designed to create "the possibility of a dignified, university-level curriculum . . . for poorly prepared students" (644). While the students were not demeaned by workbook drills, neither were they coddled into believing that their readings were valuable just because they were their own. Rather, they were given explicit instruction—"we left little to chance" (647)—in a particular way of reading that enabled them to learn to approach texts with confidence (647).[17]

In order for such pedagogies to impact upon the way reading is defined and taught, however, they need to be seen, not as somehow peculiar to special interest groups or as relevant only to particular kinds of texts in particular kinds of courses, but as part of what it is to read a text of any kind from a critical perspective. Although I certainly do not advocate that culturally informed theories of the reader and the text be taught wholesale to all students, I do believe that such theories need to be seen as being as automatically relevant as cognitive or expressivist theories when it is time to develop pedagogies for the teaching of reading in the schools and the universities. While so often the schools and the universities seem quite separate, it is primarily the research carried on in the colleges and universities that drives the reading lessons students are given in the schools. If feminists, theorists of race and gender, and cultural studies teachers and researchers in the universities were to begin to engage in more active dialogue with the developers of reading programs and the teachers who have to teach students—young and older—"how" to read, it might be possible to begin to change the dominant significations of reading in the schools—so that more students could begin to learn to read the world simultaneously with learning to read the word, so that readers can begin to see themselves as interdiscursive subjects, to see texts as always "in use," and to recognize that different ways of reading texts have consequences.

Notes

1. For developments in Britain see, for example, C. B. Cox and Rhodes Boyson's *Black Paper 1975* on education; the report of the National Curriculum English Working Group, popularly called "the Cox report," and discussions of it in *Critical Quarterly* 32.4 (1990) by Colin MacCabe and Simon Frith. For developments in the U.S., see essays collected in James R. Squire's *The Dynamics of Language Learning;* Harry Singer and Robert B. Ruddell's *Theoretical Models and Processes of Reading;* Judith A. Langer's *Literature Instruction;* Suzanne de Castell,

Allan Luke, and Kieran Egan's *Literacy, Society, and Schooling;* Nancy L. Stein's *Literacy in American Schools;* and John Willinsky's *The New Literacy.*

2. See, for example, statements from such different theoretical orientations as those by Charles A. Perfetti, "Reading Acquisition and Beyond" 58; Louise Rosenblatt, *Literature as Exploration* 32; Suzanne de Castell and Allan Luke, "Defining 'Literacy' in North American Schools" 173–74; David Morley, "Texts, Readers, Subjects" 171.

3. For such arguments in the field of education, for example, see Willinsky 65–91; Smith; Goodman; Mills; Walkerdine; and Hirsch. In psychology, see Bransford; Anderson; Rumelhart; and Crawford and Chaffin. In literacy, see Barnes and Barnes; Resnick and Resnick; Heath; and Szwed. In literature, see Durant et al.; Rosenblatt; Bleich; Fish; Holland; Iser; Donahue and Quandahl; and Rocklin.

4. See, for example, Langer; NAEP; Bloom; Hirsch; Anderson et al., *Becoming;* and Giroux.

5. See Langer; Giroux; Shor; Freire and Macedo; Barnes and Barnes; Resnick and Resnick; and de Castell and Luke. I should note that "critical literacy" should not be confused with "critical thinking, which generally assumes that objectifiable truths exist in the world and that one can evaluate arguments solely on the basis of their logic, purpose, and lack of bias." See, for example, the essays anthologized in Golub et al., *Activities to Promote Critical Thinking.*

6. My organization roughly follows James Berlin's typology of rhetorics of writing instruction (Berlin, "Rhetoric and Ideology"), except that I argue that there is more potential overlap among these approaches to reading than Berlin necessarily suggests in his discussion of approaches to writing, and I will suggest that they exist on a continuum and in dialogic relation to one another. This continuum also represents the likely chronology of a student's reading lessons from elementary school through college, and two of the many questions I will be raising are about the institutional reasons for why particular theories dominate particular educational sites and how it might be possible to get more exchange among positions at different points in students' education.

7. Most agree that cognitive science was officially recognized in 1956 at the Symposium on Information Theory held at the Massachusetts Institute of Technology (See Gardner 28).

8. As Dykstra notes, there are over 1,000 articles published per year on reading (quoted in Willinsky 160), and in the United States, funding for empirical research on reading outstrips research on writing by a ratio of 100 to 1. Moreover, the textbook industry for teaching reading that grows out of this research is massively profitable. Anderson comments that "an entire basal reading program would make a stack of books and papers four feet high" (*Becoming* 35). It has been estimated that "basal" reading "programs"—books or "readers" designed to teach children reading in the United States, organized by grade level from kindergarten through eighth grade—are used in 90 percent of all reading classrooms for 90 percent of their instructional time (Shannon, quoted in Willinsky 163).

9. See, for example, Fish's discussion of "interpretive communities"; Fetterley's analysis of the "resisting reader"; and the essays collected in Nelms's, *Literature in the Classroom.*

10. See, for example, the essays collected in Kintgen, Kroll, and Rose's *Perspectives on Literacy;* de Castell, Luke, and Egan's *Literacy, Society, and Schooling;* and Beach and Hynds's *Developing Discourse Practices in Adolescence and Adulthood.*

11. Again, I wish to emphasize that the models I am setting out are on a continuum. When, for example, Barnes and Barnes argue that "learning to read includes the whole of the reader's understanding of the world" (51), they are not in conflict with models developed by Smith, Goodman, or reader-response critics, and in principle at least, many cognitive psychologists would probably agree with them; however, these researchers actually attempt to analyze the reader's "world." They recognize, following Paulo Freire, the need for the teacher to understand and speak to the actual conditions in which the learner exists: "words should be laden with the meaning of the people's existential experience, and not of the teacher's experience" (Freire and Macedo, *Literacy* 35). And they see their goal in teaching literate behavior as enabling students to develop the capacity to *transform* that world, not simply to be able to function within it.

12. See, for example, Morley, *Nationwide* and *Family Television* 43; Hobson "Housewives," *Crossroads;* Pribram 5; and Masterman 30.

13. See, for example Eugene K. Garber's "'My Kinsman, Major Molineux': Some Interpretive and Critical Probes," in Nelms 83–104; James Butterfield's "Seventh Graders Making Meaning: A Historical Approach to Ray Bradbury," in Nelms 121–28; Kyle Fiore and Nan Elsasser's "'Strangers No More': A Liberatory Literacy Curriculum," in Kintgen et al. 286–99; Sharon Crowley's *A Teacher's Introduction to Deconstruction;* the essays collected in C. Mark Hurlbert and Samuel Totten's *Social Issues in the English Classroom;* Kathleen McCormick's *The Culture of Reading and the Teaching of English;* and Kathleen McCormick, Gary Waller, and Linda Flower's *Reading Texts.*

14. For a similar type of cross-cultural reading lesson, see Walter Hesford's "Overt Appropriation."

15. Donahue and Quandahl do clearly mark themselves as teaching reading, perhaps, in part, because they are working with "basic studies" students who are generally perceived as needing instruction in reading.

16. The authors note that had the quarter not been ending, this could have been the basis for a fourth project (646).

17. For examples of other uses of psychoanalytic pedagogy for similar ends, see McGee; Jay; Brooke.

Works Cited

Anderson, Richard C. "The Notion of Schemata and the Educational Enterprise." *Schooling and the Acquisition of Knowledge.* Ed. Richard C. Anderson, Rand J. Spiro, and William E. Montague. Hillsdale, NJ: Erlbaum, 1977. 415–31.

———. "Role of the Reader's Schema in Comprehension, Learning, and Memory." In Singer and Ruddell 372–84.

———. "Schema-Directed Processes in Language Comprehension." *Cognitive Psychology and Instruction.* Ed. Allan M. Lesgold et al. New York: Plenum, 1978.

Anderson, Richard C., Elfreida H. Hiebert, Judith A. Scott, and Ian A. G. Wilkinson. *Becoming A Nation of Readers: The Report of the Commission on Reading.* Washington, D.C.: National Academy of Education, National Institute of Education; Champaign, IL: Center for the Study of Reading, 1984.

Barnes, Douglas, and Dorothy Barnes. "Reading and Writing as Social Activities." In Beach and Hynds 34–64.

Beach, Richard, and Susan Hynds, eds. *Developing Discourse Practices in Adolescence and Adulthood.* Norwood, NJ: Ablex, 1990.

Beck, Isabel and Margaret McKeown. "Application of Theories of Reading to Instruction." In Stein 63–83.

Bennett, Tony. *Formalism and Marxism.* London: Methuen, 1979.

———. "Texts in History: The Determinations of Reading and Their Texts." *Journal of the Midwest Modern Language Association* 18 (1985): 1–16.

Bennett, Tony, and Janet Woollacott. *Bond and Beyond: The Political Career of a Popular Hero.* London: Macmillan, 1988.

Berlin, James. "Contemporary Composition: The Major Pedagogical Theories." *College English* 44 (1982): 765–77.

———."Rhetoric and Ideology in the Writing Class." *College English* 50 (1988): 477–94.

Bleich, David. *The Double Perspective: Language, Literacy, and Social Relations.* New York: Oxford UP, 1988.

———. *Subjective Criticism.* Baltimore: Johns Hopkins UP, 1978.

Bloom, Allan. *The Closing of the American Mind.* New York: Simon, 1987.

Bransford, John D. "Schema Activation and Schema Acquisition: Comments on Richard C. Anderson's Remarks." In Singer and Ruddell 385–97.

Bransford, John D., and Nancy McCarrell. "A Sketch of A Cognitive Approach to Comprehension." *Cognition and the Symbolic Processes.* Ed. Walter B. Weimer and David S. Palermo. Hillsdale, NJ: Erlbaum, 1974. 189–229.

Brooke, Robert. "Lacan, Transference, and Writing Instruction." *College English* 49 (1987): 679–91.

Butterfield, James. "Seventh Graders Making Meaning: A Historical Approach to Ray Bradbury." In Nelms 121–28.

Cox, C. B., and Rhodes Boyson. *Black Paper 1975: The Fight for Education.* London: Dent, 1975.

Crawford, Mary, and Roger Chaffin. "The Reader's Construction of Meaning: Cognitive Research on Gender and Comprehension." *Gender and Reading: Essays on Readers, Texts, Contexts.* Ed. Elizabeth A. Flynn and Patrocinio P. Schweickart. Baltimore: Johns Hopkins UP, 1986. 3–30.

Crowley, Sharon. *A Teacher's Introduction to Deconstruction.* Urbana, IL: NCTE, 1989.

de Castell, Suzanne, and Allan Luke. "Defining 'Literacy' in North American Schools." In Kintgen et al. 159–74.

———. "Models of Literacy in North American Schools: Social and Historical Conditions and Consequences." In de Castell et al. 87–109.

de Castell, Suzanne, Allan Luke, and Kieran Egan, eds. *Literacy, Society, and Schooling: A Reader.* New York: Cambridge UP, 1986.

Donahue, Patricia, and Ellen Quandahl. "Freud and the Teaching of Interpretation." *College English* 49 (1987): 641–49.

———, eds. *Reclaiming Pedagogy: The Rhetoric of the Classroom.* Carbondale: Southern Illinois UP, 1989.

Durant, Alan, Dara Mills, and Martin Montgomery. "New Ways of Reading : A Course Innovation at the University of Strathclyde." *Critical Quarterly* 30.2 (1988): 11–20.

Eagleton, Terry. *Criticism and Ideology: A Study in Marxist Literary Theory.* London: Verso, 1976.

Easthope, Antony, and John O. Thompson. *Contemporary Poetry Meets Modern Theory.* Ed. Antony Easthope and John O. Thompson. New York: Harvester Wheatsheaf, 1991.

Fetterley, Judith. *The Resisting Reader: A Feminist Approach to American Fiction.* Bloomington: Indiana UP, 1978.

Fiore, Kyle, and Nan Elsasser. "'Strangers No More': A Liberatory Literacy Curriculum." In Kintgen et al. 286–99.

Fish, Stanley. *Is There a Text in This Class? The Authority of Interpretive Communities.* Cambridge, MA: Harvard UP, 1980.

Freire, Paulo. *Pedagogy of the Oppressed.* Trans. Myra Bergman Ramos. 1970. New York: Continuum, 1989.

Freire, Paolo, and Donaldo Macedo. *Literacy: Reading the Word and the World.* South Hadley, MA: Bergin & Garvey, 1987.

Frith, Simon. "The 'Cox Report' and the University." *Critical Quarterly* 32.4 (1990): 68–76.

Garber, Eugene K. "'My Kinsman, Major Molineux': Some Interpretive and Critical Probes." In Nelms 83–104.

Gardner, Howard. *The Mind's New Science: A History of the Cognitive Revolution.* New York: Basic, 1985.

Giroux, Henry A. *Schooling and the Struggle for Public Life: Critical Pedagogy in the Modern Age.* Minneapolis: U of Minnesota P, 1988.

———. *Theory and Resistance in Education: A Pedagogy for the Opposition.* South Hadley, MA: Bergin & Garvey, 1983.

Golub, Jeff, chair, and the NCTE Committee on Classroom Practices. *Activities to Promote Critical Thinking: Classroom Practices in Teaching English, 1986.* Urbana, IL: NCTE, 1986.

Goodman, Kenneth. "The Reading Process: Theory and Practice." *Process, Theory, Research.* Ed. Frederick V. Gollasch. Vol. I of *Language and Literacy: The Selected Writings of Kenneth S. Goodman.* Cambridge, MA: Harvard UP, 1982.

Graff, Gerald. *Beyond the Culture Wars: How Teaching the Conflicts Can Revitalize American Education.* New York: Norton, 1992.

Hall, Stuart. "Encoding/Decoding." In Hall et al. 128–38.

Hall, Stuart, Dorothy Hobson, Andrew Lowe and Paul Willis, eds. *Culture, Media, Language: Working Papers in Cultural Studies.* Boston: Unwin Hyman, 1980.

Heath, Shirley Brice. "Protean Shapes in Literacy Events: Ever-Shifting Oral and Literate Traditions." In Kintgen et al. 348–70.

Hesford, Walter. "Overt Appropriation." *College English* 54 (1992): 406–17.

Hirsch, E. D., Jr. *Cultural Literacy: What Every American Needs to Know.* Boston: Houghton, 1987.

Hobson, Dorothy. *Crossroads: The Drama of a Soap Opera.* London: Methuen, 1982.

———. "Housewives and the Mass Media." In Hall et al. 105–14.

Holland, Norman. *5 Readers Reading.* New Haven: Yale UP, 1975.

Hurlbert, C. Mark, and Samuel Totten, eds. *Social Issues in the English Classroom.* Urbana: NCTE, 1992.

Iser, Wolfgang. *The Act of Reading: A Theory of Aesthetic Response.* Baltimore: John Hopkins UP, 1978.

Jay, Gregory S. "The Subject of Pedagogy: Lessons in Psychoanalysis and Politics." *College English* 49 (1987): 785–800.

Kaestle, Carl. "The History of Literacy and the History of Readers." In Kintgen et al. 95–126.

Kastle, Carl, et al. *Literacy in the United States: Readers and Reading Since 1880.* New Haven: Yale UP, 1991.

Kintgen, Eugene R., Barry M. Kroll, and Mike Rose, eds. *Perspectives on Literacy.* Carbondale: Southern Illinois UP, 1988.

Knoblauch, C. H. "Rhetorical Constructions: Dialogue and Commitment." *College English* 50 (1988): 125–40.

Knoblauch, C. H., and Peter Johnson. "Reading, Writing, and the Prose of the School." In Beach and Hynds 318–33.

Langer, Judith A. "Literacy Instruction in American Schools: Problems and Perspectives." In Stein 111–36.

———, ed. *Literature Instruction: A Focus on Student Response.* Urbana, IL: NCTE, 1992.

Liston, Daniel P. *Capitalist Schools: Explanation and Ethics in Radical Studies of Schooling.* New York: Routledge, 1988.

MacCabe, Colin. "Language, Literature, Identity: Reflections on the Cox Report." *Critical Quarterly* 32.4 (1990): 7–13.

———. "Realism and Cinema: Notes on Brechtian Theses." *Popular Television and Film: A Reader.* Ed. Tony Bennett et al. London: British Film Institute, 1981. 216–35.

Masterman, Len. *Teaching the Media.* New York: Routledge, 1985.

McCormick, Kathleen. *The Culture of Reading and the Teaching of English.* Manchester, UK: Manchester UP, 1994.

McCormick, Kathleen, and Gary Waller, with Linda Flower. *Reading Texts: Reading, Responding, Writing.* Lexington, MA: Heath, 1987.

McGee, Patrick. "Truth and Resistance: Teaching as a Form of Analysis." *College English* 49 (1987): 667–78.

Mills, Collin. "Making Sense of Reading: Key Words or Grandma Swagg." *Language and Literacy in the Primary School.* Ed. Margaret Meek and Collin Mills. London: Falmer, 1988. 27–52.

Morley, David. *Family Television: Cultural Power and Domestic Leisure.* London: Routledge, 1986.

———. *The Nationwide Audience: Structure and Decoding.* London: British Film Institute, 1980.

———. "Texts, Readers, Subjects." In Hall et al. 163–73.

National Assessment of Educational Progress. *Three National Assessments of Reading: Changes in Performance, 1970–1980.* (Report No. 11-R-01). Denver, CO: Education Commission of the States, 1981.

Nelms, Ben F., ed. *Literature in the Classroom: Readers, Texts, and Contexts.* Urbana: NCTE, 1988.

Perfetti, Charles A. "Reading Acquisition and Beyond: Decoding Includes Cognition." In Stein: 41–62.

Pribram, E. Dierdre, ed. *Female Spectators: Looking at Film and Television.* New York: Verso, 1988.

Resnick, Daniel P., and Lauren B. Resnick. "The Nature of Literacy: A Historical Exploration." In Kintgen et al. 190–202.

———. "Varieties of Literacy." *Social History and Issues in Human Consciousness: Some Interdisciplinary Connections.* Ed. Andrew E. Barnes and Peter N. Sterns. New York: New York UP, 1989. 171–96.

Rocklin, Edward. "Converging Transformations in Teaching Composition, Literature, and Drama." *College English* 53 (1991): 171–94.

Rosenblatt, Louise. *Literature as Exploration.* 4th ed. New York: MLA, 1984.

———. *The Reader, the Text, the Poem: The Transactional Theory of the Literary Work.* Carbondale: Southern Illinois UP, 1978.

———. "The Transactional Theory of the Literary Work: Implications for Research." *Researching Response and the Teaching of Literature: Points of Departure.* Ed. Charles R. Cooper. Norwood, NJ: Ablex, 1984. 33–53.

Rumelhart, David. E. "Schemata: The Building Blocks of Cognition." *Theoretical Issues in Reading Comprehension: Perspectives from Cognitive Psychology, Linguistics, Artificial Intelligence, and Education.* Ed. Rand J. Spiro, Bertram C. Bruce, and William F. Brewer. Hillsdale, NJ: Erlbaum, 1980. 33–58.

———. "Toward an Interactive Model of Reading." In Singer and Ruddell 722–50.

Sarris, Greg. "Storytelling in the Classroom: Crossing Vexed Chasms." *College English* 52 (1990): 169–85.

Scribner, Sylvia. "Literacy in Three Metaphors." In Kintgen et al. 71–81.

Shor, Ira. *Culture Wars: Schools and Society in the Conservative Restoration.* Boston: Routledge, 1986.

Sinfield, Alan. "Give an Account of Shakespeare and Education. . . ." *Political Shakespeare: New Essays in Cultural Materialism.* Ed. Jonathan Dollimore and Alan Sinfield. Manchester, UK: Manchester UP, 1985. 134–57.

Singer, Harry. "Conceptualizing in Learning to Read." In Singer and Ruddell 239–55.

Singer, Harry, and Robert B. Ruddell, eds. *Theoretical Models and Processes of Reading.* 3rd ed. Newark, DE: IRA, 1985.

Smith, Frank. *Understanding Reading: A Psycholinguistic Analysis of Reading and Learning to Read.* 4th ed. Hillsdale, NJ: Erlbaum, 1988.

Spivey, Nancy. "Constructing Constructivism: Reading Research in the United States." *Poetics* 16 (1987): 169–92.

Squire, James R., ed. *The Dynamics of Language Learning: Research in Reading and English.* Urbana, IL: ERIC/RCS and NCRE, 1987.

Stein, Nancy L., ed. *Literacy in American Schools: Learning to Read and Write.* Chicago: U of Chicago P, 1986.

Szwed, John. "The Ethnography of Literacy." In Kintgen et al. 303–11.

Turner, Graeme. *British Cultural Studies: An Introduction.* Boston: Unwin Hyman, 1990.

Walkerdine, Valerie. "Progressive Pedagogy and Political Struggle." *Screen* 13 (1986): 54–60.

Weiler, Kathleen. "Teaching, Feminism, and Social Change." In Hurlbert and Totten 322–37.

White, Sylvia L. and Ruie Jane Pritchard. "Students Examining Values in the Study of *Huckleberry Finn*." In Nelms 205–34.

Willemen, Paul. "Notes on Subjectivity: On Reading Edward Branigan's *Subjectivity under Siege*." Screen 19 (1978): 41–69.

Williams, Raymond. *Marxism and Literature.* Oxford: Oxford UP, 1977.

Willinsky, John. *The New Literacy: Redefining Reading and Writing in the Schools.* New York: Routledge, 1990.

19 Teaching in the Contact Zone: The Myth of Safe Houses

Janice M. Wolff
Saginaw Valley State University

some other where
alchemists mumble over pots.
their chemistry stirs
into science. their science
freezes into stone.

—Lucille Clifton (from "Quilting" 3)

As teachers, we sometimes see ourselves as alchemists, trying for the right mix; sometimes as scientists, classifying, typing, ordering the chaos of the classroom. But often, the work in the laboratory places us in a most unsettling environment, attempting to produce good teaching. Lucille Clifton recognizes the dangers of such "pseudo-science" and points out the stony results of such endeavor. The story that follows is a journey of a teacher into alchemy, the search for gold, for a "contact zone," for a "safe house" in which to teach.

Three authorities influenced and continue to influence my alchemy: Mary Louise Pratt and her contact-zone theory; Henry Giroux's critical pedagogy; and Toni Morrison's novel, *Beloved*. Pratt has borrowed the anthropological term "contact zone" and made it a metaphor for the imaginary spaces where differing cultures meet. Very often the cultures have different languages and certainly different values, and very often one culture will dominate the other as it privileges itself. The "contact zone" is where the two come together, sometimes in situations of conquest and sometimes in conversation. Giroux outlines a project aimed at democratizing the classroom, a project enabled by a "critical pedagogy," one that is self-aware and self-critical, a pedagogy that talks about itself and is cognizant of the power relations in the classroom—teacher has all power and students have none—and aims to equalize those inequalities. "Border pedagogy," too, comes into Giroux's project for the

316

classroom: it is the sort of pedagogy that admits the ideological geography of the classroom—again, the arrangement that puts the teacher at the center and the students on the margins, the borders of the space for learning. Visions of Pratt, Giroux, the "contact zone," and "border pedagogy" were very active upon my teaching as I began a recent fall semester, as I began rereading *Beloved* for the term ahead. Contact-zone and border theory and critical pedagogy made sense to me and taught me that

> where there are legacies of subordination, groups need places for healing and mutual recognition, safe houses in which to construct shared understandings, knowledges, claims on the world that they can then bring into the contact zone. (Pratt, "Arts" 40)

Constructing that "safe house" for learning, an environment that would encourage knowledge making and risk taking, would be my alchemy.

Toni Morrison is a teacher herself, one who works at the intersection of print and oral cultures. As Joyce Irene Middleton has pointed out:

> Through her playful intermingling of an ancient, oral storytelling genre with a modern literate one, Toni Morrison draws on the creative dimensions of both oral and literate language, giving us new and stimulating perspectives on oral memory in her accomplished modern novel. (74)

Though Middleton writes of *Song of Solomon,* her point applies as well to *Beloved.* Morrison, in the way that she brings orality and literacy together and in the way that she blurs the distinctions between the two, implies the presence of the "contact zone" for those interested in the relationship between theory and pedagogy. This essay explores the ways contact-zone and border theory inform the teaching of a novel such as Toni Morrison's *Beloved* and, by extension, inform pedagogy.

After having immersed myself in reading her theory, I began to see Pratt's concept of the contact zone insinuating itself into my courses: in my American literature course, a survey spanning several hundred years of written material, a course that was all but unmanageable in its scope—pre-Columbian to 1900—I began by asking students to think about cultures in terms of oral and literate. I am using oral and print cultures as Walter Ong has presented them for us: orality representing a culture that is "innocent of writing," and print being that which has an established chirographic representation of text (18). Admittedly, the idea of "oral cultures" and "print cultures" sets up a dichotomy, a system of binaries that will not necessarily hold, but one which seems to make the idea of "contact zone" knowable. The students and I spent some time listing the possible features of each, where they might overlap, and so on. (We returned to the notion of print vs. oral cultures at the end of the semester when we read *Huck Finn,* so the concept never really went away.) When we read explorers' narratives, I asked students to write about which voices seemed most intent on conquest, which best exemplified "the Monarch of all I survey," as Pratt tells it to her readers. We explored Eurocentrism as it manifested itself in the readings and looked for the naturalistic impulse to list and classify the flora and fauna. We recognized this impulse as we read Cabeza de Vaca and saw his tendency to place European comparisons on places and things in the new world: the newly "discovered" islands remind him of "springtime in Andalusia." Pratt asserts that science, particularly that Linnean brand of classification, had a central part in the colonization process, that

> natural history set in motion a secular, global labor that, among other things, made contact zones a site of intellectual as well as manual labor, and installed there the distinction between the two. (Pratt, "Science" 27).

At the same time that Pratt's contact zone was informing my pedagogy in the American literature class, her earlier work on natural narrative was informing my pedagogy in the section of "Literary Analysis" that I was also teaching (a general education course required of many of our majors). But contact-zone theory coalesced when we came to the reading of *Beloved.* On the first day of discussion, students told me of their difficulty with reading the novel. The first sentence, "124 was spiteful," stopped their reading cold. Some pushed forward, allowing their reading to teach them that 124 was an address, a house, a metonymic accounting for a building. One student even asked me to lecture, to tell the book to the class. Two pages further on, students confronted yet another semantic stumbling block: the presentation of Sethe's sexual bartering for the letters on the tombstone: "Ten minutes for seven letters. With another ten could she have gotten 'Dearly' too?" (5). It seemed to me that this was the sort of textual fragment, unreadable though it was for students, that represented the meeting of print and oral cultures. It seemed, too, that Sethe was at the mercy of the individual who "had" print culture on his side.

Because contact-zone theory informed my reading of Toni Morrison's *Beloved,* I thought that that reading would establish a "safe house" in which to discuss the novel. "Contact zone," as Mary Louise Pratt explains it, refers to

> social spaces where cultures meet, clash, and grapple with each other, often in contexts of highly asymmetrical relations of power, such as colonialism, slavery, or their aftermaths as they are lived out in many parts of the world today. (Pratt, "Arts" 34)

Those asymmetrical relationships of power obtain in the confines of Sweet Home; the blacks live a colonized existence under both the Garners and Schoolteacher. When Sethe's nonliterate "rememory" meets the Linnean print classification system of Schoolteacher, contact-zone asymmetry is evident. He asserts power, and she, through the course of the novel, rememories the violent events precipitated by the clash of cultures. Sweet Home is the first site of contact-zone counter-pedagogy, teaching methods that capitalize on the asymmetrical relationships of power, but the novel is punctuated with incidences of print culture colliding with oral culture.

In addition to thinking in terms of the contact zone, my students and I agonized over some of the unsolvable narrative issues in the novel: Is the ghost real? Is Beloved real? How could a mother murder her child? But I kept returning to the idea of the contact zone, the site where print culture meets oral culture. Pratt provided us with language that allowed us to speak about the print culture as it reproduced the oral culture, as the one asserted its scientific, naturalistic, textual might, as the one appropriated the Other. Pratt's metaphor of the "safe house" allowed students to examine the political in light of the historical and the pseudo-scientific. Morrison's already masterful subverting of the narrative, coupled with Pratt's questioning of the colonizing impulse, allowed for some thoughtful discussion of the insertion of the self into culture. Students began to see that out of the fragmented narrative, the recounting of slender threads, that a tapestry of meaning might occur.

Our reading, our impulse to create order out of seeming chaos, paralleled the naturalistic impulse in the novel. Nowhere is the "systematizing of nature," that impulse that supports the "authority of print, and . . . the class which controlled it" (Pratt, "Science" 30), more evident than in the character and behaviors of Morrison's Schoolteacher. His presence at Sweet Home is the presence of the empiricist, the one who must make order out of the chaos of the plantation, the one who records and measures and writes, the one who privileges text and colonizes the unread. Schoolteacher becomes "the (lettered, male, European) eye that held the system could familiarize ('naturalize') new sites/sights immediately upon contact, by incorporating them into the language of the system" (Pratt, "Science" 31). Pratt further characterizes the naturalist-collector-scientist as a "benign, often homely figure, whose transformative powers do their work in the domestic contexts of the garden or the collection room" (33). In addition to spotting the evil he engenders, my students identified his impulse as a scientific one, a way of producing "a lettered, bourgeois discourse about non-lettered, peasant worlds" (34–35). Schoolteacher uses that lettered, narrative impulse to exert power and to create

the slave class as Other. Ultimately, he exposes "our impulse to organize in power lines that create false distinctions and class/race hierarchies" (Barnett 2).

In order to "rememory" power lines and class/race hierarchies, Sethe
tells Denver the story of Schoolteacher:

> Nothing to tell except schoolteacher. He was a little man. Short.
> Always wore a collar, even in the fields. A schoolteacher, she said.
> That made her [Mrs. Garner] feel good that her husband's sister's
> husband had book learning and was willing to come farm Sweet
> Home after Mr. Garner passed. The men could have done it, even
> with Paul F sold. But it was like Halle said. She didn't want to be
> the only white person on the farm and a woman too. . . . He brought
> two boys with him. Sons or nephews. I don't know. They called him
> Onka and had pretty manners, all of 'em. Talked soft and spit in
> handkerchiefs. Gentle in a lot of ways. (36–37)

But more than narrating the past, the "rememory" enables Sethe to
continue with the job of living. After having been colonized,
marginalized, and nearly erased, she narrates herself into a historical
subject. It is as if characters must narrate or must resign themselves to a
mute (or dead) state: consider that Denver, after being asked about her
history by a schoolmate, becomes speechless for a number of years. Sethe
sees that "book learning" is a privileged position; she also sees rightly
that Mrs. Garner didn't want to be in the minority, on the margins of
the farm community, even with the power of being white. Sethe's assessment of the culture as represented by Schoolteacher reveals gentil-
ity as a veneer. She "reads" him very well, indeed. The narrative goes
on, though, and describes the site where the two cultures meet and blur:

> He liked the ink I made. It was her recipe, but he preferred how
> I mixed it and it was important to him because at night he sat down
> to write in his book. It was a book about us but we didn't know that
> right away. We just thought it was his manner to ask us questions.
> He commenced to carry round a notebook and write down what we
> said. I still think it was them questions that tore Sixo up. Tore him
> up for all time. (37)

Schoolteacher's pedagogy is one neither Pratt nor Henry Giroux would
support, though it is consistent with the classifying, taxonomizing, naturalistic impulse. It is a pedagogy that is immoral, a false attempt at knowledge making, a counter-pedagogy that exploits its subject even as it
studies it—forcing Sethe to make the ink that produces the signifiers that
render her family into text. Schoolteacher's methods make Sethe
complicitous in her own objectification. Giroux proposes a pedagogy that
undermines Schoolteacher's:

> At the heart of such a pedagogy is the recognition that it is important to stare into history in order to remember the suffering of the past and that out of this remembrance a theory of ethics should be developed in which solidarity, compassion, and care become central dimensions of an informed social practice. (Giroux 102)

Schoolteacher's methods may be historical, in the way that he inscribes and measures and records the subjects, but never ethical. His pedagogy, rather, constitutes a "narrative act of colonizing that is finally disabling and tyrannical" (Barnett 3). His science is pseudo-science and othering.

Bit by bit Sethe's remembered narrative returns to her: "Easily she stepped into the told story that lay before her eyes on the path she followed away from the window" (29). Remembering the pregnancy that was key to her run from Sweet Home, the bodily sensations, the swollen feet that nearly kept her from running, she recalls that

> she waited for the little antelope to protest, and why she thought of an antelope Sethe could not imagine since she had never seen one. She guessed it must have been an invention held on to from before Sweet Home, when she was very young. Of that place where she was born (Carolina maybe? or was it Louisiana?) she remembered only song and dance. (30)

She wonders about the choice of the metaphor "antelope," and it shapes more memories of the oral culture:

> Oh but when they sang. And oh but when they danced and sometimes they dance the antelope. The men as well as the ma'ams, one of whom was certainly her own. They shifted shapes and became something other. Some unchained, demanding other whose feet knew her pulse better than she did. (31)

The clash of cultures has removed the young Sethe from her mother, an assertion of asymmetrical power.

As if the fading antelope metaphor isn't enough, as if the erasure of one's mother isn't enough, as if linguistic othering isn't enough, Sethe has a dim memory of the language that once was hers:

> The woman who cared for Sethe as a child was Nan who used different words. Words Sethe understood then but could neither recall nor repeat now. She believed that must be why she remembered so little before Sweet Home except singing and dancing and how crowded it was. What Nan told her she had forgotten, along with the language she told it in. The same language her ma'am spoke, and which would never come back. But the message—that was and had been there all along. Holding the damp white sheets against her chest, she was picking meaning out of code she no longer understood. (62)

The lived experience, her narrative, supplies the meaning even though the signifying system is all but gone. Hanging up damp sheets becomes the memory trigger that contains traces of the past.

There are other instances of the contact zone, where print culture privileges itself and colonizes those who are unread: the newspaper clipping that contains the picture and the account of Sethe's murder of her child sends Paul D out of the house and away from her. Even though he cannot read the alphabetic representation of the event, Paul D "reads" the implications of the text: for people of color to become textualized means something very bad indeed. When Beloved, or the incarnation of her, arrives at 124, she spells her name in a way that identifies her illiteracy. But it is at Lady Jones's school that the more positive features of the contact zone are realized:

> For a nickel a month, Lady Jones did what whitepeople thought unnecessary if not illegal: crowded her little parlor with the colored children who had time for and interest in book learning. The nickel, tied to a handkerchief knot, tied to her [Denver's] belt, that she carried to Lady Jones, thrilled her. The effort to handle chalk expertly and avoid the scream it would make; the capital *w*, the little *i*, the beauty of the letters in her name, the deeply mournful sentences from the Bible Lady Jones used as a textbook. Denver practiced every morning; starred every afternoon. She was so happy. . . . (102)

In spite of the more common travesties found in the contact zone, Denver enjoys, for a short time, the "safe house" that Lady Jones provides, the safe house on the margins of the educational system. Prior to the "rage, incomprehension, and pain" that Denver ultimately experiences, she also finds "exhilarating moments of wonder and revelation, mutual understanding, and new wisdom—the joys of the contact zone" (Pratt, "Arts" 39).

In many ways, the contact zone and its inherent terrors and triumphs inform our reading of *Beloved,* and, in many ways, *Beloved* shapes our reading of contact-zone theory. The more crucial question is where were my students in the quest for the contact zone? To be very honest, most were resistant to the reading, as was evident in many of their reading journals. Most could not abide the nonlinearity of the book. Many were shocked by the idea of bestiality and, shocked too, at the suggestion of oral sex. Many wanted me to supply a plot summary; many, I suspect, wished for *Cliffs Notes* to accompany their reading. A few said that they stuck with the book, read as if they knew what was going on, powered through, and were rewarded at around midpoint with meaning. Fragments were beginning to add up for them. It was with and through that fragmented reading experience—a reading that made demands on the students, a reading that disrupted their conventional notions about narrative patterns—that students began to see not only what was privileged in the 1850s slave culture, but also what sort of reading is privileged in the academy. Students admitted that their reading history included texts that progressed logically from point A to point B to point C; their reading experience did not include narrative fragments, out of time, out of sequence, just as their education did not include material out of time, out of logical sequence. The subverted narrative of *Beloved* confounded the conventional, orderly presentation of material to be learned, what the students had come to expect from the classroom environment.

Because they weren't ever sure of the "what occurs when" in the novel, students worked on fragments of knowledge—they had to. *Beloved* denies a reading that supports conventional reading behaviors. We had to invent some new tactics. Students worked in small groups to frame boundaries for the characters, that is, to define characters according to their relationships to one another. For instance, one group worked to define Sethe according to Paul D; another group defined her according to Schoolteacher; another group created Sethe through Denver's eyes, Beloved's eyes, Amy's eyes, and so on. We filled in the gaps where we could; we wrote Halle's narrative, told his story. We talked about the novel in terms of cultural and political boundaries, too, seeing the moral and legal ramifications of a slave culture. But it was the day that the small groups were still at work on the identities of Sethe that I met with some contact-zone resistance of my very own. I was circulating, listening in on the small groups, when I came to a group that seemed to be finished with the work at hand. After asking whether they were socializing—a valid thing to do in a "safe classroom"—a member of the group looked up at me in all sincerity and asked: "Why did you assign this book?" Embedded in her question was the resistance that both Giroux and Pratt speak of, but something else was at work, something that the journals evidenced, too. My style of teaching had changed, yes; no longer was I telling students the meaning of the novel through the medium of lecture. Small groups and initiatory writing (Elbow's concept) and journals were better ways for "constructing meaning." I imagined myself teaching in the "contact zone," where

> every single text we read stood in specific historical relationship to the students in the class, but the range and variety of historical relationships in play were enormous. . . . All the students in the class had the experience, for example, of hearing their culture discussed and objectified in ways that horrified them; all the students saw their roots traced back to legacies of both glory and shame. . . . (Pratt, "Arts" 39).

Pratt is speaking specifically about a course she teaches, but it informed the way I heard the question from my student, the one about why I had them read *Beloved*.

Her resistance was honest and compelling for me. Why did I select that novel? What was my intent? Aside from the fact that *Beloved* is one of my all-time favorite novels, and aside from the fact that my professional title gives me the power to put selections on the syllabus, I discovered that I depended upon the always already institutionalized reasons for my choice. *Beloved* became a part of the syllabus because the novel says both loud and subtle things about our history and our culture; it carries the literary and artistic features that English teachers relish; it is weighty enough to bear multiple readings (and needs rereading). Beyond those elements, it supports and exemplifies other literary structures that the "Literary Analysis" class had been reading about and testing out: natural narrative, literary anecdote, metaphor, intertextuality, and naming—all concepts mapped out for us in Scholes, Comley, and Ulmer's *Text Book*.

Text Book was a force to reckon with all semester, and it provided us with strategies for making meaning from *Beloved*. Knowing that the novel is a story woven from a nineteenth-century news account of a former slave who tried to kill her children rather than let them live a slave existence made the novel intertextual for the class. Metaphor, and our special attitude toward it, allowed us to see the figurative impulse of the writer. But more than seeing the historical or literary structures in the novel, my hope was that students might begin to see the boundaries that are so defined in Sethe's story, boundaries as they are presented to us in *Text Book*. The reading of *Beloved* uncovers cultural, legal, and institutional boundaries that support racism. Identifying those boundaries so apparent in the novel might allow us as a class to confront our own racist positions. The idea of the contact zone, the reading about historical contact zones, and becoming part of a contact zone in the "safe house of the classroom"—if such a space is more than myth—allow students and teachers "the opportunity to engage in antiracist struggles in their effort to link schooling with real life, ethical discourse to political action, and classroom relations to a broader notion of cultural politics" (Giroux 141). I wanted students to recognize racism; I wanted "to make antiracist pedagogies central to the task of educating students to enliven a wider and more critically engaged public culture." I wanted "students not merely to take risks but also to push against the boundaries of an oppressive social order" (141). The irony seemed to be that the oppressive social order that students pushed against was me.

Teaching in the contact zone can be fraught with danger, and sometimes establishing a "safe house" is little more than myth. For every exhilaration, there seems to be a corresponding downward spiral. Using contact-zone theory as a screen through which to read a complex novel was one thing, but realizing that the metaphor of the contact zone was also active upon the classroom itself was daunting. It was never clearer than the day I had the terms "print culture" and "oral culture"—those arbitrary and imaginary classifications—on the board. I was asking students to help me characterize the two, to list the features of a culture rich in print—libraries, newsstands, alphabetic writing, text of all sorts—and the features of oral culture: people innocent of writing, those dependent upon oral language, people studied by anthropologists. We were doing fairly well, listing, pulling ideas from one another, when a student suggested a third category, that of "video culture." No problem. The twentieth century surely does make room for such a classification. Father Ong's notion of secondary orality was active upon me as I took the liberty of aligning myself with print culture as it appeared on the chalkboard, showing myself to be one with that culture. The rest is fragmented memory, somewhat repressed. Next, I asked students to align themselves with the appropriate category, making the assumption that video would be their choice, or possibly even oral culture. In effect, what I was doing was saying that I was representative of print culture and that students were something Other.

A discerning student responded with some petulance to the way I was constructing the categories, saying that he felt students straddled categories, had to, in fact, in a culture that demanded literacy. He went on, as I found later in a journal entry, to say, in effect: "I felt excluded when you said you were the print culture and students were oral. I read, lots. In fact, the word 'condescending' comes to mind. I felt cheated. Here, all semester you have been saying in 'Literary Analysis' you were going to give us access to literature, and in a very few minutes, you seemed to close doors to us."

What had I done? Up until that moment, I felt I had been working to give students access to literature, to allow them entry to that literate world. I felt that my pedagogy had been a critical one, a democratic one, one that Giroux espouses:

> Pedagogy that replaces authoritative language of recitation with an approach that allows students to speak from their own histories, collective memories, and voices while simultaneously challenging the grounds on which knowledge and power are constructed and legitimated. (105)

But in the very telling of contact-zone theory, I had centered myself and relegated students once more to the borders of knowledge making. By naming myself the representative of the print culture, I had emphasized the false dichotomy of print culture and oral culture; I had bought a bill of institutionalized goods. Instead of teaching against the grain, instead of practicing a critical pedagogy, I had subscribed to one that undermined what I had hoped to do.

As problematic as that moment was, and as perplexing as it was for someone interested in critical pedagogy, it became a real object lesson in what it had to say about contact-zone and border theory. The moment we center ourselves and privilege our discourse, whatever narrative it may be, we may be constructing counter-pedagogy. Morrison's "School-teacher" is a metaphor for all of us working in the contact zone. Bringing theory to bear in the classroom is critical to our work. Researching ethnological approaches in the classroom must also teach us that we are the "Schoolteachers"; we are the latter-day naturalists trying to produce text about the reading and writing processes of our students. When we consider the work that we do, we must not forget that theory that informs the way we read literature is also theory that is analogous to the classroom. Students know marginalization when they see it, and perhaps not even classrooms that want to be "safe houses" can be very safe, either for students or for teachers. Ethics is key to a discussion of critical pedagogy. Where Giroux outlines critical pedagogy, he stresses that "ethics must be seen as a central concern of critical pedagogy. . . . Ethics becomes a practice that broadly connotes one's personal and social sense of responsibility to the Other" (74). My alchemy for the classroom was getting a bit ahead of my ethics.

Perhaps the best that teachers can do, when concerned with matters of pedagogy and theory, is to read theory and then problematize it. For instance, reading Pratt's contact-zone theory and seeing it as an analogue for the classroom is good. Thinking of the classroom as a "safe house" is also good. To read Giroux and to understand that one must maintain a self-critical pedagogy is also a positive move. But then one must read them against the grain. We must, as readers and teachers, employ the "greatest gift of deconstruction: to question the authority of the investigating subject without paralyzing him . . ." (Spivak 9). This deconstructionist gift allows the reader of Pratt to say, "Well, yes, she critiques the naturalistic impulse to classify and hierarchize, but doesn't she allow herself the same privilege of classification?" And might not Pratt create classifications that are purely imaginary? And is Giroux political enough? Might his narrative support the very authoritative hierarchies that he seems to oppose? My best advice is to read theory but refuse to privilege it. Read about the "contact zone," use it as a meta-phor for the classroom, let it inform pedagogy, but always with a Derridean caveat: Use the term under erasure.

Works Cited

Barnett, Marianne. Response to an early draft of "Teaching in the Contact Zone." January 1993.

Cabeza de Vaca, Alvar Nuñuz. Selections from his journals. *The Heath Anthology of American Literature I.* Gen. ed. Paul Lauter. Lexington, MA: Heath, 1990. 89–99.

Clifton, Lucille. "Quilting." *Quilting: Poems, 1987–1990.* Brockport, NY: BOA Editions, 1991. 3.

Giroux, Henry A. *Border Crossings: Cultural Workers and the Politics of Education.* New York: Routledge, 1992.

Middleton, Joyce Irene. "Orality, Literacy, and Memory in Toni Morrison's *Song of Solomon.*" *College English* 55.1 (January 1993): 64–75.

Morrison, Toni. *Beloved: A Novel.* New York: Penguin, 1988.

———. *Song of Solomon.* New York: Knopf, 1977.

Ong, Walter J. *Interfaces of the Word: Studies in the Evolution of Consciousness and Culture.* Ithaca: Cornell UP, 1977.

Pratt, Mary Louise. "Arts of the Contact Zone." *Profession 91.* New York: MLA, 1991. 33–40.

———. "Science, Planetary Consciousness, Interiors." *Imperial Eyes: Travel Writing and Transculturation.* New York: Routledge, 1992. 15–37.

Scholes, Robert, Nancy R. Comley, and Gregory L. Ulmer. *Text Book: An Introduction to Literary Language.* New York: St. Martin's, 1988.

Spivak, Gayatri Chakravorty. "Subaltern Studies: Deconstructing Historiography." *Subaltern Studies* 4 (1985): 3–32.

20 How Literature Learns to Write: The Possibilities and Pleasures of Role-Play

James E. Seitz
University of Pittsburgh

> Of course performance includes the imitation of past accomplishments, sometimes as emulation, sometimes as parody. . . . In either case, however, imitation in performance is only part of a larger activity: of shaping a self out of the materials in which it is immersed. . . .
>
> —Richard Poirier (*The Performing Self* xxii)

A colleague of mine at the university where I used to teach recently told me that he flatly refuses to assign writing in his literature classes anymore. "If they are to write for me," he said, bristling with anger and resentment, "it's going to be in class on tests—not at home. All I ever get is that garbage they take from *Cliffs Notes* and *Masterplots*, and I'm not going to accept it anymore." As he spoke, I imagined a revision of the scene in the film *Network*, wherein watchers of the nightly news would be transformed into teachers so thoroughly enraged by the dullness of term papers that they would raise their windows and shout into a dark and tempestuous night, "We're mad as hell, and we're not going to take it anymore!"

The degree of frustration and boredom teachers of literature often experience while reading the student papers they assign is really quite remarkable, given most teachers' love of literature and, in many cases, their love of teaching. Why do these papers make us so miserable? A fairly obvious explanation may be that hardly anyone can claim to enjoy reading weak argumentation, which defines a good deal of what teachers encounter in student writing. After all, to compose a sustained argument for a particular reading of a literary text can be a challenging, even intimidating, task, especially for students who have been taught to regard the essay as a "report" rather than a rhetorical endeavor. One of the most acute difficulties is that students do not seem to know for whom they are writing—what, on the one hand, they can assume is common knowledge and what, on the other hand, needs to be explored in detail. Papers that begin "William Shakespeare was an important writer of the sixteenth century" or "*The Great Gatsby,* written by F. Scott Fitzgerald, was published in 1925" don't signal much promise; we know from the start that we are in for a bad read. And there seems to be no immediate method for setting such students straight. We might scratch in the margin, "This is unnecessary" or "Believe it or not, I already know who Shakespeare is," but such comments will not give students a means of knowing *in general* how to determine what should be included or excluded in their future papers. We can blame it on their lack of experience and hope that time will do its work, but meanwhile we are stuck with papers that create in us sudden desires to clean out old drawers or to reread *Paradise Lost*—anything but to confront student writing.

Yet the issues at hand—as is usually the case with pedagogical matters—are not only practical but also theoretical. The estrangement teachers experience when they encounter student appropriations of academic discourse reflects more than burnout; rather, it signals the need to consider closely the dynamics of reader-writer relations. Since writing is always constrained by the writer's image of her reader, by the expectation of how her text will be read, it is imperative that textual analysis examines the reader(s) which the text has prefigured. A teacher's reading of student writing should therefore include an interpretation of the characteristic teacher-reader whom the student appears to have envisioned. Conversely, as Roland Barthes indicates in *S/Z*, reading is itself "a form of work . . . a labor of language" (10–11) by which readers *write* their readings: reading is a process of active composition. Given this productive feature of reading, the teacher-as-reader must be alert to the constraints on his own approaches to "composing" the student texts he reads—particularly the ways in which he may insist that student writing compose *itself,* in the sense of disciplining itself, of gaining calm self-possession. In other words, as in more general studies of reader-writer relations, the crucial questions facing a serious exploration of student writing share with recent critical theory a concern for issues of expectation, imagination, and desire.

If, as Barthes claims, "every reading is steeped in Desire (or Disgust)" (*Rustle* 35), it may be that, in certain respects, we teachers have created our own disgust. As readers of student writing, we occupy the peculiar position of having sharply curtailed, through our "assignments," the possibilities for the texts we read before they even come to be written. While it is clear, as I have noted, that any writer's intended audience surely influences her discourse even as she composes, few readers hold the control that teachers exert over a writer's objectives and methods. "Tell us what you want" is the most common student demand, not simply because students are mercenary but because they discern, correctly, that teachers, to some degree, anticipate the texts they desire their students to write. Even if the assignment is so designed as to disguise these desires—usually by offering students the "freedom" to choose their own topics—"what the teacher wants" will emerge in corrective commentary on the texts themselves, where students are often instructed to rewrite their essays with an agenda directed (or even dictated) by their teacher-reader. In other words, by the end of the semester—if not much earlier—we have done much to ask for what we get. It is not only our students' capabilities but also the nature of our own assignments and responses that lead to agitation and disgruntlement when we read student writing.

None of these remarks would come as a surprise in the field of composition, which has long been concerned with the relationships between assignments and their results and between teacher commentary and subsequent student revision. But such concerns do not appear to be very prominent among teachers of literature, who often seem to imagine that there is no assignment they *can* give other than to ask that students read texts and write interpretations, sometimes with the help of secondary sources. There are also, of course, the familiar variants on compare-and-contrast papers, and essays based on specific themes, symbols, or characters. Some teachers even ask students to keep reading journals—but this is about as far as experimentation with writing goes in most literature courses. Yet, while teachers of composition continue to discuss all that recent literary theory has to offer their freshman writing classes, teachers of literature typically have little to say about what composition theory's imaginative engagement with pedagogy has to offer their literature classes.

At this point, however, it might be useful for me to move away from the composition versus literature dichotomy, particularly in light of the fact that so many teachers (such as myself) teach both. What I have found most intriguing in recent years are the possibilities born of teaching these courses as though there *were* no distinction, as though a course in writing should concentrate equally on reading and a course in reading should concentrate equally on writing. This essay will examine the latter predicament, primarily because it has not received the attention accorded the former. I want to consider what happens when we ask students of literature to reconceive not simply the literary texts about which they write but also the particular identities *through* whom they write. Might there be something to gain from inviting students to write not as themselves but as others?

If the act of writing is a social drama, a negotiation between the writer and imagined readers, then it may be useful to create writing assignments based on the role-play through which we participate in all other forms of social interaction. Though Jane Tompkins has called for an end to pedagogy based on "the performance model" (653–56), I would claim that performance, on the part of students as well as teachers, should not nor cannot be escaped. Tompkins apparently would have teachers relinquish performances before their students in favor of what she calls a more "maternal" presence (660). Yet this view fails to acknowledge the ways in which any revised conception of the teacher's activity will inevitably inaugurate still another performance, another role. Once we accept that there is no recovery of the authentic self, we have no choice, it seems to me, other than to embrace the multiplicity of roles through which the self performs and constitutes itself. As Richard Poirier notes, performance is "inclusive of all kinds of versions, absorbed from whatever source, of what the self might be" (xxii). In the context of the literature class, this means that teachers may offer students the opportunity to assume, as have the authors they read, any number of textual identities. Rather than requiring them to write in the frequently banal student-to-teacher voice to which they have become accustomed, we might ask them to adopt discursive roles that call upon their reservoir of cultural funding—that is, what they already know about language, rhetoric, and power from their own social experience.

Before proceeding further, I want to provide a few examples of what I have in mind. The list below offers a small sample of writing assignments I have used in introductory-level literature classes during the past few years:

- Choose a story from the newspaper and retell it in poetic form that resembles the style of Homer. Rely on formulaic devices, have speakers adopt noble attitudes, etc.

- After reading Swift, write your own "Modest Proposal," complete with the appropriate irony, in response to a contemporary political or social issue. Attempt to follow Swift's textual and syntactical structures as closely as possible.

- Play the role of an adolescent Walt Whitman writing to the elderly William Wordsworth after Whitman has just read "Tintern Abbey" and hopes to make contact with the great poet. Then write Wordsworth's cranky reply to whom he presumes to be a would-be imitator.

- Write a parody of the famous "Hemingway style," with its deceptively simple, direct syntax, and plain dialogue.

- You are Godot. You have been watching Vladimir and Estragon from behind a tree. Write a letter to them (to be delivered by the boy).

These assignments represent only one approach to role-play, that of writing in the guise of the author under study. What I should make clear from the start is that I do not subscribe to a position criticized by René Wellek and Austin Warren over forty years ago—namely, the idea that "one cannot understand literature unless one writes it, that one cannot and should not study Pope without trying his own hand at heroic couplets" (15). Our students need not become poets in order to study poetry, nor need they write like Beckett in order to read him.

On the other hand, I have found that asking students to attempt their own versions of the discourse of a literary text often brings them "closer" to the text in ways that reading it on its own only rarely accomplishes. Until they are asked to grapple with the formal and syntactical features of a particular work, students often engage with literary language in only the most conventional ways—following the plot, searching for "hidden meaning," figuring out a character's "psychology," and so on. In assuming the author's textual identity, student writers must, if they are to create convincing imitations, attentively observe and enact not only the thematics but also the linguistic moves, the tonalities, and the discursive characteristics of the literary text at hand. When students convert a newspaper article of their choice into the style of Homer, the disjunctions between journalism and epic poetry place the gestures of Homer's discourse into sharper relief. (Furthermore, the comic possibilities are endless; my students have had great fun turning politicians into unlikely figures of mythic grandeur.) Similarly, by attempting not only to compose their own "Modest Proposal" but also to make it *sound* like Swift's, students must do more than simply find a current debate to satirize; they must explore the differences between eighteenth- and twentieth-century diction, phrasing, and reader-writer relations. Language thus becomes denaturalized, an element of human culture and history.

The assignment in which students write letters as Whitman and Wordsworth, however, takes this form of role-play a step further, for here they are asked to leave behind the stylistics of specific literary works and to envision these authors as writers in another genre. What students have gleaned from these authors' poems surely comes into play—but the imagination is granted considerably more license for invention than in the previous assignments. This loosening of formal constraints leads me to imagine any number of objections to such an assignment:

1. that the assignment creates a fictional scenario and is therefore frivolous;

2. that students who have read a few poems by Whitman and Wordsworth, and have but a cursory knowledge of their lives, could not possibly understand these figures well enough to write in their places—therefore the assignment is presumptuous; and

3. that it sets up so many artificial constraints that it restricts how students might respond to "Tintern Abbey"—therefore the assignment is counterproductive.

In other words, we should not waste our time on such nonsense.

Yet each of these objections can be satisfactorily answered. In response to the charge that fictitious writing scenarios are frivolous, I would reply that the scene of writing in the classroom is always, in effect, artificial and fictional; it is always a rehearsal. The kinds of papers that students write for teachers are usually of the sort that they will never write again in contexts beyond the university. Even the very few who go on to write for professional literary journals quickly discover that much of what they learned about writing for teachers or even for dissertation committees no longer applies when writing for readers of a specific publication. But this fictional nature of student writing need not be seen as a mistake to be corrected, but, rather, as an opportunity to engage students in a whole spectrum of imagined trials and roles. The point is not to make our assignments completely conform to "real world" writing—for how do we know what worlds our various students will eventually enter?—but to help them learn how to make the necessary shifts and turns required of all writers each time they confront a new contextual dynamic. In other words, I want to teach my students not just to play by the rules of a single game but to attend to the ways rules change—and how they might challenge them—as they move from game to game. They need both to work within a variety of frames and to perform what Erving Goffman calls "frame analysis"—a reflexive critique of the social, institutional, and cultural contexts which enable and limit their performances.

To those who would object that students know far too little, especially in an introductory course, about Whitman or Wordsworth to succeed in representing these writers' epistolary styles, I can only say that historical accuracy is not the point. Our sense of Whitman and Wordsworth is as fictional as this imaginary correspondence between them; what students know of them—indeed, what we know of them—is only enough to invent creative versions of what actually "being" these people might have been like. All I am asking my students to do is to construct letters which reflect viable images of Whitman and Wordsworth based on the poetry and biographical sketches they have read—and with their own social knowledge of cocky young aspirants and cranky old men. As it turns out, students know a lot about such things, a lot about ambition and flattery and rejection and irritation, and they can even figure out how to include an argument about poetics—on the conflict between meter and free verse, for instance—in the middle of it all. Though I generally object to quoting a single student in order to assert the value of one's pedagogical methods, it may be useful here to give an example of how students might "inhabit" the identities of authors in order to explore the dialogue their poetry inaugurates. Playing the role of the youthful, impetuous Whitman, this student writes to Wordsworth at one point in her letter:

> "Tintern Abbey" has brought back memories of my childhood when I was still a boy. Now I am a man, and yet that boy's life still remains deep in the confines of memory. I know that you share my heart's emotion because I also feel that the fever of this world has lost its soft inland murmur. . . . In my days of labor, the woods, the streams, and the trees have brought me more pleasurable moments than all those acts of duty to man's demanding will. And these same moments have provided me considerable hours of reflective recompense.
>
> How is it that you, sir, are able to speak so well in England what I feel here in America? Is it not likely that the two of us own that unusual intellect, that significant capacity to write what most men can only learn to experience? Being a writer like yourself, I know you value this talent for what it is.

Even in the midst of having her Whitman borrow significant terms from "Tintern Abbey" such as "murmur" and "recompense," this student captures precisely the presumptuousness that might irritate the older poet, whom she later has reply:

> Dear Mr. Whitman,
>
> I have just read your letter and find your inflated words rather distasteful. You seem to be under the impression that poetry is a simple expression of emotion. I'll have you know that much work and devotion goes into the writing of a poem. It is not something that flows from the fingertips of the average fool.

And the student goes on to take up the issue of the poet's relationship to nature, the process of composition, and Whitman's need for hard-earned maturity rather than lazy days in fields of grass—all of which strike me as displaying this student's serious interaction with the issues that arise in "Tintern Abbey" and in Whitman's challenge to traditional poetry.

The final objection I mentioned above, though I imagine there are others, is that of the constraints which control such an assignment. But this charge overlooks a crucial feature of social life and of writing—for it is the existence of constraints that paradoxically creates the possibility of discursive production. Without sufficient constraints, students find themselves in the position I noted earlier, wherein they are unsure of their audience and of which matters ought to warrant their attention. Such uncertainty accounts for one of the reasons why fiction writers invent various kinds of narrators who constrain the otherwise infinite options for telling a story. As Barthes claims, writing is "that *play* whereby I turn around as well as I can in a narrow place" (*Roland Barthes* 137). In a similar vein, he asks:

> Can one—or at least could one ever—begin to write without taking oneself as another? . . . the origin of the work is not the first influence, it is the first posture: . . . I begin producing by reproducing the person I want to be. (99)

In other words, we *must* devise boundaries so that we can *read* our writing even as we are composing. When students attempt to enter a role, they recognize immediately that the nuances of their language must be adjusted to "fit" the specific predicament—which, in the case of the imagined Whitman-Wordsworth correspondence, includes issues of gender, age, history, literary tradition, narcissism, and so on. These traces of social performance give us, as teachers, a place to situate our commentary, for we can indicate the ways in which the semantic and syntactical movements of various sentences either capture or fail to capture what one would expect in such a role. In other words, we can draw on students' own knowledge of the "ways of the world"—of psychic, cultural, and discursive negotiations—in order to respond to their work.

Finally, and perhaps most importantly, role-play assignments offer students an avenue for writing about their own writing. I ask my students to include a critique of their own text when they turn in each assignment, wherein they describe the features of the role they are trying to inhabit and they identify those features in their texts. For example, in one section of the critical commentary on her Whitman-Wordsworth correspondence, the student I quoted above discusses her strategies and evaluates what she has achieved—including a very interesting reading of her imaginary Wordsworth's unconscious identification with Whitman:

> Replying as Wordsworth, I tried to attack all of Whitman's voicings
> by destroying his credibility as an experienced writer. In doing so I
> think I was able to create a character in Wordsworth who did identify
> with Whitman though he didn't openly reveal it. . . . Though
> Wordsworth tries to hate Whitman for being rude and pretentious
> it is difficult for him to admit a complete lack of interest. In the end
> Wordsworth reveals more of his own self than he intends to.

This analysis of her own text strikes me as a savvy interpretation, the
kind we look for in literary critics. At the same time, I was in the position to indicate places in her letters where it seemed to me that she was
allowing Wordsworth to make his case with little more than easy clichés
about writing, such as when she has him reply to Whitman: "You cannot write poetry until you go out into the world and live." Rather than
turning us away from issues of poetics, these fictional letters provide an
intriguing social space in which we can attend to them.

But scenarios like these, in which students are asked to take on the
language of authors or of their literary characters, describe only one
realm of possibility. Another form of role-play—one that many teachers might find more suitable in an academic setting—asks that students
assume the part of someone professionally involved in the interpretation of literature: a literary critic, a book reviewer, or even (the gods for-
bid!) an English professor. Along these lines, the following assignments
have challenged my students' resources:

- The editor of an academic journal has invited you, a respected literary critic, to submit an essay for a forthcoming issue on contemporary literature. Write an argument in favor of your interpretation of one of the contemporary stories or poems we have read this
  term. Then write a letter to the editor from the *author* of that story
  or poem who strongly disagrees with your interpretation of his/
  her work.

- Go to the bookstore and pull from the shelf a novel you have not
  read. Take note of the title, the author, the table of contents, the
  opening page, the cover design and commentary. Then, *without
  reading the novel,* play the role of a book reviewer writing a review
  of this novel for *The New York Times.*

- You are an English professor writing in an academic journal about
  why, given the limited amount of time in an introductory literature course, you prefer teaching one text rather than another
  (choose from the texts we have read this term). Then write as another professor who disagrees.

Again, I expect that these assignments might be seen as unusual at best
and impossible at worst. How can lower-division undergraduates play

the role of someone writing for an academic journal or a major newspaper (a task that academics themselves find sufficiently difficult)?

My experience is that students can play these roles surprisingly well—not usually well enough to merit publication (which, in any case, is not the objective), but well enough to appropriate the characteristic gestures of literary critics, book reviewers, and English professors. In order to make such appropriation possible, however, we must ask students to do something that is seldom part of introductory-level courses, that is, to carefully read literary criticism—not just for "research" papers, but for class discussion and scrutiny. It is indeed surprising, once we stop to consider it, that we often expect students to write effective criticism without having *read* any; and we commonly assume that the articles we write for academic journals would be of no interest to anyone who is not part of the profession. In fact, when articles for class discussion are chosen with care, students illustrate ample curiosity about this hidden dimension of their teacher's professional life, and they are happy to have it demystified. Once they see that critics have no special hold on the "true meaning" of literary texts, students seem much more willing to join the debate and to resist the positions of "specialists" to whom they have presumed they should submit. Furthermore, they are astonished, intrigued, and amused by the passion with which professors argue over minute details in the back of various journals. This affective component of academic work leads students to recognize that the rhetoric of literary criticism works much like the rhetoric of politics: contentious argument fueled by participants who are "interested"—not just in the sense of desiring to gain knowledge, but also in the sense of desiring to gain influence, power, and prestige.

I do not mean to suggest that I want my students to think of literary critics as scoundrels. But I do want them to see that criticism is a conversation like any other—one in which roles are adopted and negotiated, and conventions are established and challenged. The assignment in which they are asked to write a book review without reading the book is intended not to encourage deceit but to invite students to exhibit the rhetorical procedures, maneuvers, and gestures that characterize most reviews. Once we have discussed a number of reviews in class, it becomes apparent that the book review is an unusually predictable genre, one whose basic structure and typical variations are readily deciphered. Students quickly learn to mimic the reviewer's practice of noting the author's reputation and earlier works; providing a brief plot summary; discussing their own expectations and whether they were satisfied; considering the book in relation to others of its kind; and so on. If students can do such things convincingly *without* having read the book, then I would contend that they are prepared not only to write proficient

reviews of books they have read but also to read book reviews with a
critical understanding of what generates and regulates their power as a
form of writing.

Role-play thus provides an entry into the social, rhetorical, and
performative dimensions of reading and responding to literature. But it
also offers many students something else, something they don't anticipate: pleasure. The pleasure of writing-in-role seems to come from the
liberties and tensions of inhabiting a fictional space, of having the context for writing so sharply defined even while the possibilities for text
remain open. As Judith and Geoffrey Summerfield note:

> Within the constraints, guidelines, and frames of role, our purposes
> and our means are clarified. We can do things well that we might
> fudge *in propria persona*. . . . Role-play creates a strong, clear sense
> of environmental determinants: all those factors of context or
> situation that, when recognized, make an appropriate/effective
> utterance what it is and not otherwise. (199)

Students are paradoxically freed to make all kinds of imaginative moves
precisely *because* of the constraints that limit the field. Furthermore, when
assignments are structured so that two or more roles come into dialogue
with one another—as above, where two professors take opposing views
on the value of certain literary works, or an author disputes a critic's
interpretation of his or her text—students are afforded the opportunity
to locate their work in the realm of "real" social activity, where writing
converses with other writings. While the institutional context in which
students and teachers work is never fully escaped or transcended, role-
play does offer students the pleasure of temporarily displacing their all-
too-familiar discursive position in order to inhabit another, in order to
be what they are not but might eventually become.

Yet, I have encountered colleagues who are disconcerted by my emphasis on finding ways for students to take pleasure in writing; they
question whether I should not stick to justifying role-play on supposedly "higher" grounds. In the midst of all the concern that we use the
classroom, as Patricia Bizzell contends, "to promote social justice" (6),
pleasure may seem like a matter of little significance. But should pleasure be approached simply as a supplement, as something that we hope
our students experience on occasion as a bonus of fortune? Rather, I
would argue that pleasure should play an important part in the conception and design of our courses and assignments. The pleasure of parody,
for instance, is an experience which all students should have the opportunity to explore, for parody is a cunning means to forging simultaneous
distance and intimacy with a particular discourse. We cannot parody an
author's stylistics or the features of a particular genre unless we have

swallowed them, digested them, made them our own. Parody is *reflexive* role-play, a form that many students enjoy above all others.

On the other hand, I am not one who believes that our job as teachers is to produce happy, contented student writers of the type that standard textbooks apparently endorse. Writing is almost always a more or less uncomfortable act—as even professional writers admit—and my vision of the pleasure to be had in student writing does not presume that role-play will make writing in response to literature any easier. What it can make writing, however, is less alienating—more connected to what students already know about people and the ways they interact. When they are asked to take on specific roles, students often experience the pleasure of entering a field of play, a landscape of possibilities constructed by the assignment's parameters. This imaginative territory becomes what Thomas Pavel calls a "fictional world"—that metaphoric realm in which writers and readers travel through texts, both departing from and referring to the "actual" world of social relations (136–48). To *become* Godot, as one of my assignments asks, leads students to enter into the strange dislocations and multiple ironies that comprise Beckett's bare terrain. The act of recomposing this fictional world brings many of them to a closer understanding of the text than they usually achieve in a more conventional academic essay; for rather than merely writing *about* a literary work, students must write one themselves—and their own work becomes subject to the same critical analysis, the same conjecture, with which we approach literature.

But it is not just *students'* pleasure that I have in mind. While I disagree with Tompkins's conception of "performance," I nevertheless embrace her admonition that we teachers consider *our own* pleasure in the classroom (660). As Barthes notes:

> [The intellectual] is not a proxy, he doesn't speak in the name of the proletariat: he must speak in his own name, in a revolutionary perspective, to account for what he needs, what hinders his intellectual activities, the alienations imposed on him as an intellectual by our present society. He will be all the more a revolutionary if he measures the extent of his own alienation, and not just that of others. (*Grain* 163)

While Tompkins asks what we need to do to confront our own alienation as teachers in the classroom, I want to ask what we need to do to confront our alienation as readers of student texts. Perhaps, I have suggested, this is an alienation we bring upon ourselves. I must confess that one of the reasons I use role-play in writing assignments is because the results are papers that give me far more pleasure as a reader than I have ever had with traditional prompts. Should I feel guilty about this? I would answer no, for two reasons: first, because I believe students always enter a role in order to write, whether or not they are aware of it; and second, because I believe that attention to pleasure may begin to heal the ascetic imagination which often dominates our vision of writing in the literature class. Our students need not dread to write, and we need not dread to read.

Works Cited

Barthes, Roland. *The Grain of the Voice: Interviews 1962–1980.* Trans. Linda Coverdale. New York: Farrar, 1985.

———. *Roland Barthes by Roland Barthes.* Trans. Richard Howard. New York: Noonday, 1977.

———. *The Rustle of Language.* Trans. Richard Howard. Berkeley: U of California P, 1989.

———. *S/Z.* Trans. Richard Miller. New York: Noonday, 1974.

Bizzell, Patricia. "The Politics of Teaching Virtue." *ADE Bulletin* 103 (Winter 1992): 4–7.

Goffman, Erving. *Frame Analysis: An Essay on the Organization of Experience.* Cambridge, MA: Harvard UP, 1974.

Pavel, Thomas. *Fictional Worlds.* Cambridge, MA: Harvard UP, 1986.

Poirier, Richard. *The Performing Self: Compositions and Decompositions in the Language of Contemporary Life.* New Brunswick, NJ: Rutgers UP, 1992.

Summerfield, Judith, and Geoffrey Summerfield. *Texts and Contexts: A Contribution to the Theory and Practice of Teaching Composition.* New York: Random, 1986.

Tompkins, Jane P. "Pedagogy of the Distressed." *College English* 52.6 (October 1990): 653–60.

Wellek, René, and Austin Warren. *Theory of Literature.* London: Penguin, 1978.

21 Making Connections: Theory, Pedagogy, and Contact Hours

Beverly Sauer
Carnegie Mellon University

For participants at the early NCTE Summer Institutes for Teachers of Literature, theorizing involved the larger issues of canon definition and the textual politics of textbook selection and curriculum development. Most early participants felt personal and institutional pressures to increase "minority" enrollments and expand their multicultural horizons; more urgently from an institutional perspective, declining enrollments and new demographics challenged educators to revise traditional course structures to attract changing student populations on campus. Coverage anxiety met political incorrectness; the realities of departmental politics intersected curricular debates about the nature of liberal education; academics struggling to define courses in Western Civilization confronted issues of civility, inclusion, and a non-European perspective; a new canon threatened to displace the great books and the great men of Western Civilization. Encouraged to teach diversity in a multicultural curriculum, participants exchanged lists of texts and syllabi. In Gerald Graff's words, the debate centered on the cafeteria, not the food.

In defining the new canon, however, Institute participants confronted new questions: Is there a difference when new theories play in the classroom? Do theories imply politics? Who is authorized to teach new texts? Does a canon imply agreement? Does culture have a place in the English curriculum? Have culture and politics ever been absent from the diffi-

This essay was based upon contributions from participants in the pedagogical materials exchange at the 1992 NCTE Institute for Teachers of Literature. The author especially wishes to thank the following workshop participants for their submissions and comments cited in this article: Anonymous, "Eng 347: 20th Century American Literature: Response Journal Assignment"; Robert Felgar; John Getz, syllabus for "EN 381 American Renaissance: 1830–1865"; Theodore and Grace Ann Hovet, "Weaving the Fabric: Textual Studies as an Interdisciplinary Pattern," unpublished paper, 1992; Sharon Howard, comments, *Conversations*, 8 June, pp. 4–5; *The Iowa Student as Critic Conference* (brochure), University of Northern Iowa (3 April 1992); Dan Sheridan; Joel Wingard, "First Paper Assignment: English 109a (6 March 1991)" and "Third Paper Assignment"; Susan Yunis, "LLE499 Independent Study" (syllabus).

cult task of teaching students to read and appreciate literature? Do new texts require new strategies and new curricular practices? How, in short, can a traditionally trained Anglo European Milton scholar teach the new texts and new literatures of the multicultural curriculum?

In describing the "Race for Theory," Barbara Christian articulated the frustration that many teachers of the Institute felt in encountering "theories." For Christian,

> [T]he race for theory, with its linguistic jargon, its emphasis on quoting its prophets, its tendency towards "Biblical" exegesis, its refusal even to mention specific works of creative writers, far less contemporary ones, its preoccupations with mechanical analyses of language, graphs, algebraic equations, its gross generalizations about culture . . . silenced many of us to the extent that some of us feel we can no longer discuss our own literature, while others have developed intense writing blocks and are puzzled by the incomprehensibility of the language set adrift in literary circles. (53)

If the conference promised "theory" for teachers of literature to undergraduates, the conferees wanted pearls, not abstract theorizing about canon, center, correctness, conflict, coverage, and culture. In criticizing the authoritative discourse of new theoretical criticism, conferees raised questions that would ultimately form the central focus of each successive Institute:

- Who is authorized to speak in the classroom?
- For whom are we doing what we are doing when we do literary criticism?
- How does theory practiced in academic criticism reflect the kind of thinking we would like our students to do?
- How can student assignments reflect the kind of theorizing that we would like students to do?

Their comments, published in a daily journal called *Conversations*, demonstrate the engagement of participants with issues of theory in the classroom and the creativity of classroom teachers working to develop effective syllabi and classroom assignments that meet the needs of a diverse and challenging classroom environment.

Generating Conversations: The Institute's Curricular Exchange

To help participants incorporate theory in the classroom, Institute planners organized an informal "curricular exchange." Held in the late afternoon following leader-led sessions and beach activity, the first exchange attracted about twenty-five teachers who swapped syllabi and course lists and exchanged anecdotes about successful teaching strategies. The following year, NCTE formalized the exchange and invited participants to bring copies of course assignments and course lists to exchange with other workshop participants.

During these late afternoon sessions, participants discussed the implications of the morning's theorizing for classroom teachers at two- and four-year colleges. Most of the participants had full-time teaching loads; some taught as many as four or five classes per semester. Few had the released time available to faculties at large research institutions which would enable them to conduct extensive research in a new field—especially a field so broad and ill-defined as "multiculturalism."

As the curricular exchange demonstrated, however, these teachers rarely stopped theorizing about what happens in the classroom. Their formal and informal theorizing helped them to shape the content and method of assignments, and the intellectual framework of course syllabi.

In describing their own experiences shaping curriculum, pedagogy, and politics within the framework of course outlines and class assignments, participants who submitted materials for the curricular exchange revealed the resourcefulness of teachers who theorize constantly about how to teach students to (1) "think critically" and (2) "engage in" the process of reading and writing. As the syllabi and assignments revealed, the notion of "applying" theory entails diverse activities: teaching theories, defining theories, teaching students to apply theories, helping students articulate their own theories, making theories (theorizing), arguing theories, understanding the theoretical differences in arguments, and helping students negotiate theoretical differences in the larger college curriculum. In articulating the practical application of theory in the classroom, these voices from the classroom demonstrate how curriculum, pedagogy, and the politics of the classroom are continually shaped and reshaped by the practical realities of contact hours, administrative requirements, and student/teacher interactions in the classroom.

During the curricular exchange, participants discussed each syllabus and assignment from the point of view of how to develop students' understanding of Theory (with a capital "T") in general and such specific theories as feminism, reader response, cultural criticism, and deconstruction. Although the curricular exchange focused on a number of issues related to politics and pedagogy in the classroom, I will focus on two questions raised during the sessions: (1) Who is authorized to speak? and (2) How can student assignments reflect the kind of theorizing that we would like them to do?

Who Is Authorized to Speak in the Classroom?

In the newest round of the culture wars, David Bromwich asks: "Who after all, is better qualified to know the obligations that come with a given subject than the professor who has chosen to spend a career in that subject?" (29). Bromwich's authorization of a single point of view in the classroom contrasts with the "radical heterogeneity" which Mary Louise Pratt imagines in describing the "pedagogical arts of the contact zone" (Pratt, "Arts" 40). For Pratt, the lecture became "anomalous and unimaginable." Instead, each person in the class had to work in the knowledge that "whatever one said was going to be systematically received in radically heterogeneous ways that we were neither able nor entitled to prescribe. . . . The very nature of the course put ideas and identities on the line" (Pratt, "Arts" 39).

Within the contact zone defined by student contact hours and classroom configurations, ideas and identities are clearly "on the line." As the language of the participants' syllabi reveals, learning to speak of, with, or for "others" demands that faculty understand how the pedagogical texts of the contact zone encode political and pedagogical assumptions about power relations in the classroom. In examining the following course descriptions, syllabi, and assignments as "textual artifacts" of the contact zone, we can understand how those texts express conflicting messages about politics, curriculum, and pedagogy in the classroom.

In the following course description, for example, Sharon Howard describes her experiences with community college students who focus on "a single part of the text" and "essentially ignore how the *entire* text modifies the meaning of the part":

> This zeroing in on a part of the whole is usually followed by an immediate flight into connections from the student's personal experience, leaving the text in the dust. How does one even get to the point of applying theory when the meaning(s), various paraphrases of the text, remain so murky.

Yet theory is clearly at work in Howard's classroom. From a theoretical perspective, Howard's pedagogy involves two approaches: the first, based on reader response; the second, based on deconstruction. The classroom is a pedagogical contact zone, a negotiated space where the personal experience must be transformed into the institutional discourse of textual analysis. Yet the underlying politics of pedagogy in the contact zone—expressed in the oppositions between student experience and text—silences students' participation in theory making. In asking her students to distinguish between "personal experience" and "the text," for example, Howard authorizes "the text" as a kind of icon with an existence independent from the personal experience of the reader. Although Howard despairs—like many other faculty at the Institute—of her students' "murky" paraphrases of the text, the parenthetical "s" that transforms "meaning" into "meanings" paradoxically prohibits her readers from reducing her own meaning to a singular, unmuddied paraphrase.

As participants concluded, however, by making problems transparent, students and faculty can use their own texts to demonstrate how theory works in the classroom. In articulating for her students the theoretical questions that drive the practical problems she faces, for example, Howard can authorize her students to analyze the relationship between textual meanings and their own personal experiences and to construct their own theories of meaning in the contact zone. In helping students define their own "linguistics of contact," Howard can, in Pratt's words, "take the much debated slipperiness of signifiers for granted, and . . . be much concerned, as students of contact languages are, with the improvisational dimensions of meaning making" ("Utopias" 62) as well as the differences between speech production and reception.

Syllabi also demonstrate how the linguistic artifacts of the contact zone establish power relations in the classroom. John Getz's syllabus for "EN 381 American Renaissance: 1830–1865," for example, illustrates the best notion of "putting an instructor's assumptions up front." In addition to listing the "goals" of the course and the format, he describes his "approach" to the texts and a premise for consideration. The language is subtle, flowing, poetic, literary; students and faculty participate together as "we":

> *Premise for consideration:* That literature is written and read in history, not in a vacuum, and that aesthetic concerns cannot be separated from political and social issues. Accordingly, as we read texts, we remake them, so that our responses themselves become texts for us to study.

In the same syllabus, however, details concerning course attendance and grading still reflect a power differential between student and teacher in the pedagogical contact zone—a power differential expressed in the forceful commands and sharply punctuated language of authority and power. Here, students are clearly "others":

> Classes will follow a discussion format, sometimes involving group work. Students will come to class prepared for thoughtful discussion of the readings. In-class writing and reaction papers will be one measure of this preparation, but I will also feel free to call on you even if you don't volunteer to answer. . . .

From a student's perspective, the syllabus establishes two separate and conflicting relationships that, in the end, authorize faculty as the empowered voice of the classroom, a tension that John felt as much as his students. Once we understand such tensions, however, we can examine how changing the discourse of syllabi might improve student/faculty communication in the pedagogical contact zone. What would happen to the politics of the classroom, for example, if we expressed our commands in the poetic and encompassing language of our theories? How can we adapt our pedagogies to enable students to speak with authority in the classroom while still meeting the administrative requirements of student contact hours?

If syllabi construct the format of the classroom, assignments construct how students will write, read, and respond to texts. They define how students will speak and in what form. As cultural texts, assignments also transmit encoded meanings and traditional assumptions about authority and politics in the classroom. Here, however, the very slipperiness of language and the complexity of signs work against us. We hope to convey to our students that their own voices and opinions have a place in the classroom, but the complexities of language in the pedagogical contact zone and the embedded politics of student/faculty power relationships complicate the task of helping our students learn how to read "for themselves." It's no wonder that conservative opponents seize upon complaints from students who feel pressured to assume a "politically correct" posture.

In his "First Paper Assignment: English 109a (6 March 1991)," for example, Joel Wingard differentiates between a traditional reading, which "pretends that it is 'faithful' to the text or the author's intention," and a strong reading, which "actively seeks to take a distinctive position in relation to the text, even reading it 'against the grain.'" Within the contact zone, however, faculty must teach real students to read against the grain. Read as a "textual artifact of the contact zone," Wingard's "Third Paper Assignment" reveals the paradox inherent in any attempt to write clear instructions that will enable students to read against the grain.

In the third paper assignment, Wingard asks students to discuss how a literary perspective changes their reading of the text. In providing examples—necessary from a pedagogical point of view to help students understand the nature of the assignment—the effort to broaden his students' perspectives leads Wingard to warn his students:

> (I would hope, of course, that you have learned that what an author thinks is not the final word or even the highest word on the meaning of a text, that you would acknowledge that the reader has something important to contribute to the meaning of a text, so that you would

not claim that the case is closed now that you found out something about Ibsen's theories of drama.)

But who is the reader? Wingard's message separates reader from student, "reader" from the "you" he addresses in his suggestions to improve the breadth and scope of his students' reading.

From a student's perspective, the message conveys three commands: (1) learn that what an author thinks is not the final word; (2) acknowledge that the reader has something important to contribute to the meaning of the text; and (3) do not claim that the case is closed. Like Getz's syllabus, these comments appear within the context of the clear commands of the administrative aspects of the assignment (date due, number of sources, etc.) and directions for using the library ("Once you have identified such potentially useful sources, locate them in the Reeves Library . . . and read them, taking notes." "I want you to read at least three secondary sources"). If we teach students to read against the grain, however, we must expect them to resist all texts—including our own instructions.

To create an academic community where students and faculty are authorized to speak from radically heterogeneous perspectives, then, we must reinvent the language of the contact zone. In the meantime, we can "lay our own identities on the line," articulating for our students how our own assignments, course descriptions, and syllabi can be read as cultural artifacts in the struggle to express meaning between writer and reader.

How Can Student Assignments Reflect the Kind of Theorizing That We Would Like Students To Do?

As Institute participants came to realize, the question of how student assignments can reflect the kind of theorizing we would like them to do begs the question: "What is the theorizing we would like students to do?" and, more importantly, "What theories do we do?" As the pedagogical texts of the contact zone demonstrate, "who speaks" in the classroom depends ultimately upon how we as instructors can theorize about how our own texts resolve the tensions of politics, pedagogy, and power relations in the curriculum.

Many faculty at the Institute embraced a well-defined theory such as feminism or reader response. Others invented assignments to meet particular course needs or borrowed effective assignments from colleagues and mentors. Still others replicated the assignments and course structures of their own graduate or undergraduate education. For many, the new textual readings based upon reader response or cultural critiques or deconstruction were, in practice, indistinguishable from older, carefully considered New Critical readings, though the European American men at the conference joked uneasily about the problems of reading literature from a "white hegemonic perspective." For others, however, the new theories helped participants reconsider the problems of meaning and significance in the classroom.

As the Institute workshops demonstrated, politics, pedagogy, and curriculum intersect in many ways: traditional canonical texts read in new ways; new texts read alongside traditional favorites producing new meanings; greater diversity in course content; greater freedom in course structure. A new vocabulary described a pedagogy where power is decentered, students read against the grain, faculty develop space for resistance, and students and faculty alike discover themselves as Others. In learning to teach a new canon, however, participants discovered that new texts demand new theories. Assignments that grew out of workshop activities thus reflected the consensus of workshop participants that

- nontraditional texts demand nontraditional pedagogies;
- faculty can and must educate themselves to read new texts in new ways;
- the notion of self as "Other" could have a profound influence on the reading of a text; and
- the formal syllabus or course list reveals little about the politics, theories, and pedagogies operating in the classroom.

As Dan Sheridan discovered, radical politics may be at work in traditional courses—hidden beneath titles that sound like chronological, sequential coverage models of the traditional "English" curriculum. In other cases, however, courses with a clear "multicultural bias" in their course descriptions retained traditional pedagogies: genre-based assignments, traditional power structures in the classroom, lecture formats, and canonical readings. The number of traditional paper assignments in such courses suggests that, although texts and curricula have evolved to include greater diversity, faculty still embrace traditional conventions of style and organization (the essay, for example) that may, from a noncanonical perspective, reflect and reproduce underlying power structures, social and economic values, and class differentials.

But the most creative assignments clearly reflected the kind of theorizing most of us would like our students to do: foregrounding issues of power, refiguring traditional courses, enabling students to engage in critical debate with their peers and to understand the role of texts as cultural artifacts.

Foregrounding Issues of Power

Susan Yunis, for example, foregrounds issues of power in her "LLE499 Independent Study." As the course description explains:

> Our course will explore arguments about power which have been made through cultural "texts" as diverse as fairy tales and myths, circuses, philosophical essays, parenting books, films, novels, zoos, and classrooms. The students will be invited into arguments about power and control, to examine, present to each other, and discuss the implications of specific kinds of power relationships in their families and friendships, in their school experiences, in male/female communication styles, in environmental issues, in the experiences of Black and Native Americans, in the professional worlds they are about to enter, and in the disciplines which they have studied.

Her course list combines both canonical and noncanonical authors, including Tannen (*You Don't Understand Me*); *The Breakfast Club* (film); *The Magic Flute* (opera/film); and Toni Morrison's *Beloved,* alongside Aristotle; Bondourant; Hobbes; La Botie; Locke; Marx; Plato; Wolff; Robert Paul; Charles Merriam; and Evelyn Fox Keller (*Reflections on Gender and Science*).

Assignments in the class also encourage students to examine cultural texts from canonical and nontraditional perspectives. Before analyzing *Field of Dreams,* for example, students discuss Aristotle's and Plato's rationales for hierarchies of power in small-group discussions, followed by reports to the class. The syllabus includes units on power relations in politics, families, education, gender, and the environment. In a unit called "The Black American and Native American Experience of Power," students examine theories of power in relation to the novel *Beloved.* As a senior "capstone" course, the final unit appropriately discusses power relationships in the world of work.

Refiguring Traditional Courses

Inspired by the three core texts of the Institute, Dan Sheridan developed an imaginary course based on the concept of "others" and a grammar of "othering": I other you, her, him, them; you other me, etc. "In the 'grammar,'" he writes, "are the germs of writing assignments" that raise questions about the cultural construction of subject and object in relation to each other: How are men and women, for example, constructed by literary conventions to see each other as objects? What has to happen to our concept of literature if we are to empower "others" as fully participating subjects in society, in the classroom, in politics, in the workplace? For Sheridan, the grammar of othering allowed him to rethink his own Victorian literature class. The traditional "Studies in 19C. Victorian Lit" suddenly became a new course that, according to Sheridan, "might possibly be called "Victorians and Others," including alternative texts, such as *Wide Sargasso Sea,* which explore similar subjects from a non-Eurocentric perspective. If we see ourselves as others, however, Sheridan's class and his new grammar suggest additional possibilities for courses. From a non-Western, non-Eurocentric perspective, Victorians become the Others in courses that require new vocabularies to name—"Africans and Others" (Victorians/Americans/Europeans); "Caribbean Peoples and Others" (Europeans)—turning "Others" into "we's" and the "us's" into "Others," ultimately deconstructing the "we's" entirely.

Participants also refigured traditional course structures based upon univocal, chronological assumptions about influence and period. New course structures reflected nonlinear, nonhierarchical metaphors in which juxtaposition and montage would allow faculty and students to engage in a play of difference. In place of a traditional, romantic study of love, one participant used feminist critical theory to examine the interplay of power, gender, race, economy, and love in literary and nonliterary texts. Juxtaposing Byron and Barrett Browning within a feminist theoretical framework produced more lively discussion and critical engagement than in the traditional, linear "great masters" survey.

Robert Felgar uses traditional texts like *Paradise Lost* and *Oedipus Rex* to demonstrate how, in his words, "if I can't change the curriculum, I can change pedagogy, which, in a sense, changes the curriculum after all." In teaching *Oedipus Rex,* for example, he asks students why a man shouldn't marry his mother and kill his father. In *Paradise Lost,* he raises questions about the text's ability to represent a "perfect person" in a postlapsarian world. In challenging traditional assumptions, he writes, "cultural criticism makes available for analysis issues that really matter to students." But, Felgar notes, cultural criticism can raise questions about liberal ideologies as well. Thus, in teaching *Native Son,* Felgar examines how a racist environment constructs the behavior of oppressor and oppressed alike. The resulting debate demonstrates how race and gender are cultural inventions with powerful political, social, and moral consequences.

Enabling Students to Engage in Critical Debate
with Their Peers

According to Gerald Graff, students also need space outside of the class-room to discuss theoretical issues of curriculum, politics, and pedagogy that occur in faculty conferences and lounges. To provide such a space, the University of Northern Iowa has designed the "Iowa Student as Critic Conference," which clearly attempts to "encourage and reward critical thinking and writing in Iowa's high school, community college, and college and university students." Organized by the University of Northern Iowa's Group of Critical Theory and Practice, the conference includes small-group discussions of student essays and a memorial lecture. In 1992, the conference included student essays on "Imagery as Agency," "Critically Reading Media Texts," "Criticism in Context: Literature in the Middle East," and "Narrative Lives in the Work of Leslie Silko." According to Theodore and Grace Ann Hovet, the conference, "with a ten-year record of successful and stimulating practice," provided the impetus for Northern Iowa's proposed interdisciplinary certificate in textual studies.

Enabling Students to Understand the Role of Texts
as Cultural Artifacts

When Susan Gubar, Sandra M. Gilbert, and Henry Louis Gates, Jr. described the textual production of their *Norton Anthologies* at the NCTE Summer Institutes, they described how the limits of the binding, the weight of the text, and the thickness of the paper determined how many pages a volume could contain. From this perspective, defining a canon depended ultimately upon technical, economic, and physiological factors (how much weight an average student could carry, for example). As a technical writer teaching a course in "Major British Authors," I designed a final assignment to demonstrate how cultural politics and textual practice constrain the definition of a "major author." If major authors were those included in a major anthology, I explained, then no new authors could be added to the text unless an equivalent number of pages from another author were removed. Students acting as "editorial advisors" were required to choose a noncanonical author to include in a revised version of the anthology. To justify their choice, I required them to write a report explaining the criteria they used to define a "major author" and to explain how their author fit those criteria. In a second report, I asked students to justify why they chose to replace a canonical author with their noncanonical substitute. As the final assignment in the course, students were asked to consider how editors weigh issues of genre, social class, gender, politics, aesthetics, religion, and morality in the construction of an anthology. In the *Norton Anthology* that I used for the course, students discovered that poets were generally overrepresented because poems are shorter and thus easier to include. One student argued that the anthology contained only one novel—*Gulliver's Travels*—that could easily have been represented in an abridged version. In another course, students discovered that the inclusion of Dickinson's poem, "Wild Nights," radically transformed their image of the Amherst spinster. From a feminist perspective, the assignment allowed students to articulate the codes and assumptions that govern issues of canon and curriculum. More importantly, they discovered how silences and exclusions are a necessary part of any anthology, regardless of political perspective.

John Getz has adopted this assignment for a course in the American Renaissance based upon the *Heath Anthology of American Literature,* the first anthology, he tells his students, which was "thoroughly committed to opening the American literary canon by region, race, class, and gender." In the final assignment of the course, Getz asks students to critique the content of his course, justifying the selection of one canonical author and one noncanonical author in future versions of the course. Students must explain the criteria for their selection and justify the removal of one author or work studied in the course. Getz's assignment helps students understand how courses—like texts—have coherence and direction, how time constraints affect course content and pedagogy, and how new juxtapositions produce radically different readings.

Conclusion

In describing "the linguistics of writing," Mary Louise Pratt suggests that "the tendency to postulate social subgroups existing separately from each other" produces a linguistics that defines "identity," but not the "relationality of social differentiation" ("Utopias" 59). For Pratt, dominant and dominated groups are not comprehensible apart from each other. Their speech practices are "organized to enact their difference and their hierarchy" (59). Although they share a "social referent" in the dominant group, speech practices are not homogeneous, and this nonhomogeneity produces a "split subjectivity" which forces dominated groups to identify with the dominant group and simultaneously to dissociate themselves from it.

For students—minority and majority—the classroom is a contact zone where, in the few contact hours allotted to each student/teacher interaction, they enter a world of "split subjectivity" that asks them to speak in authentic voices while learning a new language that will enable them to succeed within the academic institution. As poet June Jordan notes, however, few students—majority or minority—have ever encountered a language that expresses the truth of their existence. For minority students, Jordan explains:

> Mostly Black kids ran into a censorship of their living particular truth, past and present. Nobody wanted to know what they felt or to teach them to think for themselves. Nobody wanted to learn anything from them. (29)

But majority students find themselves at odds with what Jordan calls "Queen Mary's English" as well. For Jordan, the problems of language in the classroom are clearly connected to a larger institutional politics— "[the] problems of a currency that someone has stolen and hidden away and then homogenized into an official 'English' language that can only express nonevents involving nobody responsible, or lies. . . ." In a "true" democracy, Jordan argues, "We would make our language conform to the truth of our many selves and we would make our language lead us into the equality of power that a democratic state must represent" (30).

As the participants' syllabi and discussions revealed, however, faculty working in pedagogical contact zones throughout the country are hard at work helping students find a language that will help them learn the truth about their many selves. Like poets, they must reinvent language, construct new meanings, and struggle with the limitations that words, texts, and time impose. They are not, in the final analysis, politicians, sociologists, economists, and historians. Yet they recognize that politics, history, and culture have shaped them and the literatures they love. Regardless of the particular theory they embrace, new theories demand that they articulate the assumptions and politics that guide their teaching.

As the syllabi reveal, new theories demand that faculty and students confront hard questions about cognition, reality, and the role of texts in constructing the world in which they live: "What does the text contribute to my response? Why does the text contribute to my response?" They ask students to reexamine old notions and traditional interpretations: "What does it mean to 'discover America'?" "Where do we stand in relation to this material?" I try to imagine myself as a sophomore responding to the following assignment in "Eng 347: 20th Century American Literature":

> You can talk about the effect of whatever critical position you are reading from, which of course requires you to be aware of that position. . . . Analyze your response. . . . What does it tell you about

354   *Beverly Sauer*

yourself as a reader? What does it tell you about the culture that
either you or the text or both is/are written by?

Happily, however, the study of literature demonstrates that the most
productive periods of literary achievement have occurred in the contact
zones: in the blending of Christian and Celtic discourse that produced
Beowulf; in the new Latin cognates that produced the English Renaissance; and in the flowering of language in this country during the Harlem
Renaissance. It is as hard to imagine a Milton without politics as it is to
imagine an English curriculum without Shakespeare. In engaging ourselves as others in the kind of theorizing we would like students to do,
faculty can construct a world of difference for students in the few precious hours of the contact zone.

Works Cited

Bromwich, David. *Politics by Other Means: Higher Education's Group Thinking.* New
    Haven: Yale UP, 1992.
Christian, Barbara T. "The Race for Theory." *Cultural Critique* 6 (Spring 1987):
    51–63.
Cooper, Marilyn M., and Cynthia L. Selfe. "Computer Conferences and Learn-
    ing: Authority, Resistance, and Internally Persuasive Discourse." *College En-
    glish* 52.8 (1990): 847–69.
Gates, Henry Louis, Jr., ed. *The Norton Anthology of Afro-American Literature.* New
    York: Norton, 1990.
Gilbert, Sandra M., and Susan Gubar, eds. *The Norton Anthology of Literature by
    Women: The Tradition in English.* New York: Norton, 1985.
Graff, Gerald. *Beyond the Culture Wars: How Teaching the Conflicts Can Revitalize
    American Education.* New York: Norton, 1992.
Jordan, June. "Problems of Language in a Democratic State." *On Call: Political
    Essays.* Boston: South End, 1985: 29–30.
Lauter, Paul, gen. ed. *The Heath Anthology of American Literature.* 2nd ed. Lexing-
    ton, MA: Heath, 1994.
Pratt, Mary Louise. "Arts of the Contact Zone." *Profession '91.* New York: MLA
    1991. 33–40.
———. "Linguistic Utopias." *The Linguistics of Writing: Arguments between Lan-
    guage and Literature.* Ed. Nigel Fabb et al. New York: Methuen, 1987: 48–66.

Index

Editors

James F. Slevin is professor of English, chair of the English department, and director of the writing program at Georgetown University, where he has taught courses in composition, literary and rhetorical theory, and eighteenth-century literature and culture since 1975. His most recent publications include several co-edited volumes, *The Future of Doctoral Studies in English* (1989) and *The Right to Literacy* (1990) among them, and a monograph, *The Next Generation: Preparing Graduate Students for the Professional Responsibilities of College Teachers* (1992), which focuses on graduate programs of study. He has served on the executive committees of the Conference on College Composition and Communication and the Association of Departments of English, and on the steering committee of the NCTE College Section. His essays dealing with the politics of teaching and the curriculum have appeared in *College English, Rhetoric Review, ADE Bulletin, Liberal Education, The Politics of Writing Instruction: Postsecondary, Understanding Others: Cultural and Cross-Cultural Studies in the Teaching of Literature, Writing Theory and Critical Theory,* and *Composition in the 21st Century.* He was program chair for the 1991 NCTE Summer Institute for Teachers of Literature.

Art Young is Campbell Chair in Technical Communication and professor of English at Clemson University in South Carolina, where he teaches a variety of courses in literature and composition. His recent co-edited books include *When Writing Teachers Teach Literature* (1995), *Programs and Practices: Writing Across the Secondary School Curriculum* (1994), and *Programs That Work: Models and Methods for Writing Across the Curriculum* (1990). He has long been interested in the connections, in theory and in practice, between literature and composition. He has published book chapters and articles on using student writing to teach literature in the *Journal of Language and Learning Across Disciplines, ADE Bulletin, Approaches to Teaching Frankenstein,* and *Approaches to Teaching Shelley's Poetry.* He was the program chair for the 1992 NCTE Summer Institute for Teachers of Literature, and he currently serves on the executive committee of the Conference on College Composition and Communication.

Contributors

Wendy Bishop teaches writing and rhetoric at Florida State University. Her recent books include: *The Subject Is Writing: Essays by Teachers and Students* (1993) and *Colors of a Different Horse: Rethinking Creative Writing, Theory, and Pedagogy* (co-edited with Hans Ostrom, 1994). Her current projects include *Genres of Writing: Mapping the Territories of Discourse* (essays co-edited with Hans Ostrom, forthcoming) and *The Process of Ethnographic Writing Research* (forthcoming). During the rest of her life, she writes poems, gardens, and plays with her kids, Morgan and Tait.

David Bleich teaches a one-year seminar and practicum in pedagogy for doctoral candidates in the English department at the University of Rochester. He recently guest edited volume 14, number 1 of the *Journal of Advanced Composition*, "Collaboration and Change in the Academy," and co-edited, with Sally Barr Reagan and Tom Fox, *Writing With: New Directions in Collaborative Teaching, Learning, and Research* (1994). His book, *The Double Perspective: Language, Literacy, and Social Relations* (1988), is available in paperback from NCTE.

Eric Cheyfitz is professor of English at the University of Pennsylvania. He is the author of two books: *The Trans-Parent: Sexual Politics in the Language of Emerson* (1981) and *The Poetics of Imperialism: Translation and Colonization from* The Tempest *to* Tarzan (1991), which was chosen as one of the outstanding academic books for 1992 by *Choice*. He is currently at work on a book, of which the essay in this volume is a chapter, entitled *What Work Is There for Us to Do?: Towards an American Studies of Social Vision and Social Action*.

Barbara T. Christian is professor of African American studies at the University of California–Berkeley, where she has taught since 1971. She is the author of *Black Women Novelists; The Development of a Tradition—1892–1976* (1980), which won the Before Columbus Book Award and is the first book to explore black women novelists; *Black Feminist Criticism: Perspectives of Black Women Writers* (1985); and a *Monarch Note* on *Alice Walker's Color Purple*. She has also edited a casebook, *Everyday Use/Alice Walker* (1994). She has worked in curriculum development in the areas of women's studies and African American studies for the past twenty-five years and was co-author of the prize-winning volume, *In Search of Our Past: Units in Women's History* (1980).

Peter Elbow is professor of English at the University of Massachusetts at Amherst. He has taught at M.I.T., Franconia College, Evergreen State College, and SUNY–Stony Brook, where for five years he directed the writing program. He is the author of *Oppositions in Chaucer* (1975), *Writing without Teachers* (1973), *Writing with Power* (1981), *Embracing Contraries* (1986), *What Is English?* (1990) and (with Pat Belanoff) a textbook, *A Community of Writers* (1989) and a peer-response pamphlet, *Sharing and Responding* (1989). He edited *Landmark Essays on Voice and Writing* (1994) and *Nothing Begins with N: New Investigations of Freewriting* (1990). He won the Braddock Award in 1986 for "The Shifting Relationships between Speech and Writing" (1985) and the James Berlin Award for "The War between Reading and Writing and How to End It" (1993).

Anne Ruggles Gere is professor of English and professor of education at the University of Michigan, where she directs the joint Ph.D. program in English and education. A past chair of CCCC, she has served on a variety of NCTE committees. Her recent publications include *Into the Field: Sites of Composition Studies* (1993) and *Language and Reflection: An Integrated Approach to Teaching English* (with Colleen Fairbanks, Alan Howes, Laura Roop and David Schaafsma, 1992), which received the Richard Meade Award.

Gerald Graff is currently George M. Pullman Professor of English and Education at the University of Chicago. Previously, he was John C. Shaffer Professor of Humanities and English at Northwestern University, where he served as English department chair and director of the Northwestern University Press. Graff's books include *Professing Literature: An Institutional History* (1987), *Literature Against Itself: Literary Ideas in Modern Society* (1979) and *Beyond the Culture Wars: How Teaching the Conflicts Can Revitalize American Education* (1992). *Teaching the Conflicts: Gerald Graff, Curricular Reform, and the Culture Wars* (1994) is a collection of essays on Graff's educational ideas edited by William E. Cain, and *Falling Into Theory* (1993) is a textbook by David H. Richter which applies Graff's ideas to a textbook. Graff's work in progress includes a book-length critique of "pedagogies of empowerment" with Gregory Jay, and a volume on criticism since 1945 with Evan Carton for the *Cambridge History of American Literature*. Graff has lectured at approximately 170 colleges and universities.

Keith Hjortshoj teaches in the John S. Knight Writing Program at Cornell University and is the director of Writing in the Majors, an interdisciplinary program that supports innovative language instruction in advanced courses, especially in the sciences. As an anthropologist, he has published essays on Shi'ism in India and a monograph on the cultural history of an Indian city, *Urban Structures and Transformations in Lucknow, India* (1979). With his colleagues at Cornell, he is also the author of *Teaching Prose* (1988), a guide for teachers of writing.

Paul Lauter is Allen K. and Gwendolyn Miles Smith Professor of Literature at Trinity College (Hartford). He is the general editor of the revisionist *Heath Anthology of American Literature* (2nd ed., 1994), author of *Canons and Contexts* (1991), among other books, and a member of the editorial board of *Radical Teacher*. His current projects include books on new pedagogies for new canons and on the rise and fall of academic cultural authority, as well as a variety of articles on multiculturalism. Lauter currently serves as president of the American Studies Association.

Min-Zhan Lu is assistant professor of English at Drake University, where she teaches composition, literary and cultural criticism, and autobiography. Her stories about life in China and essays on the use of cultural dissonance in teaching have appeared in such journals as *College English, College Composition and Communication,* and the *Journal of Basic Writing.*

Kathleen McCormick is associate professor in the Department of Rhetoric, Language, and Culture and director of Freshman Reading and Writing at the University of Hartford. Her most recent book is *The Culture of Reading and the Teaching of English* (1994). She is the co-editor of the MLA volume on *Approaches to Teaching Joyce's* Ulysses (1993); the co-author of *Reading-to-Write: Exploring a Cognitive and Social Process* (1990) and the textbook *Reading Texts* (1987). She is also a contributor to a number of contemporary volumes linking theory and pedagogy, including *Pedagogy Is Politics* (1992) and *Cultural Studies in the English Classroom* (1993).

Daniel Moshenberg directs the expository writing program at George Washington University. He is a founding member of the Tenants' and Workers' Support Committee of Alexandria, the GWU Marxist Studies Group, the Popular Education Process of Alexandria, the *D.C. Area Writing Center Newsletter,* and the Washington Area Working Committee for Critical Teaching. He translated Paul Virilio's *Lost Dimension* (1991) and is the author of *Policing Coherence* (forthcoming). He is now writing a book on the rhetorics of national literacy, liberation, and composition campaigns, as well as editing an issue of *Pre/Text* on prisons, literacies, and cultures, and also co-editing an issue of *Radical Teacher* on pedagogies in postrevolutionary places.

James Phelan teaches English at Ohio State University. The editor of *Narrative,* the journal of the Society for the Study of Narrative Literature, he has recently published *Understanding Narrative* (co-edited with Peter J. Rabinowitz, 1994) and *Beyond the Tenure Track: Fifteen Months in the Life of an English Professor* (1991). The working title of his current project is *Narrative as Rhetoric.*

Mary Louise Pratt is professor of Spanish and comparative literature at Stanford University, where she has chaired the program in Modern Thought and Literature. She is author of *Toward a Speech Act Theory of Literary Discourse* (1977) and co-author of *Linguistics for Students of Literature* (1980) and *Women, Culture, and Politics in Latin America* (1990). Her essays have appeared in such volumes as *Race, Writing, and Difference; Writing Culture;* and *Colonial Discourse/Postcolonial Theory.* Her most recent book is *Imperial Eyes: Travel Writing and Transculturation* (1992). A long-time participant in debates about culture, curriculum, and Eurocentrism, both at Stanford and nationally, she has spoken widely on the subject and published several essays on multiculturalism and educational reform.

Jacqueline Jones Royster is associate professor of English at Ohio State University, where she teaches courses on rhetoric, literacy, and language. She is a member of the editorial collective, Sage Women's Educational Press, Inc., which has published a semi-annual journal, *Sage: A Scholarly Journal on Black Women* (1984–1994) and an anthology, *Double Stitch: Black Women Write about Mothers and Daughters* (hard cover, 1991; soft cover, 1993). Her other publications include *Writer's Choice* (1994), a textbook series in language arts for middle school students; *The Anti-Lynching Campaign of Ida B. Wells* (forthcoming); and numerous articles in books and scholarly journals in literacy studies and women's studies. In addition, she is also quite active in English professional organizations. She is currently chair of the Conference on College Composition and Communication and a member of the executive committee of the Division on Teaching Writing of the Modern Language Association.

Beverly Sauer is assistant professor of English and rhetoric at Carnegie Mellon University, where she teaches technical writing and Renaissance rhetoric. A regular participant in NCTE Summer Institutes, she has conducted workshops on applying literary theory in the classroom. Her own research focuses on the cultural analysis of risk communication and on the ethical analysis of discourse in large-scale technological disasters. Her most recent publications analyze technical communication from a cultural and historical perspective. She is currently developing a theory of rhetoric in public policy under grants from the National Science Foundation and NATO.

Robert Scholes is professor of English at Brown University. He has published widely on the intersections of literary and composition studies; his book, *Textual Power* (1985), received the Shaughnessy Prize of the Modern Language Association.

James E. Seitz, formerly director of writing at Long Island University (Brooklyn), teaches writing and literature and coordinates the training of new teachers in the Department of English at the University of Pittsburgh. His publications include articles in *College English* and *College Composition and Communication.* His forthcoming book, *Metaphor, Reading, Writing: A Fragmentary Study of the Teaching of English,* will be published in the Pittsburgh Series on Composition, Literacy, and Culture.

Gary Waller, dean of Arts and Sciences and professor of English and interdisciplinary studies at the University of Hartford, is the author of twenty books and over 100 articles, mainly in the fields of early modern literature and culture, and cultural theory, curriculum, and pedagogy. His most recent books are *The Sidney Family Romance* (1993) and *Edmund Spenser: A Literary Life* (1994). He has been both a Guggenheim and Newberry Fellow. He is currently working on gender and psychoanalysis, Shakespeare, and trying to construct interdisciplinary organizational and curricular structures that will improve student learning and help universities to survive.

John Warnock taught for many years at the University of Wyoming. At different times, he directed the first-year composition program, the Writing Center, the

Wyoming Conference on English, and the Wyoming Writing Project and also taught in the law school. Since 1992, he has been at the University of Arizona, where he directs the doctoral program in Rhetoric, Composition, and the Teaching of English.

Janice M. Wolff is assistant professor of English at Saginaw Valley State University, where she teaches undergraduate courses in composition, literature, rhetoric, and women's studies. She has published articles in *Reader* and *College Composition and Communication,* and she is editing a collection of scholarly essays in which contact-zone theory is brought to bear on the teaching situation.

Morris Young is a doctoral student in the joint Ph.D. program in English and education at the University of Michigan. His interests include Asian American literature, the politics of literacy, and contemporary rhetorical theory. He is currently working on a study of literacy narratives in Asian American literature and is teaching a course on literacy and reflective learning and teaching.